Dearest Moosie

Dearest Moosie

David H. Mickey

David H Mickey

Agnes: with fond remembrances, Dick,
Dave

iUniverse, Inc.
New York Lincoln Shanghai

Dearest Moosie

Copyright © 2006 by David H. Mickey

All rights reserved. No part of this book may be used or reproduced by any means, graphic, electronic, or mechanical, including photocopying, recording, taping or by any information storage retrieval system without the written permission of the publisher except in the case of brief quotations embodied in critical articles and reviews.

iUniverse books may be ordered through booksellers or by contacting:

iUniverse
2021 Pine Lake Road, Suite 100
Lincoln, NE 68512
www.iuniverse.com
1-800-Authors (1-800-288-4677)

The views expressed herein are the sole responsibility of the author and do not necessarily reflect the views of iUniverse or its affiliates.

ISBN-13: 978-0-595-41199-3 (pbk)
ISBN-13: 978-0-595-85555-1 (ebk)
ISBN-10: 0-595-41199-1 (pbk)
ISBN-10: 0-595-85555-5 (ebk)

Printed in the United States of America

Contents

May, 1942—December, 1945

Ft. Leavenworth	1
Camp Shelby	6
Camp Barkeley	108
Camp Lee	131
St. Louis	143
San Francisco	158
St. Louis	169
Ft. Lewis, Washington	174
APO. N.Y.	209
Voyage	212
Chilbolton	217
Treviéres	242
Pantin (Paris)	276
Dijon	327
Foug	336
Camp Philadelphia	416
30-Day Leave	420
Ft. Leavenworth, Kansas	421

Ft. Benning, Georgia 422
Just a Bit of Travel. 425

Preface

When called to serve one's country in a war against a combination of formidable foes, one ought not be filled with such degree of self-esteem that he feels nearly all he has to say about his experiences should be preserved for future reference. Yet, that is what happened, for I had suggested that my family keep my letters. My chief correspondents were to be my mother, my sister, and my brother-in-law—Moosie, Bindy, and Don. They lived at the same address, and it was often convenient to write them in a collective sort of way. From a later date, my fiancee and wife to be, Miriam S. Hodgson, of Hyde Park, Massachusetts, likewise saved most of my letters.

As given name, "Donald" is well known. But, how about "Moosie" and "Bindy"? Here, we need some explanation. We shall turn first to time of origin, rather than to age. My sister was christened "Mary," after our mother. As a small child, she could not pronounce the consonant "M" as "muh," but would say "buh." When asked to say her name, "Mary Mickey," she would respond, "Bindy Binky." My father, a great one for nicknames, latched on to "Bindy"; and, so, it remained. I came along four years later and knew her only as "Bindy" and never used the other name.

My father, Benjamin, died in 1930, and my maternal grandparents, David and Janet Hanna, in 1931. We lived in the small town of Wood Lake, in the "Sandhills" of north central Nebraska. The years of our "Great Depression" followed in the 1930s. My mother, forced by circumstances to resort to her own resources, moved into the large parental house. This magnificent home was completely furnished and sat above a full basement. Its two major levels provided for gracious living. Four of its five bed rooms were large and with closets. The attic above was a "walk through" and had five dormer windows. My mother would board and room some of the teachers of the public school and usually two boys attending the high school. Others who wished to join at the table did so. The crowd for a noon meal averaged fourteen.

Conversation about the table never lacked for wit, and warm friendship led to some terms of endearment and to nicknames, even. For our purpose, we need remember but one name, that given to my mother. A very pretty woman, with a gentle and round face, she gained the sobriquet of "Mooseface"—eventually to become "Moosie," and it, in time, became a term of endearment for nearly all who knew her within a "family circle."

To write her, only on rare occasion did I address her as "Mother"; it was to be as "Moosie." The ordinary "Dear" would, as the emotions of wartime intensified, level at "Dearest." Therefore, "Dearest Moosie" serves to provide title for this collection of excerpts from many, many letters—written to "folks at home," May 12, 1942 to October 3, 1945.

One may wish to note, at this point, that my letters began at Ft. Leavenworth, KS, and then followed from Camp Shelby, Hattiesburg, MS; Camp Barkeley, Abilene, TX; Camp Lee, VA; Medical Depot, St. Louis, MO; Medical Depot, San Francisco, CA; Medical Depot, St. Louis, MO; Ft. Lewis, WA; APO, NYC; Chilbolton Downs, near Winchester, England; Trevieres, France; Paris, France; Dijon, France; Foug, France; Camp Philadelphia, near Reims, France; Ft. Leavenworth, KS; and Ft. Benning, GA.

Preface

Staff Sergeant

1st Lieutenant

Ft. Leavenworth

May 12, 1942

Dearest Moosie, Bin & Don,

Well, here I am—in Leavenworth—the Fort. This reception center is really quite a place—just plenty big. So far, our program has been exceedingly unpredictable—will be this way until we get definitely placed, I guess.

Left Ft. Crook last evening at 5:20 and got here about 9:30. Then we had to wait here until after midnight—then to bed and up at a quarter to five. Judas, but it was ornery—but such is the life of your soldier boy—and my bet is that he can take it. Eh? One thing is certain—is that we are all in the same old buggy.

One thing that surprised me is the certainty of so many of the fellows that this mess will be over in, at the most, six months. I'm afraid they are optimistic. Haven't really seen or heard much news since I left, but guess we won't need any. Humph! Sure miss it, though.

Well, there really isn't, as yet, anything to write. I'm sitting on a bunk, a book on my knee, and trying to make this writing intelligible. We had our fingers stuck this morning for our blood counts and tests and so far I haven't been shot. I'd certainly like to know just all of what we will be getting.

Well, you must have had quite a rain up there. Did you get home before it broke. From what it said in the papers, it must have been quite a downpour—old Salt Creek—really on the rampage.

It will probably be 7-10 days before we will be moved, and they desire that we not be written to. It adds considerable confusion and extra work, I guess. It already seems like a week since you left me at Ft. Crook, but, when this darned milling around is over, I'm sure that the time won't pass so slowly.

They showed us two or three short movies this morning—hygiene, courtesy, etc. Were really quite interesting. Visual education is really a part of any instruction.

This confounded pen is just about dry, but I doubt if I'll get this mailed today, but I know you are anxious to hear from me, eh?

Be sure to keep track of all that I might be interested in. I'll remind you later of all my things that I want you to do for me. Eh? But most of all, see that any Uni. fees are paid that are "called to my attention." That absentia fee, in particular—but I really shouldn't have to pay it.

Well, if I get a chance to mail this, I will; if not, will add some more tomorrow.

Ft. Leavenworth, Kansas May 13, 1942

Now, a bit after 8:00 a.m. We have been up since 5 o'clock. They do know how to rouse us up and out at an early hour. This is going to be quite a life, methinks. We are quite a mixture of persons. I'm going to enjoy it. We have no program, as yet.

We took our I.Q. and "Mechanical Aptitude" tests, yesterday. Results are to be posted by serial number. I answered 143 of a possible 150 for the first, and all but two in the second. Do not know how well I did, but for the second I guessed all over the place—all about pulleys, metal-cutting, etc. We got to bed about nine, and I feel much rested this morning.

We are to be issued our clothing. I shall be sending home my "civies"—and things will be quite wrinkled. As for the tweed suit, just hang it in my closet. It has been worn to nearly a frazzle.

Saw Stan Essman this morning. He taught Vocational Agriculture at Oshkosh. Then, I ran into Tat Bowman, fellow Wesleyanite—debater and Phi Tau. Ross Allen, one of our group of 46 who came down from Omaha, thinks that those who scored well in the tests will be assigned soon and shipped out. We shall see. You are to be notified right away as to my "address." I sort of hope I shall be assigned for "personnel" work.

Ft. Leavenworth May 14, 1942

Just a note to tell you the latest. All is O.K., though.

Our courier from Omaha did not have our papers with him, and there has been a mixup. So, they will not process us until they have our papers—for the 46 of us. They will do nothing with us, except feed us. Ha! The food is good, and we are going to be putting on pounds—in a hurry. We have been told that at least three days will be required to find our papers. Meanwhile, we have just played cards, gone to movies, and become somewhat bored.

Two groups following us have been processed and sent along their ways. We are getting a good rest. But, we may soon become "permanent fixtures." We continue to wear what we have on.

Ft. Leavenworth May 16, 1942

We are still here. Two of us went to see the "Company Commander," a Captain Clemens. He called the 46 of us together to explain our situation. The courier, who brought us from Ft. Crook, had picked up the wrong set of papers, and until they had our papers we could not be "handled." We have been passed over and will not be processed until they have, here, our papers. So, we must wait. We are getting plenty of rest, and our food is good and plentiful. But we sort of complained of boredom.

So, the captain asked us to clean up the unit barracks—five of them, each two storied. This we did—wearing our civilian clothes and attracting quite a bit of attention. We then stood "inspection," and passed with flying colors. We are now known as "The Lost Battalion," and we seem to be attracting quite a bit of attention.

The captain decided we should have some drill. So, two sergeants lined us up, marched us to a field, and we had a long session of instruction and practice in drill. These two sergeants had as good a time with this as we did, and it was almost a relief from the boredom.

Until our papers arrive, we shall have no interviews with respect to assignments. But, once our files get here, then action will take over.

Ft. Leavenworth May 17

Nothing to write home about. The call home was delightful. Our papers are still elusive. We have been given the run of the camp, almost a special status. We just cannot leave the grounds.

As one of the officers said, without our papers they, here, have no proof that we are really in the army. Ho! Ho!

And, no trouble with the teeth which you recently filled, Don. So, I think I shall have no pain, whatever. So, no need to take a "pain killer."

Talk circulating about rationing of gas. So, you'd better take your summer trips while you have no restrictions. Have been strolling all over this base, and it just amazes me—all of the motorized equipment! Whew—but it is going to take an ocean of gasoline to keep all this stock a-rolling.

Some of us have been doing lots of hiking—just to take a look into the corners of this base. And, some nearby horseshoe pits have provided us with good fun. I played about 15 games at one stretch.

May 19, 1942, Ft. Leavenworth (but this letter would be mailed from Camp Shelby, Hattiesburg, Mississippi, the 26th)

Well, I've just completed my first day in uniform, and we spent most of the day in "fatigue suits"—work clothes, silly hats, etc. Someday, I'll get a picture to you of me in them.

We really get the clothes issued to us; and when I am in a writing mood, I'll give you a full description. I wish they would hurry up and get me stationed. I saw an interviewer yesterday, and he recommended to be an "instructor." On my I...Q., the score was 138—comfortably high out of a possible 150. My mechanical aptitude score was 140 out of 150. I don't quite understand, for I guessed like a fool in the second test; but, maybe I'm just mechanical at heart. Ha! The interviewer said the two scores were very good. He also asked if I would object to being put in the air corps. I said "No." However, what instruction I could give there would be a joke. (Maybe I'll meet up with Major Ralston, my Uncle Orville, if I get in the AC.)

As soon as I get my shipping orders, I'll phone you. From indications, it should be tomorrow (Friday, or Saturday). We have been here nearly a week too long, and we will probably be hurried out. Some of the fellows have told their folks to write them here, and have received letters. I think it is better not to write. Phone calls are more fun.

In full uniform I attended my first retreat this evening. While in formation, the Star Spangled Banner was lowered, and I must say it gave me a thrill. I'm quite certain that I'll not dislike army life; but, you can bet I'll be glad when it is over. Yes!

We don't hear much news—just a rumor now and then. Actually, we don't have much time for news. We must have spent from three to four hours drilling today, and these big army shoes are just the stuff. My shoes fit just swell, and I doubt if they will bother me any.

Camp Shelby

May 25, Camp Shelby, Mississippi, Hattiesburg

Well, it will be quite a lapse of time since you last heard from me, but I didn't write another letter from Ft. L.—because I thought I'd be able to call you before I left. As it was, we were given about an hour's notice, had to pack our barrack bags, line up, go to "chow," back to the barracks, pick up our bags, get checked out, march about a mile to a RR station, and thence away. Darn! I didn't have more of chance to call you than a monkey. But, here I am, and no one can do anything about it.

We left Saturday evening and arrived here this morning (Monday)—two nights on the train; but, we had sleepers and really rode in state. However, it was a dirty train, and none too easy to ride. Our route—via Kansas City, St. Louis, Cairo, Illinois, Memphis, Tennessee, and then to Hattiesburg, Miss. We are little more than hundred miles from the Gulf. Boy, but it is Deep South!

I'm going to heah jes' plenty of this Suthun Tahlk. Didn't do much today—missed out on a six-mile hike I was supposed to have been on, but the Sergeant said it was all right. So, I went on a detail duty. It is very sultry here—very damp, and my cough has begun again. They have placed me in the Medical Detachment of the 328th Artillery Battalion, in the 85th Division. I don't know if I'll like it. If not, I can seek change.

We will have about three weeks of drill, and I am told that will be about all. We've been told we'll be very busy. I still just about fly into a spasm every time I pass a commissioned officer and have to salute. I shall get over this. Ha! Officers here are very nice, but we should know a few things, and they will expect us to be ever so efficient.

By the way, Moose, keep all letters I write to you, for I might want to remember many incidents, etc. So. I shall keep putting events into the letters. I'm in the deep, deep south, and feel just plenty far away from home; however, I think it is just a part of this whole business. From all indications—after this next three weeks is up, I will know more about army life.

May 29, 1942 Camp Shelby, Miss.

Whew! Let me tell you that this is just about the hottest place I have seen for some time. I'm going to seek a transfer as soon as my period of training is over. Believe me, this sultry weather certainly saps one's vim and vitality. But, perhaps I'm to be toughened up a bit. Ha!

We continue to have classes of instruction, and drill and march, etc. So far I've avoided the six-mile hikes they hold every evening. We Privates are sort of "the Freshmen" about camp, but it isn't so bad, really.

They are certainly fussy about the way our beds are made. So far, mine has passed inspection. There are five of us in this tent—along with me the following: Charles Gladue from N.Dak.; Louis Dvoskin from Jacksonville, Flo.; Martin D'Onofrio from New Rochelle, N.Y.; and Clayton Goodyear from Omaha. We're pulled into this together.

This Southern Drawl is quite interesting. By the time I get home, I should be able to give you a good demonstration. I have no trouble understanding it. Do not know, yet, what I may be doing ultimately, but from indications it will be non combatant. An instructor has told me that glasses are too dangerous in battle zones because they reflect and thus attract.

Every one is certainly hoping that the Russians can hold Hitler. It will mean such a vastly shorter war, and, too, that is what all are hoping and praying for.

I'm going to try to look up some of the fellows who came down from Leavenworth—about 15 of us were in the group held over for so long, and most of them were swell guys. I'm having no trouble with my feet, and I'll make the grade after all. A man in the army is no better than his feet when it comes to this army business. It's no later than 8:30 in the morning, but is has seemed like a long day thus far—for the sun is already overhead, nearly. My serial number is 37123304.

May 29, 1942 Camp Shelby

Well, tomorrow is Memorial Day. It won't seem much like it, I'm afraid.

This sort of life is not distasteful—really not so much different from camp life about which I am familiar. But, it is terribly hot down here. Really, it just drives one to a melted away feeling. We have been working on a 105mm howitzer, and running through formation, etc. It is all part of the basic training which every one has to take. The "drill" is thrown in 2 or 3 hours per day.

I'm expecting mail tomorrow. Write me long letters! This three weeks' lapse has been the berries. I had to substitute on K.P. after supper tonight. It wasn't bad, just annoying, for I had wanted to see a Charlie Chaplin movie.

I still haven't found any of the bunch. Maybe I'll have to raise a little Cain if these buzzards can't tell me where certain people are around here. Ha! From what I hear, new rules are going to call for "stricter observance." I believe I can endure. That seems to be what we are doing—anyway. Oh, well. If it would just cool off! I'll never live permanently in the South!

They put us through some paces, today, but we had a pretty good time. This cabin group of ours is the berries. We spend most of our spare time just sitting around and laughing about each other's great troubles.

May 31, 1942 Camp Shelby

Well, my first Sunday, here. Sundays are our own time to spend as we desire, and I guess I'll go to church at 10:00 this morning. It hardly seems possible that it is three weeks since you took me to Ft. Crook, does it? Well, I was just sitting here and thought that I might just as well babble a line or two to you.

I still do not know just how I have come to be placed in this Med. Detachment. I'm quite certain that I might as well get this basic training here as any place. We had rifle drill yesterday, and it was interesting. As far as I can gather, we'll be in training—classes and drill—for about 13 weeks; but some have said that orders are to push down to eight weeks. Anyway, after I am a little better orientated, I'll inquire about officer's training. If my five years of college won't mean anything, then I'll just have to explode, eh? Ha! Well, enuf.

There are a number of movies in the camp, and also a very large auditorium. Every Saturday evening there is a broadcast from Shelby, and I think it is on a national hookup. Anyhow, when I know more definitely, I'll let you know. There is certainly one advantage to the being of a private, and that is one doesn't have to do anything but follow orders. Also, it is a restful procedure, mentally. Believe me, these officers are faced with considerable responsibility.

Well, I must start for some church, or chapel, and will put my mind at rest, I hope. Sundays are bad days for the army, maybe. It isn't so bad when one is busy. I'll have to get out and explore the camp this afternoon. I sure hope I can run on to the fellows I know. I'd give a lot to know just where about four of them are. This camp is about 15 miles square. So, it isn't a big chance that I could meet them.

Am still waiting for a letter, dern it! But I fear mail service here in camp is slower than the devil.

June 2, 1942 Camp Shelby

So much has happened since I wrote yesterday. First of all, I received my first letter from home, and it was a thrill—from you, Mother. I was just about to go into distraction, for three weeks without a letter is bad. BAD! Your two diaries were just about perfect, for I think I've missed very little.

You probably wonder how I got hold of this typewriter. I guess I'm going to be a sort of clerk in this Med. Det. As far as I can gather, until my basic training is over, I'll "train" in the morning, and then type and file in the P.M.s. Anyhow, things are beginning to take form. It all started when I asked our Sergeant if I could use one of the typewriters in the Dispensary (Infirmary). He didn't answer my question, but asked if I could type—not by "hunt and peck?" When I said I could, he just rushed me right over. Well, I get out of a long, dirty hike every afternoon; but, today, I had to type over twenty letters which requested medical attention for soldiers at the Station Hospital. All in all, I don't know whether to prefer hiking or typing. Ha!

Well, I no sooner got up here yesterday afternoon when a Major stepped up to me, for he had noticed I came from Nebraska and that my name was Mickey. He asked if I was relation to the former "Governor of Nebraska," and I told him I was a grandson. His family name is HAWES, and he originally came from Fairbury; his father and Grandpa Mickey were very good friends. So, there was one good acquaintance that came my way.

Another surprise came when I received your big air-mail letter, the one you wrote after receiving my first letter from Shelby. On the face of the letter was written—"See Cap't Munger, please."

I hardly knew what to do, for I didn't think I knew any "C. M." It so happens that Dr. Horace Munger is a Cap't down here in the medical corps (and, Bin, you know who he is). We've had a couple short visits; and believe me, it is nice to meet someone from the "old home town." It is not something to be sneezed at! People are really thrown together in strange circumstances, aren't they!

As I've said before, weather here is atrocious—just so warm and humid. I just about sweat off my skin, but I guess I can take it as long as I can keep sweating. Boy! When a lieutenant comes rushing in with a patient and wants an order for treatment typed, I have to flag it. On one set of papers, several of them, I got the dates for admission to the army typed instead of the date for admission to the Station Hospital, and our poor Sergeant had to get the mess straightened out. We later laughed about it, for it was all new to me. But, it had better not happen again!

By the way, did you receive the Army Insurance policy I took out—making you two the beneficiaries, first and second? It is for ten thousand dollars. You should have received it by now. Let me know, if not, and I will check on it. Don't know what I'd do, but I could try.

Don't send any cookies, for it is just too warm and humid. I'd much like to have them, but I think hard candy would be better. Cooked stuff might spoil before it is ever delivered.

To give my address, this is correct as I know it—Pvt. David H. Mickey, Medical Detachment, 328th Field Artillery Battalion, 85th Division, Camp Shelby, Mississippi. These abbreviations can be used—Med. Det. and F.A. Bn. The 328th must be there, for it tells which Med Det I'm associated with, and will speed up delivery. They are switching soldiers much, but I guess I shall remain where I am. If the war is a short one, I doubt if I'll be interested in officer's school. A couple of our lieutenants have asked me about it. If they ask me again, I may put my name on the list. I do not want to appear to be too eager. Will wait to see. One must wait about thirteen weeks before being admitted, anyhow, and then only a chance.

Well, this is a terrible war! Hardly any breeze here, but it is cool during nights. I haven't had a bad night's sleep since I arrived. I still have not found any of the fellows who came down here with me. We are soon to have a roster available, and then maybe some success.

I went to church, Sunday, and it helped immensely. I was pretty blue all morning—just thinking about home. But, the sermon sort of straightened me out, a bit. I may go over to visit with the Chaplain some evening.

June 4, 1942 Camp Shelby

Well, we had a darned nice rain here yesterday, and today it is quite cool. Really, the heat has been something terrific down here. But, the life of a soldier boy is one of taking whatever is dished out to him—and that is that.

I see Capt. Munger every day, and we exchange greetings. His wife, as you know—Margaret Buell of Randolph. I believe he is to be head of the medical division—or something. I feel that I'm not just started out with someone I never knew.

Our Sergeant—in charge of us—is quite a fellow (Johnson); he gets rather excited, but I'm beginning to make fewer errors, I hope. He had to chase all over camp the other evening to correct some dates I had put in wrong—the first time I tried to do it. He just said it was all in the learning of the game. I think he felt he was getting the initiation, not me.

June 5, 1942 Camp Shelby (Friday)

Will try to snatch a few moments to drop you a few lines. I'm busy most of an afternoon and evening, but things at the moment are a little slower. Time seems to be slipping by rather rapidly, and I can't say that I really dislike any part of this sort of life. Of course, I have long insisted that any thing can be just as bad or as good as a person lets it become, and that may be that.

Monday, a Lt. from the Medical Corps is to begin to teach us that which we in this Med Det are to know. We will have about two hours each morning, while the others have exercise, drill, clean up, etc. The rest of the time we'll study on our more specific duties. Of course, I wouldn't mind knowing more about all the guns; but, after all, if we are going to be good at this MED game, we can't spend too much time on this drill. Much of what we do is nonsense. Drill does keep us alert and responsive; but, a good bit of what we get is just exactly not up to snuff—seems to me.

I'm poohed tonight. Cap't Munger had me make a week's training schedule—all lined and neat for next week—four pages, and it took me over three hours. At times, I was at my wit's end, but it turned out OK. My hunch is that it will never be used, for there still seems to be some mixup on just when and where we Meds are to be trained—and by whom. Anyway, a General wanted a tentative schedule by this evening, and I did flag my fanny around.

Too, I'm to be typist for our "doctors," and this will keep me very busy. Come what may, I think I can keep up with them.

We do get substantial food, here, and I'm not kicking one bit. Sometimes things are not just exactly tasty, but we can hardly expect to be too pleased, can we?

My cough never did get very bad. I still continue to spit up a lot of stuff, but not much more than normal.

I get amused at the fellows who can't stay in step, and it is so easy to get "out" if one takes his mind off what he is doing. This morning our old Sergeant was giving us some different "directions," and I glanced across at some of the other fellows and turned right instead of left. Old Sgt. wanted to know if I had two left hands. I told him I did, and grinned. He told me I'd better switch one of them to the right side. I told him I would. It wasn't all that bad.

So far, we haven't been bothered by too many mosquitoes. I've been told they are about as big as bombers, down here—especially when they get organized. We'll get them later. The chiggers have been after us lately, but I've had just a few.

Please send me my little red camera and my brown shoes (the ones I sent home from Leavenworth). Also, I'll need my polishing set—the dobber, shiner, and brush. There is not a one of us who wanted to come into this army, but only a few want to get out until all is finished up and those darned maniacs are laid low.

June 7, 1942 Camp Shelby

A Sunday afternoon again, and the one easy day we get. It is a sort of day off, for we are not as busy as usual. We have more time to think of things other than the army, etc. But, sometimes Sunday may not be an easy day. It has rained off and on, and I do not like rainy days "in the army." Went to a movie this afternoon—Jackie Cooper, Adolph Menjou and Bonita Granville in "Syncopation." It wasn't bad. I am waiting to see that Skelton picture that you liked so well.

From what you write, Major Ralston must be in there really pitching. It is wonderful that Cy Bo (Aunt Charlotte) could make the trip to see him. Later, he may not be able to choose "a time" for her visit.

This typing job is going to be a devil of a lot of work, and most of it is going to be on the side. I hope I can get some kind of a rating out of it, but don't suppose so. There is not much chance for advancement in this type of service—as I understand it; but it isn't going to be as hard a training as the other would ordinarily be. However, I'm going to be plenty busy, and I don't mean maybe. The medical instruction begins tomorrow, and with the exception of the mornings and evenings, when we are doing drill or calisthenics, we will be entirely free from the Artillery group. As I understand it, our work will be taken up with the application of medicine in the army and field, treatments of various diseases and injuries, etc. By the time I'm out of this army, I should know quite a bit about the art of medicine. All of our instructors will be Doctors—not regular army men, and I think I'll like them a good deal better. At least, they aren't shelled with the crust of professional army men. Ha! Ha! Well, whatever.

Cap't. Munger, I think, is to be head of this particular medical detachment, and he will probably have a good deal to say about things. I typed a class (instruction) schedule for him the other day, and from the sound of things we are going to have our hands full.

Your last letters, via air mail, came through in two days. Since you now address them correctly, Ahem!, they do arrive a day earlier. Unless they are "just so," they may "lay over"—even for two days! I have tried the razor sharpener, and it works fine.

From all indications, we are going to get a raise in pay, if the House and Senate can ever make up their minds on the subject. It certainly amuses me the way these American politicians can throw the bull and get nowhere, fast. Also, all of the red tape it takes to get anything really done in this government amazes me. However, this is the American way, and I don't believe that we would trade it for any other way that is now existing on the face of the earth.

The news concerning the Japanese naval losses west of Midway seemed to be pretty good and authentic. I hope we can soon give them some more good doses—and maybe they will wish like thunder that they had never heard of Pearl Harbor.

Well, I feel quite adjusted, here. I really feel fine. My cough is O.K., but I still croup around a little. Maybe I'll just sweat it out. This muggy climate is enough to kill or cure, and I believe it might cure me—anyway, that is the way I am betting.

June 9, 1942 Camp Shelby

Tuesday—I guess the best way to write these letters is to all of you, for what I have to say is to all of you. So, that is that! The more I see of this man's army, the more I think I'd like to do just a little cleaning up around the edges. But, I don't think I know just where I would commence. I shall tell you about it sometime. Feel pretty good tonight. It rained most of the day and was very muggy. It hasn't been so warm, but sweat just does not evaporate. I can not say much for this Mississippi climate.

We are being instructed entirely by the Medical Corps lieutenants and captains, and it is much better. I also liked our other instructors. We have drill and calisthenics every morning from 7:10 to 8:30, but that is just duck soup—at least, I don't mind it. My two summers at Camp Waldron must have given me a little wind to go on.

This darned typing takes all afternoon, and usually each evening. I think I put in more hours than any other Private around these "here parts." However, my work may be a little "softer." Ha! This "darned typing" may well be the thing I had in high school that is really going to be worth a good bit.

I finally ran onto one of my "Lost Battalion" pals, Sunday evening. We had quite a time comparing adventures. We aren't more than three blocks apart, but our paths just had not crossed. .Now, ain't that the old devil!

The news seems pretty good right now. Sure hope it continues. Yes, I read a paper nearly every day. So, you should not send me the "Journal," for I do not need it. Thanks, anyway.

June 12, 1942 Camp Shelby

I believe I haven't written for some time. We have been terrifically busy, and I've been pounding out the old typewriter "music." I now help to run through the cards for "sick call" in the morning. So, it has now become an all day job in the dispensary. We hold about seven hours of classes each day, and if I ever get into my noodle all of this medical stuff, it will be a miracle.

The weather has been so very muggy, and terrifically sweaty. I guess that as long as I can sweat, I'll be OK. I expected to get my box today, but it didn't come. I'm surprised you couldn't find my shoe-shining brush. I'll bet you thought it was a clothes brush—wooden back, with rather long soft bristles.

When the camera gets here, I'll get you some pictures. But, I'm not going to have any good photos taken until I can wear my O.D.s.

We are being moved tomorrow, or Sunday. Will be to another area, but close by. They like to move us around. Just don't want us to get too comfortable.

June 15, 1942 Camp Shelby

The weather, so hot and disagreeable, is about the only complaint I can, at present, make. Got four letters, Saturday—so, quite a day!

Also, I located the fellows that I have been trying to find. Yesterday afternoon, as result of the mail system here, we managed to get together. Four of us went to a Service Club, about 5:30, and ordered sirloin steaks, each for 75¢, and were they good! Honestly, they were the best tasting morsels, and must have been "Nebraska grown." Each of us blew half of a private's monthly salary, and that is not much, I assure you. Yeah! By the time $6.70 each month is reduced from my paycheck, I don't have much of the original 21 to spend. But, I still haven't cashed my last "school check." I really do not need much money. But I'd need some extra were we to take off for New Orleans, or Jackson, some weekend—on a "leave," of course.

We got moved, but it certainly messed up our schedules. It seemed rather disgusting and unnecessary; but, we must get used to these sorts of orders. There seems to be so much waste and duplication of time. Of course, this is just my own observation and idea—a Private's. Ha!

No news to speak of, but I have a hundred things to do on this typewriter this afternoon; so, I'd better close this. It seems to me that the days are getting busier and busier, with less time to think about much—other than to attempt to crowd about twice as much into the time-space we have. Well, the busier I am, the better off I am, methinks.

P.S. Did I understand that Don may be going into service soon? If so, some thoughts from me. The best place for you, Bin, would be right there in Lincoln. Really, the officers' wives, who are living down here, pay atrocious rents! (I think Margaret Munger is to arrive, here, soon.)

PSS Didn't get this mailed; so, will add a bit. It is so hot down here! But, I really think that I am beginning to get acclimated, for it doesn't seem to bother me like it did.

It was a long and drawn out day, today. I really kept this typewriter "hot." I wish I could get "lined out"—to know just what I'll be doing.

As for homesickness, I just try to think about other things, and about all I have to do here. I can't believe that it has been a month since Ft. Crook. I'm glad they keep us busy—less time to become homesick.

June 16, 1942 Camp Shelby (to Bindy)

Well, I finally found my old pals that I met at Leavenworth. Four of us hit it to a service club and had sirloin steaks. Oh, boy—good, good, good! We really gorged. Mine was nearly three-fourths of an inch thick, and cooked just this side of rare, the way I like it!—to perfection! It was a rare treat, yessirree! We think this should be a regular Sunday affair, and just for 75 cents, each. Aah!

As for Don's going into the service??? What's the general public going to do when so many, or most, of the doctors and dentists are "in service"? Nevertheless, we are short of medical and dental help, here.

So much written work to all of this, and my knowing to type has come in handy. Every Tuesday and Thursday consultation reports, all in form, to be written and typed—often more than twenty at a time.

Saturday, June 18, 1942 Camp Shelby

Tomorrow is Sunday, and I'm ready for another of those sirloin steaks, and I'm certain I'll do it justice. It is a grand, cool evening—rained most of the afternoon and should be quite decent to go nosing around camp tonight.

I'm beginning to feel quite like a doctor. The Sergeant is to be gone tomorrow, and he put me in charge of sick call. So, I'll be running about twenty fellows through the gauntlet in the morning—and the main job will be to put dope on the chiggers. Of course, our battalion doctor, a lieutenant, will be there, but Doc Mickey will sort of herd them around.

We have been "typing" blood the last two days, and three of us have been helping the lieutenants. My job, one of them, is to stick the finger, push out the blood, and get the drop into the solution. Ah! I have a mean look in my eye, for it gives me some satisfaction to jab some of these new and cocky drill corporals. Ha!

Yesterday was a sort of punk day for me. About 10:30 in the morning, I felt droopy, but nothing serious or sharp. Ate lunch, but while we were having gas-mask drill, things began to go round and round. I just moved out, made it to the dispensary, and to the toilet. Ah! but did this little soldier heave—almost everything but his back-pack. Mercy, but I thought I was to turn inside out. However, I kept my "natural form," pulled myself together, and ventured forth. I really looked like a ghost, and felt like ten of them. Well, the lieutenant on duty—not knowing that the worst was over, and he thought I had really been hit by something. He made me sit down; and, before I could get him to listen—that I had merely eaten something that didn't agree with me, he was of mind to call an ambulance. He gave me a stimulant, a little ammonia in water, and in thirty minutes I was O.K. Later, he told me that he thought I was going to collapse—that he didn't want me flat on my back, because we had about 105 men "to type" that afternoon. Ha! This morning he gave me the "once over." Again, I assured him that my stomach knew what is could not take. It crossed my mind, that maybe some of the cookies from home had been the culprits. Actually, I was overdue for a good, old-fashioned heaving spell. Humph!

There is talk around here that some of us, maybe six of fifteen, are going to be moved over to "Medical Headquarters." From what I gather, about three from our group of sixteen will probably go—myself included. As of now, this is mere speculation, and nothing is to be said until finally accomplished. I could finally be out into clerical work. After all, it is what I can probably do best. From the amount of typing I have been pouring out for lieutenants (doctors), etc., I'm certain I can keep up. I hope it all will turn out just right.

It is interesting to hear the fellows speculate as to the endurance of the war. Such varied opinions and reactions. We all want it to be over in a hurry. But, some think Hitler and Japan are practically done for. Personally, I can't see it. So, usually I just sit, say little, and answer questions if asked. Every once in a while, somebody will make such an outlandish statement that I feel the urge to attempt to give some enlightenment. In general, we agree that we have at least another "year of army life."

Well, I'm going to meet Wallace Holen, the fellow from Holdrege, and we are going to bang about a little this evening. He is one grand fellow, and one of these days I'll get a picture of us snapped and will send it to you.

My hair is actually almost back to a combing state, but it is still quite a bush. The wave is definitely back. So, the next time you see me, I should look my natural self. Ha! Those pictures make me look impish. Eh?

June 20, 1942 Camp Shelby

At 2:30 in the afternoon, I have my typing done. Isn't it wonderful! Now comes the fun of catching up on filing.

I must invest in a couple of new summer uniforms. It will cost me about eight dollars each, but I must have them. I can't continue to wear a uniform for a week and expect it to last very long. A person can easily sweat one to pieces, here.

The cookies arrived, with some crumbled a bit. Most whole and nice, but they wont last long—just this evening.

Two days until Sunday, Friday and Sat in between, and than I can sleep in the morning.

Still don't know what my job will finally be, but it looks as if it were definitely shaping into some sort of a clerk's position. Of course, if the Division moves overseas, the clerks will have to go along to keep the records—just as usual. I haven't taken a hike for at least ten days, for this office-work keeps me busy all of the time. But, just in case we should have to take a long, overnight hike, an assistant in the Dental Clinic and I take long walks each evening after supper. Last evening, I walked more than four miles, each way, to seek one of the fellows I so much like and who came down from Leavenworth with me. When I got back, I was ready for a little rest.

I know that some of the others around here do not like it because a few of us get out of a lot of B.S.—all of which most have to go through, do things that have to be done, spend hours on this and that, etc. So, much seems to be in spite of whatever one tries to do to avoid it.

Each must have his blood typed, and my job yesterday was to alphabetize the entire "Division Artillery"—four battalions. The Sergeant thought I'd be working until after midnight, but it took only an hour and ten minutes—about five hundred names—the whole shootin' match. Maybe all the sorting I did for Miss Reynoldson, down at the University, gave me a little method with which to employ a little madness. Anyhow, Sarge wouldn't believe it was done when I told him.

Margaret Munger is here, now, and will be for some time—as I understand. They have a residence somewhere. For a change, I got Capt. Munger's training schedule for us medics all typed up in time yesterday afternoon. It took me more than three hours the first time, but only 40 minutes yesterday. So, I guess familiarity with procedure shortens one's time requirement for getting something done.

Again, it is starting to rain, and I must once more shut the window. The darned rain comes so very quietly here, and then it just pours down with density. Sometimes, things just sweep before the flow, and I don't mean maybe. Most of the gang are out somewhere, and I feel sorry for them—but such is the life of a soldier. So far, I haven't had to do much soldiering.

Major Hawes is certainly a fine person to be working for. I was much amused the other morning. We privates are not supposed to be hauled around by the officers, or even by the NCOs (non commissioned officers). Well, it so happened that we were delayed a bit in coming from our present barracks across about half of camp to the dispensary and were late in getting sick call under way. To get two of us to the dispensary in a hurry, the Sergeant and Major Hawes picked us up. In open touring car, we passed General Haislip. Major Hawes, quite certain that the general had seen us, started to worry—certain that the General would say something to him about it. To me, it was funny—that such a matter could cause so much concern. There was no "fall out," apparently. But, I was much amused.

Must write the Edwards, to thank them for the candy. Along with theirs, three other boxes of candy into the barracks, and we are still putting it where it is intended to go. Those sweet things do hit the spot! There are 16 of us in our barracks. Honestly, I think I have drunk more pop since I came down here than I have in all the rest of my life. But, doggone it, there is so little to spend your money on. I will get a pass when I go to New Orleans—should I so desire. Some of the gang have gone into Hattiesburg, but from report there is not much there, other than a big crowd. With the new pay increase, maybe I can afford to go to New O.—just something to plug for.

Every Saturday evening, at 9:30, there is a Victory Salute Program from Camp Shelby, and I think it is on a national hookup. Perhaps, you can locate it somewhere on the dial, particularly if relayed via a closer station. I haven't had a chance to get near a piano since I left home, and I certainly miss the darned thing. Now, I want you to remember something, for you told me that anything I wanted you would send it to me—RIGHT AWAY! The next time you send something to me, do put in my old glasses-case. I left my other one at Leavenworth. One of these days I'll be unlucky enough to break my glasses; but, I try to be very careful. Why don't you just send the case, and put the piano on the inside? There now, it is all settled!

I see they are beginning to tear down our old tent-stand. They are starting to clear space for new hutments. Then, maybe we will move back to our locality and wont be traipsing all over the country to get from barracks to dispensary.

I spent over an hour this morning fixing the typewriter, for there was one of the keys that would not print. As result of a "hair raising" investigation, I found that one of the little connecting wires had slipped off. Luckily enough, I found it on the floor under the desk. Maybe someone was monkeying with the machine last night, after I had put it away. Had we been rushed this morning, we would have been "in a pickle." And, I don't mean maybe!

Am waiting for Clay to come, for we go to buy new clothes. I wish this rain would stop. I hope the tailor shop is open, yet. I'd hate to wear these sour clothes another day. Our laundry is two days overdue, and that is why some of us are in such deplorable state. Ha!

P.S. I always get plenty to eat—just not enough pie and cake. Ha! We get lots of fruit for breakfast. For noon and evening, always salad—cabbage, cukes, etc. No—I make no complaint about our meals. Of course, not too often cooked and seasoned to suit my taste. Don't worry, Mrs. M., your little boy is not going hungry!

June 23, 1942 Camp Shelby

How time does fly! The days seem to slip by so fast that I can hardly keep up. I guess we are just pretty darned busy. Eh? But, the past two or three days have been almost civil, and without extremely warm weather. It rains nearly every afternoon, here, and I hope it continues to do so—for it makes it very comfortable to sleep. I will say this, that this army program makes one ready for the old army cot when 9:30 rolls around each evening.

At present, I am Charge of Quarters at the Dispensary, or Battalion Infirmary. Each of us, there are fifteen in the Med. Det., has to take his turn—so, it comes only every two weeks. We go from noon to noon; so, it carries a 24-hour duty. But, very little happens—at least it hasn't so far. There is always a lieutenant to be called in case anything serious comes up, but we usually handle something in a way that we can. Now, isn't that clear? We must paint chigger bites, doctor athlete's foot, etc. However, the other day a fellow nearly cut off the end of his finger with a razor blade, and one of our Meds, by keeping the wrist artery tightly held, stopped the bleeding—which was severe. Well, when the Lt. came to dress it, he got it started again and couldn't get it stopped. He called in us recruits, and we again effectively administered first aid. Our lieutenant was a little put out, for the soldier thought it rather queer that a doctor couldn't stop the flow. Ho!

I got your letters—written on the 19th and 20th. As you may guess, I certainly do not just wait until the next one comes. Letters mean so much, and are just one of the necessities of a soldier's life. Lincoln seems so darned far away, and, yet, when I close my eyes, I can see all of you so very plain. If I take out the two pictures that I kept, I can just about be back home. Anyhow, I think of you so often, and sometimes wonder if I am where I happen to be.

Sunday evening, Wallace (Holen) and I went to the Service Club to have another feast. He got half a fried chicken, and I had stuffed crab. Both were darned good, and you can bet that we did enjoy them. It is relief to get away from the hurry-scurry of the mess hall. One of the theaters here in camp is going to give a single showing of "Gone With the Wind," Friday evening. Wallace and I bought tickets—20 cents for a reserved seat. Now, isn't that some price! I should enjoy it as much as I did before—about two years ago. I'm looking forward to it, even though I will have to sit for four hours on an old hard bench. Yes! Wallace has never seen it, and I'm certain he will enjoy it.

I think all packages have arrived safe and sound. The oatmeal cookies were great, but some a little bruised. No crumbs escaped munching. The butterscotch didn't last long enough to get sticky. There wasn't much danger of that.

I do not understand just how this government insurance policy works. You are supposed to receive the policy. I imagine it may take it some time to go through all of the red tape this government procedure requires. As you may know, a new bill has passed, and no salaries will be paid until it has been determined that a soldier has dependents—or not. We will receive about fifteen dollars this month, and the remainder with our next month's wages. I still have a school check to cash, but I don't think my three and a half dollars will last me until July 10th. Anyway, I am happy that I have that reserve. Many of the fellows have been borrowing quite heavily.

My sinuses are not causing me any trouble—just a little drainage. As long as they do drain freely, there isn't any danger. If they ever stop up on me, though, I'll not hesitate a bit to get my head pumped out. The heat doesn't bother me any more; so, I guess I am just getting used to it. I'm sure I will always be a "damned Yankee"—as far as this weather and climate are concerned.

The war news doesn't sound very good lately. The loss of Tobruk is played a little too much, I think. But what worries me is the serious condition of Sebastopol, on the Black Sea. That is one place the Nazis just must not gain control of—in my estimation. The whole key to the Caucasus seems to lie right there. But, let us hope and pray that this last desperate offensive of Hitler will fail dismally. The next two or three weeks may determine the length of this war—in terms of months or years.

Soon, there are to be some appointments in our Med groups—for transfers over to the headquarters of the 85th Division Med. Det. I wouldn't mind getting one of those transfers. It would be some sort of office work. I'll let you know as soon as I hear anything definite. A promotion might come, and I could strut around with a couple of stripes on my sleeve.

This old building is a real quiet place right now. No one here but me, and this old typewriter is a bit of company. At least, the noise is company. I don't know if I shall be able to sleep without all of the snoring that one gets used to in the barracks. Anyhow, I'm going to give it a try pretty soon—and should enjoy an extra hour of sleep in the morning. Ha! This is one advantage to being the C of Q.

There was a notice given the other day that no furloughs would be given in the 4th Corps Area until after the fall maneuvers. There may be exceptions. Certain groups may not be called for maneuvers, but will be broken into cadres to organize medical units in new Divisions. Only time will tell. Anyhow, the furlough I'll plug for will be the Christmas one, and then I'll hope it will be for twenty days. Anyhow, I think that will be the soonest we can plan on. Just six months until Xmas—I'll have to start saving my dimes.

Well, this has become quite a letter. I'm just about run down. I thought I would get about six letters written tonight, but my peepers wont keep open. We did go through the Gas Chamber today. Tear Gas, and does the stuff ever smart! The first time we went in, we had to wear our masks—to check them for efficiency. The second time, we opened them a little—to test for gas. The third, with masks off, and then to put them on. Of course, the gas hit us, but it is not harmful. We held our breath, but those masks went on in a hurry—for it was quite unpleasant. It was quite educational.

June 25, 1942 Camp Shelby

I'll start you a note on this piece of scrap paper. This is one of the days when we send fellows to the hospital for consultation, and pretty soon the diagnoses will start rolling in. You"ll probably get this letter when you receive my last one, for I did not mail it right away.

From all indications, it is going to warm up considerably, and I'm not looking forward to it. I can wish I were in Alaska, as far as this temperature is concerned. It wasn't so bad as long as the rain kept up. But, when the sky clears, it gets atrociously hot.

As you have found out, when I sit down to the typewriter, I just write as I think, and in about ten minutes it is all over. I typed at the Dispensary until nearly 9:30 last night, and made out next week's training schedule, and this typing is never a picnic. I sort of dread a Wednesday, for it is schedule day.

No news, really; and, I can't seem to make up any. It must be the heat, er sompin. Did you ever know anyone by the name of Castile—as in Soap? It seems there is a Major Castile here in camp; he knows the Mickey family, and was looking for me the other day. I can't recall having heard of that name—a person who was a family friend. If you can think as to who he might be, let me know.

You seem to be so worried about the boxes you send me. Heavens! Haven't you received any of my letters—that they have arrived? So, rest on your oars, Moose! Will write some more when I return to the barracks this evening.

8:30 pm Well, I just got my hair cut, but just around the edges. It is still short, but not as it was. I just doctored up a fellow who had been getting no relief from chigger bites. I applied something quite different from the usual, and I hope it cures. Ha!

Now back to my hair. I want it long enough to comb, and I don't think it will take me long to train it. It has been unbearably warm today, and everyone is running around with his tongue out. I'd certainly like to hit the North Pole for a brief stay. I'm just about fagged.!

Everyone seems to get a kick out of my fancy pajamas. Anyhow, I wear 'em. The nights are cool, but it is almost too hot for a blanket. So, the pajamas come in handy. I had the green ones laundered last week. Our laundry—things look much of the time as if they had been thrown at an ironer and then rolled into whatever shape or form they might take.

There is a lot of athlete's foot around here, and we sure keep feet doctored up. It has no excuse to let it advance to the extent that some do. When maneuvers start, we will be rushed to death—just painting and dabbing.

June 28, 1942 Camp Shelby

Well, I have quite a bit to tell you. Don't know just where to begin.

As you may have noticed, my title has changed. As of the 26th of June, I am a Technician Fifth Grade, and called a Corporal—though strictly speaking, I am not. I'll have two chevrons and a "T" on my sleeves. It will certainly look better than nothing. I'll be a medical clerk, also a sick and wounded clerk, a "Technician." There are several government forms I must become familiar with, and I shall have them under my thumb—you can bet.

We (and I could cautiously say "I") have the dispensary office pretty well organized. Last Wednesday and Thursday, I washed it from top to bottom; then, rearranged and labeled all the shelves, restacked all forms above the labels and in the process found many forms that had been lost. Now with the filing up to date, it begins to seem that we have "a system." I'm beginning to feel at home in this place. Maybe I can do a little "regulating"—now that my stripes will be on (as of Monday).

Our Lt. in charge of the Med. Det. had quite a talk with me today. He wants we to apply for officer's training and urged me to act immediately. So, tomorrow I'll go through the files and attempt to get my information in order. Perhaps by Monday or Tuesday I can get the ball rolling. I'm trying to see ahead a little and feel quite encouraged. I don't know which branch I'll seek, but there is a Medical Administrative Corps. I'm beginning to think that one of the smartest things I ever did was to get the master's degree, for on our medical staff some of the officers take notice of it. I hope it will turn in some dividends—Eh?

I guess my promotion has made me just a little puffed up. Only two of us in this detachment received promotions at this time. Another encouraging thing is that our little old Staff Sergeant is turning over to me just more and more stuff to do—jobs most "clerks" never get to do. So, he says I can do it and leaves it up to me. And, enuf of this bragging!

As for all of those fresh vegetables from the garden! It makes me hungry and homesick to hear about them. Of course, I'm a little homesick all of the time. It seems so far to home, and I just sort of gulp every once in a while.

It is very warm, and all of us sort of lounge around in the barracks. Most of us are in our shorts. The 16 of us in our Med. group (there are 4 such groups in the artillery part of this Division), hit it off very well. We are a varied group. One fellow hasn't had more than a 4th-grade schooling, and I have had over five years of college. I don't believe there is any consciousness of it. We just seem to enjoy each other. We're mostly a mixture of New Yorkers, the South, and the Midwest, and the jabbering is something to hear. As for me, I believe the old "r"s should be sounded as "r"! Ha!

We are doing a lot of drilling, now—to get ready for a 4th of July review. Do not know whether I'll have to march in parade, but will be with our unit. It will be rather warm, but I'm about used to this climate, now—at least, I think.

Any more news on Don's status? Most of these officers have a good time, here. But, home is far superior. But, this war must be won, and whatever we are called to do, we must do it as best we can and willingly. One of the fellow's girl is coming down from Joslin, Mo., to see him, and is he ever excited. Ha! He's been eating nails all week, and we've been laughing at him.

It is almost time for chow, and I wonder what we'll have thrown at us tonight. Since we have been housed in this temporary area, there has been no improvement in our eats. But, it will be better when we return. But, it is still satisfactory, nevertheless.

Had to cash a $25 school check—was just getting too low. No one has an abundance of cash, but plenty of spending seems to be going on. I've eaten more boughten ice cream and drunk more pop since entering the army than in all times previous, believe me. Anything cold just tastes and feels good.

I just washed out a couple pair of undershorts and a couple undershirts, and also my wool socks and leggings—then shaved and took a shower. The water was cold, and I cooled off. It was the closest thing to a good swim—refreshing! Our Saturday p.m.s are really scrub days. Many of the gang are scrubadubbing, and how the dirt does fly! Most of us will really know how to SCRUB when we get out of this man's army.

Remember, it is now Corp. Mickey.

Monday, June 29, 1942 Shelby

This routine becomes quite varied, with some days almost terrifically full of just rushing around. Today, I was busy constantly from 7:00 to 5:00. Our Lt., doctor, has practically turned over all his files to me, and notifications are left to me to do. Sometimes the routine is quite boring, but I suppose some boredom is to be part of my job.

Had quite a talk with Capt. Munger, yesterday. He was the Med. Off. of the Day, and we held "sick call" for the battalion. He wants me to apply right away for officer's training and thinks I might be admitted within a month. He was insistent, but I do not think so—for we are to be in the service about six months before acceptance. So, I am to make application this week—maybe for the artillery. I think such would be more interesting than many other branches. But, I wouldn't mind the Air Corps. But having had basic training in the Field Artillery—????? But, I'm sure it will be Christmas time before any sort of notice. But, wouldn't it be something! So, I'm going to work for it.

As for my promotion, it is nice to have something other than Pvt. before my name. Maybe I'm on my way and just started—Ha!

The officers in our service battery are, in my opinion, somewhat snobbish. But, from what I can learn, they are an exception. Wallace said his officers were just swell, etc. Well, should I ever become an officer, I want the men's respect and friendship. Of course, there must be a "line"—but, it doesn't need to be as wide as an avenue.

This job of mine is certainly a wild game, sometimes. You get things thrown at you from every direction. But, I'm keeping up with them, and shall continue to do so.

Did Moose go to Petersburg? I hope so. She needs to get away. I suppose she and Janetta have many swell chats—and maybe some weeping, over "the boys" being so far way.

June 30, 1942 Shelby

Have Archie and Echo heard from Archie Wayne? I think he is in Australia, and says the people there treat Americans swell. Also, Jim O'Halloran is now in England—reached there the 5th. I guess it took about 10 hours by bomber to make the crossing—pretty swift. People from our little home town are really spreading out.

Down here, things are busy—just gushing. But, I'd rather have it this way. This is such a wretched climate that I'm sure I could bear up most anyplace. There are certainly many places a lot worse.

My officer's school application isn't in, yet, but it is about ready. I'm going to have a good visit with Capt. Munger about it—one of these days.

We were paid today—$20, with the rest to come as soon as "dependencies" are figured for every body. I guess I shall receive about 3 dollars more as a corporal. How about that? Our Sergeant really ran our promotions through, and two of us received our advancements a week before several others. I wore my stripes for the first time, today, and felt quite elegant. With two stripes, one can escape from some of the manure (if you know what I mean). Anyhow, it is nice to have these stripes. Our Sergeant is really a honey. One of these days I must take some snapshots.

I guess we are to parade the 4th of July, and I'll likely be in it. Quite a program is posted. Too, there are places here in Camp for relatives of soldiers to stay. Reservations must be made weeks in advance, I understand. It is somewhat of a rigamarole, I understand.—but only 50 cents per night. Is any one coming to see me? I'd certainly be surprised.

July 1, 1942 Shelby

Guess that I'm a little homesick, today. Haven't felt very well, just sort of worn out. It has been awfully warm . I'll feel better tomorrow. It will seem nice to get fully settled. My job is beginning to take definite form, and I know its duties quite well. At least, the book work is coming along smoothly, and I'm beginning to see daylight.

Am just kind of proud of my stripes, and—believe me—they are worth it. You can get a little attention, here and there. Ha! From all indications, there were no hard feelings in our group over the promotions, but in the others (the other three med groups), there were plenty. It was sort of understood and expected who would get them in ours, but not so in the others. Well, I guess that that is the army's way.

There is a fellow here from Omaha. He was a dental technician. He just missed getting a technician's rating in the Dental Corps. His Lieutenant is trying like the devil to get him a promotion—in spite of the Tables of Organization. He is very capable, and it just happened that another man had the inside track. Anyhow, it is the nuts!

I have been sewing on my stripes the last two evenings. I have about two more to do. This task is the berries, and I can see the sense to pay the 20 cents apiece to have it done. A good job for a mother!

Have been washing socks, underwear, and towels this evening. Now, I'm quite ready to begin tomorrow in a clean condition. Yassah! I'll be a jack-of-all-trades when this affair is over.

I've found nearly all the gang that came here from Leavenworth. The three I liked so well—I know where all are, and we see one another frequently. Went to church, Sunday, and whom should I see sit but another favorite. We are living not two blocks apart. Now, this is something! I guess one just must have patience.

July 5, 1942 Shelby

What a quiet 4th of July I spent—quite amazing.

The Med. Det. went out to a bivouac area with the "battery" Friday night into the woods; we pitched our tents, camouflaged all our trucks, vehicles, etc., and really carried on a little different sort of life. From indications, we shall be doing this frequently, now. They tried to spot our camp, from the air, but couldn't do it.

In the evening, about 9:00, I went out with seven others to intercept, if we could, some officers from other "batteries." These men were attempting to get into our camp. I was stationed at a crossroads, hidden in brush, to see if I could hear anything—just in case. Others of our camp found an officer's jeep, brought it back and hid it—right close to me. Too dark for me to know who the men were; so, I just hugged close. They knew I was supposed to be somewhere nearby, but I didn't dare make a sound because I didn't know who they were. After they quit the jeep, I did some sneaking around and chanced upon a radio operator and was no more than five feet from him when I let him know I was there. It was then that I put my glasses on. I had found out how much good I'd really be without my specks on, and out in the woods at night.

No one slept much, but I got some rest. Got a few bites from various creatures. About 3:45 we were alerted to return to barracks, gathered our stuff together, and were returned to barracks by about 5:45. Then, it was a mad rush to prepare for inspection and be in position for parade by 10 o'clock… It was my turn to hold "sick call"—with no time to clean up or to change clothes, and I must have been a good example for a medical clerk. I had put powdered sulphur in my trouser legs to keep out the chiggers, and the stuff has a sort of mild rotten-egg odor. Oh, what a life we poor soldiers do sometimes have to lead!

I did have time to wash my neck, to shave—but no shower. Our shoes were all muddy, for it had rained much before we went on our overnight. I had to wash my shoes with saddle soap, and then to polish them for inspection—to make them gleam. Had time to get my pants buttoned, when our Captain walked in to tell us we had five minutes before the Colonel arrived. I was irked to have to put on a clean uniform over my dirty self. Ha! Such can become the life of a poor soldier.

Well, the parade was something! Assistant Secretary of War, McCloy, reviewed the 85th Division, and some 5 or 6 thousand marched. I really got a thrill out of it. My first parade! We really pranced along in fine style. Six weeks can make an awful lot of difference in the ability of a group of men to perform in unison. I understand we made a good account of ourselves. After that night out in the woods, we had to march from our area to the parade ground—about two and a half miles each way, I think. Many visitors lined the way to watch the action. We were well pooped.

Then, we had a turkey dinner, but the bird was a tough one. Humph! Most of us in my gang then fell on our beds, and I slept for four and a half hours. It was refreshing. Some did not sleep, for they had passes to go to town. So, that was my "quiet fourth." A few did not pass inspection and they were given special "duties" to perform. Most of us just caught up on a little more of our lost sleep.

Being Sunday, I'll wash my leggings and shined again my shoes. This is a "catch up day"; and, I'm enjoying it. Didn't go to church—no chance, really, but didn't feel very churchy. The Sergeant had gone to New Orleans; so, I was actually in charge—had to report for reveille, and this was a "new" for me. But, no trouble—sort of fun.

Think I'll go to the Service Club for supper, this evening. I'll enjoy a change of ration—some good fried chicken, maybe. I am about written out. The old hike, the parade, etc.,—all add to quite a life. But, now, I'm so sleepy I can hardly maneuver this pen. We do drink a lot of pop, and I just ate a pint of ice cream. I should be sick tomorrow morning. Oh, well!

July 7, 1942 Shelby

I will need my birth certificate—to identify myself when I make formal application for officer's training. So, Moosie, scoot around and get one for me. Will you have to write to Valentine for it? Or, do you go to the State House? I will need it in the near future, probably about the first of August. Send it as soon as you can. Someone, there, should know the process necessary.

It rained again today—does 6 out every 7, and is often somewhat refreshing. This heat is the most depressing climate I have ever endured. I'm sure I will never kick quite as much on Lincoln-weather in future.

Some Sunday I'm going to get rambunctious and call you. Don't know just when, but for about $3 we could talk about six minutes. Of course, I shall call "collect." Ha!

Got thru work about 3:00 this afternoon—first time for two weeks! I must pinch myself, for I'm certain something has been overlooked or missed. We shall see, if so.

Again, don't forget to send me a birth certificate, but don't have a wreck doing it.

July 9, 1942 Shelby

What a hot day! I'm just about melted away. No news, from here, really. Anything I think about is quite muddled.

After supper, we had an hour's lecture from the Colonel, and then we were all so hot that we went to the PX for pop and ice cream—one way to cool off. That's one way to spend money—on pop and ice cream. Most of the fellows buy lots of beer and fill up on the stuff. As for me, I've just never liked it—the taste.

Tomorrow, we send our laundry in, and I shall send all I can gather together. We move back to the new area about next Sunday or Monday, and the more I can push into the laundry, the less stuff I'll have to carry across camp. Yes!

I'm just about ready for sleep when 9 o'clock rolls around—rather, it is 21 o'clock. We are on the 24-hour basis, now, and we'll need some time to make adjustment. It is now July 092157—or rather, July 9th, 9:57 p.m. Get it? If not, I'll explain further some sometime.

I wonder about Don's status. Major Hawes notes that there must be left for the populace a sufficient number of doctors and dentists. I guess the army officials are making a close study of this.

Thanks, Bin, for the candy and gum. We are really enjoying! Are now getting ready for snoring, and the lights will soon go out. Last night, about 2:30, on went our barracks lights. Poor guy had a tooth ache. So, I got up and gave him several aspirin. Must confess that I was more than just a little exasperated, for so many of these fellows hoot around about the Meds getting out of a lot of bull; but, they sure come a-running if anything hurts them. Oh, well!

A year ago the 7th, wasn't it, that Bill Hanna died? A year ago tomorrow that he was buried. I certainly hope that Phil can win the election. It will give her so much satisfaction were she to win.

July 12, 1942 Camp Shelby

No news of importance, except that I'm really bitten by chiggers. We had to lie out in the woods during a "practice alert," and it seemed sort of silly. But, we must get used to dashing for cover. Those bugs really landed on me, but I shall conquer them.

It has been very warm the last two or three days—almost unbearable. I hope we can get out of here one of these days. It is so uncomfortable. Dabbit! Guess I'll go see "Tarzan in New York"—do hope it will be good. I am just out of sorts, today. Can't think of much to write.

Am going to get my application in tomorrow—for officer's training. I hope I can get into something good. If this Russian situation grows much blacker, they will probably be enlarging their officers' classes. It will be something if I make it!

I held "sick call" this morning, again. We've been having so many hand-wounds lately. I think I shall be able to take care of most anything when I'm through, here. Most of it just requires a bit of common sense.

We shall be eating dinner in about a half-hour, and it is so warm! I don't know why I should care a thing about eating, but I am hungry. Believe me, you'll never find me in the deep South in future—particularly in the summer!

July 14, 1942 Shelby

Here we are, sweltering in this heat, and it is awful. Everyone is just about melted into spots. We shall endure, but it seems to me to be much worse than anything experienced in Lincoln, and I thought Lincoln could be the hottest place in summer.

We are sitting around in our shorts, and just sweating it out. There is no air anywhere. I expect this writing to just run together—from the wetness. They tell us that it is just beginning to get warm!

Tomorrow, I should get my application in—for officer's training. I hope it goes through. My birth certificate certainly got here in a hurry.

I don't like the Russian situation at all, but maybe something will break to brighten things up a bit for us. They should be able to make a better showing than for last summer, but I'm just speculating. We do need a "second front"—and pretty quick!

Major Castile has tried two or three times to contact me, but I do not know what he wants.

To call home—sometimes it is almost hours of delay to get a call out. But, one of these days!

I hope I can get into Hattiesburg next Sunday morning. Would like to go to the Episcopal church and go to communion. And, I may then call home. You think the $3 would be worth it, eh?

Should Don go into the service, Bin should stay home! Right there in Lincoln!

July 16, 1942 Shelby

What a day we are having. They completed our new hutments, and we moved in this morning. It was up a little earlier, pack up our barrack bags, throw them into a truck, and then clean up everything, and I mean everything. We swept, we mopped, we wiped, et cetera—until we were blue in our faces. Finally, cleanliness prevailed, and we put our packs and gas masks over our shoulders; then, across camp we marched. It was hot moving, let me tell you. I sweat it out and feel somewhat wilted.

Our new barracks are nice—considering everything, for they are full of wood chips and sawdust and all sorts of leavings. Much "finishing" to be done, and no shutters on windows. But all in process, and I hope we'll be here for a while.

This heat is really something. I wrote that I had received the candy and gum. We had a chewy time—just swell. This sort of camp is so much different than Camp Waldron. There we were sure we were in the U.S. Here, we are not certain. The environment is so different—and the climate. But, I'm just a bit out of sorts, today.

The heat does get on our nerves, and a few handles have flown—but not too far. Several are hoping to be invited for Sunday dinner—good, old Southern hospitality.

We won't be eating from our mess kits for a good while, now. It seems nice to get back to plates. I was getting used to the metal pan, but guess I will be able to change back to the other. Ha!

Took some photos with the little red camera. Its lens had fallen out, but I may have put it back correctly. We will see, eh?

Glad we are here, for it was somewhat congested over yonder. And, I got the certificate. Thanks and your service was right pert. I'll have it when I need it.

July 17, 1942 Shelby

We have been transferred to the Headquarters Battery (I may have written about this), and we have an inspection tomorrow. The new officers, for us, will have to be well impressed, and then they wont be looking for things later on—I hope.

I am so amused at our Med. group, for we are such a variety of individuals. We do have one fellow who doesn't seem to fit, but he is just the exception.

The lens of the little red camera was knocked loose, and I think it got knicked a little and blurs, I fear. It could be just dirty. Anyway, I'm afraid I can't use it anymore.

Yes, do send my Masonic ring, and also my old Eastman Kodak—the anniversary one. I hope it will work. I really want to have some pictures of this gang.

From photos, you can see that I haven't gained any weight, but I haven't lost. Am just holding my own, and feeling fine—but do hate this heat. (The short, heavy-set fellow is a Tyrolian from Wisconsin—a real character, but a very good egg. We pass a lot of blarney back and forth.)

Well, must get back to my polishing, to get ready for inspection.

July 21, 1942 Shelby

Another terribly hot day, but I guess I can take the heat—almost. From sounds of things, you have been having your share of hot weather. And, I've been waiting for the latest cookies. We will find some ways to get rid of them, and even the jam.

Went into Hattiesburg, yesterday—saw a USO show, played ping pong and shuffle board, and then was at a piano for about a half hour. It was a refreshing afternoon. Then back to the hot old barracks.

We had a heavy sick call this morning—about 35, and about 20 more than usual. I should know how to doctor up about anything, at this rate.

From all reports, MacArthur is getting quite an army built up over there. But, I think we know as little about it as you do.

It is only 9:00, and I'm ready for bed and sleep. This is such a sleepy climate, and I can plainly see why these Southerner people move so slow. I'm going to turn in.

July 23, 1942 Shelby

Am not sure when I wrote you last, but day before yesterday, maybe. This has been such a busy week. So far, I've just about run my fingers off—so much stuff to be kept track of in this man's army.

The last box of goodies came through, and all was just swell. The cookies were somewhat crushed, but they made delicious crumbs. We had lots of small pieces left, and Lt. Heath, our Med. Det. commander, came in, wanted to know whose they were, tasted them, said they were good, picked up the box with the remaining tidbits, and walked out—to his office, sat down, and put contents into his official self. Thus came swift end to the cookies, but they were good!

I'm trying to save the jam, for a spoonful now and then. As for the dills, I got just two of them, for they just walked right out of the bottle. Ha! Were they ever good!

This Lt. Heath is one of the finest persons I have ever known. He lives in Tampa, Florida, paid an income tax last year which was greater than his commission salary, and is such an interesting person to visit with. He has toured much of the U.S.

Yesterday noon, the whole battalion went out on a 24-hour problem. We camped out in the woods. Lt. Heath commanded the medical truck which was at the end of the procession. When we arrived at the bivouac area, we set up our first-aid station. The first thing we soldiers did was to pitch the lieutenant's tent and to get him settled. The rest of us had to wait until it was dark. We had everything camouflaged and were located between two artillery batteries—each attempting to sabotage the other. Whew! They were sneaking all around us. But, I went to sleep before any real action started, and didn't wake up until 5:45 this morning. So, I felt quite refreshed. We didn't get to apply any first aid; so, chief action was to board the trucks and head back to the barracks. About all we had to do was to sit around to gab—the Sergeant, the Lieutenant, and we six medics. Only in case of some sort of casualty would we have been called into action.

You should be getting that government insurance policy. I'm paying 6.70 per month on it.

A cool day, today, but one sweats just plenty, whatever. Received a letter from Uncle Arthur, for I had asked him for the prescriptions for my eyes. The government is going to issue us steel-rimmed glasses, and also a pair of lenses for gas masks. If I can furnish a prescription, then I avoid going in for an examination. Ha! Sometimes it is a bit difficult for me to believe that I am "an army man."

July 24, 1942 Camp Shelby

What a quiet Friday—hardly anything stirring. Last night I was on emergency Charge of Quarters. All I had to do was to just curl up on a cot at 9:15. I didn't wake up until 6:15 this morning—even got an extra hour's sleep out of it. So, no complaint. But, since awakening, my right arm has been numb, just feels funny at times. May have to have it checked. But it is very cool today, and what a relief. This must be the first day for a month that I haven't just sweat all day.

The jam is on its last spoonfuls, and I'm going to make a couple of sandwiches for my lunch. They will be yummy!

Mississippi is a very pretty State, and probably not as uncomfortable in summer as this camp. But, give me the northern climes!

From now on, we shall be doing over-night hiking and bivouacking. Not my favorite sport!

But, it is all in "army style," and maybe I'll learn to enjoy it. Ha! Nevertheless, on some days I feel mean enough to chew nails, and then try to be just a little meaner. Oh, well!

July 26, 1942 Shelby

It's Sunday, again, and I have an impulse to call home. But, not yet. Think I shall go to church, but not really in the mood. But. delightfully cool the past two or three days. The heat, here, when it is really hot, is almost too much for me. But, what can one do about it???

We are going to hold sick call in a few minutes, and the herd will be tromping in—and the rush will be on. This will be the first day in about a month that the Sergeant has been around. So, this is one Sunday I can sort of take it easy. We've had some funny things happen during "sick call."

The general war news doesn't sound very good, and I don't like it a bit. It could mean years of difference in the length of this war. We hope the Russians can keep Hitler out of the Caucacus.

Sick call finished, and still a half hour before church. So, time to prattle a bit. The USO show last evening was very good, and it was cool enough for us to enjoy it. The MC was a Lew some body. Now, you know for sure—slow grin!

Have begun to comb my hair again. It is still quite short, but beginning to take form as before. So, when you next see me, I will look quite natural. So, there!

July 27, 1942 Shelby (to Bin)

Your long, typed letter indicated quite a boost in the population. You will soon be in need of some vacation. Would be nice if you and Don could take a trip to Colorado. How I wish I could be in the mountains. It is enticing just to think of the coolness. It's getting much hotter down here.

A new cadre (unit of new officers and personnel to take charge of and train the enlistees of a new Division) is to be selected soon. I'd like to be put in it and be moved out of here, but nothing sure about anything. There are going to be some new ratings come out pretty soon, and I hope I can snag a sergeant's rating in the shuffle. Lt. Heath wants me to stay in his Med.Det.; so, I suppose I won't get shifted. My work won't be nearly so hard if I stay here. The 85th Division may be moved shortly after the cadre leaves. So, maybe I'll get away from here, anyhow.

Our basic training is almost over—just a week or two, yet, from all indications. I can't say that I've had a tough time . This clerk's job has really kept me busy, and free from lots. Thank Heavens!

Nearly phoned yesterday—just felt kind of blue all day. But, just thought I should wait until I had something important to talk about. It costs about $3.00 for three minutes But, to hear your voices just makes me homesick to see all of you. So, I resist calling.

July 29, 1942 Shelby

Just a note before we have a Non. Com. Officers' meeting. It is the first of a series of classes of instruction for newly made sergeants and corporals in our Med. Corps. It will be about two months before a cadre (organizing unit) leaves to begin a new "division." Those who go and who stay must be prepared to "take over" immediately.

The candy, nuts, and ring arrived in fine shape. We are enjoying the eats. I am wearing the ring, and it has a nice shine.

The heat is again discouraging. Any coolness in the breeze is most welcome.

Out in the woods, yesterday, and we dug fox-holes, and then practiced crouching in them—just in case some tanks should come rumbling through. We had to camouflage our medical truck, and then practice jumping in and out of the holes—just as if being attacked by an enemy from planes overhead. We are learning to run for cover, and are acquiring a technique for quick response. It has been fun, actually.

Well, this Army becomes more damning and more humorous day by day, and more disgusting and more amusing. I hope I can get into officer's training before many more weeks pass. But, I shall have to wait for some time, yet. But, the pace of things seems to be stepped up a little, and will be so from now on—from many indications.

It is swell to have your letters coming in—at least, every other day. One fellow's sister wrote and said that all info was urging people to write the soldiers to keep up their morale, but that his letters home were keeping up their morale. A two-way street. Right????

August 1, 1942 Shelby

Well, I have been in the Army three months now. It hardly seems possible, but it is! How the time does pass swiftly. Whew!

It rained this afternoon, and maybe we'll have some coolness for a change. I was out in the rain and got wetted down; so, must dash to the barracks and put on some dry clothing. But, I've been just as wet from sweat. Oh, well!

Was asked last evening, by our chaplain, to play for church, tomorrow. Not being an organist, I readily accepted and then hurried over to practice—all by myself for nearly two and a half hours. I did enjoy it! It is a Hammond electric, and easy to play. I thought I was pretty good at it.

Ahem! I trotted over this afternoon for about 45 minutes, and had another good time. It was returning from the chapel that I got wet.

Must finally do something with my letters from you, and others. They are filling my foot locker. Got paid yesterday—$90.50, and am going to send a $100 bond home—via registered mail.

Some of the fellows get into crap games, and are soon "busted." Just no sense to it, methinks. But, it is their money! Two of our gang just can't hold on to their money, and then they have to keep borrowing in order to have cigarettes. So, it goes

"Tis now getting late, about 10:00 at night, and I'm sleepy, but must keep awake. So busy today, and had no time to call home. And this is Sunday evening. I played the organ for the morning service, and it seemed to be OK. Since 1:00, I've been C.Q. I think I'll visit that organ about twice a week. I might have you send some music, but do not know just what I might need, and how long I will be doing this. So, we shall just wait to see.

And, Don is going to pursue further this army business, eh? Maybe the next time I see him, he will have a bar or two on his shoulder. But, I'm going to kick him on his left shin if he doesn't write me one of these days.

The latest movie with Abbott and Costello must have been good. I can hear you wheezing, while laughing, Mother—just like a little steam engine.

One of my pals from Nebraska, Walt Klute, dropped by this evening, and we had a wonderful visit. I really like him, and he has common sense—more than umpteen others put together. He'll soon be a corporal or sergeant in mechanical maintenance; he is in the infantry, is in a cadre, and will be leaving Camp Shelby in September. I shall miss him. He is one swell egg. Haven't seen Wallace Holen for over a month, and will have to "run him down."

More rain, but quite cool. I should get a good night's sleep. But, often several of the fellows come carousing around. Others come in, complain of headaches; so, I keep a supply of aspirin in my locker, and pass out the pills, and send them back to bed. Just part of a day's work.

Aug. 4, 1942 Shelby

Just a note to accompany the bond. A busy day and hot, and no disturbance last night—and had a good night's rest—while being Charge of Quarters.

Sent my application for officer's training over to hqs, and I hope things pan out. Major Hawes took it over for me, and I hope he will give me the boost I'll need. Will just have to wait to see.

Bought a new Parker fountain pen, for 95 cents, one marked for $3.00—as reduced for us poor soldiers

My hair is quite natural; and, Mother, I'll never forget how you looked at me when I had it cut—to go into the service. It seems that I have been in the army for ages. Have been out of high school for seven years. Time has flown along so fast, and so much seems to have happened. Our world had become so unsettled.

From reports, the Germans continue to forge ahead. The tide will certainly turn, and then this agony will cease to be so severe.

The last candy sent is gone—for the gang here at the dispensary quickly saw to it. One of the fellows got a peck of peanuts in a burlap sack. We collapsed that in a hurry—Ha! We are just a bunch of pigs, at heart, and I'm not complaining.

Rumor is that we shall be in Camp Shelby for some time, yet. Hot weather is predicted., and I think I should write our congressman!

Cut my thumb this morning. Was cleaning a sink in one of our laboratories. It wouldn't drain. I found it was plugged with cigarette butts, and proceeded to clean them out—but hit a razor blade down in the mess. I bled nicely, and then got all bandaged. First aid always comes in handy, and what we learn is to our advantage. So, maybe I was lucky to be placed in this medical detachment.

August 5, 1942 Shelby

Sent the bond to Bin at the Stuart Bldg. She can put it away for me. Maybe I can buy another in about three more months.

A wild day, today, and more such all the time. It is keeping the men plenty busy. My officer's application came back, for one of the endorsements was not correctly placed. So, after changes, Major Hawes took it back for me. Hope it will go through this time. The Air Corps is my favorite, but have my fingers crossed.

While at the post office purchasing my bond, others were there to do the same. One purchased both a $100 and a $25. So, many of us are trying to save a little, here and there. Lots of us get $66 per month. So, there!

Looks like rain again, but not nearly so warm. But, I've been too busy to notice temperature.

Saw John Payne, Betty Grable, and Victor Mature in "Footlight Serenade." Enjoyed it, and could just relax. Do enjoy all mail from home, and can't kick about neglect from you. Erma Jane keeps me posted on all that goes on in Wood Lake.

Now it is raining, and we go on a ten-mile hike tonight. So much mud to hit, and my poor shoes will be in need of much cleaning. Much wind, too; and the poor guys not under cover are in for a soaking.

August 8/9, 1942 Shelby

Another Saturday. It has been dreadfully warm, but I'm about to believe I can take almost any kind of heat.

That ten-mile hike wasn't bad., and we get one of fifteen miles on Tuesday. Yup!

Had almost to play for a wedding last evening. Went to the chapel to practice, and Chaplain Leudke asked—"Would you help me out and play for a wedding tonight?" So arranged, but the couple never showed up. So, I just practiced some more. Howzabout that?

Hope the bond I sent arrived before Bin and Don left on vacation. Being registered, my letter might just lie around in the P.O. for a week.

Do you enjoy my stationery, for I use whatever scraps of this and that—found lying around.

August 10, 1942 Shelby

Was just swell to talk to you, but we seemed too excited to get much said—Eh? I guess I was a bit homesick. So, I just went to one of the camp theaters and saw "Invisible Agent." It was a good picture and lifted me from my doldrums. Could hear you so well on the telephone; it hardly seemed possible that we were so far apart. Tomorrow will be another busy day, and I will be back on track.

Played again at the chapel, for two services. Really enjoyed it, and hope it will continue. But, our "sick call" was a long one, and I just almost missed getting to the chapel to play.

Had do put in my application, again, for officer's school—something wasn't correct! Well, maybe it will move along this time.

About time for lights to be out; so, must close this. Will need my rest, for we have a fifteen-mile hike scheduled for Tuesday evening. So, we must be ready.

Was so good to hear your little old voice, Moosie, come piping through the old phone. Bravo!

August 13, 1942 Shelby

We have been as busy as beavers, around here. And, I missed out on the fifteen-mile hike we had this evening. About 3:30 this afternoon, they phoned from the Division Artillery Hqs. and told me to report to the Message Center at the Hqs. at 7:00 this evening. It had something to do with my application for officer's school. I got over there, and six others were also waiting. After about thirty minutes, I was called in.

Well, I saluted the colonel who headed a group of five officers, told him who I was, and was told to sit down. The questioning began, and I hope I made a favorable impression. We'll know soon and if accepted, I shall be called for a physical examination—a sort of last step before being assigned to a class. I certainly have my fingers crossed. It will be for the Air Administrative Corps or the Medical Administrative Corps. Do not know which, but will be tickled to get either.

They asked if I knew anything about motors, and I told them that I had driven considerably, and that was as far as it went. Ha! The colonel said: "In other words, you can herd them around, but no further." We all laughed. Then he noted that in Medical Corps I might be assigned to motors, and I said that such would take considerable work on my part. And, it would!

It was quite an informal interview, and I hope I made the grade. Anyhow, here's hoping!

Went over and played the organ yesterday evening—just to enjoy myself and relax. No more news to dig up.

Sunday evening, August 16, 1942 Shelby

So good to talk to you and Bin, and sorry that your head is bothering you, again. I called from the USO in Hattiesburg, and had stayed in town at night with Walt Klute, a fellow Nebraskan. We had a good night's sleep, and I called right after we had had breakfast.

Am sending this photo, of our beds getting a sunning—see me on the left, second; am on my bunk, in front of the barracks.

The call went through in about three minutes, this morning. Not bad! But, no more extravagance for a while. To call from a booth—it is simpler to call collect. So!

Am eager to know about Don's status. Much cooler, here, today. This poem amused me.

MY LIFE IN SHELBY

I am sitting here and thinking of the things I left behind,
I hate to put on paper what is running through my mind,
But there is one consolation, gather closely while I tell,
When we die, we'll go to heaven, for we've done our hitch in hell.

A place, it seems, that God forgot, forgetful, yes, was he,
If Ponce DeLeon had been the name, how happy I would be,
It is a known fact, on the seventh day God did rest,
But it seems he left the devil here, and let him do his best.

We've dug a million ditches, cleaned a million miles of ground,
A meaner place this side of hell is waiting to be found,
We've built a million kitchens for the cooks to stew our beans,
We've stood a million guard mounts and cleaned the camp latrines.

We've cleaned a million mess kits, peeled a million spuds,
Baled a million blanket rolls and darned near drowned in mud,
The number of p'rades we've stood is mighty hard to tell,
But, we don't parade in heaven—we've done our hitch in hell.

We've shaken out a million bugs from underneath our sheets,
We've killed many a roach and ant that galloped through our eats,
We've shaken out a million miles, and made a million camps,
We've tugged and pulled at cactus that harbored in our pants.

But when our work on earth is done, the folks back home will tell,
They're bound to go to Heaven—they've done their hitch in Hell,

When the final taps have sounded, and we've lain away our cares,
We'll do that final last parade right up the golden stairs.

The chow will be much better, the harps will play all day,
We'll draw a million canteen books and spend them any way,
And when old St. Peter sees us, we'll be welcomed by his yell,
"Take the front seats, boys from Shelby, you've done your hitch in Hell."

August 19, 1942 Shelby

Just a note before I hit the hay. No real news.

My sinus problem seems to be all cured, as far as I can tell.

I dropped my glasses today, and they didn't break. I'm beginning to think they are charmed.

So pleased to see the photos Bin sent. So nice to see them.

August 20, 1942 Shelby

It has rained since about 3 o'clock this morning, and I wouldn't attempt to wager the amount we have had—but, it is plenty up to now—at 11:00.

The whole battalion, except the Med. Det., are out on the firing range. Our Doc and two aides are with them. I feel sorry for them. They had a mighty wet night of it. Of course, Lt. Heath will have slept in the ambulance, as well as the two "aide" men. But the rest of the poor boys! We really haven't had much to do in here.

The cadre is moving out in about two weeks, but I will not be going—thus, no promotion. But, all who are going had to sign an agreement that they would not apply for officers' training before February 15, 1943. So, had I been picked, I couldn't have gone on the "Cadre"—since my officer's application was already in.

No word, yet, from the committee, but our Med officers think I'll be called . I hope so, for the suspense is a bit wearing. Ha! I'd prefer the Air Corps Administration, but expect a call for the Medical Administration. It was on that score that most of my questioning was based. I'll keep you posted.

The Allied raid on France created quite a stir, but, as I thought, it was only an experiment to test the strength of German entrenchment A shame that it had to be done, but the only way to know how well we must be prepared—and for what. It foretells action to come. Sure hope the Russians can hold! Their success will whittle so many months off the war. We must keep our fingers crossed!.

This rainy day has given us Medics a breather. Should I be called for the M.A.C., I should get in on a lot of good, practical experience.

May see a movie, tonight—Ronald Coleman and Cary Grant in "Man About Town." Fellows who have seen it say it is good.

Walked over to see Wallace last evening—about a mile and a half each way. We just think nothing of such an evening's stroll! But, next week we have a 25-mile march slated, and we will be dragging ourselves in!

One of our Nebraska boys, Klute, a little red headed fellow, is being promoted to sergeant. He is in infantry and will be charged with motor maintenance. He is a whiz at mechanics, and he was just sort of picked from the ranks. He is tickled pink, for he is now doing just what he wants and hoped for.

Do not know when next to call, for it makes me too homesick. Seems so long since I've been in the army, but time has gone swiftly.

August 23, 1942 Shelby

Am only a few feet away from a phone booth, but no call today. I'm enjoying a nice quiet weekend in town, and it is a relief to get away from the camp. Hope to see a movie or two, and then will head back to the grind.

Six of us are in this large room—in a large, old home. A bit crowded, but lots of fun. Three of the boys just got a little too many bottles under their belts, and the other three of us did what was needed to keep the M.P.s from "closing in." Ha! Now, it is off to dinner.

August 25, 1942 Camp Shelby

Have a bit of a breathing spell this morning, and will take advantage of the lull. I did enjoy the weekend in Hattiesburg, despite my playing nurse maid to a couple drunken brethren. It was all for the good of the cause. But, their heads were not in good shape Sunday morning, and neither cared to eat dinner at the boarding house—and it was a humdinger of a good meal, and just beat the stuffing out of what we call "army chow." But, really, we fare well, from day today!

No letter from any one this morning, but had a letter (letters) each day last week. So, no room for complaint. But, I'm really a bit spoiled, and I do want to receive mail each day.

Am back from dinner. We were supposed to have a "gas test" today, but has been delayed until tomorrow

Have been having an itch in "various places," but seem to have it on the down grade. This darned place just gives you one thing after another. Several of the fellows are having ringworm, and it has become a sort of siege. My itch is not ringworm, but I'm just as eager to get over it.
The chiggers have just about run their course. Over-night bivouacs are never pleasant when one has to be crawled over by all sort of creeping creatures. Yes! One can really feel them!

The battalion is going into the field for three days "firing"—practice. We medics do no firing, and we may get a break. I do like my little army cot, for it is so nice compared to the ground!

The Army is dreadfully short of doctors and dentists. Don can rest assured that there is a place for him—as an officer.

August 27, 1942 Shelby

The past 24 hours has been rather harum-scarum and mostly "on the double." Yesterday afternoon I received notice that I'd been approved by the officer's candidate board. So, now I will go before a final board for my physical. Went to the hospital and was told to report back at 8:00 this morning, which I did.

Several of us were to be checked over, and it was much more thorough than at Ft. Crook—blood tests, x-rays, etc., and etc. Because of my history of sinusitis, my head received special attention. I will know if things are clear, and do hope so.

I tried to stretch my eyesight. Could almost remember the chart, and did score at 20/l00, but could hardly see the letters. But, with near sightedness my only problem, I should not be kept from officer's candidate school. Whichever school requests me, I shall accept. Maybe, the dust will fly.

I weigh the same as I did when coming into the service—158 lbs. Posture is good. Blood pressure came in at ll4/72—certainly not high; And pulse was 84 (sitting), 102 (after exercise), and 80 (after two minutes' rest). Then, chest measurements were 37" (at rest), 39" (inhale), and 36" (exhale). My waist rounded to 30". So, I guess all of that adds up to normal.

Several of us are heading into Hattiesburg this evening. Camp-life does sort of get on one's nerves now and then. One of the boys wants to look up train schedules. I know that it takes about 34 hours to get to Omaha. A three-day pass wouldn't do me any good. Most of us have long distances to go to get home. I'm going to plug for a Christmas furlough, and no need of any other.

The weather seems to be cooling somewhat, and almost seemed a bit frosty this a.m. But, this summer heat has been enough to kill my love for this southern climate.

From barracks to our station hospital is a bit over a mile, and I have walked it four times on hard-surfaced road—today. I think I've done my walking for the day.

Have my filing all up to the hour, and am ready for another quiet weekend in Hattiesburg. I do enjoy my Sunday morning snoozes—in town. I think I am spoiling myself. You will hear from me pronto, should anything exciting happen.

August 3l, 1942 Shelby

Received the book, and will give it a thorough investigation—to see what notations I "can't" make for the sake of posterity.

Received the box Saturday, and contents didn't last long—candy, nuts, and cake. I had to refrost the cake, for the frosting stuck to the paper. I just scraped it off and spread back on, and it was really GOOD. The pickles, as with the first jar, were just right and didn't last any time at all. So, Dearest Moosie, it was so sweet of you to send it. Noticed the postage—80 cents; so, you sent us an expensive treat. Ha! But don't desist if you get the urge to send another.

My itch is nothing serious—just a little rash in "conspicuous" places—too numerous to mention. I put salicylic acid solution on; this burns like thunder, but it kills the itching. Don't worry, for I swear I'll be immune to nearly everything before I leave this "great place."

If I pass that physical exam for officers' school, I'll be put on a waiting list—which means I am in line. They are checking my sinuses, and was called in for a consultation with one of the doctors who examined my head. All showed clear in the lights, and I'm satisfied that they have cleared. Should know fairly soon.

Just sat around most of yesterday in Hattiesburg, and just seemed tired and restless. Returned to camp about 6:30.

We were paid, today, and I'm going to send another bond, soon. Neither you nor Bindy has told me that the other bond arrived, and that she had put it in the bank for me. So, please let me know. I sent it by registered mail, and she was on vacation.

War news is heartening this evening, and I hope it continues. Things simply must brighten for our side. So, until later this week.

Sept. 2, 1942 Camp Shelby

A nice day—sunny and bright and cool. Maybe our real hot days are over.

Sure wish I could find out about my OCS standing, particularly with respect to the physical part of it. Most rejections come from physical reasons, but I hope to squeeze through. This waiting just sort of gets to one. Ha!

Guess we are going on a 25-mile hike tomorrow, unless they postpone it again. It seems to me that the officers must not want to take it, for they keep hedging.

They set a date, and then they cancel. It is supposed to be a sort of final in the training program. Will finish this letter before we go hiking—may not be able to write for a week after the hike. Ha! Oh, well!

Doesn't seem possible the we are now in to September, but the calendar doesn't lie. Not long until Christmas, and I hope I will get a furlough. Some of the fellows get three-day passes which they put before or after a weekend, and these enable them to get home—if not over 500 miles to travel. I must await a furlough, for Lincoln is too far.

Capt. Munger is to be our battalion medical commander. Lt. Heath, whom I have liked so much, is being transferred. Not that it should make any difference, but he was so much fun to work with. He just spoiled us. But Munger will be OK. (I think Margaret Munger has returned to Nebraska. Believe me, the army is no place for a wife to be hanging around. It is a mistake for the wives to follow their husbands, and this seems to be the essence of the talk around here. These nearby towns are so overcrowded; it hardly pays to put up with the inconveniences, and rents are cut-throat.)

When the dental man examined my teeth, at time of my physical for OCS, he asked me where I had my work done, and by whom. He said I had one of the "best looking mouths" he had seen for a long time. He must have liked my inlays. So, Don, you haven't lost your knack. Ha! My teeth wont keep me out of officer's school.

Word is around that I am an applicant, and so many ask if I have heard anything. Rumor has it that officers are under pressure to recommend candidates. With my myopia, I shall probably be considered only for a noncombatant field, but we must just wait to see.

We went out yesterday and dug "fox holes," slit trenches, and other conveniences. One of our gang referred to "hole-fighting." Well, I hope never to get the opportunity to see just how fast I can dig a hole and then crawl into it. Ho! Ho!

And, I've rattled on long enough, but just got wound up. Our Sergeant is getting a five-day pass, and I'll be plenty busy to get the weekly reports out—all by myself. If I don't, there will be some skin flying, and I know whose it will be. Yeah! And almost four months in the army!

Sept. 7, 1942 Shelby

Just remember, that my letters are always to the three of you—Moosie, Bin, and Don.

One of these days, I'll make it to a postoffice before it closes at 5 o'clock—to send a fifty-bond to you, for me. I just don't seem to get the time to get it done.

And, still no word about my physical! I've been told that one hears soon if he fails the physical.

I really do not care whether I'd be taken for Air Corps Adm. or Medical Administrative. If for Med., my further training would probably be at Carlisle Barracks, in Pa.

Thus far, we are not very well satisfied with our new medical commander. Munger may be from Lincoln, but he is a bit on the high and prancy side of the fence, I would say. He is now the ranking medical officer in the 85th Division Artillery, and I would say he needs to enlarge his hat size. He may get over it, and I hope so—the sooner the better.

Our Sergeant was gone, and another non-com and I had to make up the weekly medical "sick and wounded" report for the 85th Division Artillery. We worked Friday evening about two and a half hours, and double-checked everything; and, we had to get it to the Division Surgeon "on time" Saturday morning. Our final event was sick-call Saturday a.m., and Capt. Munger was 45 minutes late and much "on edge" about something—to such extent that he checked only about half the sick cards. We went ahead with the report and gave it to him to sign—at which time he informed us that 12 hospital cases had been transferred to the Division Artillery, and these had to be included in our report. So, all was now changes, new figures in every column, etc., etc., etc.

So, we had to call the Station Hospital to find whether the cases were diseases or injuries. Of course, we were now quite late, and the Division Surgeon's office called and wanted to know about "things"—particularly the delay. Well, we put the report together, and then the phone rang—the hospital registrar informed us that the transfer of the cases had been rescinded.

Well, we were burned up, and I, the file clerk, particularly. I was angry, and felt like holding my nose in the air! Had I had my choice, our dear commander would have received "plenty." I just had to get out of the place!

Then, today, Labor Day, according to "regulations," about 25% of our detachment could receive passes. We had a drawing to see who could go, and I had all typed to be ready by 9:30 this a.m.

Well, Capt. Munger didn't show up until after 1:30 to sign them, and half the fellows just stayed in camp. The Captain doesn't seem to think much of his "detachment," and our men in plain language can tell you what they think of him. I just keep my mouth shut, and I don't blame the men—not a little bit!

Things are not really so dark, but our change of officers hasn't been a good one—in my estimation. It is just one of those things which this old army life is going to dish out to us, and we just have to take it. But, too bad!

Camp Shelby broadcasts to the nation, over Cincinnati, each Saturday evening at 9:30 standard time. Each broadcast lasts thirty minutes, and it may be good—or otherwise. Haven't been to one for over a month, but must go from now on—unless in to Hattiesburg.

We do work up a game of bridge, now and then. And, one or our gang, from North Dakota, is a cribbage player. We have been at it, and I am fourteen games in the lead, and he is about "cooked." All my practice with Uncle Arthur has not been for naught. Ha!

And, I've just about worn out this typewriter for this sitting.

Sept. 10, 1942 Shelby

Well, we seem to be back into routine, after all the switching around. I was a bit roiled the other day, but everything on even keel, now.

We went on a "firing problem" last Tuesday, but not much for us Medics to do. I had my board and a deck of cards in my sack, and Capt. Munger and I had some good rounds at cribbage. He likes the game, but hadn't played for years. So, it will now be routine—to take along board and cards when out on field problems. It's the best two-handed game a-going!

News from Wood Lake—that a glider field is being constructed near Johnstown, and there is already a housing shortage, there and in Ainsworth. An army officer was to W.L., and wanted to know if 18 houses could be available for rent. Could be that an increase in rents will come to pass. Ho! Ho!

An officer on the examining board for OCS met me along the way, and he said my master's degree would be much in my favor to get into "school." He thought I'd hear soon, for the more education one has the better the chance. Well, we shall see and will keep fingers crossed.

But, I was in a growly mood when I wrote, the other day. Basically, "things" were not so dark—just my disposition. Capt. Munger is a good egg, but so different from Lt. Heath—and it just is going to take some time to get used to the change. To take over, he just wanted to assert himself into place. But, he did annoy me, in the process—Ho! Ho! Things are much brighter. (I think Margaret is still here.)

So, in a better mood. That Russian front needs to improve for our side!

Sept. 13, 1942 Camp Shelby

Well, another Sunday. Have a mind to call, but will not.

It has turned dreadfully hot, here, lately, and is nearly unbearable. Seems to be almost worse than it was, and it makes we sweat—just to think about it.

Went into Hattiesburg, yesterday, and bought me a pair of shoes—$6.85. I like them, and they are a plain military-style oxford—just what I was looking for. Went to one store and tried on nearly every shoe there, but no luck. Then, I asked if any store in H. had Freeman shoes, and was referred to a store that did. I then walked out with the first pair I tried on. It's strange, that a certain make of shoe will just fit so much better than other makes. So, I was fortunate.

Would you send me some music—particularly my CHOICE SACRED SONGS, the collection with "The Publican" and "The Penitent." Then, also that green book of assorted songs (my old one). No particular hurry, but I just want to have some songs here—may practice a bit.

Will be sending some negatives home, to be developed. Then, just keep the photos for me. Will send you some descriptions of where and whom, etc. And, I'll be sending some more home.

Am hungry for a steak, or some good fried chicken. So, Klute and I are going together, and each of us will "blow" a dollar.

Have been at the cribbage board often. Two of our gang have learned the game, and four of us are at it, often. It is as good a four-handed game as it is for two. Lots of fun!!

The war news is a little more encouraging, and we do so hope those Russians can "hold"! Their success will shorten this war considerably, I'm sure.

Sept. 15, 1942 Camp Shelby

Saw "Bambi" the other evening, and really enjoyed it—to an extent. Didn't think it was as good as "Snow White"—but it was good entertainment. Some mixed opinions as to the "Pied Piper." Maybe I can catch it in future.

Well, Moosie, you seem to have been bitten by the travel bug—may want to come down here to see me. Much to be said about such a trip, and about accommodations, here. Better to wait until October, and maybe "things" might be a little surer. But, one time is probably as good as another. Would you attempt to drive? A car would be nice, and we could go to New Orleans.

The gasoline issue may create difficulty, and to drive may be out of the question. As for passenger service on the railroad, priorities fall to freight and to troops—so, it will take some planning ahead, very likely. I understand that reservations, here, for guest rooms, are difficult. So, let me know, and I can attempt to get you a room at our guest house here at camp. Also, do not come for a first or second weekend in the month, I am told—just more crowded, for some reasons.

Another angle with my officer's application. I must sign a waiver. X-rays showed scar tissue in spots of my sinuses. They are now clear, but the government wants to be free of any liability—in future if I were to receive a commission. In other words, should I be assigned somewhere and should sinusitis recur because of conditions, and with infection to come,—get the drift? Without the waiver, I will not be accepted. An officer at our Adjutant General's office was certain that, with the waiver, my application would "go right through." So, I guess I shall soon be on the "waiting list." Maybe I should feel encouraged. This lieutenant told me that about 35% of applicants do not pass their physical exams. I had to laugh, for I remembered that I was at first rejected for the army because of my flat feet and myopia. I wonder if standards have been lowered.

Keep me posted about your plans, for I'll need some time to make arrangements.

Sept. 17, 1942 Shelby

An off-day for me, today. Nothing has really gone wrong, but I'm just unsettled. Maybe I just need a change. Would like to get this O.C.S. matter settled favorably.

So very disagreeably warm again. Maybe I'm just fed up with this weather. I do keep free from any sinus trouble, and with all this humidity I should be somewhat bothered. But, no!

The war news is so dark, and I guess that is why I'm so depressed. Seems to me we need a second front. If we don't do something, the Russians will make a deal with Hitler—and, in a way, I can't say I'd blame them. I do hope the big guys who are running this affair know what they are doing.

So, I'm OK, but just kicking plenty. We just need to land some boots in a good many places.

And, I could name some that are too obvious to mention. I could get some real pleasure from it. Ha! Ha! And, it is time to sign off.

Sept. 20, 1942 Shelby

Will now finish our conversation which I began on the phone. Am back in the dispensary, and the typewriter is just waiting to be used, and it is faster than pen and ink.

So much disturbance during the first part of our conversation—just could understand but little for about two minutes. Someone just kept butting in—from some source.

Sorry to learn that Don's application for a commission was rejected. He is certainly disappointed—as I know I'd be were mine to be turned down

As for this waiver business—the government just will not be responsible should I have a sinus flare up attributable in some way to the circumstances or nature of my assignment. So, I must take the risk, for the examining board found I had evidence of a serious infection in the past. Thus, the waiver. My application should move right along, now. Don would have been serving in a center, somewhere—not out in some swamp. So many of our men in service need lots of work done on their teeth!

The lieutenant, a dentist, who checked my teeth when I had my OCS physical, wanted to know all about the work done on my teeth, and who had done it. So, I told him—about Uncle Orville and Don. He said mine was the best inlay-work he had seen for months. Now, isn't that some-thing!

Our conversation really bolstered my spirits, but I don't know why. Today, I feel just as light as a spring zephyr—really "in the pink." The call proved to be a real "upper," and I was not down in the dumps afterward. It cost me just $2.20, and was worth every penny!

I've become quite pleased with Capt. Munger. He has a rather abrupt manner, and he got under my skin at first. He believes in and insists on efficiency, and we can always have it "on hand."

When he finds somebody not performing up to snuff, he gives forth with both barrels. But, I've heard him give some excellent counsel and advice—and encouragement. When he finds some kinks, he proceeds to straighten out. He knows how to pay a compliment.

I scrubbed some clothes this afternoon—actually, after supper. These darned bites, as well as the itch, require some salicylic acid and alcohol, and clothing gets stained and somewhat discolored. So, it takes rubbing and bleaching. What matters is that we get things clean! Some of our men come in just covered with bites, infected by ringworm, and badly scabbed from lots of scratching, etc. We do a lot of doctoring and give a lot of instructing. Several come back for second and third rounds. So, it keeps going!

Went into Hattiesburg, yesterday, with Holen and Klute. We feasted on ice cream, hamburgers, junk, etc., saw a movie, and then went to bed at the boarding house. Wallace and I may go to Biloxi some weekend; he knows people, there, and he wants me to go with him. It will be a treat to see the Gulf—something different.

The war news seems better recently. It has been so discouraging and seemed to be, at times, on the brink of desperation. I keep hoping that a corner has been turned.

I read an interesting excerpt from the prophecies of Nostradamus—the monk who in the 1500s predicted this war and predicts the final downfall of the union between the Eagle (Germany), the Roman (Italy), and the Sun. It was encouraging, but I can't put much stock in it. The English keep this document in underground vaults. You might want to see what encyclopedias say about him.???

Fifteen minutes to chow, and a little chilly. We had stew, cold pie, and cookies (good, too). The world even seems a bit brighter, now. Word is that furloughs will begin, soon; and, I'm still hoping for Christmas. But, should you prefer another time, earlier, let me know, and I'll try.

We have a foursome for cribbage all lined up for this evening. Nice!

Sept. 22, 1942 Shelby

Just about 48 hours since I called you. Seems, now, just like a nice dream.

Furloughs for the 85th Division to begin October 3rd. Each will last ten day, plus travel time. Only 10% of a "command" can be gone at one time. So, for our little group, just one or two. I still hope for Christmas!!! But, I may just have to be away when told to go.

Boxing tournaments have been flourishing nearby—in a large field house. The bouts come about twice a week, and some have been quite good—even exciting.

Some knockouts and some slow matches. Oh, well! But through it all, we just yell like "thunder"! Sportsmanship has been remarkably good.

Just wish the mail arrived more evenly—nothing for a couple days, and then three or four letters the same day—almost in piles. Ho! Ho

Captain Munger is searching for a time when he can take Margaret and the boys back to Lincoln. He says that home is definitely the best place for her and the boys. He suggested that I could ride along—if I could "stand Mike" (who is their youngest, I think). Ha! Wouldn't you be surprised were your doorbell to ring unwarned? The Captain is certain that I'll be called soon for OCS. But, my guess is that it is more like two or three months in future.

Nights are getting quite cool, now. But, this heat can be something else. And, the good cribbage games continue!

Sept. 24, 1942 Shelby

It is beginning to feel a bit chilly in the evenings, but it can get plenty warm again. Lots of juggling going on about furloughs. Mine should come later, and not before November. And, Mother, as for your coming here, it must be for a weekend, for no chance for me to have time off during week days. We might be able to hit New Orleans—for a day or two.

Your letters have been coming in bunches—none for three or four days, and then a cluster.

Not much news. The Russians seem to be doing more than their share of the fighting. I find it difficult to understand Anglo-American policy; but it isn't my job to understand. Ha!

Must go to the Division Surgeon's office again to a class—this evening. Most of these meetings are for me wastes of time.

Sept. 26, 1942 Camp Shelby

Wallace and I are going to Biloxi, and I am waiting, here, at the Dispensary and have time to scribble a few lines.

Wonderfully cool today, and I seem to feel much better when not so hot. With football season underway, I would give a pretty penny to be able to hear the Nebraska games. Just must find the score in a newspaper.

Yesterday we had to parade (a practice) before the commanding general of the Division—Haislip. We had to march nearly three miles to get to the reviewing stands, and it was very warm. The General rode around in his car, inspected the various organizations, as we stood at attention and saluted, etc., and then took his position for us to march before him.
We were away from our quarters for more than two and a half hours.

As yet, we haven't taken our 25-mile hike, and it was again on the docket for last evening. I'm of a mind that our officers just do not want to have to take it. They would be embarrassed if to need to "fall out." Humph!

October looms as the time for my furlough. Capt. Munger will be returning his family to Lincoln and has asked me to ride along—to be after the 15th. You may just be hearing my footsteps upon the porch! But, no furlough if an OCS call is on line. Then, we can try to figure a time for you to come. It is nearly five months since I've been in this man's army.

Nearly three o'clock, and Wallace hasn't arrived. He has probably been put on some sort of duty. So, I may just take a nice, long walk. I always have letters to write, and owe about four.

Have some kind of dermatitis on a leg—not poison ivy, but something that does not itch much. So, must apply some ointments. Have given up on the trip to Biloxi.

Sept. 29, 1942 Shelby

Rumor has it that President Roosevelt is to be in camp, today. Most of the 85th Division is now being reviewed by higher ups, and a long string of cars just drove by about two streets away. We think F.D.R. was in the group—quite certainly. Men of our medical detachment were to be used only if needed to fill in the ranks of one of the batteries—for a parade. So, we had to doll up—in khakis, leggings, helmets, pistol belts, and first-aid packets. They didn't use a one of us. We were somewhat disappointed, for it would have been a bit special to be "in review" for the President of the United States. We are certain he was here.

Temperature is getting coolish, and we are wondering when we will be ordered to change into our O.D.s. It doesn't make much difference to me—when we change over.

This is the end of a month, and all the reports cause me to run this typewriter nearly to death. Oh, the red tape! One just about loses his mind. Our reports must summarize the "sick and wounded," sorts and numbers of "health examinations," equipment counts, all sorts of rosters, etc., etc., etc. And, we must keep up with all the daily routines.

As for Don and his rejection! To sign a waiver means, simply, that should his ear again become suppurative, the government could not be held liable. It is logical. As much as our services need surgeons and dentists, his willingness to sign such waiver should take care of the matter. It seems a bit strange to me!

October 2, 1942 Shelby

Yes, President Roosevelt was here!

Tomorrow, some special Army Inspectors are coming around, and many are quite nervous. Ha! One would think that something unusual was really in the offing. But, who knows??? Some "big shots" and "brass hats" are going to give our Med. Det. "the once over."

It has been a busy time—with all the end-of-month reports to get in; almost enuf to make a person sick. I've persuaded myself that I do need a vacation. Ha! Ha!

Saw the movie, "Wake Island"—and the American marines fought to the last man and really made the Japs pay dearly for the island. Those "little YBs" will be receiving lots of "interest"—methinks.

No news about furloughs. As for OCS, Captain Munger expects me to be called soon. But, I'm sure it will not come before Christmas.

Have had a cold, but have it on the run. Do have to watch my sinuses.

October 4, 1942 Shelby

It is again most uncomfortably warm, and I'm sort of on needle's edge. Was restless, went into Hattiesburg; though I'd see a movie, but none looked good; so, just turned around and came right back—and that was that. And, our basic training was supposed to finish, as of yesterday.

Walt Klute has his furlough, and he will call you should he have the time while in Lincoln. He is an awfully nice guy. Should he have the time, you might pick him up and take him out home for supper or lunch. He comes from near York, and is really OK. We've had many good times! But, he is going out on cadre to form and to train a new Division, and wont be back here. I'll miss him!

So, Don had been called to report to Omaha. Maybe, he'll make it this time. If so, he'll probably come in as a 1st Lt.

Could be seeing you about the 19th. Of course, Capt. Munger could slip away without me; or, I could be up for OCS. And, one of the fellows wants to go for some pop. So, I 'll go.

St. Louis, Missouri October 18, 1842

(Fn.—had been home on first furlough.)

Here I am, with 3 ½ hours until my train pulls out. Hardly seems possible that I've been home. But, so it is. Really had a swell train clear through to St. Louis—just like the one from Lincoln to Union, only larger. Now, I shall ride a sort of old buck-board to Jackson, Mississippi.

Didn't have to change cars in Kansas City, and had only 15 minutes. So, no chance to call Martha. But, wanted to.

The train was on time to St. Louis, with but 20 minutes to catch a train south—but, it was Pullman only, and cost extra. And, I ran into 5 fellows from the 85th—so we are now six of us to return together. They are in the infantry, and nice guys—one from Winner, So. Dak., and the others from Nebraska.

No chance to eat until St. Louis—arrived at 5:40 this evening. We walked about a mile, found a cafeteria that a lady told us about, and ate plenty. Mine cost 94 cents, and it was worth it—Swiss steak, corn, tomatoes, grape juice, buns, lemon cake, etc. I feel quite content, but sure wish I were home. Doggone it!!

It wasn't so difficult to leave, this time, for I knew where I was going and what I would be doing. Now, I hope I can get into OCS, but the waiting will be sort of like pulling teeth, though.

What a boost to my morale—to be home! Maybe it wont be so long before my next return.

So many soldiers are traveling, and the train was half filled with us. We'll be a large group of returning furloughers by the time we reach Camp Shelby.

From now on, just send my letters by regular mail, and they will arrive just as soon. So many of the air-mails took three days.

So many folks I just didn't get to see. And, don"t bother to send my razor and blades. Have the replacements already purchased. Or, have you already sent them?

It was just grand to be home, and I love all of you so much.

October 21, 1942 Camp Shelby

Got here at11:00 last night—40 hours to get back (from Lincoln). The trip was rather uneventful, except for the multitude of long waits I had to endure—6 hours in St. Louis, then 3 hours in Memphis, and an hour in Jackson—where about 30 of us boarded a bus for Hattiesburg. The darned bus had a flat tire, a real blowout with about an eight inch slit in it; but the bus had no spare, and we had to call Hattiesburg to send one. What the man brought was the wrong size. So, some more sitting around and walking around—to the tune of another two hours So, you see, nearly a third of my time to return was spent in just waiting. More fun! But I can't say I am so terribly tired out, but just a little dizzy!

From the looks of things, here, we will be plenty busy. New recruits are just arriving to replace the cadre. We'll be giving lots of shots, and new cards will be named for the records, etc.

Except for one, we have new officers. I'm not sure that Capt. Munger will be with us when he returns—and I was really liking him a lot! Dern it all, anyhow.

Again, it was wonderful to be home!

October 22, 1942 Camp Shelby

Not much news. Will type a quick note, for I have to eat before relieving the Charge of Quarters.

Tomorrow, I'll be CQ for the day, and plan to write several letters. Had many waiting for me, and must begin to answer.

Well, I'm really back in the groove, and I do mean BACK. Once home, it didn't seem that I had been in the army so long. Now that I'm back here, my visit home was so short. One can hardly keep up with himself, I guess!

Several of the fellows close by have been accepted for officers' candidate schools, and the rest of us are speculating. It's a gamble, I guess, but we are eager to get away from here. We will welcome change.

We have three new medical officers, and our new C.O. is a Capt. Mark J. Hughes—and I like him very much. Capt. Munger is to be our new Division Artillery Surgeon. As you know, I was liking him much; but, he will be around and about—just no longer with us.

Very dry down here, for no rain for all the time I was gone. Lots of wind, I guess. Dust covers nearly everything, but I'm not ready to dig out—yet. Want to wait until it rains.

Must get busy with my letter-writing!

October 26, 1942 Camp Shelby

Went into Hattiesburg, yesterday, and went to the Episcopal church—had met the minister the day before, and he wanted me to come and also to sing in the choir. So, I did, and it was nice. The church is very shabby, of old brown bricks, with plain white plaster—much blotched and damp in appearance on the inside. Not over 25 at the 11:00 service—very few, for a town of more than 20,000.

This minister is a little fellow, and seemed rather meek and mild. Two of us soldiers sang in the choir, and we went to the parsonage for dinner. We met his wife, who, in my estimation, is a "battle axe." First impressions are often wrong, but she struck me as being anything but a minister's wife. They have a little girl, probably about two years old; and the way this woman about ate up the little thing, two or three times, should have put the wee one in "fear and trembling." The child is very nervous, but as cute as can be. But, this woman is quite a character. Didn't really enjoy the meal, for just couldn't feel comfortable.

Three other friends of the minister were there, and they didn't strike me as being too friendly. The rector told me that, until a few years ago, the Episcopalians in Hattiesburg were a very "select" group—wealthy and clannish, and to such extent that the church suffered much. He must be trying to do something about the situation. This church is in a pretty bad state.

While in town, I saw Zazu Pitts in "Miss Polly"—as cute as it could be, and with Slim Summerville—lots of chuckles.

Am getting impatient with OCS, and wish things would begin to move. This med office work sort of gets on my nerves, now and then. It is such a dead end. Did get caught up on my letters, and can now relax and listen to my little radio. I must get a new aerial for it.

Work at Dispensary seems to be slowed—with no more than about 30 "active" cases on our books. But, new recruits are coming in, and we have quite a bit of training to do. We have new cards for them—to record shots, blood types, ailments, etc. More fun!!

October 31, 1942 Camp Shelby

A Saturday, and payday. Two of our fellows are heading to Hot Springs, Arkansas, to attend a Medical Specialist Training School; and two are on furlough. Things are somewhat calm. I plan to go to the chapel and play the organ this evening.

Haven't written for several days, for we've been unearthly busy! So many recruits into the Division, and all the shots to be given, cards made, records begun—for over a hundred men! So, an explanation.

Too, we had to take the hike—one over twenty miles, and we were gone from the barracks area for more than six hours. It was a humdinger. My right hip tuned up, and I guess I must be getting a bit rheumatic, er sompin. My feet bothered not at all; so, I guess that one with flat feet can get along in the army. Of course, there are two sorts of flat feet—one with fallen arches, and the other with arches that are just naturally flat. I have the latter—so, hurrah!

Did find out that my sinus waiver was granted. This removes the government from being responsible for any consequences which might arise from past infection. In other words, I can never sue the government for a pension, on the grounds that I had developed sinus trouble as result of my endeavors in the service. This is what I learned at our camp's Adjutant Office.

Weather has been quite balmy and nice. I'll now mosey over to play the organ, and haven't been over for a month. So, it's about time to practice again on those ethereal pipes. And it is BOO-TO-YOU This is Hallowe'en!!! And, please save this Willkie speech for me.

Nov. 3, 1942 Camp Shelby

Am still kicking. Hope I can hear some election returns, tonight. Would like to see how Norris runs—this time as an "also ran"! Difficult to get excited over an election when one is not there and really voting. I should have registered when I was home, and could have voted by mail. It would have cost me nothing.

Rumor has it that we will have our 28-mile hike this coming Friday. This one will be a corker, without a doubt. I can hardly wait to get it behind me, and then to find out just how crippled I will be. Ha! But, maybe not much more than the one for 18 miles.

I wonder about the Japs in the Solomons, for I don't like the atmosphere of that place. There seems to be an essence of bad tidings, but I hope I am mistaken. My hunch is that MacArthur has something up his sleeve.

Nov. 7, 1942 Shelby

Things have been so busy! When evening comes, I just hit the bunk. So, a few days since writing. I listen to my radio and quickly fall asleep. Did see a couple movies in camp theaters, and this sort of thing one can do on a moment's notice.

Last evening, I returned to the barracks, and turned on my radio—to listen to the "Little Rascal." There was a flash of light, and I knew something had burned out. I was just this side of furious. Oh, well!!

Be sure to send me a newspaper which gives all the Nebraska election returns. I do know that Norris was not returned to the Senate, and that Bryan Q. didn't wiggle his way into office. The Republicans seem to have made large gains all over the nation.

The British are advancing against the Germans in north Africa, and I hope this will continue. That large fleet, an armada, that passed through Gibraltar will keep the Axis guessing, and my belief is that they will land behind Rommel. We shall see. There could be an attempted invasion of Italy or Greece, or an attempt to pass through the Dardanelles into the Black Sea. We shall find out; but, first of all, I think the Axis must be bumped out of north Africa. It would be too risky to leave Rommel in Africa if a strike at Italy is to be made. Things are beginning to look somewhat brighter. If we can just succeed against the Japs in Guadalcanal!

These recruits are keeping me very busy. So many records must be kept for them. We are receiving several who are in for "limited service only," which means they were inducted with certain physical defects which disqualifies them for full field service. They must be examined in a clinic, appear before a "limited duty board," and then be transferred to a suitable unit. It takes a lot of time, and we also give them many of their shots. It was a real whirl all day today.

This morning, I had to get in our weekly report of the sick and wounded—of ours for both in quarters and in the hospital. We are training two new clerks to take over the job that I have been doing for the past eight weeks, but nothing has been stirring—to indicate any change-over. My report was delayed, because the Division Surgeon's Office did not report to me on time—to confirm a case of gonorrhea. It tickled my funny bone to be able to put blame where it belonged. Ha!

Then, about eleven this morning, we received notification that at 1:00 this afternoon our office was to give eye examinations to new recruits. Also, since a new supply of serum was in, we were to give shots, also; but, the new serum was still at the Station Hospital. Nicholas Lukatchik put the eye charts up and was prepared to run all 67 of them through, and it turned out to be quite an affair. Of course, we had to send an emergency vehicle to the hospital to get the serum—both typhoid and tetanus. As if by some miracle, we managed to have enough time for dinner. By the way, we call Lukatchik our "mad Russian"! And, we took care of it all in the afternoon.

Yesterday, we had our 28-mile hike, and it was a scorcher. I did all but a mile, for I had to make a run back to the Dispensary by ambulance to get more salt tablets. I just happened to know where they were stored. It took all of ten hours of walking. Our cooks met us at a half-way point with a hot dinner, and we had an hour's rest while eating. The final two hours for several men seemed to be quite grueling, but most made it in with flying colors.

With our Sergeant away on furlough and our Corporal having departed for a medical school, I was more or less "in charge." One of our men, a new one and a little red-head, proved to be quite a problem. He had begun to make it his practice to do just what he wanted, and seemed to resent our older and firmly established men. For our long march of 28 miles, five of us were to go with the five batteries to be the "first aid men"—mostly to take care of blisters. Well, Louis would not go with the battery selected for him, but insisted he go with another. He became more and more abusive "in language," and demanded to know by whose authority I had assigned him to this particular battery. My "Irish" blood began to boil a bit, and our match became a shoving one. I ended the match on top of him, with his back to the barracks' floor and with a mark or two of battle. The scuffle over, he got up and left the barracks. I supposed he would head to the assigned battery. The rest of our gang had literally pulled me from him. We then departed for the various batteries, and it was seven in the morning.

Upon our return to the barracks area, here was Louis dressed and groomed—shoes polished and his canteen full of water. He had not been on the hike! I said nothing, but went to the barracks of his assigned battery—just to double check. The next morning I informed Captain Hughes and requested that he refuse to sign a weekend pass for Louis. Hughes said he would apply the penalty to our "mutineer." Later, in the morning, Hughes confronted Louis, denied the pass, and told him: "Just for your own good, remember that Mickey is boss in your outfit!"

Well, it proved to be quite an incident. Louis will get no pass to leave camp if he does not do what our duties require. I think he now knows he must do as requested. I dislike the idea that differences cannot be settled amicably, or at least through arbitration. We shall see, but I will not put up with his refusal to cooperate. There always seems to be a first time for everything. Well!

Yes—the long hike is over, the week's work is done, and I think I have the situation, here, firmly in hand. News indicates that the British are making the war a bit brighter. My spirits are pretty good this evening, and I'm ready for a night's rest. So, Moosie, your "warring" son has learned a few things this past week—at least he did have to put his foot "down"!

Capt. Munger told me that he had left pheasants for you while in Lincoln. As you may guess, I think more highly of him all of the time.

Nov. 8, 1942 Camp Shelby

A Sunday, and I just returned from Hattiesburg. Saw two movies, ate a $1.25 meal, and ain't I extravagant!

I forgot to tell you what was wrong with the radio. A tube burned out, and got it replaced... Am sending the dead tube to you. Take it to Dietz to see if you can get a new one, for I hadn't used it a week, and the radio was never jarred. Should you get a new one, send it to me; and I'll return this borrowed one.

All is quiet around here and seems to be quite firmly in hand. Our little difficulties should blow over, I hope.

The American invasion of French Africa is something, eh? And, Montgomery's drive into Libya is beginning to look like success, seems to me. Things should begin to swing better for us and our side!

Music on the radio is very nice, tonight, and I really enjoy it. And, I'm all over my aches and pains—except that my hip is about as sore as it could be, and just gives me a little Hell. Ha!

Nov. 11, 1942 Camp Shelby

This is going to be a hurried note. Things are rolling along pretty smoothly, now. We are pleased with the progress of the American troops in Morocco, and that is quite enlivening. My hope is that the French will stiffen toward Germany, but there is so little that Vichy can do but just be carved up for the present. But, they could get that fleet out of the harbor and away from Hitler!

Typed our weekly training schedule today, and that is one big job out of the way. Friday, we must take our recruits to 'blood type' them, and then we will "shoot" them—all 65. It is going to be a busy day for the four of us who will have the most of it to do. Two of us do the recording on the cards. Whew! Haven't sent the tube, yet. It will get there when it gets there. It must have been defective, and it would cost me $1.67—or, thereabouts. The borrowed tube just plays right along.

Too bad about Don's army business, and we do need him in the service.

Nov. 15, 1942 Shelby

Sunday, again. I'll be taking it easy. The weather has been quite chilly, particularly in the evenings. Nice and warm in the daytime. The heavy woods nearby must have something to do with it.

Four new recruits for us. After two weeks of basic training with recruits for the battalion, we'll take over and give them their medical instruction. They look pretty good!

One of our boys, a medical man from the 329th, was called for M.A.C. officer's training. I'm still hoping for Air Corps, but do not expect to be called before January. One never knows. Capt. Munger still thinks it will be soon. We'll just wait to see, but my guess is—after Christmas.

And, Moosie, was pleased to know you've been honored as a "War Mother."

From reports, it is now to the place that American manpower is none too plentiful; and, those not in service are either physically unfit or have "some pull"—the gist of opinion around here.
This army is big business; and as these recruits come, it is evident that induction centers are not checking these men carefully enough. We, here, have had either to get medical discharges or to put several fellows on limited duty. They should never have been inducted. Some are clearly too handicapped.

Our poor recruits! Have we ever been giving them the works—here a shot and there a shot! I gave it to about 65 yesterday, and I'm getting more blood thirsty all the time. And, to type their blood, we must draw out some. Do the poor fellows hate that!

Went to the dental clinic to get my teeth cleaned—Thursday. The oral hygienist looked in my mouth (get Don braced), and said, "Say, Corporal, did anyone ever tell you that you have a pretty set of teeth?" She called over another gal, who observed, "My, but those inlays are just beautiful!" Three dental officers then came over to look in my mouth, and a Major said: "Corporal, you have no idea how refreshing it is to look into a 'well kept' mouth!" They proceeded to clean the teeth, and insisted it was a pleasure. So, now, Don, you may strut around! I just acted as unconcerned as I could—just as if I were used to it. Ha! Ha!

Please send me clippings about the election. I'd like to read all about the voting in Nebraska—particularly as to what Norris had to say about his defeat.

We have been so darned busy! Sgt. Johnson got back, today, and now I won't have the whole load. I had it all to do, nearly; and now he will have me. But, we must keep up with all the work, and the records. And, I'm about 15 letters behind in my personal correspondence!

Nov. 18, 1942 Shelby

More shots, all the time, is the order of the day. These new recruits must receive their allotment, and I'm the guy to give it to them. They call me "the executioner," and look at me as if to say, "Just wait until I meet you in the dark!" I just let them groan. Must have given over a hundred shots, today—typhoid and tetanus. Not much of a knack to it, and it has to be done. For me to give them relieves the doctors of considerable duty here in the Dispensary, and they instruct many classes, here and elsewhere.

Weather is again quite warm and sultry, and tiring. Had no time to get the schedule typed today; so, must do it first thing in the morning. Capt. Munger wants it posted "on time." He is O.K., and I like him better all of the time. He keeps wanting to know about this and about that, and it keeps me busy looking up stuff for him.

Another left for OCS, today, and I wish I could go with him. This routine just gets rather tiring. My job is a sort of blind alley, and I'm waiting somewhat impatiently for the next Air Corps Adm. quota to come out. As rapidly as the Air Corps is growing, it should be needing more administrative officers.

Will go to a movie this evening—nothing better to do. No fun to sit around.

Nov. 20, 1942 Shelby

Is now a full month since I was home, and it hardly seems possible. Just don't know where the time has gone!

We have been so very busy—with "limited duty" reports, immunizations and shots, special physical exams, etc. My time is fully occupied... Must have given over 250 shots last week. Each of our artillery battalions received about 50 new men, and nearly each had to have a tetanus and a typhoid shot. So many really hate to have that needle stuck in. Most get along fine, but some have bad reactions and become ill.

The war news has been heartening. Seems to me that the naval battle over in the Solomons was, perhaps, a real victory. Did you read about the cruiser, "Boise," and all that it did? It was just like a story-book account. Also, I'm getting optimistic over the African outlook. The Axis will be knocked out cold, there, and Rommel is taking a beating from the British. The old "Desert Fox" no longer has much choice. Old Hitler will no longer be "calling the punches"—I think. His struttin' days are about over.

This OCS business has me sort of stumped. The quotas remain small. I wonder how much "pull" has to do with it. Capt. Munger told me that he had made some inquiries, but information is all tied up. Our Det. staff sergeant is soon to go to the Field Artillery officers' school—in about four weeks. I shall probably be advanced to be staff sergeant, and that will look better on my OCS application. I'm going to the camp adjutant's office to see if I should reapply—if promoted to be staff sergeant.

Just returned from noon chow—liver, green beans, banana pudding, etc., and it was a satisfying meal. Yesterday, at noon, it was awful, and another fellow and I went to the service club for supper—just had to get the bad taste out of our mouths. Ha! It was worth the 70 cents. Some of our foul meals just about lay us under the sod. Well, I hadn't "eaten out" for over two weeks.

Will be playing the organ, Sunday, at the chapel, but this will probably be the last time. I want to go regularly into Hattiesburg and will try to make the choir practices each Friday.

Received a great, big box of Xmas hard candies the other day, and have we had a good time melting them down. Postage on the box cost 40 cents, parcel post. It came from Boston! Guess who? Awfully good candy, and the fellows here make it disappear as if by magic.

I need some white woolen socks, like basketball players wear. The ones Uncle Sam gave me have no holes, but they are worn to a paper thinness. I wear size 11—just plain white ones. You can put the cost on my Christmas bill—all totaled up.

Lots of field work coming up for us, and I shall be "out" most of the day times. The battalions (field artillery) are to start firing over the heads of the infantry. It should be interesting to see.

Must be in the Dispensary most of tomorrow, to complete the training of two men who are to take over the reports to be regularly compiled. Once they are ready, then I can relax a bit.

So, this about winds it up or down for today.

Nov. 21, 1942 Camp Shelby

Another Saturday afternoon, and not much is brewing. The entire Division Artillery is out on the range, firing—except me, and I'm left in to get out the weekly reports and to be CQ for the day. I had a wild morning, but this afternoon has been serene.

Have been fighting drowsiness, and have had a couple cat-naps. Now I feel as if someone had hit me on the head with a brick. Just finished eating the last of the candy Joe's sister sent me; but, how it did disappear! It was in a round tin box, about two inches in depth.

We should all feel heartened over the African news. Rommel should soon be wiped out. It will startle the Germans when Hitler has to announce that the "Desert Corps" is no more. Now, with the Suez secure, the British can catch an extra breath or two. Sergeant Johnson and I are real news hounds—just want to keep up to date!

May run in to Hattiesburg—just to eat out. But, the spirit may move me to bide my time here. I am to be relieved pretty soon, for I've been pinch-hitting. Will probably go to a movie, and I'm getting to be quite a movie-goer!

Do keep the letters rolling!!!

Nov, 22, 1942 Camp Shelby (Tuesday)

Well, your little boy is about to lose his mind. The trying experiences I have had in the last 48 hours have about got me down. I will start with this morning, and then jump back to yesterday.

It has rained since seven this morning, and the crease in my O.D.trousers might well have been on those of the "Ancient Mariner." First, I went to breakfast. My two fried eggs were cold, and one of them, I suspected, may have been about ready to hatch before being cooked. But, I was hungry! The toast was soggy. The eggs needed some salt, but the humidity kept the salt from shaking. So, I had to resort to the finger-pinch method, with its uneven distribution. The first bite was decidedly flat; and the second was so salty it took my breath away.

I was due at the Dispensary for sick call—8:30. The rain came down, and I had almost to swim for it, and I made it, but nearly in a dead faint. The "sick and wounded" came rolling in, and they tried to tell, or show, me what was wrong with them. I was too nearly drowned to comprehend, and proceeded to give aspirin to those who had broken legs and to put splints on those with colds and headaches.

At 10:00, Sunday, I went to church, and played the organ for the chaplain. He likes to sing at slow tempo, and I prefer it "up to time"; so, we had a tug-of-war with each song. As to whom Victory gave her smile, I do not know; but, I played the organ as loud as possible. Maybe I won, for no one was continuing to sing when I finished playing each final stanza.

The rain continued to pour. I returned to the Dispensary, shook myself, and swam to the barracks to await chow (noon). The whistle blew. So, over to the mess hall and picked up a cup of coffee and a bowl of soup—the kind that always has grease floating on top. Yes! While sitting down, I let my tie fall into the soup—but didn't notice until I had grease spread all over the front of me. Ha! Ha! With disgust, I finished my dinner, anyhow. The world was dark, and I was wet and greasy. What a nice way to work my way into a happy Sunday. I shall try harder next Sunday.

Yesterday, I was alone in the Dispensary, from about one in the afternoon, to about 8 in the evening. The Division Artillery was out on the range firing, but I had stayed to make out weekly reports. Recruits drifted in every now and then; so, I couldn't do much snoozing. One fellow came in—with a sore ankle. He gave me a history of his family—about his ancestors, and his uncles and aunts, and all. He didn't stop for breath for forty-minutes. Finally, I put an adhesive strap around his neck, gave him some Epsom Salts, and told him to return to the barracks and soak his ankle in hot water. He did depart, but not until I was ready for a "nut house."

Then another recruit came in. He looked at me, and I at him. I finally had courage enough to ask him what he wanted... His lips moved, but I heard nothing. I next asked him for his name, and he looked at me as if to say, "Will that help me?" Again, I asked—"What is your name?" But, no response. I pressed further: "You do have name, don't you?" He said, "What?" I said, "A name—you have one, don't you? Is it Jones, or Brown, or Smith?" He said, "Uh-huh, that's it." And he then sort of grinned—like a sick mole. Well, I asked which it was, and he said "Smith"—but I couldn't believe him, but was mentally not capable to begin the process all over again. Then, he told me he wasn't sick. I then asked him the reason for his coming to the Dispensary. He did not know. He really didn't know WHERE he was, but he did remember where his barracks was. So, I sent him to his barracks, and I collapsed! Maybe I have recovered, somewhat.

When they start sending fellows like that into our army, it must be for one purpose—to hope the Nazis could capture them, and then lose their minds trying to interrogate them!

Such has been the life of your Medical Soldier Boy. I'm ready for the barracks, an evening's show, and then some sleep. Ha!

Nov. 25, 1942 Shelby

Almost a spring-like day, today. But, as you know, this has never been my idea of a suitable climate.

The stuff came through in flying colors, and down the gullets most of it went in a hurry. Ha! Ha! And, were those dream-bars good! A million thanks!

Was called in for an interview, today—with the officer in charge of a Special Services Commission (entertainment). They are dreadfully short of personnel for dramatics and skits. It would be interesting work, but higher ups won't let them take non-coms and OCS candidates. So, two strikes against my chances. But, I'm not too eager for it. Several things seem to be pending. So, we shall just wait.

The tube arrived, and I shall now return the borrowed one. You must have had no trouble to get a new one. Bravo!

Just had chow, and it is Thanksgiving Day. We are to have our feast tonight, and some trimmings are promised. Our cooks have been working "like sixty" the past two days, and we are to eat at a later hour than usual. It will be good.

Almost a flood of colds besieging us. For me, it is more like my frequent sinus drainage. But, I keep my fingers crossed. Have had to get out a report on our men who, for whatever reasons, are on "Limited Duty." This was a new one. Maybe I'll feel better, tomorrow.

Do not expect me to get home for Christmas. It is out of the question. Quotas for furloughs do not end until January 20th, and no chance for anyone who has had one.

Was at this typewriter at 7:00 this morning; so, the day has seemed long. Can't do anything about anything, except gripe to myself. So much for my woes!

Hope I can make it in for choir practice tomorrow evening. But, something always arises to keep me right here in "Dear Old Camp Shelby"! And, don't ask me if I am on a grouch! Ha! Ha!

Nov. 28, 1942 Camp Shelby

Your letter of the 25th arrived today—three days by airmail. So, just send letters regular from now on, for the planes do not speed delivery. The government has utilized air to such an extent that regular letters just have to wait.

So, Don did strut around when you read to him what the dental people, here, said about my teeth.

Not bad!

We are giving all sorts of shots, and the poor fellows just have to take them. Personnel for the Division are now up to strength (T.O.), and should soon be whipped into shape to be shipped out. No new men, now, to come in.

Lots of speculation as to the length of the war—until this mess is over. Capt. Munger has wagered that we will be home in 15 months. He talks about hiking into Berlin, possibly being sent to India, perhaps a push through China, and a "hike into Tokyo." The Allies are way in the lead in this production game, and British bombing of Germany has so reduced German production that odds for our victory begin to loom. Our armies of occupation may not just hover above the Germans, but also the Yugoslavs, Bohemians, Czechs, and others. Yes, things are in pretty good shape, seemingly.

The "blowing" of the French fleet was certainly done in direct defiance of Hitler. Now, the Allies no longer have to watch it, and the Mediterranean is practically secure. The Italian fleet is virtually nil, and the poor Italians are about ready to call it quits. We shall see! Eh?

Went into town for choir practice last evening. Now, the minister and I are going to sing a duet. Besides the organist, we were the only ones there. We will have to lead out for all the chants he wants rendered. I do not know just what it all will be like. I hadn't been in town for about three weeks.

Certainly, no bid for me for OCS before January. It will be nice to help with the Christmas music at the church in town.

We had full field inspection of our equipment on the bunks, this morning, and our new boys came through with flying colors. According to Capt. Munger, our barracks was the only one to pass. Our new boys are going to be all right. Now, we can become a little conceited. Ha!

More rain today. My ODs will constantly need repressing. So, it goes. I must look neat for the services in town!

December 2, 1942 Camp Shelby

You folks have really been up to some high ideas—about my flying home for Xmas. Three hurdles must be jumped over. First, that our Division will permit it; second, that Capt. Hughes and Capt. Munger will consent; and third, that I can get plane transportation. I have no problem with Hughes and Munger, but no word from Division,, yet, and my military status is so low that I could have no priority for a flight. We shall see what can be done, but do not plan on it!!! I will not plan on it because of the transportation difficulty. You will hear nothing more from me about this—unless I shall be coming. You'll receive a telegram.

Busy around here, as of late. Several of us are taking "driver's lessons." An army license could come in handy one of these days. One can never know ahead when some sort of emergency may require him to drive, and I would be protected with a license. I guess drivers are being checked to see if they are "licensed"—to drive military vehicles.

Cold here last night—with a heavy frost, actually. As for me, I am more comfortable cold than with heat. I just don't care much for this overnight stuff, whether cold or hot. We shall see!

Mussolini made a speech to his "House of Deputies"—said that the President of the U.S. wanted this war all along, and that Roosevelt had certainly broken his promises to American mothers that "no American blood would be spilled again on European soil." Poor old Benito can do little more than just moan and wail away. He has lost most of his bluster and "boistrosity"! I wonder what he will think when Hitler moves into Italy to ward off an Allied thrust there.

Sick call about to begin, so I must close. Just do not expect me to make it home for Christmas.

Dec. 4, 1942 Shelby

Just a hurried note to let you know that I'm still kicking. Am at the Service Club in Hattiesburg and am going to choir practice in about a half hour.

And, I am full of aches and pains. That 28-mile hike was just a breather compared to what we had today. This was another, but with just 8 hours to walk it, instead of 11&1/2 as before! And did we have to travel—just had to pick up the little footsies and lay them right down in quick order. We had a five-minute break at end of each hour, and then thirty minutes for lunch. We started at 7:00 and finished at 2:45—on our feet about 7 hours and 20 minutes. Average steps per minute was about 120, instead of the usual 106. So, some aches and pains, afterwards.

My hip didn't bother at all, but knees really tuned up—and remain painful. No one fell out, and about 400 participated. But, so many limping around, and we appeared to be centuries old. Ha!

I had only two small blisters, on tops of toes. Some of the fellows had bad blisters on the soles of their feet, with feet and ankles swollen. My hands swelled, strangely enough, but feet and ankles were practically normal.

Yes—please send the Christmas cards. I can use them. And, I have called the air company in Jackson. Will not know for two or three days if passage can be arranged. If not, I shall help with Xmas music at the Episcopal Church in Hattiesburg, and then spend my $100 on a bond. Do not send me any money, but you'll have to stake me when I get home. IF!!!

A sad thing happened for one of our medical men. He timed his furlough to be home when his wife was due to have their baby. He was there, but the baby died—and his wife nearly so. Poor guy, and he was 20 hours late in return. Had he requested, he could have had an extension. A late return automatically results in loss of some "ration money"—about $8, and this is a regulation which is automatically exacted after a "morning report." Capt. Munger would do no more, and all of us felt just so sorry!

Dec. 6, 1942 Shelby

Sunday afternoon, and not much to write about. Of course, an American soldier can always find plenty to kick about, and he is on the average supposed to be a far superior griper than any other soldier. We always have plenty to kick about. We just look around!

This week our Med. Det. has the duty to keep the Dispensary clean—just an extra for us. This morning we had 54 for sick call, rather than the usual 25, and we didn't finish until about 9:40. Inspection of barracks was to be at 10:00, and the fellows had to rush back to have clean mess kits, and all, on display. Capt. Munger thought the Dispensary needed another mopping, so back came a crew to make things ready for 11:00. Our new recruits, four of them, were out on a four-mile hike, and did not return in time to display properly their equipment, and to be dressed in their O.D.s. Inspecting officers really chewed out Sgt. Johnson, and directed that none of the men be given passes for the weekend. It was a dirty deal, and something will be said about it tomorrow night when we have our Officer-NonCom meeting. I think I shall speak a little piece. Capt. Munger doesn't know about all of this, and I want him to know.

Used my "honor pass" to leave camp and come in to Hattiesburg for communion at the Episcopal church, and had been asked to sing "The Publican." It went well, the organist is an excellent accompanist, and all seemed to like it. It was the special music for the offertory.

No info from the airplane company as to a reservation. We've heard that extra planes are being put on to handle the Christmas traffic. It is likely that I won't make it home.

Dec. 8, 1842 Camp Shelby

Socks and candy came through, and all in order. I much appreciate it. The candy is gone, and the socks will last considerably longer, I think. They appear to be my size, and should remain so, unless they shrink.

Our Christmas passes cannot begin until the 24th, and Capt. Munger told me he would see to it that I got one. The Chicago & Southern Airlines at Jackson, Mississippi, sent me my reservation, but they had it for the night of the 22nd—a day too early. So, I had to request a change, but asked them to hold my reservation for me—Omaha, to Jackson, via Chicago, on the 27th. Will reach Jackson about 5:30 in the afternoon. Not bad! Now, if we can just get something arranged for Wednesday evening or Thursday morning! It is an extravagance, but money does not mean much to an army man, so I am told. Must just as well spend it while I have it. The ticket costs about $120.

You might send me about fifteen dollars; this will give me a little margin in pocket. I could borrow, but do not want to. The fellow who lost his baby owes me twenty dollars, but he can't pay me until payday at the end of the month.

Sergeant Johnson is to report next Monday at Ft. Sill, Oklahoma, for officer's training. When he goes, I guess I'll be made Staff Sergeant. My salary will be about 96 dollars per month, instead of 66—minus, of course, what is taken out for insurance, laundry, etc. There is a big M.A.C. quota going out the 22nd of January, and I'm going to attempt to be on it. One nice thing about it—that I shall receive a staff sergeant's pay instead of a corporal's. So, nice!

Capt. Munger is planning to fly home, too, for Christmas. It would be something were we to be on the same flight together. It is a day-flight, and only about eight hours. Hardly seems possible.

Went in for communion to the Episcopal church last Sunday, as you know, and then went to the Rector's for Sunday dinner. His wife, who I at first thought to be somewhat of a nitwit, is really much different after you get used to her. Mrs. Morgan is really a clever woman—to sew, to cook, and to make all sorts of gifts for members of the congregation. Must admit that my first impression was pretty tipsy

And, Bin, in case I do make it home, would you buy some knick-knacks for me—to put under the tree for Don and the Moosie? Thanks.

Dec. 9, 1942 Shelby

Will call Sunday morning and should know by then if I'll be coming home. And, Mother, I know you have a birthday coming up, soon. Are you to be 58 or 59? But, if born in 1884!

As for the READERS DIGEST, just hold the copies at home for me to read, and do not throw any away.

Am to be C.Q. tonight, and hope for a quiet time. Sometimes my "beauty rest" gets interrupted.

On Monday and Tuesday evenings, I must hold classes on the medical forms and reports we use and are to make. Capt. Munger thinks I'm the one who knows "the stuff." So many new recruits and changes in personnel, and so much confusion with the paper work. So, it appears that my first duties as a staff sergeant will be instruction. Sergeant Johnson departs this Friday, and I'll be made Staff Sergeant on Monday. Now, isn't that something! And, the fellows in our Med. Det. are such a grand gang!

Lots of reviewing about "Pearl Harbor" going on. Some hold it to have been a real disgrace for the U.S. to have been taken by such surprise, and Republicans are trying to breathe on the heels of the Democrats. Well, things should brighten up—as far as efficiency is concerned.

This rationing business is getting to be "something else," also. You see it, hear it, feel it, and wonder about it! It is a necessity, but we hear the government is storing large quantities—to be prepared to ship much to lands as they are liberated.

What do you think of Darlan? He certainly came in handy for the Allies. DeGaulle and Darlan will certainly reach some kind of an understanding.

So, no more whipping cream to be available, eh? If I get home, we'll have to make "ice milk."

Typed the training schedule this morning, and then had time to play in about fifteen games of volleyball this afternoon.

As for Christmas, you might get me one of those pants creasers—electric. Can use it as long as we are the U.S.

Dec. 11, 1942 Camp Shelby

A letter, yesterday; and another, today.

Wallace and I were going into Hattiesburg for church, but he hasn't shown up. So, I'll go to the nearby chapel this a.m.

We are now to become involved in training problems, and "evacuation of casualties" will keep us moving, and I do mean "moving." Our Dispensary must have a C.Q. on duty all the time during the next two weeks, and this means that our squad will be short a man in the field. But, we'll be getting some valuable experience, and our drivers will be busy bringing in the "wounded…"

Am off to the chapel.

Well, Wallace arrived just after my return from chapel, and into Hattiesburg we went. We went to a hotel, had $1.00 dinners, then to a movie, and then back to camp. Quite an excursion, eh?

The candy and scarf arrived. The scarf is not "regulation," But I'm going to wear it, anyhow. Maybe some general will be driving by, see me, and tell me to take it off. Oh, well!

Dec. 13, 1942 Shelby

Wanted to call, Sunday, to wish you a happy birthday, for today. But waiting time for the telephones was too long. May try tomorrow evening, and will hope you are home. I never know when a lull in action around here will permit me to sneak away for a call. Terrible, the way these army duties interfere with what one wants to do. We can always blame "Old Schickelgruber"!

Wanted to tell you that my trip home seems to be set. Have my plane reservation, and ticket cost $118.75—not bad! By bus to Jackson to catch a 9:17 p.m. to St. Louis—the 23rd. Then, Thursday morning, a MCA flight gets me to Omaha about 11:30. So, will meet somebody there.

Capt. Munger said that the Division had not placed any restriction on Christmas passes. I must be back for roll call the 28th. So, I must leave Omaha about 9:00 Sunday morning, to be back in Jackson by 5:45 that evening—the 27th. Sure hope the connections work out. It will be just scrumptious to be home for three nights and 2 ½ days. Will need decent weather!

Had to shoot a gang of recruits, Saturday—about 110 shots altogether. I feel like a real veteran with this needle!

Fellows are getting Xmas packages, and we have so much candy, nuts, and fruit cake to eat. It is just great! We are going to become fatter and sassier by the day! Pretty hard to keep "in training"—Yessirree! And, will try to call this evening.

Dec.18, 1942 Camp Shelby

Should be my last letter before I see you. Capt. Munger is letting two of us have the passes. It is just swell of him to do it, and each of us must cover a lot of ground—distance. The regulations really do not permit such distances—for such passes, actually. The Captain is really an "old pal," isn't he? He wanted to slip to Lincoln, too, but the General in control of his command refused an absence. So!!!!

Remember, Omaha, about 11:30, the 24th. But, when you first wanted to know if I could get a pass to come home for Christmas, I thought you were out of your minds.

The Xmas packages keep coming in, and things get eaten in a hurry. However, some cheeses and canned olives get secreted away for future.

Am not used, yet, to being called "Sergeant." But, it certainly has a different ring to it than "Corporal." So, until Thursday morning!

December 28, 1942 Camp Shelby

Well, by hook and crook, I did arrive here by 10:30 Monday morning. Wasn't bad at all, for having to travel by train. Got into Chicago on time, a good sleep on the train—just snuggled under my heavy overcoat . Etc.

A limousine took about 15 of us to the airport, but planes had all been grounded into St. Louis and Memphis because of weather. Jean Craven Mickey, at the airlines desk, did her best to find a plane for me, and there were about 20 others needing to go south. A plane was circling over the airport, but heavy fog prevented any descent at Chicago. So, no chance to get us up and away. So, Jean called the Illinois Central, to see if reservations could be made on the "Panama Flyer." But. In no way—and the only thing possible was a slow old coach train, to leave Chicago at 5:55 and to reach Jackson, Mississippi, 26 hours later. It seemed that I could not get on the "Flyer," so, I wired you folks and Capt. Munger.

Most of the other fellows were heading to Camp Livingston, in La., and we were all in the same boat and somewhat ticked off. The air company sent us back, by limousine, to the Illinois Central R.R. station, and we were at the ticket office about 2:50. But, no reservations—as before. I went back to the window and said: "Mr., we just can't take NO for an answer... Our plane is grounded, and we must all get back into southern Mississippi or Louisiana by tomorrow morning at reveille. We'll even ride in the engine!" One of the other fellows added: "Yeah! I'll even ride in the can!" We all laughed. But, I think we all appeared kind of green around the edges. The agent looked at us and said: "Well, I'll see what I can do."

He went into an inner office and returned after about five minutes—to say that he would give us tickets, but that he did not know where we could ride. We exchanged our airfares for the train, and rushed to the track—at 3:10, and the train had not departed. The conductor looked at our tickets and asked: "Don't you have a car number?" We said, "No, but any car will do, and we are not choosy!" He then asked, "You going back to camp? When you got to get there?" We told him, and he told us to crawl right on and to go "back to the lounge car." Did we ever "crawl on"!

The lounge car was filled, and suitcases were everywhere. We exchanged seats as the people moved around. We felt we had more than a break and a half. This "Flyer" is a wonderful train, and one of the newest. The staterooms are like private "suites"—just quite elite. I had to sit on the floor, near the tail-end, but I knew I'd be in Jackson about 5:30 next morning—all that I really cared about. I was on my way!

Connections to Hattiesburg took but 45 minutes, and I was in by 9:30 and to camp by 10:15. And, I sent you a postal telegraph. I think I may have made record time from Lincoln.

No officers were around; so, I just started to work; and, didn't clean up my dirty self until chow time in the evening—about 5:15. Capt. Hughes asked me if I had encountered bad weather, and this I affirmed. He made no comment. Capt. Munger is ill with a bad cold, and he did receive my telegram, and he had been told I had arrived. I went to see him, and he felt I had made some "pretty good connections"—to get here when I did.

So, every thing is OK, and what a wonderful Christmas in just every way. It was a hair-brained idea to begin with. But, we did get in our Christmas together—just wonderful for me! It was a wild dream come true. I was lucky with it all!

While on the train, rolling south from Chicago, three of us in uniform were along side a man whose plane had been grounded. About 6:30, we three (the other two were also sergeants) went to the diner for chow. We found a table, just vacated. This man had followed us and joined us at the table. He then insisted that he be our host. With exchanged glances, we sort of concluded that we could not refuse. He ordered "full dinners," and I had trout with all the trimmings—$1.70. This gentleman appeared to be quite prosperous—was wearing two large diamond rings, etc.

We were at the table about an hour, and had a good time. He was most gracious, paid the bill, tipped the waiter generously, and thanked us for having joined him. Of course, we let him know how much we appreciated his generosity. We then exchanged names, and we had another good chuckle—for I was David Mickey and he was J. H. Rooney.

Well, I had more than my share of good luck on this trip. I could have hugged the last breath out of that ticket agent in Chicago. And, I didn't have to be AWOL—at least, no one reported me as such. Now, it is back to "normal"—whatever that means.

December 31, 1942 Camp Shelby

(To Bin and Don, in Lincoln)—Have been in somewhat of a stupor since Moosie called me this morning. I know she has gone to Valentine. It's such a shame about Uncle Orville, and I'm just stunned. We just do not come to grips with something like this until it strikes at home.

Have just written Aunt Charlotte, but couldn't say anything the way I wanted to. Just hope to bolster her a bit, and Janet, Robert, and Patsy. WE are never prepared for such as this! Mother said that Janet had left for Valentine the evening before, and I suppose she did not know of her father's death until she arrived. What a greeting for her!

When they phoned the Dispensary, here, the operator told me to get to nearest pay station as quickly as possible, and to call operator 13, in Lincoln, Nebraska.

Our camp phones do not work very well with outside connections. I was about petrified, for I knew something real bad had happened. I guess I made such a pitiful sigh that one of our lieutenants just handed me a five dollar bill and said I was to use it if I needed it. I rushed to our nearest Service Club and placed the call—and it took about ten minutes, but seemed like an hour.

Mother answered the phone and asked: "Hello, David, how are you?" Her voice sounded just heart-broken, and she could say hardly more than a word between gulps. She was going to drive right away to Valentine.

I have been just puttering around, and can't keep my mind focused on anything here. Cy and the kids have so much to be proud of. Uncle Orville did a courageous thing, for he knew what he might be getting into. They can keep their chins up high.

(Fn. My mother's younger sister, Charlotte, married Orville A. Ralston, a dentist. He had been a pilot in World War I, and was Nebraska's only "Ace"—quite a distinction. His dental practice was for many years in Ainsworth, and then in Valentine. A few months after the attack on Pearl Harbor, he applied for a commission in the Air Force and received an appointment as Major, and was assigned to a station at Great Falls, Montana—with air ballistics being his forte. He and several of his associates were on flight eastward to spend a New Year's recess at their homes. For whatever cause, the plane after lift-off failed to clear a mountain ridge. That was it! My aunt was waiting for his arrival at a government training airfield which had been laid out between Johnstown and Ainsworth. She was told, simply, that she was to return to her home. She felt something had happened, but she did not know what. A few hours later she received official notification.)

Well, Bin, we know all about this, don't we? How often I have wished that Dad were still alive. Yes, we understand what CyBo and Janet and Bob and Pat must now endure. Mother will be such a comfort to Aunt Charlotte, and she will stay there just as long as she needs to. Such things do happen, and they seem to be just too much.

Yes, my trip from Lincoln back to camp was a wild one. The fellow who went home to Pennsylvania was a corporal, and he was 26 hours AWOL, whereas I was only 3 ½. His was caught in Atlanta, Ga., because of a bridge wash-out; but he was not penalized. Nice!

Payday, today, and I received $75.80. So, back in the money! Will be sending a money order, soon, and would appreciate, Bin, if you would take from it what I owe you. Don, you see that she "dood it.'

I feel so insignificant—this news about Uncle Orville.

January 6, 1943 Camp Shelby

Received letter from Mother at Valentine. Rushed over to pay phone and called Valentine—and visited with her and with Aunt Charlotte. It was worth the $5.18. Just feel so blue and so sorry for little CyBo.

These field problems and simulated casualties are training at the darndest! The tags are made out ahead of schedule, and then are distributed to the batteries of the battalions. Lots of transporting of "wounded" by litter and by ambulance. We are to be "out on training" again tonight, and again Friday night. This is valuable experience. Yesterday my nose was running and I was certain I had some temperature. But, today, am just back to normal. Ha! I guess I can still take it.

Over the phone, Moosie said, "Your birthday present is going to be a little late. I'm so sorry!" I gave her a lecture, of about ten seconds in length; and, she agreed with me. We then had a wee chuckle. Isn't the telephone a wonderful thing!

January 9, 1943 Shelby

My first Saturday afternoon free for some time. A beautiful day—with the sun out in full force.

These overnight problems with all the evacuations are to continue for a while. Trucks must transport infantry and haul the artillery. Our medical unit's command car was both pulling and hauling. Due to some problems, we had sick-call at the Dispensary this morning, and I slept in my bunk last night! We had been slithering about in Mississippi mud and wobbling across swamp bridges built by the Engineers. Two or three accidents proved to be not serious. One of our lieutenants was run over by a jeep, but hardly a bruise in evidence on his leg; so, not so much as a sprain.

The rain continues, and we would welcome some dry weather. Schedule requires us to be out in the rain nearly each day. Maybe we wouldn't mind if we could hunt ducks. Humph!

January 11, 1943 Shelby

Am enclosing this money order and this check. Please get them deposited for me. Also, would you let me know what funds I have. This check is the refund from the air company, and is the difference between airfare and trainfare—Lincoln, via Chicago, to Jackson. Refunds to enlisted men must have endorsement by an officer; so, Capt. Hughes signed. This means that if a check bounces, the officer must pay up. So, if the bank wants to know about the double signature, you can explain. So far, I know of no officer who has been "stuck"—!!!

It was nice to know that Uncle Orville knew of Janet's engagement to Warren and had given his consent to the "nuptials"—Yes! Also, was so content that you were in Valentine for more than a week with Aunt Charlotte.

January 13, 1943 Shelby

Two letters from you, today, Moosie—your final one from Valentine and the one after your return to Lincoln. So much to be said about Uncle Orville. It was satisfaction to know he was buried in the cemetery at Wood Lake. And, I so much appreciated your telephone call to inform me of his death, for I should not have wanted to read of it, first, in the newspaper. But, what a numbing shock to receive that phone call! Had I not have been home so recently, I might have asked for an emergency furlough. However, such is supposed to be for illness or death of a member of an "immediate family." Knowing our officers, I probably would have received one.

Three new men transferred into our Med. Det. We had been so short-handed, and now we can again function almost properly. It has been difficult, particularly with two of the fellows ill and in the hospital. We were constantly pinch-hitting and doing, often, double time.

January 15, 1943 Camp Shelby

In the field all day, today—with 20 simulated casualties to tag, to administer first-aid, and to transport in certain cases to forward station or "hospital." It was a rugged day, but sunny and warm. Time passes much faster when busy "on the front"—rather than to be in camp.

Many rumors, that another cadre is to be called from this Division. If so, I'm going to attempt to get into it. I'd much prefer such change to OCS. From what I have learned, it would be almost financially better for me to move up in administrative ranks within a new division. My guess is that OCS for me will be the Medical Administration Corps (MAC), and promotion comes very slowly. Should I be selected for the cadre, I will cancel my application to OCS. Too, I have concluded that something a bit underhanded has been at work with regard to my application. Do not know for sure, but???

Have a new guy fully ready to take over this records business for the Battalion, and he has eased my load of work considerably. He will be promoted to a Technician, 5th grade (corporal), my old rank—and which has been vacant since my promotion to be staff sergeant. I'm all for him, and am pushing for his advancement.

January 20, 1943 Camp Shelby

Have I been having a time! On our last over-night problem, I must have bedded down in some poison ivy. Monday I began to break out with the nicest rash and itch—both hands, wrists, and forearms, along with face and neck. I've become quite a sight, and all dobbed up with calamine lotion. Have injected serum, and am much improved. This serum is remarkable stuff, the best remedy I have ever seen. The doses are daily over several days, gradually increased in strength, and sting like the dickens for about two minutes each time. But, does it help!

Another of our medical boys has it, and we shoot each other each morning, and then moan and groan in harmony. Happily, two of our battalion lieutenants got into it, and it is my happy privilege to give them the shots, and they, in turn, just about hit the ceiling each morning. Such good fun! My right hand was badly blistered, but soon so much better. The itching has stopped. This serum is a miracle, really.

Wish to call this evening, to wish Bin a happy birthday, but will not if the waiting time is to be too long. My package will arrive a day or two late.

Also, I should be sending some funds home each month, for will not be spending much of my $88. I'll either buy a bond, or send a money order. We'll all be rich. Ho! Ho!

Saw the show, "Commandos Strike at Dawn," with Paul Muni. It was a good, anti-Nazi film, and deals with the ruthlessness of the Nazi. Was well played.

No let up in our being busy, but the poison ivy has kept me in camp. My replacement with the book work is in full swing, and no worry about it. I gave him some typing lessons, and he has really grabbed hold. He's not yet ready for typed correspondence, but he will be.

We've been ordered to send all cameras home. Mine will be arriving, soon. Training projects within the Division have become somewhat indicative of future action, and especially so. So, we are to be conscious of secrecy.

The British have been pouring it on Berlin, and I hope they level the "joint." Hitler had promised the people that Berlin would never be bombed. Reports are very good for our side. Hope the final blow will be dealt in N. Africa, and I wish we could get Rommel—would be a real blow to German ego and morale.

Quite a bit of flu and colds around here, and my sinuses are draining plenty; but, as long as they keep draining and open I have no worry. But, "to stuff up" can be bad!

January 23, 1943 Shelby

So, you have had some frozen pipes? One of these years you should figure out where the air sifts in. The direction of the wind has to have a lot to do with it. But, no pipes leaking?

The last three days, here, have been just balmy and nice. My head has ceased to flow. So, all sorts of things are clearing up. Our real chilly spell may be over.

Saw the movie, "Shadow of a Doubt"—lots of suspense. The actors were good—all around.

Have been hoping that CyBo's finances are secure and sufficient. I've been told that she will receive six months of Uncle Orville's salary. He must have had insurance. I feel so concerned for Aunt Charlotte.

This is Saturday. I feel grimey, or is it "grimy"? Ha! Am heading over for a scrubbing.

We now have doubled-decked beds, and I have an upper—with my radio on top of the clothes rack—right at ear's level. Not bad!! Electric outlet is below in floor, and do not need batteries. So, I wont be buying new ones for a while.

January 24, 1943 Camp Shelby

Not much, today. We held sick call. Then, I wrote some letters, had dinner, saw a show, visited around to bat the breeze, had supper, and am now writing to you—half sitting and half lying down. You may need a translation.

William L. Shirer says there is something big in the news, and he speculates that the Americans, English, Russians and Chinese are about to enter into a united action—to get this ended. I think it will be a long affair, and I do not plan to chew my teeth on air. So, there!!

Capt. Munger is in the hospital, sick with the flu. He had a high temperature; but, my hunch is that he was just worn to a frazzle.,

Of all things, last evening—I got KFOR on my little radio. Just closed my eyes and seemed to be in Lincoln. The first time this has happened. The airways must have been just right. Sure was a surprise.

Tomorrow I'm going to see if I can get on the next quota for M.A.C. officer's school. Our Division's adjutant thinks I should recheck my papers, to make sure all are in order. He implied that Capt. Munger could have had me on the list any time he chose. The implication was almost clear and caused me to wonder a bit. The Capt. did say to me, once, that I had to get somebody ready to take over the records before I left for school. Now, I think I understand just what he meant. But. I'd hate to believe he put a sustaining hand on my application! I may have to use some lung power and make inquiries. The next class is to begin March 5th, and to be in it will require me to make a move.

Another big field problem coming up, and predicted weather is for cold and rain. I'll be glad when it is over.

Didn't shave this morning. So, must reap my harvest the first thing tomorrow.

January 28, 1943 Shelby

Just a shorty, today. Was out in the field for two days. We were a cold, but cheerful, lot. We did some shivering in our timbers, and the scarf came in handy

Poison ivy is gone, but some itch continues around the spots where the shots went in.

Am now heading to the barracks for some sleep.

Not surprised that Janet and Warren will be married in Lincoln.

No attempt to call this evening—just couldn't get to a booth early enough to avoid long delay.

January 30, 1943 Camp Shelby

A hectic week, with little chance to write much. We continue to be in the field this week—sort of. Engineers have been building roads and pontoon bridges to provide ways to get through swampy areas, and the units are expected to use the new ways.

We continue to gather and to evacuate simulated casualties, and ambulances were constantly coming in and out of our Clearing Station, and we average about 20 each night. We acquired a large pyramidal tent and have been using it as shelter—keeps us much warmer, just to roll up in our bedding and enjoy the cover. Had we received an order to evacuate, at night, we would have had a real mess on our hands. Ha! These nights are just cold, and we were able to keep quite snugly. I am still amazed at the impact this scrum had with the poison ivy. The shots are taken over six days, and they are effective from the first. Without them, I would have been a real mess!

Another fellow in our 328th Bn. came to see me. He, too, suspects he has been getting a "run around" with respect to OCS. He proposed we go to the Adjutant's office to make inquiries. His was for a different OCS. We shared our disgusts, suspicions, and resentments. So, to the office we went. Each of us was more than just mildly suspicious! He had been teaching philosophy and speech at Notre Dame. Between the two of us, we expected to find some explanations.

Well, we made our inquiry, and I think we were just quite blunt. We wanted to know if our papers were in order, if they might have been misplaced, and why so much time had elapsed since applying, etc. Well, the sergeant, who was there at the desk, talked about re-organization, about some files having been mislaid, and about all being now in place. Then, almost as an after thought, he told me that I had been slated for the January 6th "quota"—but had just been "squeezed out"! Well, my dander began to rise, and I asked him what he meant by "squeezed out"! Two nearby lieutenants were listening in, and they were laughing. Well, we sort of joined in the mirth, for it seemed quite clear there had been something a little off-color with the "squeezing"! It was evident that much skullduggery had been at work, and the mischief had not been to our advantages. Both of us asked if we should reapply—to start over. Officers and sergeant assured us to the contrary.

Some other factors at work, maybe. Seemed a bit evident that perhaps a certain religious qualification would help considerably. Further check with my application revealed that I had submitted it more than three months before, and that I had to have another physical examination.
Then came the assurance I was slated to be on the list for March 5th, along with just one other from the 85th.

So, I shall be heading for OCS on March 5th. Had I not come in to headquarters to press things and to threaten almost to expose that my file had been put aside, etc., nothing would have changed... I'm quite certain that my application was put aside as result of request, and I know whose!!!

No problem with the physical, but I had to sign another waiver on my sinuses. Now, we shall just have to see if I'm on that list for March 5th. I'm mad enough already with some of the "brass hats"! G-r-r-r-r-r-r-r!

Really is a nice day, today. Tomorrow is payday, and I have $1.50 in my pocket. I still am due to receive a check for $10.60 from one of the air companies—refund for unused ticket on return after Christmas. So, will have a little extra, maybe.

Was impressed by the news concerning the President's journey to Morocco. Seemingly, the troops didn't know that Roosevelt was in the limousine to pass before them while they were standing in formation. Officers were not informed, and some groups were not standing at "attention"—even. But, it would be something to stand in formation while the President of the U.S. passed before you. Roosevelt has also swung by Brazil. He does get around! It must pay to keep on the move!

But, so much waste!—and just about everywhere.

Haven't been into Hattiesburg for about two weeks. Will plan to go in next Sunday, for church.

Our Battalion commander was just in to get his booster shot, for typhoid—about 3:15. It was my pleasure to drill it in. Ha! It is so much fun to shoot our officers!

January 31, 1943 Shelby

We are to be out about four days next week, and I won't find much time to write. Weather has been warm and sunny, but much colder in the offing. So many have colds, and we've had a couple cases of pneumonia.

February coming up, and three months from tomorrow I shall have been in this man's army for a year! Much has happened in the past nine months, eh? Wonder what it all will be like after another nine months.

There seems to be an intensification in a "war of nerves"! Recent British raids seemed to have been timed to interrupt speeches by Goebbels and Goering. The British must have been tipped off—as one newsman said, as if some witness had pushed a signal-button, the very second each speech commenced. I think we are beginning to get the jump on "Uncle Adolph"!

Am reading Ralf Boswell's NOSTRADAMUS SPEAKS. You'd find it quite interesting. This 16th-century "prophet" made some uncanny and accurate predictions. Of course, Boswell's effort is to point out the accuracies of his subject.

February 4 & 5, 1943 Shelby

Out in the field for a fourth day, and we have had our little typewriters for about a week. So, I shall give this one a try. But, we have been moving around on the double—to simulate offensive, then defensive, then offensive, etc., postures. Our Division is not slated for maneuvers until sometime in April. By then, I should be in OCS.

Our simulated casualties average about 20 per day. The captain in charge of our clearing station has noted that the Division Artillery is sending in more casualties than the infantry of the division and that it should be just the reverse, about three to one. We do not know what is at work, but we may just be better at what we are supposed to be doing.

Monday night it was rainy. So, I curled up in the back seat of our command car, usually used by our Captain, and slept snugly—but, a bit cramped. For Tuesday night, another of the gang and I joined our shelter halves together, at the bottom and along one side, and had beneath a veritable double sleeping bag—of sorts. We really sawed our logs!

The next night, about eleven, we had to change location, and didn't get settled until after one o'clock. I awoke too late for chow. Our three medical vehicles had been misdirected during the night, and some of us were out on a flank of the battalion. Those of us who were "lost" could not find even so much as our chow wagon. Quite a grand mix-up, with casualties lying unattended. Some of us were about two and a half miles away from position, and it was just quite a mess. According to some experts, the Division Artillery had some new "ninety-day wonders" who had become confused. Ha! Anyway, we returned to proper locales, and with casualties again being correctly cared for.

One of our new men in the Med. Det. had complained about pain in his back, hips, and upper legs. As diagnosed, he suffers from sclerosis of the sacroiliac and lower lumbar facets. He has been a very good B'try Aid man, and we are going to lose him. He thinks that constant riding in trucks has caused his trouble. He is now in so much pain that he can hardly walk.

Was called in to sign another waiver on my sinuses, and the explanation sounded a bit fishy to me. Rumor has it that there has been far too many applications for the various candidate schools, and that a cut-back is in order. Too, I was again advised that my normal 20/200 vision in each eye limited me to an OCS for administrative purposes, only. But. the sergeant at the Adjutant's office assured me I would be next. So, we shall see!

We are about twenty miles from camp. Our vehicles have been little used, and rumor has it that we have a shortage of gasoline. Surmises hold that too much running around has been permitted and that vehicles will be moved only upon specific order. Others reason that the several new lieutenants must be taught to conserve. Maybe these restrictions are just a part of the training of new officers. This little Corona is not as good a machine at my portable Royal at home—I think. Just can"t put it to as rapid a pace.

It is now Friday, and about three this morning did the rain come pouring down! Just no let up! Things were quiet. Capt. Hughes was away. Then came trouble. A jeep came tearing into our Aid Station, and the driver had orders to pick up our doctor. I directed the man to an Infantry "Collecting Station"—about a half-mile away. We learned, later, cause for such urgency.

Two officers, a sergeant and a corporal from a Quartermaster Corps unit within the Division were in a jeep, with the lieutenant at the wheel. Officers are not supposed to drive these vehicles—only the designated NCOs and enlisted men. Well, according to report, speeding was involved and a sharp turn came up at the bottom of a hill. A crash followed, and the lieutenant was killed and the sergeant critically injured, with the other two thrown clear. Capt. Hughes did gain word of the accident, but was not the first medical officer to reach the scene; and, he, therefore, did not have to make out the official report. (On a previous occasion, I once had to stay up nearly half a night to write up a report on an accident, with casualties. So, I was spared.)

These training accidents are just woeful, and nearly always because of carelessness. We are informed that the lieutenant who was driving and who was killed will have no government insurance paid to his family, for his being at the wheel of the jeep was against regulations. This is probably the way it is. A very saddening affair!

February 6, 1943 Camp Shelby

As for magazines, I really do not have time to read extras. I do pick up a mystery novel now and then. And am trying to finish Boswell's book on Nostradamus. Do not send any—just keep "Readers Digest," "Newsweek," and "Pathfinder" until I get home. Stack them in the attic.

Rains returned with intensity, and we got in from the field just in time.

So, Bin and Don are going to "rassling matches"—eh? Good for them!

Plan to go into Hattiesburg for church and communion, tomorrow. Then, after, will go to a movie or two.

February 9, 1943 Shelby

Am sending my tax return, and was surprised that I owed nothing—had expected about $48. So, I'm pleased to know that I am richer.

Fine weather, here. And, about February 22nd, we are to be in the field for about three weeks. Do not know the nature of the program. Local people inform us that a windy season is about to begin.

No word about OCS, but I'm sure hoping. Do not think it would do any good to go back to that office to do more complaining.

At church in town, yesterday, one of our camp chaplains was the speaker, and he was very good. I was invited to the parsonage for dinner, also, and it was roast chicken with many trimmings—and excellent. Three other boys from camp were there, too, and we had a good time—didn't begin to depart until about 1:45. Then, I hit two movies—"Young and Able" and Noel Coward's "In Which We Serve." This latter was a wonderful picture—story of the British navy and the devotion of a crew to a certain ship. It is sad, but well worth seeing. I think it shows the British quite accurately as they are.

Three men are being transferred to us, today. We have been short of manpower. Five of the battalion, including me, are to depart in about a month's time. So, new men are needed.

News continues to be encouraging. Bravo!

Feb. 13, 1943 Camp Shelby

Have been out in the field for about a week.

I know the house is to be full of "relatives" for the wedding, but they are pretty good relatives to have come to visit, aren't they? Wouldn't have it any other way, eh?

Seem to have some sort of stomach ache—just don't know what it is all about. Not severe.

About the 22nd, we are to go on extended bivouac—to be for about three weeks. Do not know about me with this OCS pending—at Camp Barkley (?), in Texas. Do certainly hope I'll be going, but I understand it is a tough school. But, the change of atmosphere will be welcome. We received word that the Staff Sergeant whom I replaced resigned from OCS. We hear that many candidates do. He was a plucky little fellow, and I am surprised that he didn't make it. And, we also hear that much is "rigged"—for or against one.

Again, the candy, tea, and stuff arrived, and the cute Valentines. The candy didn't last long, for the barracks is full of wolves with sweet teeth. And, I'm actually in Hattiesburg, here at the USO. May, yet, decide to phone.

February 14, 1943 Camp Shelby

Really hit the jack pot, this morning; for, I got to talk to all of you!

Am still waiting for my summons to attend OCS. Took two hours to get through, and I started at eight—with my call to you.

I wish this portable was as smooth as my little Royal. Sometimes it works more like a small threshing machine, but not as noisy. Ho! Ho!

War news continues to be good. Those Huns are again on the run. I'm sure Hitler will attempt an another offensive, of some sort. This Russian campaign has certainly sapped much of his reserve. We understand, here, that fuel has become critical for Germany. I hope so, for it means he will collapse the sooner.

All these typographical errors I blame on this darned typewriter. But, I'm a little "mad"—nohow!

Feb. 15, 1943 Camp Shelby

I'm really banking on this OCS business for the 5th of March. If it doesn't come through, I shall have to do a lot of howling. It has become a sort of stalemate, I fear. We go for a week of maneuvers, the 22nd, and the change of pace will be interesting. I may be left behind, and could have much time to write.

We are pouring on the instruction for our new men, and some of them seem to be mixed up. But, they are learning. It is sticking, too!

This cold weather continues, and is often freezing—just chills one to the marrow of the bones. I sure hope Texas will be better. Oh, well!

I know Janet's wedding was very nice. How I'd liked to have been there! Yes, I would have had some singing to do. We'll have to blame it on the war.

Just do not have much to write about, today.

Feb. 16, 1943 Shelby

We are to be in the field the next two days. So, will scribble a few lines, now.

More maneuvers this coming Monday, and slated to be for about three weeks. If I go to OCS, I shall miss all or most. Do keep your fingers crossed!

We are going to give some of "the boys" luetic shots. In this past month, our battalion has had two cases of syphilis show up—the first since our activation. Several compounds to be used, and the injections are made via the rear end. I understand that it takes 26 weeks to cure. Some of the gang is going to have some fun, eh?

Americans seem to have received somewhat of a drubbing in Tunisia. Seems that the Allies had enough time to prepare. The news has made me both sad and angry. And, some of our Congressmen are really beginning to express themselves. We shall see!

February 21, 1943 Camp Shelby

We've been "in field" getting ready for maneuvers. We have been flagging our fannies around, and I don't mean maybe.

But, I won't be going. My orders came through, yesterday, for officer's training, and 13 of us are to leave March 3rd. I have been put in charge of the group, and must handle the tickets, meal passes, reportings in, etc. Several telephone communications involved, and my time before departure must be spent here. This means that I won't be able to get a "delay in route"—to enable me to swing by Lincoln. But, at end of the training at officer's school, in May, I should have several days. So, will see you, then!

As for the maneuvers I'll be missing, we've been assured, by those experienced in such doings, that 999 out of a 1000 survive them. How do you like those odds?

The past few days, weather here has been just scrumptious. Maybe winter down here is about over. But it has been a bit nippy, and the warmth of the barracks has felt just great.

About a dozen of us will be separating from the battalion. For chow, we probably will have to go to a mess hall clear across camp. But, we may get in on some late morning snoozings—do you suppose? This could be nice!

My last field trip involved travel along dusty roads. Wind shields for all vehicles were covered and open, and did the dust flow in. I spit mud nearly all day, yesterday. But, no more of such for several weeks. We shall see.

From what I have learned, OCS will be darned, hard work for three months. So, pleasure may not be part of the project. So many do not make the grade—that no more than a third of each class will gain commissions. Such weeding out is a way to determine that the caliber of new officers is high. I'll have to put on my study hat and really get ready for hard work.

Had supper at the Service Club with Wallace last evening. We had trout, and it was real good. We need a good meal, such as this, just every once in a while. Really, our regular chow is quite good, but one likes to relax in a "dining room."

Should keep up on correspondence this coming week. May run into Hattiesburg a time, or two. With so few of us around, it will be pretty quiet.

February 22, 1943 Shelby

No rain, today, for a change. Just a note to let you know I'm kicking right along. Almost, except for me, our entire outfit is out on maneuvers. I'm the only one to sleep in our hutment, and it seemed a bit lonely—without the other 15.

Will be leaving for Abilene, Texas, the 3rd of March. I'm to carry the tickets for passage and meals, and have been in touch with the others who are also to depart.

For combination of reasons, quite a group from our Division have remained in camp, and we ended up with a shortage of non-coms. So, the powers that be appointed me to be Sergeant of the Guard, and to take charge of our eighteen artillery prisoners—soldiers convicted of various misdemeanors. This requires me to carry a loaded pistol. I must make certain that these men are always accounted for—busy and "cheerful"; and, I have had quite a day.

A medical soldier isn't supposed to stand any guard, nor to carry arms of any sort. We certainly ignored regulations. When the officer assigned me to do this, I just took it—it being good army policy to finish a detail and object after its completion. The thing that both irked and tickled me was that we medics are never given any sort of target practice, and here I was placed with a loaded gun. The two officers left to be in charge were 2nd Lts and new from school. Neither seemed to know what the score was. This putting a medical sergeant in as "Sergeant of the Guard" is something different. Under dire circumstances, it might have been necessary—but hardly here. Ha! Ha! Thank heavens, we didn't have to have a formal guard mount, or I'd really have been up a creek. Tomorrow morning I shall be off the detail, but must spend the night here in the "guard house"—and back in the barracks tomorrow. Well, what is one day on guard! But, it is amusing—the way some of these new officers just don't get some things straight.

One thing is certain, that I won't be in Camp Shelby much longer. My old gang is out on maneuvers, and I may not be seeing some very good friends again. They will probably be in camp, Saturday, for payday, and then I may never be with them more. We have been through a lot together, and it is going to end so suddenly.

News from Tunisia is not good. I just want Rommel to be swatted once and for all. The weather there seems to interfere with our efforts to eliminate him.

Am sending a new photo of me—it is good, but sober. But, a surprise in it for you—Ha! Ha!

I do not expect to receive my mail regularly, for it will be delivered to the Division in the field.

My tentative address will be—OCS Class # 16, Med. Adm. Corps, Camp Barkeley, Texas (Abilene). And, from what I understand, we candidates will have three months of "Blood, Sweat, and Tears" ahead of us.
On guard duty, I must sleep in a large tent—not so warm as the barracks.

February 23, 1943 Camp Shelby

Am now off guard detail. Have swept out this hutment, and will be all alone tonight. I do not enjoy being alone.

Was over to the Dispensary, and then went to the transportation office. Our tickets to Camp Barkeley are in order, and we leave here March 3rd. I report in there the 5th.

Clear and warm, here, today. No mail for me, because it all goes to the Division—in the field.

February 25, 1943 Camp Shelby

Well, I am on guard duty, again—and will be through tonight. About all we do is to just sit around, to watch our prisoners, and to keep them busy.

Spent some time with a couple of the fellows going to Texas—they are fine, and we agreed that a real grind probably lies ahead for us.

Went to the service club for supper last evening and had quite a feast for $1.40. I hadn't eaten since morning, and was hungry. It was all good. Ha!

News seems better. From indications, Rommel is on the run in Tunisia. A quick victory for our side would put a real blight on Germany's morale. Will listen to the news this evening, and then I should be up to date.

Feb. 27, 1943 Camp Shelby

Saturday evening, and the guys are back in camp—and payday to be tomorrow. I'm in a better mood, for it is nice not to be alone. We opened the Dispensary, and I'm in charge. It will close after all depart, again, for maneuvers.

Got my mail, and several letters. So nice!

Rommel, the "fox" is on the run in Tunisia, and I hope we push him into the Mediterranean. Then, we shall soon be putting a second front on the European continent.

Am sleepy!

Feb. 28, 1943 Camp Shelby

Just think—tomorrow I"ll have been in this man's army ten months. Doesn't seem possible. A lot of water has gone over the dam. Much has happened, and some of it is a bit tremendous!

Today, Sunday, may well be the last day for me to receive mail here at Shelby. It will be forwarded to Camp Barkeley, and over a week could pass before letters reach me.

Rationing for you seems to be a little stiff, now. However, Moosie, you complained about only one aspect of the rationing—me! So cute!

The gang departs again, today, for maneuvers, and I'll be alone—until I depart. I am persuading myself that this OCS will prove to be interesting. It seems to be a sort of policy to put fear into the minds of those heading for these schools—to be a sort of harangue composed of GI manure.

Of course, GI means "Government Issue"—Get it?

News of the war seemed pretty good today—from all directions. But our men had it pretty rough in Tunisia—woefully costly! More reason to really go after Herr Schicklegruber! Yes!

March 1, 1943 Camp Shelby

Rained all night, like the dickens—but grand and spring-like this morning. No flowers in bloom, yet. So, I can't be a Ferdinand!

The Division pulled out this morning, to be in the field for about two weeks. This was the final weekend to be with some good old pals, and I may never see them again. It makes me a bit sad! We have been through some good times together—and about four of these men I really hated to say "Good bye" to. Some little pang, here, and we hope all turns out for the best.

Had quite an evening, last, at the Dispensary—sort of commenced about 9:00. When in from the field, some of the boys get polluted with this stuff some call "beer." Ha! Some of it smells like something pigs wouldn't want to drink. Well, one of our batteries has a pair of fellows who, when they imbibe too much, become belligerent and seek out and corner some poor bloke and proceed to give him a good beating. It happened again last night, and the poor victim was brought to the Dispensary. He was quite drunk and may have started the ball rolling. This poor fellow was half crying, half cussing, half angry, half feeling very sorry for himself (too many halves, here), and bleeding from nose and mouth—and multiple bruises evident on face and head. I cleaned his face; and, others of our medical crew checked pulse and other parts of body. Pulse was strong and regular, and we found him to be in no serious trouble.

The men who had brought the victim to the Dispensary were quite excited and upset, and seemed a bit peeved because I wasn't so excited. Well, I had been through such as this before, and I tried to inject some humor into the situation. Our Battalion Commander, a Major Burton, heard of the incident and came to the Dispensary. He was more than mildly irked, and insisted that we call in Capt. Hughes. So, in he came, examined the bruised victim, and made note that the guy was more drunk than hurt.

But, the Major was not satisfied, was very peeved, and pointed out that this had been the sixth such incident in recent weeks. Well, it had been the same two men who had given the beatings. Burton went to their Battery, called forth the First Sergeant, ordered him to summon all his noncommissioned officers and direct them to take the culprits, one at a time, and give each a thorough beating! Of course, this was done, and these NCOs did their work well! Before the punishment was administered, the Major told each of the offenders that, should they ever repeat their offense, they would be more extensively punished.

This Major seemed to know what the situation required. One after the other, the two men were taken out and given their beatings. The NCOs did their job! Proper and effective measures were administered. The Major was pretty blunt about it—that the army had ways to take the wrong kind of fight out of a man. The executioners brought the two men in, one after the other, and I sort of presided over the caring of the more recently wounded. The "mean little kids" had to be taught their lessons. In about an hour and a half, we administered more first aid than we had given in several weeks. One of the two had the flesh between thumb and forefinger split on one hand, and this required suturing. Without anesthetic or nitrous oxide, I just sewed the lips of the cut together, put a band of adhesive tape "around" to hold thumb and finger somewhat together, and told the fellow to keep his hand closed and to keep in touch with his "medics."

All in all, we did have quite a time of it. By morning, when the Division pulled out, everybody knew about the affair. It was quite a way for me to close my sojourn at Camp Shelby and with the 85th Division, etc.

Final mail for me, here, this weekend. I suppose it will be some time before my next. Sent a package home, today—my little red camera, some books, and my pajamas which I hadn't worn for months. Am keeping my radio, but a rumor has it that at Barkeley the candidates are not permitted to have radios. We shall just have to see. I have kept my little Kodak.

Hope you have enjoyed the photos. And, as you know, Camp Barkeley is near Abilene, Texas.

And, I shall plan to be home for the end of May.

March 2, 1943 Camp Shelby

My last evening, here. It is for the best, but I am just a wee bit sad about it.

Today was a wild day—had to check in field bag, web belt, gas mask, mess kit, and other stuff and equipment. Tomorrow, it will be all my bedding. Had to go to the camp Adjutant's office to pick up my WD AGO form 32. And, I had to check with the fellows going with me—that all of their Service Records were in order, etc. We had a few problems, and some officers had simply not taken care of a few matters. But, we did get all set and ready to go!

Some will be going by auto. Another had received a delay for one day, but changed his mind. So, we had to work him in to be with the rest of us. There always seems to be a hitch to be uncovered somewhere! Then, for our group, I was to have a letter of authorization for use for meals—on and off train. Well, I had to wait for two hours for our camp Adjutant to return to office and sign. I was a bit furious, but didn't have any place to go—Duh! Duh!

Will be alone in my hutment this final night, here. It has turned cool, and I may light a fire. And, it's off to Barkeley, tomorrow.

Camp Barkeley

March 4, 1943 Abilene, Texas

Here I am, and do not have to report into camp until tomorrow morning. The wind is blowing a fierce gale.

I think I shall like it, here—the air is fresh and cool. I am now, of course, after higher stakes.

Thirteen of us, in my group, are put up in the Hilton Hotel. I'm with another sergeant, but he is not of our group. I expect to sleep well. No berths were available for us on the train, although our tickets specified such. So, it was sit up and curl up! Our coach was one pulled back into service, and it was rough to ride in—and dusty. We just had to ride along as best we could. First thing for me, now, is to take a shower.

The dust on the train must have given my sinuses the devil. The dust was bad! Maybe my head will clear with a good night's sleep. The four men who drove from Shelby arrived OK. The rest of us on the train had seats, but the dust.

(Later)—We've looked over this town, a bit. It reminds me of Scottsbluff—wide streets and neat business section. First impression is that it is much nicer than Hattiesburg. Some of us went to the USO, and ladies were serving cake and coffee—really good! These women almost surround one, and they want to know where your home is, where you have been stationed, and what your reason for coming to Camp Barkeley is all about. None of us have any secrets, as yet. Ha!

Tomorrow morning, we shall call the Commandant to find out where we are to report. We are to be on our toes and good behavior, and for three months. Yup!!

We walked some streets, just to give this town a bit of a once over. My room mate is a Sgt. LeClair. He was at Pearl Harbor, December 7, 1941. He said it was just terrible!

Am going to send home the rest of my chevrons—hadn't taken all of them from my khaki shirts. Sure hope I wont need them again. So, keep the stripes for Technician 5th Grade and Staff Sergeant as souvenirs.

Am not sure of the date of our graduation, but it will be near the end of May. Wouldn't it be nice if I had my bars and then be home for Memorial Day! Sure hope so! And, now for some shut eye.

March 6, 1943 Abilene, Texas (Saturday)

Went out to camp yesterday and registered. In town at the Hotel Grace.

We new fellows get the impression that this OCS is going to take plenty to get through it. Every now and then I get a sort of sinking feeling. Ha! Nearly all of us got passes to come back into town. Starting Monday, we'll have to be on the ball, and I do mean ON THE BALL.

This is practically like coming into the army again. One feels the tension. Will soon know a lot more about it.

Until further notice, my address will be—MRTC OCS Class # 16. We are all candidates, and to be abbreviated as Cdt. We are to remove all chevrons and organizational insignia from clothing. We are just plain candidates!

Camp Barkeley is about ten miles SW of Abilene, and right out on the plains—and no trees. We will have no relief from the sun. But, it has been cold, and we were told that it would be down to just 10 above tonight. Fires were burning away in stoves at camp.

Will keep you posted about the "torture" we have been through. This may be a case of the survival of the fittest. Gee whiz!!!

March 7, 1943 At USO in Abilene

From all we can learn, this OCS business is going to be quite a grind. Have been without mail for nine days, and my spirits will bounce up a bit when some arrives.

Plan to go to church, today. An Episcopal church is about five blocks away. We should have communion.

Candidates in classes ahead of us tell that we will be marching every where we go, and we will be yelled at to straighten up, to watch our arm swing, etc., etc., etc. Purpose seems to be to get a candidate rattled! Here's hoping this cookie can keep on the level.

Abilene is a typical western town of about 32,000, and does remind me of Scottsbluff and of Cheyenne—and much nicer, somehow, than Hattiesburg. People, here, seem to be a bit more eager to please us—it seems to me. Food prices, here, are much more reasonable, and people do not try to bleed the soldier. A good, evening meal will cost about 65 cents—about half of what we usually paid in Hattiesburg.

Had to get my hair cut real short, again, but not quite as short as last May. The dust blows all over, and the hair must not be long. So, Mother, you wont need to groan quite as loud as you did before. Ha!

Am certain that my writing time is going to be quite limited, certainly during week days. We will have a required "Study Hour" from 7 to 9 each evening, Monday through Friday. We have been told that the examinations are tough, and that many flunk out—particularly if one had not attended a "prep school", which we did not have at Camp Shelby. So, those of us who come directly from active units are to be more sorely pressed. I shall just have to see!

My hotel room is so warm and comfy. Was so tired last evening, and slept from eleven until nearly nine this a.m. And, tomorrow we shall find out about the routine we are in. It will last for three months. I'll just have to keep up.

March 11, 1943 Camp Barkeley

Got mail, today!!! Found this card and will write a wee note. We have been busy, and the wind and dust are something terrific. Am now in our "study hall"—with a ten-minute break. Do write me often!

March 14, 1943 Camp Barkeley

A Sunday morning. As you see, I'm using some Camp Shelby stationery.

Am in 1st Platoon, Co. F. So, add this to my address—after OCS Class 16.

I'm not just clicking my teeth when I say we have been busy. We must pass inspections, and the least little error will bring a demerit—and we dare not average more than one a week. Our classes run from 8:00 to noon, and then from 1:00 to 5:00—and later the study hall. Our barracks must at all times be in excellent condition. Lights are out at 10:00, and we are up at five to have time enough to stand reveille at 6:20.

We have about 45 reference pamphlets, field manuals, and technical booklets which must be lined up on our shelves in a certain order and exactly at the edge of the shelf—not a least bit, in or out—if you get what I mean! Our beds must be made, with sheets and covers pulled so tight that the inspecting officer is unable to get ahold of the blanket with his thumb and index finger. The sheets must have exactly an eight-inch fold from the top, and this is to lap 3 inches under the top edge of the blanket. The pillow is to be two inches above the edge of the fold.

Then, everything—shoes, valises, footlockers—must be exactly in line with the edge of the bed, and in a specified order. All clothes must be buttoned and hung in proper order, with exactly the same distance between hangers, and with the clothes facing the wall—nothing in reverse, and no vacant hanger. It all begins tomorrow, in earnest!

From what we hear, about 30 of the class have resigned during this first week, and as many others will call it quits during this week. Too, military drill and "bearing" are very high on the performance scale. I have had no experience in the giving of commands. This could prove to be a difficult hurdle for me to jump. On a questionnaire, I noted that I had never drilled a platoon, at all. Also, we were asked to tell of our relationship with motors and vehicles—to which my response was that, except to drive and have a car serviced, I knew nothing. As for drilling and giving commands, we are already out to practice on each other. Just will see!

We shall be studying sanitation, keeping of military records, the organization of the army, the medical facilities within the service, identifications of airplanes and tanks and all ground vehicles—with concentration eventually to settle on those of our enemy. Our instructors are excellently prepared, and seem pressed to give about three hours of teaching in one hour. We are going to have to scurry to keep up, to take notes. At the end of eight hours of this pace, one is really bushed . But there is lots of determination to meet the challenge. We compare notes and agree that we must stretch. Everything seems to be so intensive. Some of the fellows in my hutment think that we are being subjected to a sort of purposeful harassment. I think my nerves can hold out. Inspections of barracks are always "white glove"! Yup!

M.R.T.C. stands for Medical Replacement Training Center, and we are in the officer training part of it. Camp Barkeley is the largest of this sort in the country—with about 12 classes for OCS at all times. I guess about 5,000 of us are currently in the OCS, here. Do not know how many men and officers are stationed here; but, I do know that I will certainly be glad to get this school behind me. It shouldn't be much more difficult than getting that M.A. degree completed before military duty summoned. I must just be certain to make all "connections." Whew!

Not a tree in sight, here, and the dust blows constantly. Terrain is absolutely level. We must keep our hutments clean and dusted, and regularly mopped... It may well be a grueling experience. But, I'm out to make it. We have been told that many candidates lose quite a bit of weight while here. We shall see, eh?

Once we make this, we get a 10-day leave. Enlisted men receive furloughs, and officers get "leaves." Howzabout that!
A special course will be in "map reading," and I understand it is a "rascal"! We shall see.

I don't like the looks of that German offensive around Kharkov.

St. Patrick's Day Camp Barkeley

About fifteen minutes before study hour begins, and could sneak in a little more time to write. So busy, and I hope it keeps this way. After nearly two weeks, I feel more secure and that this is going to work out O.K.

From the south, and then from the north, the wind has been howling—and always full of dust. So little rain. I keep expecting my sinuses to act up; but not so far.

Want to get into town this weekend. Do look forward to a long night's sleep. This getting up at 5:00 each morning is rather tiring! Ha! But, so much studying ahead, for we have several exams coming up next week. One dares not wait until the "last minute."

We now have a formation—about seven times a day roll is taken, and we get gigged (black marks) if late. So far, I've managed to keep under the line—but with some close calls. We really get herded around, and I don't mean maybe. Ha!

This dust almost drifts into our hutments, and we must keep everything free of it—constant use of damp mops and cloths.

Gee! But they do throw the information at us. We really have to stay awake.

I need six more hangers, wire ones. So, please send. The lieutenant who inspects has hinted that double hanging of shirts and jackets, although in proper order, is a bit "short." Can't find any at the PX.

Most of us seemed to be so sleepy in class this afternoon. Our instructors use many films, and most are very good. Our first big exam comes up this Friday, in Sanitation; but, I do not expect to have any trouble with it. Also on Friday comes our first "unit inspection"—one in which they go over us to find any hair that might be out of place. These inspecting lieutenants will be wearing white gloves, carrying yard sticks, and looking for "gigs" to give. Our hair-cuts are all down to where mine was when I first came into this army.

March 19, 1943 Barkeley

We have been hitting the paces, Bin, and it is a matter of being able to stand the grind. We just do not have time to study enough and to get enuf rest! One must depend upon his wits. We really need the seven hours of sleep each night.

An inspection, today, in parade formation, and our Company Commander really went over us with a fine-toothed comb. I received no gigs, but several did. OH! But, my time will come, I think. Tomorrow comes a "white glove" inspection of our barracks. So, this evening we will do scrubbing and going over everything with moist clothes.

Things seemed to be timed so that we must nearly always run to get into formations on time. Our platoon has been sticking together, with much mutual support, and most of us are still here. Some other platoons in this class have lost half of their men. Too bad! It's rough business!

March 21, 1943 Camp Barkeley

Am in town at Hotel Grace in Abilene. Was just great to talk to all of you, and it took but about two minutes to get the call through. Yes, I sure hope I will have bars on my shoulders when I next come home. So many fellows are resigning, and most of the trouble seems to be plain old nervousness. To drill the platoon has caused some to falter. I have never drilled a platoon, and I stated such in the questionnaire. One poor guy gave us a "column left" command; then, when we were only about half around the corner, he gave us a "to the rear" command—and this caused us to split into two columns. The next afternoon, he was packing his suitcases. But. he had said on his questionnaire that he was an experienced drill-master. Whew!

Am sending several things home, for I do not need them here and they just have to be kept away and out of sight. Couldn't find enough packing to keep stuff from moving somewhat. But, it is all expendable. Ha!

Weather is cold and then hot, and we freeze and then we roast. This is supposed to make us tough, I suppose. When we dress up for inspection, it is a matter of shined and polished shoes and buttons, pressed pants and coats, smoothed collars, and whatever. This morning, we had to stand at attention for about a half hour—and the temperature was at 30 degrees. It was brutal! Our inspecting officers expressed some concern about our discomfort, but they handed out the demerits—lots of them. Humph! But only two from our squad of 13 received any.

The Episcopal church, here, is much like Holy Trinity, in Lincoln—quaint and English-like. Two of us have been relaxing in our hotel room, and we saw a movie last evening. Had a big steak—at cost of $1.85, and was it good!

Had to buy another pair of woolen trousers, for I needed a pair for reserve—cost $10.95. For our formal inspections, we wear nothing that is soiled. So, a pair of absolutely clean trousers, well creased, must be extra. Everything is now cuffless. At first, this seemed a bit strange, but now it is the only way.

Am all scribbled out.

March 24, 1943 Barkeley

Just a note on this card. Things are moving right along, here.

Quite damp. Cloudy and drizzly, but dust will probably be blowing tomorrow.

Program is advancing, and I do admire the efficiency of so much that is done.

Had a good weekend. Saw two good movies in town, and had two very good meals. Just returned to camp all primed for action. We do need these weekends!

March 28, 1943 Barkeley

Another Sunday, and am in town at the USO. Beautiful day, today—bright and sunny and not much wind.

This OCS is a real grind, and we do have to keep "on the ball"!

Will have a nice dinner this noon, and then to a show this afternoon. Should go to church, but am not sure. Lots of commotion at this place—radio blaring, and a couple pianos being kept busy, and it is a bit difficult to concentrate.

Have been trying to figure out what causes one to be pushed out of OCS. Have seen several men who seemed to be darned good officer-material just get asked to resign. It really makes one wonder. Perhaps these officers are looking for "types"—and if one doesn't fit into the picture, it is "out you go"! One keeps his fingers crossed. I hope I can figure out what makes my lieutenant tick and what will keep him satisfied. I've noticed he wears a Masonic ring, and he may have noticed mine. Ha! As if such should or would help! We will have to wait to see.

The mud seems to be drying,, and the dust just drifts over it. I learned to keep on the walks. Needed tooth paste and went to the PX to buy a tube. The cute little clerk was enamored with some handsome soldier, and she kept me waiting too long. A formation was due, and I had to run for it and took a short cut across a ditch—only to find that it was a mud trap beneath the dust on the surface. So, I was into mud well over the top of my shoes. But, into formation I went, and our lieutenant gave me a several times over from head to foot. He said nothing, but I sensed his amusement. I expected some demerits, but none were posted. I felt encouraged, for it seemed to me that this officer had a sense of fair play, somehow.

Of course, my shoes had to be scrubbed and repolished. After the scrubbing, they had a grayish color and needed some browning. I put on a liberal application of ox-blood, and they came out to be the prettiest pink—really, quite dainty. But, they passed inspection. Nonetheless, I have purchased a can of brown polish. So,there!!

Boy! But my nine hours of sleep last night have given me quite a boost. And, time is really flying right along. We've been enjoying the maple sugar you sent. Yessirree!

March 29, 1943 Barkelely

Another of your cards, today. Sun is out and bright. Welcome it is. Was on guard duty last night, and had just enough time to get ready for formation and inspection. I really had to flag my fanny around and about.

On the agenda is a "gas alert"—practice to carry along our gas masks, and then "by the numbers" to remove from cases, put on, test for gas, remove, recase, and resling on backs. We will have quite a drill. When overseas, I'm sure we shall have our masks with us constantly.

(And, this letter, later)—Received the hangers and the candy. We are now in "study hall," but my concentration is way off base. Has been very warm, especially "under the collar"! So, it seems to be.

We are to move to another area, and we will be out of these little "green dragons." Am keeping my little radio, for we will now have outlets available to plug in.

A couple stiff exams coming up in near future. So, we are doing some hard reviewing. Some of us have begun to count days until we may graduate.

April 2, 1943 Barkeley

This week has been a busy one. No spare time to scribble an extra note. So very warm, here. We do plenty of sweating—more from the pressure, than from temperature. One feels often quite "bedripped"!

Will be going into town tomorrow, and hope to find a room. When at Shelby, it was almost preferable to return to camp, rather than to stay over-night in town. Haven't had recent news from any of the old gang back there, and they are on maneuvers. Am wondering which is tougher—to be on maneuvers, or to be in OCS?

Our platoon is gradually being lessened—some fellows being told they lack the "bearing" and others are not making passing grades in the exams. The rest of us just keep plugging along and do our best. I do not look forward to the time when our lieutenant asks me to drill our platoon.
But, "we" are practicing!

Your letters keep just coming in regularly. Seems to me that you are spoiling me quite rotten! But, I love it, and each letter means so much to me!

Tomorrow, an 8 ½-mile hike for us—with full pack. We are quite of the opinion that we have done it before and we can do it again. So, there!!

It appears to be dark for Rommel, and I shall be very pleased when that old "Desert Fox" has finally been out-foxed! We can then begin to concentrate on Der Fuhrer. But, my guess is that it will take a long time to corner him.

We have several big tests coming up. To date, I have two "A"s and two "S"s—not bad! I do not want to receive any "U"s. So, over the weekend some extensive reviewing. One coming up will be in map-reading could cause me some trouble, and we have been told by candidates ahead of us that this is one that must be passed—no failure permitted. It is new ground for my plow, for all is far cry from reading a road map… Me-oh-my! And, how we do have our eyes focused upon May 27th. All still here do not want to miss getting those gold bars!

April 4, 1943 Camp Barkeley

Another Sunday morning, and this to be a sort of continuation of Friday's letter, which I didn't get mailed until with this .

Our hike, yesterday, was a hot one—especially since we had full packs on our backs. We are to have at least two more, and longer and with additional equipment.

With some darned exams coming up this coming week, we hoped to have a quiet room for a few hours of review. We were late getting in, and the only "room" two of us could find was in a home—to sleep on a daybed in the living room. So, no chance for study, but the lady was very gracious to put us up. We will return to camp earlier today than we had planned.

Paid $1.35 for an excellent turkey dinner last evening, and then we went to a show.

At the USO, and was here in time to snag one of the typewriters. So, can put more in. Bright and cool, and we agreed that it would be a good day for golf. Ha! Ha!

Will go to church, and we should have communion.

April 7, 1943 Camp Barkeley

Some rather important examinations just ahead for us. Next week will be the one on map-reading. We are told it is crucial. Resignations, now, come almost entirely from difficulties with these tests. I have three more "S"s. Another just taken didn't seem to be very difficult.

Saturday, I saw the movie, "The War Against Mrs. Hadley." Then to church, Sunday morning, and we had communion. I like this minister, too.

Well, they really run our pants off in the OCS. Everything is "on the double"! And, in seven weeks we have our graduation. Gee! Sure hope I'll be here.

April 11, 1943 Barkeley

Am again in town—my weekend escape from the tortures of OCS. Again, at the USO, and here soon enough to snag a typewriter.

We have had some scorchers for examinations. They seem to come in bunches, and they are purposefully difficult. I hit a 78 on one of them, with 75 being passing. 55 of 195 were under the line. So, you have an idea as to the pressure. We just had the one for map reading, and it was a bruiser. We never see an old examination, but just know our score and if we passed. The officer who instructs "map reading" told us he was lowering the passing grade to 70%, for so many had been flunking it. As far as I was concerned, he threw a withering attack at us. Ha! I really need this weekend to relax a bit.

One fellow in our barracks had received a fourth failure, of the ten tests we had had. So, he was asked to resign. He was so tightened up about it, the pressure of these examinations. All of us are just sick about his being directed to leave. He was solidly of "officer material"!

We have three examinations scheduled for next week, one of them for tomorrow. Along with this has been something quite interesting—to assemble prescribed material to be packed into our haversacks. We practice on each other—the clothing and various items; and the fit is snug, indeed, and it has to be just so—or it all will not go in. Whew! We'll have these carefully packed haversacks on our backs for our next lengthy hike. We have three hikes yet ahead of us, and I hope I'll be around for them. Ho! Ho!

April 18, 1943 Camp Barkeley

We are now in much nicer barracks, and we are much closer to the places we need to go to and then return from. Must continue to get up at 5 o'clock, but not so far from our mess hall, washing and toilet facilities, PX, etc. Am in Abilene at the USO and enjoying my usual Sunday. Have been to church.

This week was a real bruiser, and in so many different ways. I hardly know where to begin. We had to move, we had a full-pack ten-mile hike, and we had three tough exams. Then came the disheartening part of it, for about 1/3 of our platoon were called in and warned they were on the margin—with some requested to resign and some warned that their future as prospective officers was highly dubious. They were summoned one by one, and no one knew who would be next. We became mental wrecks!

The first part of our map-reading test had to do with military symbols, signs, and codes. It seemed to me that often there were more than one possible correct response to a question. My score was 68, and I became a "flunkie" for the first time, but we still had the second half to go. This part was up my alley, and I received a 92—my average to be 80. Another reckoning which had worried me considerably was on "motors"—maintenance and use of vehicles, and control of movement and "marches", but this one proved to be easier than I had expected.

One which was really a "bitch" (to use a good army term) dealt with property, titles, and supply. Again, it seemed to me that more than one correct answer was often possible. It is a matter of wait to see, but this one is not worrying me much. When we fellows discuss our answers, we quickly conclude that phrasing of questions often are misleading. On this one, we had few disagreements. Coming up will be Field Sanitation and Mess Supervision—and this one that I have been really concentrating on, Infantry Drill and Regulations. We must pass this one on drill and commands, and we have been practicing on each other with great zeal and purpose in mind!

Well, will give you some more information about this past week. Last Monday, we had a special formation called for 5:45 in the evening. A week before a sort of sixth-week board met to go over all reports in preparation for a seventh-week board's analyses of the candidates. This special formation was to make certain announcements. We had heard rumors that some axes were to fall, that there were to be some "beheadings." The platoon leaders, our array of First Lieutenants, had summed up and had made their recommendations. Our officer addressed us as to purpose of formation, and then proceeded to read a list of names—about one-fourth of us. It was unnerving, to say the least. A combination of demerits and poor grades had taken the toll. Some others were alerted to their being near the borderline. Tuesday, with the exception of those who were marginal, the rest of us were informed that we should order our uniforms for graduation as second lieutenants. Lt. Nunnelly told me that the chance was 90% that we would be commissioned. Well, I guess I haven't passed the hump yet, but I can now see it.

We moved, Wednesday, into our much nicer barracks. It took me five round trips, afoot, to get my stuff transferred—maybe three-fourths of a mile each way. Whew! We were all in the same boat. We were tuckered out. What really irked us was that these barracks had just been vacated by the last graduating class and were left in miserable shape. What a job to clean the place!!! Beds, shelving, and cabinets were different from what we had, and we had several decisions to make . We were exhausted by time for lights out, but somewhat in shape. For Thursday, a scheduled ten-mile hike—a full-pack and "forced march"!

Friday brought a white-glove inspection. We had special instructions with respect to suspending sack, belt, canteen, and gas mask at the foot of the bed. As for making of bed, hanging of clothes and arranging of books—just as before. Gee, and how we did work. Then, did those officers hand out the "gigs"! I received three, because my arrangements off the foot of the bed were not quite suitable. My internal fury cooled when the repeat inspection Saturday morning found me to be in proper order. In the previous weeks, I had received but two. My turn had just come up!!

Last Sunday, the Episcopal minister took me by the arm and told me I was welcome to sleep in a house which was the former parsonage. He had noticed my frequent attendance. So, when in town, I would have a place to sleep, at no charge. Mattresses were on the floors of several rooms, and at least 12 could be accommodated. Bedding and towels were also available for us . About eight of us were in the parsonage last night, and it was nice. So, no more hunting for a room and paying for it. This is real hospitality, it seems to me. All of us were Episcopalian, and we are from all over—I being the only Nebraskan. Isn't this just great? And, it will be back to the grind later this afternoon. I'm hungry.

April 20, 1943 Camp Barkeley

We went into our summer uniforms, yesterday, and are now all bedecked in our khakis. We will graduate in khakis. I am not going to make any great expenditures on clothes—just a nice dress suit of tropical worsted. Our pinks and greens seem so much dressier, somehow. Oh, well!

The so-called Seven Weeks' Board handed down its verdict, and about 45 fellows are dismissed.

Our lieutenant assured us that we are now over the peak of the bad hurdles. But, the next two weeks will be toughies—with two major exams this week and four or five next week. And, coming up tomorrow is an eleven-mile hike—with full load. Those of us still in the ranks seem to be able to prance along with the best. Ha! Also on the horizon is a two-day bivouac, and this will provide a welcome change from the usual routine.

As you may guess, I can hardly wait for this to get over with. This may be what one has referred to as "the strenuous life"! Once I relax, it may take a long time to pull myself together.

Easter Sunday, April 25, 1943 Camp Barkeley

Just finished talking to you… Sorry the call woke you up, but to have waited would have resulted in hours of delay. It was thirty minutes, anyhow. And, put it through as "Collect", for to use a pay-phone requires us to have so much pocket change handy. Will just settle with you when next in Lincoln. Ho! Ho! And our visit was for five minutes, and it didn't seem nearly so long. Your voices were so clear! These telephones are wonderful things, aren't they?

Well, I've ordered new uniforms—to the tune of $181.00. The government has given us an allowance of $250, and I have taken a good hunk out of mine. So far to be expended:

Green, winter blouse	—	45.50
Summer blouse, tropical worsted	—	35.00
Pair of green pants	—	18.00
Pair of pink pants	—	18.00
2 pair of pants, tropical worsted	—	25.00
2 shirts, tropical worsted	—	25.00
2 caps, tropical worsted	—	7.00
1 visored cap, green	—	<u>7.50</u>
		181.00

Now, you can see, somewhat, as to this business. I still have the wide belt, new shoes, some more khakis, and other things to buy. I won't make any profit on these transactions. Ho! Ho!

This coming week is a sort of "hump"—with four exams and the two-day bivouac. Our platoon has just 32 left of the original 54 men. I'm quite sure I'll make it; but nothing is that certain in this game! Just thirty days left!

April 28, 1943 Camp Barkeley

Did so much enjoy our visiting Sunday morning. You, Moosie, just wanted to keep on talking, until I told you the call was on "collect"—and did you run out of wind in a hurry. Ha! Ha!

I'm so eager for this next four weeks to be over—am just ready to have those little gold bars pinned on! Am just ready to get home for a few days, believe me! Have some of my uniform items to order, yet. From all reports, our two-day bivouac is a sort of good time, and to be about the final time during which we candidates are to be closely observed and evaluated. So, maybe we can just begin to breathe a little easier.

Won't be wearing those pretty pinks when I get home. So, it will be summer khakis. Of course, I might just dress for a special photo, but the fee would be high.

Several classes and other sessions are now quite often somewhat shortened, and we have a few half-hours of free time. And a funny thing happened in our barracks for inspection. We are lined up in alphabetic order—I being between Metz and Mills. For inspection, we have a watchman stationed at the corner entrance, and he alerts us to the exit of the officers from the adjoining barracks. Mills was our watchdog, gave the alert, and then had to hurry down the dividing aisle of the beds. As he passed my bed to turn in to stand beside his own, his foot kicked my carefully arranged equipment belt, canteen, gas mask, and field bag—result being that the canteen was on the floor and all else was out of line. Of course, we were standing "at attention", and I dared not make a move. The officers moved along the central aisle—examining one candidate and arrangement after the other, and they seemed, generally, to be satisfied. Then they arrived before me, and forward progress came to a halt. A captain cleared his throat, and Lt. Nunnelly checked everything—books on the shelf, arrangement of clothing, and tightness of blanket-cover on the bed, and even did the white-clove check to see if dust lay anywhere. He then looked me over from head to toe, and they moved along—eventually to exit for the next barracks.

Well, poor Woody Mills was practically on his knees to beg my forgiveness. The rest of the fellows were also gathered around to offer condolences. It was a bit unnerving! We all wondered what the "gig list" would reveal—to be posted the next morning. There were but a handful of demerits for the sixteen of us in our barracks, and not a one for me. My first reaction was one of unbelief—and then I remembered the muddy-shoes incident. (Fn. Later, when conferring with the Lieutenant about matters pertaining to graduation, he laughingly asked about the mess. I told him it was just something that gave no time for correction. He then assured me that far more dire things had occurred at this OCS.) Some of the gang raised eye-brows!

April 30, 1943 Camp Barkeley

Very hot, here, again. Return from our bivouac took 3 ½ hours, and we had to march a bit more than 13 miles. Were my poor feet hot—even had a blister on my little right toe! But, nothing serious. We were fatigued and quite dehydrated. After showering, many of us went to the PX. I downed three bottles of pop and two pints of ice cream! Ha! And, did I ever feel stuffed, but not in any way ill. Later, for supper, I purchased a quart of milk, sipped it slowly, and just relaxed.

Conferences with our officers have been most assuring, with just three weeks to go—after this one. Stress is now to improve our potential as officers and instructors, and suggestions are not to be viewed as criticisms and threats. This is very good, but we are still impatient for graduation. Saturday is coming up, and I am ready to enjoy another weekend and to relax.

Bought three bonds, today—two for $100 and one for $50. May mail them home, or may just bring them with me. And, we still have some tests to prepare for.

May 2. 1943 Camp Barkeley

Sunday morning again. A beautiful day, here, and I am feeling fine. Will see a movie this afternoon, and will keep cool if it heats up outside.

Friday, due to something served at the noon meal in our mess hall, over half of our class became sick with what was said to be ptomaine. By mid afternoon, and increasingly to 10:00 that evening, the fellows took to vomiting all over the place, to having cramps and diarrhea, etc. Even for Saturday morning, some of the guys had to leave classes. Our officers were running all over the premises, just constantly to check up on us. The poisoning seemed to come from the noon meal. Most of the fellows who got sick had skipped the evening meal—just didn't want food. At noon, I ate everything except the mashed potatoes. Nothing has hit me; so do not know what to think. Only one man had to go to the hospital, and all the others seem to be O. K. But, has there ever been a full going-over of the mess hall!

Into this man's army a year ago, and three weeks remaining here. A few in other platoons have recently resigned, but our platoon is holding solid. Just do not want to lose any of us!!

Train connections out of Abilene are pretty bad. We graduate at 10:00 in the morning, the 27th, and the first east-bound train suitable for me departs from here at 2:30 a.m. I really hate to think of losing all that time. Several of us are trying to figure out some sort of "snickeroo" to beat the problem. I'll just have to call you from somewhere—as to time of arrival, and where.

Will head over to church in a few minutes. Slept at the old parsonage, and it was eight hours of excellent rest—really awakened refreshed.

May 6, 1943 Camp Barkeley

Found this post card, and it can go "free" for me. Ha! Weather a bit better, but it has been so windy since Sunday. The dust is really something to get very tired of—covers everything!

We are all so curious to know what our assignments will be—really, we are impatient. Info is that we won't know until the final week. There is just no news from here

May 9, 1943 Camp Barkeley

Mother's Day, today, and I would so much prefer to be home! Would like to see those roses Don got for you from me!!!

Another good night's sleep at the parsonage, and awakened to feel almost half drugged. I think I slept on my face, for I looked as if I had been dragged through a key-hole. Oh, well! But, we have had two days of rain—and nice to have relief from heat and wind and dust. This rain is more like a constant drizzle, and the coolness is a blessing.

As for my assignment, nothing definite. But, Friday, four of us were called in to be interviewed.

To be "called in" usually means trouble, so we were quite uneasy about it. Well, the administration here is looking for another instructor, and we four are to be considered. Well, my fingers are really crossed, now. A week from this coming Wednesday we are to be informed. I shall let you know immediately.

Should I be asked to return to Barkeley, I will not receive any travel time to be added to my leave. Thus, I would have two or three fewer days at home. But, to be on the staff, here, would be a good deal. I just remain quite impatient to know. As graduation nears, we are all just more eager for the time to pass faster. The officers who interviewed us hinted that an assignment for the school, here, might prevent an immediate leave—should the incoming class of candidates necessitate an immediate service. The chances are, about nine of ten, that you will be seeing me soon.

May 12, 1943 Camp Barkeley

Just two more weeks to go, and then I'll be heading home, I hope, with a bar on my collar and one on my cap. Just bought three shirts as $4.50 each, and some "cadushes" (caduceuses) and gold bars for $6.00. Boy, but does this uniform business ever pile up. But, I think it will be worth it! Am so eager to know where my assignment is to be. It would be nice were something to come from that interview.

More wind and more dust, again. But living with this wind and dust has become habitual.

Were my skin to become reddened enough, I could really whoop it up!

Our officers are just very lenient with us, for they seem to be treating us as if we were soon to be officers, too. Isn't it the berries?

Perhaps a year from now we shall see the end of this ordeal, but I doubt it. The Allied victory in Tunis was most welcome, wasn't it? Churchill's immediate trip to Washington is significant to the fact that the Allied time table must be clicking. We will see what results come from this meeting, and I hope things will just look darker for Schickelgruber.

I am to be our "Acting" Platoon Leader—must be out in front to direct the platoon all over the place—when we march to classes, when we drill, etc. Lots of reporting to superior officers and lots of saluting. I was spared from this until now! Oh, Boy!

May 14, 1943 Camp Barkeley

Everything going along O.K. here. We are all so eager for the next twelve days to be over. Has been cloudy and cooler the past two or three days. I so much appreciate hearing from you—you are spoiling me, with a letter or two nearly every day, but none yesterday!

We are all faced with the same question—"What if I should be kicked out, now?" We keep hearing stories about fellows who were denied commissions with hardly less than a week to go. That is why we can hardly wait until those bars are actually pinned on! Whew!

About a week, and we shall know our assignments. I like Abilene, and would not be unhappy if assigned here. But, this dust and heat!

I hope we can go to Wood Lake for Memorial Day. I'll get home the 27th or the 28th, and we could make it.

Not a busy morning, and lunch coming soon. Had a funny thing happen yesterday. Had marched the platoon into position for roll call, and had first to receive reports from my "squad leaders" and then to report to the "company commander"—"All present and accounted for, Sir." Each report is given with a salute. Of necessity, each of us always carries all books in left hand to be free always to salute an officer if confronted. For some reason, I had my books in my right hand and proceeded to receive reports from my squad leaders and then to report to my battalion leader—each salute given by me with my left hand. My concentration must have been such that I never noticed. Most of my gang in the platoon noticed, but apparently no one else. It must have been a very crisp and correct salute. And, I heard nothing from "above"!

Just two exams to go, and 12 more days—Yessirree!!

May 17, 1943 Camp Barkeley

Just didn't get a letter written, yesterday, after I called. I had slept in the old parish house and then ate dinner with the group after the church service. All was so very nice! It just seemed that I had nothing to write about, for our visit on telephone was so good...

Should my assignment be for here, then I shall not need to ship my footlocker—full as it will be. My large case I shall bring with me—all stuffed with laundry. Ha! Will also have my small valise. Spent too much money on those bonds, and I've found myself to be almost short of cash.

For the 26th, am going to try to catch a 4:35 train out of Ft. Worth for Kansas City, to arrive there at 7:30 the next morning. A train for Omaha is scheduled to depart a few minutes before. So, I shall be hoping that its departure will be delayed, and that my train into KC is on time. This is going to be ticklish business, at best. Maybe I can get some breaks—similar to the ones for my return to Shelby after last Christmas. Shall try to get a Pullman—just so I wont be so poohed when I get home.

Was again very windy and dusty. We were out drilling for nearly two hours, and we could hardly hear the commands—let alone to breathe with all the dust.

My new uniforms have not arrived, but are due in Wednesday. So, it will be into town to have the fittings. My guess is that little will need to be done. Will bring both winter's and summer's with me. So, just see what is in store for you. Ha! If assigned to Barkeley, I must be here on June 5th, and would have to leave Lincoln on the 4th. We could be pushed a little to make the trip to Wood Lake. But, we shall see.

The cookies arrived, and did they disappear in a hurry! None were crumbled. All just yummy!

Just one more exam—one on Military Tactics. No one seems to be worried about it. And, as for getting home, should I get stranded, you may receive an SOS. Then, what would we do?

May 19, 1943 Camp Barkeley

One week from today I hope I'll be homeward bound. Last examination this afternoon, and then we turn in our books. We get our assignments Friday evening. We are all anxious . Do want to get my uniforms fitted before coming home. The winter uniform is here, but the summer is not in, yet. Time seems to be running a bit short! We must be in our barracks tonight, Thursday and Friday nights. So, no straying!

I have a Pullman (got notice today) on a 4:35 train from Santa Fe, to take me from Ft. Worth to Kansas City for a 7:30 a.m. arrival. Then, I will have to see what I can grab from there. Just will not know until I reach KC.

Our rains have ceased, and we are ready to swelter. It is going to be hot! I will be out of here before long. Hurrah! This waiting around is for the birds!! All of us seem to be fed up!

May 20, 1943 Camp Barkeley

The suitcase arrived, and this will simplify my packing. It will be an extra to carry, but I will manage—have done it before. Ha!

Gee, but I will be glad to get home. Just can hardly wait!

Be prepared to meet me somewhere Thursday, and I hope it will be in the morning, yet. I may have to wire you after my arrival in KC. Found one of the penny post cards you had sent.

May 22, 1943 Camp Barkeley

Saturday evening, and I'm in Abilene, and this should be my last letter from here. I plan to call you tomorrow, and to tell you about my assignment. If telephone is too busy, then you shall find out when I see you.

Will get my commission, Wednesday...

Received a wonderful assignment (not for here), and will tell you all about it when I see you. But do expect a wire from me Thursday morning—from KC. And, be prepared to tell me what I owe on all the reverse-charge calls.

Camp Lee

June 4, 1943 Chicago, Midland Hotel (Friday)

(En route to Camp Lee, Virginia—about 20 miles from Richmond, to begin training to manage warehousing and issuing of government supplies.)

Arrived in Chicago at 9:45 this morning, after a good night's sleep—do not remember the stop in Omaha, or any other place. So, it seemed to be a short trip. Have just wandered around, and I have until 3:15 to kill time. Mooched this stationery from this hotel. Ha! So many persons in uniform, with many writing.

Cloudy and muggy, here, this morning. Hope for cooler weather, but Virginia and then St. Louis are most certainly to be hotter than the devil. So, must get used to it.

Will probably wire when I reach Richmond, but maybe not. But will write soon, anyway.

It wasn't nearly so difficult to leave . I guess we are just getting used to it. But, we are much more certain about my work, and so much has changed. Things should be more interesting, by far.

June 6, 1943 Camp Lee, Virginia (Sunday)

Sent you a wire this evening, and you can add it to all the rest of my expenses. It is so nice, here—all the trees and green grass everywhere, and no dust blowing!

Got into Richmond on schedule, yesterday. Hotels were full. So, I called a rooming agency, and was referred to a private home. The people were very friendly and enjoyable. I went to church with them this morning. Mrs Alley introduced me to every one, and you would have thought I was a relative. She thought I sang "so well," and then rushed me right over to the choir director. Well, I promised to come in from camp and to sing—some Sunday. Quite a beginning, eh?

My understanding is that our real work at Camp Lee doesn't really begin for another week. You will be hearing from me as we go along.

June 7, 1943 Camp Lee

Have been lounging around most of the time. This camp is "divine" compared to Barkeley—grass, trees, a gentle breeze, and no dust. We had a couple "formations," mostly to receive information. It is going to be a different sort of life. Our superior officers are very friendly. The Officers' Club is darned "swanky," and our officer's mess is really O.K. For lunch today we had lobster salad, vegetable salad, fruit salad, jello salad, etc. It was excellent! Should this continue, we are soon going to be spoiled…

Each barracks is divided into "10 by 10" rooms—with just one officer per room. I don't know whether I 'm going to be able to stand the privacy. We'll be O.K. We have orderlies who make our beds, dust our furniture, and clean our floors. Talk about being spoiled stinky! I have a little shelf for my radio, which plays beautifully. My footlocker, shipped from Barkeley, came through without a scratch. Now, wasn't that something!!

Am to receive $104 "travel money," which I hope is soon. Otherwise, I shall have to draw on my bank account, or get a loan from the family resources. Ha! Ha!

Our classes begin next Monday. So, our orders just got us here a week early. As it is, we spend most of our time just sitting around and twiddling our thumbs. I've walked all over this camp, and it is spread out. I'm certain this idleness will not last long. Uncle Sam always finds things for us to do.

Our loud-speaker system plays all the bugle calls from recordings, and one can hear them for miles—no need for an alarm clock! Am going to scoot around to do some visiting and getting acquainted, and a few others from Barkeley also landed here.

Again, it was just wonderful to be home!

June 8, 1943 Camp Lee

Just must wish you, Bin and Don, a happy wedding anniversary, although it will arrive late.

Boy, am I living O.K.! Here's what we had for supper at our officers' mess—steaks, shoestring potatoes, tomato-lettuce salad, grapefruit cocktail, bread, butter, ice tea, and apple pie. I just never expected to get such meals at a G.I. mess hall. If they keep feeding us like this, you are going to have another 190-pounder in the family.

Whew! But is this ever different from OCS. Oh, Baby! A bunch of "the Lieutenants" are waiting on me—to go to a movie.

June 11, 1943 Camp Lee

Here we are with another cool, cloudy, delightful Virginia morning. We are warned that it can get hot, here. But, this fellow will not object—as long as we continue to be fed as we are, etc. I've never seen Uncle Sammy dish out the food on the caliber that he does here at this officers' mess. We are all looking forward to increased waistlines. We have three squares a day, and each has four corners! Yessirree!

No mail from anyone, yet, but I must be patient. Am hungry for news from home.

Plan to go into Richmond this weekend. Am going to give some of the city, particularly the capital building and grounds, a once over. Have called the Alleys for a room. Too, I do much want to visit Washington, D.C., but do not know when I can work it in—may not have enough spare time. We are not here to engage in a lot of sight-seeing.

Am really enjoying that little radio, for its reception is so clear. At Barkeley, we had so much static.

Not yet seven in the morning, and breakfast is soon. We have reveille sounded at six.

June 13, 1943 Co. "B", Prov. Bn.
ASF—4
Q.M. Sch.
Camp Lee, Va.

Want you to have my correct address, for sure. But, did receive a letter—my first.

Was in Richmond, yesterday, and went to church with the Alleys—and sang "The Penitent."

The people seemed to like it, and I received three invitations for Sunday dinner—had to turn down the second and third! These folk are so friendly, and I feel very much at home. They may make a Baptist out of me, suppose?

Have seen Davies' "Mission to Moscow," and it is one of the best historical movies I've seen for sometime. It reveals much about Russia that we American have not understood . Also saw

Mickey Rooney in "The Human Comedy."

Classes begin tomorrow—Hurrah! The past week seemed a bit useless, somehow.

Visited St. John's Episcopal Church, the one in which Patrick Henry made his "Give me liberty, or give me death!" speech. I stood in the pew from which he spoke—all very interesting.

Do note—it is Q.M. School, not T. M. The Q is for Quartermaster.

June 14, 1943 Camp Lee

We have just started our four weeks of G.I. courses and education. Can't say that I fully appreciate the rapidity with which these instructors feel they must throw all this information at us. It has warmed up considerably. We go into Richmond, tomorrow, to visit a large Quartermaster warehouse. I'm looking forward to it!

June 15, 1943 Camp Lee

Another short note, but more to say than yesterday. We went to the Richmond depot, and what a mammoth layout! It is just one warehouse after another—all over the place, and each just full of stuff. One can understand why there are shortages outside for the general public. These goods are constantly moving in and out. It is really a gigantic business, this matter of military supply!

Very hot here, the past two days. We just sweat and sweat. We are eating too much, and I have gained at least six pounds—weigh about 168, now.

Humidity high, feels like rain, and flies are biting like the dickens. Quite a bit of static on the radio. So, here's hoping we can have a change in weather. I feel just a bit lazy.

June 17, 1943 Camp Lee

As hot as blazes, here, and we are just sweating it out. It's really gruesome—through seven hours of classes per day, and very uncomfortable! We are getting impatient to make our move to St. Louis. We are to have rooms in hotels, and that should be an improvement.

Radio announced an invasion of Italy, if I understood correctly—largest naval concentration in history, one of more than 1 ½ million men. It is to be an attempted knock out blow, and Greece will be next—right across the Adriatic. Then, we may make a thrust into Yugoslavia. Things do seem to be happening fast. Sort of sets one to cheering, but I shall wait to see. One of the gang passed by and said it was all rumor, so far. So, do not know what to make of it. Humph!

Glad to know you saw "Mission to Moscow." I think this Davies is a remarkable person. He seems to have been about the first foreigner the Russians allowed to inspect any part of the nation that he chose. He had "first hand" information. The scenes of that Russian trial were really quite astounding. Seems to me it shows what "square-shooting diplomacy" can achieve. If Roosevelt can win Russian world-wide cooperation, peace should be maintained. I think he will do it. Wouldn't be at all surprised to hear soon of a R-C-S (Roosevelt, Churchill, Stalin) rendezvous, somewhere. The next step will be toward Germany. What things are happening!!

Have decided not to go into Richmond, Sunday—just want to laze around and write some letters.

We shall have no extra time when we leave here for St. Louis.

You asked about the meaning of ASF-4.—"Army Service Forces—Class # 4"—and, now do you understand? Ha!

June 19, 1943 Camp Lee

We need to study about an hour each evening. We are learning quite a bit, nevertheless. I wish more of our instruction were to take place in warehouses; but, there are so many of us, and we would have to be divided into small groups. But, I am quite satisfied with the set up. As I size up this situation, I wouldn't mind being stationed here.

Have written to St. Louis. Another new Lt. and I want to room together. We must get our bids in early if we want a better room and to be teamed up as we desire. We are to be in St. Louis for 30 days, and then to be sent to a full functioning supply depot for a month's duty as an apprentice—to be taught just how all this stuff is to be cared for and distributed. We are supposed to be able to step into any supply set-up—as trained officers. Does all of this not impress you!!

Nice and cool, here, today. Some of us played volleyball nearly all afternoon. My fellow officers are a great bunch. How different this sort of life is from my first ten months in the military. Yessirree!!

Am still in wonder because of the way they feed us, here. Last evening we had ham and shrimp, shoe strings, cold slaw, carrots and raisins, cucumbers, hard rolls and butter, jello salad, and beer.

This is supposed to be a meal for hot weather, I guess. In St. Louis, we will be eating in cafes and restaurants and hotels, and I do not expect to enjoy the meals—as we have here.

Am going to see the movie, "My Sister, Eileen." I understand that Laurel and Hardy are screams in "Air Raid Wardens." I thought "The Human Comedy" was excellent—an unusual picture.

Just about chow time. Was in Petersburg, but may not go back into this town—for, all we officers do is to return salutes from the men. This saluting is a real nuisance, believe me!! Ha!

June 20, 1943 Camp Lee

Spent the weekend here in camp; was just too lazy to go into Richmond. Sort of snoozed in until nearly nine. Then, as a sort of last minute idea, decided to go for a 10:00 service at the Q. M. School Chapel. The sermon was very good, and I was glad to have gone.

Very warm, today, and report is for more of the same for tomorrow. The sweating will be good!

Shame on you all for writing me about eating fresh gooseberry pie! And, you seem to be making good use of my food stamps, and you should have about a half-month's supply on hand. Didn't care for our noon meal, today—basically roast chicken, but the old hens must have been too fat, for the grease didn't agree with me. A mild nausea persisted until late afternoon.

Old Sol just beams down on us, and he is a friendly old chap.

That European front is one that keeps us guessing. That report about a great armada heading toward Italy proved to be just rumor, which probably came from a Nazi source. The Allied leaders never denied it, but Hitler and his henchmen were probably hoping that a denial would reveal certain positions, etc. But, to no avail. So, a broil of jitters has set in. Mussolini has to be in more than just a mild case of anxiety. We shall see!

Do not want to gain any more weight. Must guard my 32 inches. Ha! Ha!

June 22, 1943 Camp Lee

Am supposed to sing this coming Sunday at the Alley's Baptist church, and plan to sing "The Publican"—based on another of the great parables.

So often, our letters do not reach us for less than five or six days after being postmarked. Our scuttlebutt has it that the problem lies here—much delay in sorting and then distribution. And, it seems to make no difference—regular, airmail, or even "special delivery." And, it doesn't seem to make much difference as to origin of a letter.

June 27, 1943 Camp Lee

Into Richmond last evening. As usual, stayed at the Alley's, and then to church this morning. I sang "The Publican," and the people were so full of compliments after the service. It was 12:15 before I could get away.

Had called Don's dental friend, Dr. Chevalier, and was to catch a street car and then a bus to reach a point close to their home—for Sunday dinner. Had a bit of trouble to find Clinton Ave., but did reach the home by 1:20. So, not bad! A lovely dinner, and such wonderful people. They have two sons, good looking and so well mannered. The elder will be going into the marines the 8th of July, and the younger will be a sophomore in high school this fall. Just a grand time with them. Caught 5 o'clock bus to head back into Richmond, etc.

So, am back in my room, and it has been a very good day!

June 29, 1943 Camp Lee

Things have been so very convenient, here. Several of us have remarked that this work and schedule has been almost a relaxation after OCS. And, how I did enjoy my visit with the Chevaliers, yesterday.

I expect to spend the weekend in Richmond, and the Fourth of July. Would like to attend church at St. John's Episcopal Church (Patrick Henry's), and to take communion.

I has turned very warm, again. A little winter might feel just a bit of all right. Ha!

This Lt. Mills is one of the finest fellows I have ever known. We plan to room together in St. Louis. His father died two weeks ago—quite suddenly, of some sort of kidney infection and uremic poisoning.

Am hoping to swing by Boston on my way to St. Louis. Mr. C.O. Alley runs a travel agency, and he has my tickets all figured out for me. Will leave Richmond at 4:30 Saturday afternoon to go to Washington for an 11:30 streamliner that gets me into Boston at 8:00 Sunday morning, the 11th. We have to report in at St. Louis the 13th, Tuesday. So, I shall have some connections to make, but no difficulties. Will be nice to see Miriam, Mrs. Hodgson, and Aunt Anna.

June 29, 1943 Camp Lee

We are to go on an inspection tour for a couple days.

Plan to spend the 4th in Richmond—just to laze around.

Received announcement this evening that we are to report into St. Louis the 13th, a Tuesday. So, I plan to head to Boston, to arrive Saturday; will have Sunday there, and then to leave for St. Louis on Monday. Have reserved a room at the Mark Twain Hotel for Woody and me. And, as for your coming to St. Louis to see me, we shall have to see what can be arranged.

July 2, 1943 Camp Lee

Have about ten minutes before classes begin. A second exam comes up tomorrow, but no more than a little review to get ready for it.

Our two-day tour of inspection became one of my most interesting experiences since coming into the army. From here to Newport News (Hampton Roads) is close to 100 miles. Those old army trucks we went in became mighty rough and hard before we got there, and then back.

We first went to Camp Patrick Henry, the staging area for the port of embarkation at Hampton Roads. A "staging area" is a camp where men and materiel are concentrated, checked over, etc., in preparation for embarkation overseas. We were told about and shown many of the various problems the personnel must face and resolve, here. Unless skillfully handled, these difficulties cause much congestion and delay. We stayed the night at Patrick Henry, and then went to Hampton Roads. Here we saw them loading Liberty Ships—several of them; and lots of activity—to assemble and prepare for shipment. Yesterday, a bunch of German prisoners of war were landed here—to be deloused, clothed, processed, and transferred. We missed seeing them. We were then given a boat ride across Chesapeake Bay to Norfolk to see the installations there. This was highly interesting and eye-opening.

We were entertained by the P.O.E. band (port of entry) to give us a send-off after our visit—the first time they had done this for a visiting group. They did a swell job for us! The general in command at Hampton Roads gave us quite a speech and dealt with some very pertinent facts—strictly military and not to be told.

Altogether, I never spent two more enlightening days since my entrance into the army, with so much revealed. We felt encouraged and enthusiastic. All the docks, loading devices, stacks of materiel, etc.—just amazing. So much stock-piled! This was really quite a trip!

We did not get back to Camp Lee until 12:15 this morning, and I didn't get to bed until after 1:00. Up at the usual time, and we are sort of wandering around in a stupor. Ha! As for me, I'll be back "on the ball" tomorrow, after a full night's sleep.

Do not write to me, here, later than Wednesday. Then, c/o Mark Twain Hotel in St. Louis.

July 4, 1943 Camp Lee

Woody and I went into Richmond for the day. Visited some museums and the grounds around the State House. We picked up several pamphlets, here and there, and I'm sending some to you We also visited John Marshall's home. The Valentine Museum is in an old southern mansion, built in 1812 by John Wickham. It has a most beautiful circular staircase, and I found the house to be more interesting than the museum. Richmond is so historic, and so many places and structures to see. I must return when the future permits.

Went to church at St. John's Episcopal, and had communion. The services in Abilene suited me better, somehow.

Tomorrow, we inspect some government warehouses in Richmond. I'd like to return to Hampton Roads, for so much to see...

July 5, 1943 Camp Lee

Mr. Alley has secured reservations for my train connections to Boston. Unless the government changes my orders, I may get to the old bean town.

Woody and I ate dinner last evening at the Hotel Murphy. The baked chicken was very good, but not like a dinner at home. I showed him the Baptist church where I have gone with the Alleys, and I told him of the friendliness of the people there. I understand that some of the members have written you.

As for the long way around by Boston, it will not cost me anything more than the allowance I will receive to go to St. Louis. Is amazing, but Mr. Alley got such a good price for me to go to Boston. But I may have some close connections. We will just have to see—and all the way to St. Louis . The Alleys have become such good friends. Their son is about sixteen. We shall be writing after I leave. Her older sister, Miss Points, lives with them.

Ha! Mim thinks I wont know her when I arrive.

July 7,1943 Camp Lee

Just after supper, now. This afternoon, we shot cal. 30 Thompson sub-machine guns and cal. 30 machine guns. One feels somewhat off the beam when he stands to shoot his first round. Many of us were pretty poor at it. Ha! I laid the blame on my poor eyesight.

A bit warmer, today. I hope it will remain a bit cooler. I'm not much for hot weather.

My old outfit, the 85th, is now in California practicing "desert warfare."

When I wrote I was going to Boston by "Streamliner," I did not mean by boat! Mercy!

We are going to see Laurel and Hardy in "Jitterbugs" this evening. They will be silly, but I enjoy them.

I hope the Russians can hurl back those Nazis! What a shame it would be were those Germans to regain a lot of territory, for it would result in another year of little accomplishment for the Allied cause. But, I think the German drive will collapse quite readily, for I do not believe Hitler can make a sustained effort.

July 9, 1943 Camp Lee

No mail from you for three days. Did you misunderstand what I meant about Wednesday?

Well, after getting everything worked out just swell for my trip to Boston, we have had our orders changed! I would have been there from 8:00 a.m., Sunday, until 4:45 Monday afternoon. Now, I am doing some refiguring—like mad. Oh, this army can change your plans at the most inconvenient times! I'm about to chew nails, and I do mean NAILS. I still must leave Boston at 4:45 Sunday p.m. Ha! I did some calculating, and it will cost me $3 an hour—about as for my Christmas trip home. Ho! Ho! But, I am going!

We "graduate" from this school, tomorrow. And, I may still be furious. Oh, well!

St. Louis

July 13, 1943 Mark Twain Hotel, St. Louis

We had our "graduation" exercises Saturday a.m., at 9 o'clock—a thirty-five minute ceremony. Then, we had to get "cleared." Woody and I were taken into Petersburg by another Lt., who was driving to North Carolina. We caught a 10:10 train for Washington, D.C., and I had just enough time to pick up my ticket and climb aboard.

With several small delays en route, we hit the station in Washington at 2:50—with my train's scheduled departure at 3:00. I had to have my ticket authenticated at the "window," and the train began to move, and it was on the track next to the platform. I tossed my heavier case onto the platform above the steps of the closest car, and then climbed onto the steps of the next car. I just made it!! I'd had two close shaves and was sort of panting from the second one. I had to stand until we reached Baltimore; then I had a seat to Boston. The weather was coolish. Arrived at Boston—11:35 that night. Not bad, eh?

They weren't expecting me until 8 o'clock Sunday morning. So, I sent a telegram to Mim when the train made a brief stop in New York. A young private was leaving the train, and he refused to accept more than a dollar to send the telegram for me. So, I had a royal reception when I arrived in Boston.

The telegram had been called in about 9:30, and they (Mim, Mrs. Hodgson, and Aunt Anna) left immediately to go to South Station. With all the transfers needed to come from Hyde Park, they needed at least an hour. They had arrived at the station about 11:00. They spotted me before I did them, for there was a large crowd to meet the train. They certainly gave me a warm greeting—even Miriam. And, I'm being a bit silly. Ha!

We got out to the house, had ginger ale and sandwiches, and visited until after 2:30. It was just great! I was just filthy from all the train dust, but was too tired to do more than just wash hands and face.

About 7:30 I heard some stirring about. So, I got up at 8:00. We just lounged around, had breakfast, and visited like mad. About 11:00 it seemed time for me to make myself presentable; so, I got shaved, bathed, and into clean attire. I had sent Mim one of my pictures—of S. Sgt. Mickey sporting his "cookie-duster." She had it on display, but wasted no time to tell me that she wanted a replacement. Ho! Ho! For dinner, we had fried chicken, etc., and then fresh blueberry pie. Darned good!!

After dinner and "dishes," in came another of Mrs Hodgson's sisters and a sister-in-law, and their families. I had met all of them when I was here for New Year's, etc., 1942. We just had a regular family reunion. Just more fun!

Clara Luke lost her husband recently, and often spends Sunday afternoons, here. About fifteen of us were here for supper. All are such friendly people, and without any sophistication. Of course, they think I have a "western drawl," and I just have to take my "beating." Mim and I had expected to go hear the Boston Pops Orchestra, but I had to catch the train at 11:30.

At the station, I had to get my larger suitcase out of "check" and pick up my ticket. Had expected to be able to cash a 156-dollar government check, but we couldn't get it done. I was out of money for the ride to St. Louis. So, Aunt Anna loaned me the 17 dollars she had in her purse. I was a bit embarrassed.

When time to board came, we had our hugs. Mrs. Hodgson, with tears in her eyes, then paid me quite a compliment: "You haven't changed a bit, and it seems almost as if Joe has been home!" (He was Mim's younger brother. He and I had been fellow counselors the summers of 1939 and 1940 in a boys' summer camp in New Hampshire.)

Return route took me to Newark, where Woody met me. We went to his family's for a quick dinner, and then caught a 1:40 afternoon train for St. Louis, and we arrived here at 10:30 this morning—time to check in at the Mark Twain and then at the medical depot. One of the secretaries at the depot had made our hotel reservations for us, and she had really been "on the ball" for us.

Just one problem—I have a mountain of laundry, and it will flatten me to pay the bill. Woody and I needed to get rid of all the dirt from the long train trip from Newark. Ha!

July 14, 1943 St. Louis Medical Depot

My scribbling, today, is hardly legible. I need to practice my Palmer Method... I guess a got all tuckered out from that long train ride from Boston.

Our room here in the Mark Twain has a northern exposure. Thus, we aren't bothered with too much sunlight streaming in. We have ice water in one faucet, and an electric fan—along with ample space for our two beds. Woody and I are well situated, and ready to "fight the war" right here in our hotel room. But, all this comfort makes me feel just a little cheap. But, we will not be here long.

July 15, 1943 St. Louis, Missouri

Yes, within twelve hours, I was from Camp Lee to Richmond, Va., and then on to Washington, D.C..., Maryland, Pennsylvania, Delaware, New Jersey, New York, Connecticut, Rhode Island, and Massachusetts. Then, after all that, Massachusetts and to Rhode Island, Connecticut, New York, New Jersey, Pennsylvania, Ohio, Indiana, Illinois, and Missouri. How this being in the army does, now and then, keep one on the move!

Our courses at the medical depot, here, begin at 8:15 and run to noon; then, from 1:00 to 4:30. We are off for each evening. It is going to be strenuous! Should you plan to come down to see me, there is much to do and see—go to an opera, visit the zoo, stroll through Forest Park. This Park is a huge place. And, much more!

July 16, 1943 St. Louis

The reservations Mr. Alley made for me proved to be hardly more than permits to board trains. I had to keep paying for each ticket. But, I got through on schedule. Gee Whiz!! Then, in Boston, I ran out of cash. Ha!

This living in a very nice hotel room is the berries—after spending over a year in G.I. barracks. This doesn't seem much like "war" to me. Tomorrow, we begin more courses. Also, we are to have an hour of drill. The roof of one of the warehouse-buildings is where we drill. One of the warehouses has a tower which has about twenty floors. We receive most of our directives from the secretaries. Howzaboutthat!!

July 17, 1943 St. Louis

You asked about St. John's Episcopal Church in Richmond. It reminded me so much of Holy Trinity in Lincoln, and similar to the church in Abilene. The ministers were quite different, but highly effective.

As for my next assignment?? It will be to a medical depot, and there are 10 to which we may be sent. Chicago, Kansas City, and Denver are the nearest to Lincoln. Rumor has it that we will be placed in the area of our induction. But, no guarantee. Am not eager to remain in St. Louis; but, a medical depot is also at Richmond. So, we shall see. I think there are medical depots at Los Angeles, San Francisco, and Seattle. Do not think I am eager to hit the west coast.

You will like Mim and her family!

July 19, 1943 St. Louis

To church, yesterday, at the Episcopal cathedral, and have never seen a more beautiful altar. The front of the church is inlaid with figures of biblical renown—just striking! The sermon was good, and I plan to go back this coming Sunday. A soprano soloist was just excellent.

This life of luxury doesn't seem much like war, to me. This is so very different from my first ten months in the army! Woody and I luxuriate with all our comforts, including our innerspring mattresses.

Some other cities where these medical depots are located—Binghampton, NY, Savannah, and Chicago. Of course, I do not know to which I shall be sent for additional training.

Am going to see an opera, "Rosalie," tomorrow evening. Then, Woody and I plan to see a baseball game, the Cardinals v. the Giants—a night game. Will be my first big league game.

July 21, 1943 St. Louis

"Rosalie" was excellent. These summer performances are out in the open air. We were back in our room about 11:40.

Warming up, here, and we have enjoyed our ice water (out of a faucet) and our overhead fan. Some of our gang complain about their rooms, etc., but Woody and I have nothing to criticize. We are so comfortable.! Some way to fight a war!

My military address is—17th Floor, St. Louis Medical Depot, 12th and Spruce Sts., St. Louis. Mo.

July 22, 1943 St. Louis

We had drill and calisthenics this morning. Then, we ran a commando course and have been playing games all afternoon. This has been much better than sitting around and listening to dry lectures. One area of instruction has been interesting, and this has dealt with the government's accounting system. For the military, it is both complicated and simple. Eventually, recording is all done by machine. Units must know how to turn in their requests and accounts. Spare me!!

Am still much amused about the fuss Mim made regarding my Staff Sergeant's picture, with the moustache. I just keep wondering, :"Why?" Ha! Ha!

July 25, 1943 (Sunday) St. Louis

Mussolini's resignation has me just a little worked up! It would be wonderful were the Italians to get out of the war. Could mean much less time, in the long run.

We saw "The Constant Nymph" last night—Joan Fontaine and Charles Boyer. She should get an academy award for this. Also, "Someone to Remember," with Martha Paige. Do go see, for it is quite different.

To church at the cathedral, this morning. Another good sermon. A rather moving experience during the service. We sang what is sometimes called "The Mariner's Hymn"—with most verses ending with "O hear us when we cry to Thee, for those who perish on the sea." In the pew just ahead of me was a lady who began to weep, almost convulsively. She just sobbed. I reached forward and put my hand on her shoulder, and she then put her hand on mine. I never saw her face. One can only surmise as to the cause of her grief. A corporal sang "The Lord's Prayer," and he did it well!

Am eager to hear what Winchell has to say this evening about Mussolini. His remarks should be about as hot as little red onions.

July 27, 1943 St. Louis

It has been terribly hot! I was very tired last night. We had almost suffocated, so it seemed. Classes were called off, and we spent time with drill, calisthenics, and games—playing lots of volleyball. Then, we tossed a 35-pound ball around, and one has to be alert and agile to enjoy this sort of fun. It became a good afternoon.

Be sure to see "The More the Merrier"—with Jean Arthur, Joel McCrea, and Charles Coburn. I just about laughed my head off! It is good. Glad to know you have seen Abbott and Costello in "Hit the Ice." It gave me lots of laughs when I saw it.

Just think! Two months ago, today, I arrived home from Camp Barkeley!

July 29, 1943 St. Louis

Yesterday was miserable—heat and humidity! I do not want to remain here. My sinuses have really flared up, and I may have to go see the depot's "Doc"—hopefully to get some relief. Between this heat and my head, I'm not worth much! To do calisthenics, to drill, and to play games have become torture. A couple aspirin, once back in the hotel, did no good. Then, I became sick to my stomach, and what little I had eaten came up. I kept drinking water to have something to raise. Then, almost suddenly, it stopped and I felt much better.

We had planned to go see "The Desert Song." So, I cleaned up. We hopped a 7:45 bus for the park. I felt a little light-headed, but O.K. I really enjoyed the performance, and here's a copy of the program.

There is a chance that I could get home the weekend of August 13th. Will depend upon my assignment. Am feeling much better, today. But, I have no appetite. Can always blame the heat!

August 2, 1943 St. Louis

My sinuses have entirely cleared, and no more headache since the vomiting stopped. There must be a connection of some sort between stomach and head, do you suppose? Ha!

It just stays so hot! It's a good thing you didn't attempt to come down to see me. Still no info as to our assignments. The government just does not tell us anything until the last minute. There must be a logical reason for this, somewhere. Humph! Wouldn't it be something were I to get Denver? But, it could be to the west coast. And, Mother, you have so many old friends that live "out there."

Woody and I are heading out to eat. I think my appetite is returning. We didn't have a very busy day—just monotonous. Oh, these classes!

August 4, 1943 St. Louis

No news about assignments. So, can't make any plans. It remains as hot as blazes! We played games nearly all afternoon—about 14 games of volleyball.

Woody and I are going to see the Cardinals play Brooklyn. We are getting to be "big league" fans, I think.

Will call Thursday evening—news or no news.

And, glad to know the government refund on travel expenses finally came in. Now, I shall not hover near bankruptcy. The long trips by train do enable one to make plenty from travel pay—unless one takes too many side trips. My swing to Boston really ate into the reimbursement. But, $157 was pretty good, eh? No refund for the Pullman, though.

August 6, 1943 St. Louis

From all indications, we will not know about our assignments until next week. One rumor has it that we may have to wait two more weeks. So, I could be right in the Mark Twain for a while, yet.

The phone call was just so much fun—and such clear reception. Placed the call from my hotel room, and this was much better than being cooped up in a booth.

Our course-work now finished, with the last exam, today. It took us two hours to get through it, and I found it to be kind of disgusting. It was one of the courses which seemed to be of meager substance, and I do hope that down the line we shall find that what little we learned will prove to be of real use.

Woody and I are about to head out for supper. I'm hungry for chop suey—something Chinese. Then, we shall head out to a ball game. We will make quite an evening out of it. Tomorrow evening we are to see Herbert's "Babes in Toyland"—the Municipal Opera. And to come up shortly is "The Merry Widow," and this should be my last show before departure.

August 7, 1943 St. Louis

No news about our assignments. Seems to me we should have heard by now. These will be last-minute notifications which will probably leave us with no chances to get reservations. We blame our Washington "bigwigs." Oh, well!

You have been having a lot of rain, and we have had very little. However, it has been much cooler, and our "pep level" is up. Seven of our class went to observe the working routine of the transportation department of the depot. We received a job to do—to unload a completely full boxcar of packaged gauze. With fork-lift trucks and "skids" we finished the task in an hour and ten minutes—really ripped right through it. We were done at 10:45. One of the workmen told us, with a big grin, that their schedule called for the unloading to be finished by 4:00 this afternoon. Ha! I guess if you want something done in a hurry, just ask a bunch of army shavetails to do it. We did have a lot of fun doing it—just sort of "went to town" and with a good bit of horseplay.

Monday we shall go to another warehouse—purpose being to practice stacking of crated goods and taking of inventory. I expect this to be one of our better days.

August 8, 1943 St. Louis

A Sunday evening, and I am just back from having seen Claire Trevor, Randolph Scott, and Wallace Ford in "The Desperadoes." Very good, and in technicolor. Some of it must have been filmed in the Badlands of S. Dak.—certainly looked like that country up there. And, I did so much enjoy "Babes in Toyland"—every minute of it. All local talent, and some little girl, about seven, could really dance—along with about 20 others about her size. They had their routines down pat! Too, the butterfly scene was a dream, and so beautifully presented. The dancer was arrayed in white and then gradually "unfolded" to become a white butterfly—with a wingspread of about six feet on each side and the effect to come from the very light fabric which extended from her outstretched arms to the rest of her body. This was a sort of thing that I had never seen before.

To church this morning, but can't say I got much from the service. My mood was simply astray. Maybe the rain dampened my spirit! The altar of the cathedral is unusual, and I hope you will see it sometime.

For tomorrow evening, Woody and I plan to see Red Skelton in "DuBarry Was a Woman."

And, who knows? Tomorrow we may receive our assignments.

August 10, 1943 St. Louis

Just had lunch, and we will soon go out for exercise. This is the dullest existence one could hope to find. We've had a little rain, and it just adds to the humidity.

Woody and I saw "DuBarry Was a Lady"—a good picture for relaxing, and we had several good laughs. The hair styles of the Louis XV years (France) were something else! Quite a display of red hair. Otherwise, somewhat ordinary.
No news about assignments! It is disgusting. These "uppers" in Washington are just not on the ball. It causes me to wonder as to just how we are managing to win this war!

We plan to see "The Merry Widow"—out in Forest Park, probably tomorrow evening.

August 11, 1943 St. Louis

Well, officials at the Depot finally did a bit, today—they called Washington to see what was holding up our orders. They were told the orders were not ready. Then, a call came in to tell us that the orders were being sent by air mail. Info was that we should know tomorrow. So many places we can be sent, and we do not know what sort of time schedules we will have to meet. I could be going to Savannah, San Antonio, or Binghamton—and, who knows????? Gee! But it would be nice were I to get Denver! We can just hope!

Very warm, with high humidity—and we had an hour of drilling out in the hot sun. I think we unassigned lieutenants are beginning to feel a bit abused. It could be that we are just getting a bit soft. Ha! Maybe our little gold bars have gone to our heads! Oh, well! Boil it down—with what so many must endure, we have so little to complain about.

Some of us have been doing inventory, and we are finding that records and bookkeeping are highly inaccurate. Our reports really got the floor foremen all riled up. These civil service employees are not happy to have us around, let me tell you. We new lieutenants work fast and accurately. Ho! Ho!

Keep your fingers crossed—who knows, I could be seeing you "on the way to somewhere."

August 12, 1943 St. Louis

Our orders did not come in, today; but, they should be in tomorrow. These officials have known for a month that these assignments were to be made. Here we are, and this upper brass doesn't seem to have enuf sense to keep a pencil busy. Things are really SNAFU up above. We poor second lieuts could just chew nails. These higher ups just wait until after the last minute, almost, to inform us. I keep having to remind myself that we have, compared to so many who are in much danger, really nothing to complain about—seriously.

A nice thing in store for us for the evening. Owner of one of the largest of the movie theatres has invited all of us and depot personnel, as guests, to come see Irving Berlin's "This Is the Army." Minimum admission is $1.10. It is supposed to be quite a spectacle. I understand that part of the admission fee goes to an army "relief fund"; and, we may contribute to "the cause." Kate Smith sings "God Bless America..." She is a large person, but very graceful—and "handsome"!

None of us dares pack, for each of us might be assigned to stay. I may not be moved. But, nearly all of us in the class will be catching trains to get out of this town. So far, this place has not been my favorite location. This whole medical service, from the Surgeon General's office to this place, lacks efficiency—certainly in so many of its administrative responsibilities. So, you have my opinion—which probably isn't worth much. Ha!

August 14, 1943 St. Louis

Our orders are not in, yet, but the Surgeon General's office sent a teletyped copy. So, now we know. But, no one can be released until the copy of his official assignment arrives.

So, each of us is waiting. I am going to the San Francisco Medical Depot, and will have no opportunity to swing by Lincoln. The delay in communication has just absorbed any travel time we might have had—to permit a small detour, even.

Of course, we shall receive our travel pay. Usually, each of us is to be paid 8 cents per mile, as reimbursement. But, if we should travel by a land-grant railroad, for those miles we receive but 5 cents. For me, it is to be "land-grant" from Denver to San Francisco. The fees the government pays the land-grant railroads can be understood in the light of the grants of land which the government gave to promote construction—The Union Pacific receiving, perhaps, the most extensive right of way. We shall receive "Transportation Requests," and these are as good as "first class tickets." A transportation officer explained it to us. Some will choose to use these "Requests," and some will pay about $60 for a ticket to the west coast—but each is different for LA, SF, or Seattle. Four of us are going to San Francisco, and we are going to use the TRs.

This way, we don't have to pay out. Then, we are to receive about $60 for the trip, and this amounts to a profit. Our time to report in at the Medical Depot in San Francisco will not permit any side trips en route. I'm not certain that all of this makes sense, but think I have it straight. I shall find out later. Ho! Ho!

I missed going to Chicago by one name. Those officials in Washington just followed the alphabet somewhat to make the assignments. Woody Mills is going to Chicago. Metz, one of the guys I have much enjoyed and who often bunked close by, also goes to SF—along with another good one named Mathis. Our fourth to go to SF is one who, so far, has not been one of my closer buddies.

Gee! I'll be seeing another great corner of our country. So, I should not feel at all out of sorts. I guess Los Angeles would have suited me more. But, really no complaint. Uncle Sammy is paying for the ride, and I shall see a fascinating city and coastal area. Then, if after this thirty days of further training I should be returned to St. Louis to await further assignment, I shall make another 50 or 60 dollars. I must purchase my winter coat, and it will cost close to $60. Could be that profit from travel will pay for it.???

Francis Tische (also grew up in my home-town of Wood Lake, Nebraska) is stationed at Oakland, across the Bay. We will have to get together! Also, Mrs. Alley wrote me from Richmond that the USO sent a soldier to their house for a room, and she noted when he registered that he was from Nebraska. She asked him if he knew me, which he did—his being a graduate of Nebraska Wesleyan, and also a Crescent. Was quite a coincidence, eh? Paul was about three years ahead of me.

Didn't want to call you too early this morning. It is now after 9:30, and the delay is still holding. So, I think I'll get ready to go to church—as you will be doing shortly. This letter is now up to five pages on both sides. Whew! But, this time I have had some news. And, just think, I shall soon be seeing Barbary Coast and Knob Hill, etc.

Not a cloud in the sky, and it is going to be another hot one. But, with our fan on, Woody and I keep very comfortable in our Mark Twain room.

August 14 (yet), 1943 St. Louis

Posted my first letter here at the Hotel, and must now write more, since our call and visiting. I nearly cancelled my call about 10:50, and after I had decided to stay phone-side and not go to church. Then, at 11:15 a connection, and you, Bin, answered. And, Moosie, you had gone to church; so, no visit with you. I hope it didn't ruin your Sunday! Maybe, a little conceit,, here!

Between my earlier letter and the telephone call, you should understand the situation which will prevent my getting home on the way to SF. But, after thirty days, there, we shall be returning to St. Louis for placement, and a swing by Lincoln may be possible. We shall see! The more I think about it, the more satisfied I am with this sojourn in San Francisco.

This living in a hotel has made it very easy for some of the fellows to have troubles making ends meet—just too many nice things all around to flatten one's billfold. Some borrow and some send home for a booster. Well, it is their business, not mine. My guess is that this mess will last for another two years, and I hope to lay away some sort of a nest egg—to head back into more graduate work, etc.

We student officers are to be returned to St. Louis, and then to be assigned for full duty elsewhere. Older and experienced medical administrative officers are receiving the overseas and upper administrative appointments. We of the newer and lesser sort will receive the grunt and run spots. Oh, well! No overseas assignment in the cards for us new Lts., as of now…

No more letters to me, here. You might try me at San Francisco Medical Depot
c/o Officers' Training Division
San Francisco, California

August 15, 1943 St. Louis

Am certainly using a lot of the Mark Twain Hotel stationery. But, here we are, and do not know just when we will be getting out. Ain't it the berries!

Our orders did arrive, and we are now awaiting our transportation arrangements. These TRs of the government enable us to make quite a saving, but we do have to pay for Pullman. I shall have one all the way; so, it will be an air-conditioned and cool trip. But, with this waste of time, here, I could have had some time at home! I guess roughly that I'll make about $60 each way on the trips to and from SF, and this will pay for most of the winter attire I shall need. Good deal, eh?? Frankly, I just do not understand the system; but, I guess understanding is not necessity.

Metz and I shall be going together, and hope we can room together in SF. He is a big, fat fellow and very good natured. and lots of fun to be around. There are 50 of us 2nd Lts. in this class, and all will be returning in thirty days to St. Louis. I may have to do some finagling to get routed back through Omaha—but, maybe not until we head out again for more permanent placement. We could be talking about the end of September.

Saw the movie, yesterday, "Hangmen Also Die." It is excellent, and shows how the Nazi Gestapo works. Czech patriots manage to outwit the Nazis. The plot was so skillfully formed and developed—just the best seen of the German occupation of Czechoslovakia. It is not too gruesome for you to see, Moosie!

We received nice diplomas when we completed this depot instruction. This little piece of ribbon was attached to mine. So, put it in the scrap book. I'll keep the diploma for later deposit—when I get home. Also, send me addresses of friends in the SF area. I should have some time to seek them out.

Woody leaves for Chicago tomorrow morning. I shall be unhappy to bid him fond adieu, for he has been a wonderful associate. But, I should see him when we return to St. Louis. But, we have always been told that "All good things must come to an end."

August 17, 1943 St. Louis

Our train doesn't leave until 3:50 this afternoon. Delays along the way, I guess, and we get into SF about 10:00 Friday morning. Our reservations could be made only to Denver. We are to be back here in 37 days. And, I now understand that our "travel pay" will be $110 each way. It has to do with the figuring of mileage. If so, so much the better, eh? Will have plenty for my winter attire.

San Francisco is quite cool, and we will probably be wearing our ODs in the evenings. So, I may wire you to send my dress uniform—blouse, green shirt, green pants, and pink pants. Also, will want you to send my field-jacket—with the zipper front and buttoned. Also to be sent are my two OD shirts and three OD pants. This is all hanging together in my closet. It will be a good-sized box, eh?? Checked my footlocker and Gladstone clear through this morning. I have two shirts with me that I've never worn. And, it may be that I'll be sending my summer uniforms home after a few weeks.

So cool, here, today. It is the dickens that it has become so nice—just when we leave. I've enjoyed staying in the Mark Twain. At first, the noise from the passing street cars would awaken me, but this was a bother for just a couple nights—just got used to it. Ha! And, this month has just flown by. And, almost three months since I was commissioned. We have had many a good laugh over the sweating we did while in OCS—with much appearing to have been humorous, now, but we did sweat some blood. I have visited with some new lieutenants of the 18th class at Barkeley, and they said that only 46% of their class received commissions. Ours was about 55%, I think.

Must pick up my little grip, put on my little cap and cock it over my right eye, and go prancing over to the railroad station. Elmer Metz and his folks will be there. This will not be the sort of departure, for me, that it was when I saw you driving away from Fort Crook—May l0, last year.

We will be sharing our Pullman, and I shall claim the inside—otherwise, he will probably just crowd me onto the floor of the aisle. Too, he snores like whatever, and my sharp elbow may have to give him a good poke or two.

Well, off to see the train. Will post this in a box at the station. "Golden Gate," here I come. Will be seeing these states for the first time—Utah, Nevada, and California. Maybe I can catch up with Eleanor R., for she has seen all except N. Dak.

San Francisco

San Francisco Medical Depot August 20, 1943

Came through on schedule. Due to cancellations, we had Pullman space from Denver to SF. Had called ahead, and Aunt Bertha, H.O., Janet, and Mary Liz were at the station in Denver. We had about twenty minutes of wonderful chatting. So good to see them! Pulled out about 5:15.

At Ogden, Utah, we had time to eat breakfast at the U.P. & S.P. Café. My "hot cakes" were very good—just about my favorite breakfast. We crossed the Great Salt lake, and the tracks lie right across the middle. The scenery was fascinating. Eventually to Reno, and nearly all descended to walk around—hoping to see some celebrities, maybe. None! Then, to Oakland and to be ferried across the Bay to San Fran. Quite a view of the city from the Bay!

Arrived at the R.R. station at 9:20 this morning. Reported in at the Medical Depot, and then went to see Mrs. Tina Aarons who had a large room available for us—where our four predecessors had roomed… She is a pudgy, little soul, and would talk a leg and arm off you if possible. We shall humor her while here. Ha!

We were three nights en route and appreciated our Pullmans. Nevertheless, I feel quite weary, and will much enjoy my bed without the motion of the train. Each of us pays $25/mon for this room, and we receive $45 for rooming allowance. I think each of us will manage quite well! I have been munching an apple and some grapes, and am sleepy and trying to keep awake to finish this letter. You can write me at the depot, or here at 186 Commonwealth Ave. The SF Med Depot is at 15th and Fulsom Sts.

August 22, 1943 San Francisco

Our room at Mrs. Aarons is large, with a small adjacent room with one single bed… We have three beds in the large room—one of them a double, which became mine. The other two did not come Pullman, but we were on the same train. A call to Mrs. Aarons from the Depot, reserved the room for us, and she told us which transportation to use, where to change cars, and where to get off, etc. We had no trouble to find her place—a lower floor apartment, in a rather large complex. We are comfortably settled in for the next five weeks. We had checked our footlockers and heavy suitcases through to the Depot. Once reporting in and having arranged to stay at Mrs. Aarons, a truck and driver were at our disposal to haul our luggage to our room. So, we were helped considerably.

From what we have understood, we shall be spending a few days at Letterman General Hospital, at a Fort Mason (?), and elsewhere—most of time to be at this Medical Depot. It is quite chilly and brisk, and we will need our winter attire. So, I await the shipment from Lincoln. Thanks!Let me know the cost, and I shall send you a check. The fog is very thick in the a.m., but it thins by late morning. Then, we get some sunshine and some warmth.

August 23, 1943 San Franciso

Yesterday was my first Sunday, here. After breakfast, we bought some passes, at 25 cents each, and then went out to the beach to see the old Pacific roll in. Seal Rocks was close by, and some seals were on and about. Then, to the Golden Gate Park to see an art museum, an aquarium, and the Halls of Natural Science. This Park is a beautiful place, but not this way naturally—with much landscaping and planting of trees, etc.

We then went to Fisherman's Wharf, about two in the afternoon, where we had wonderful seafood dinners—fish, shrimp, prawns, crabs, lobsters, scallops, etc., all available in season. Just great! We rode the cable car to get there—much like a street car in appearance, but the very steep hills necessitated something very different. One just has to be here and to see what is done to clamp onto these underground cables and to be pulled along. Fascinating and so practical a solution to resolve a transportation problem. Once back to our room, two of us went to a movie, and we were back by 8:30. It was quite a day, and this air was fresh—yes-sirree! We will be having some Sundays on duty; so, I'm glad we made the most of this one.

We have been told that August and September are the nicest months to be here. Then, we have been assured that there is very little change in the climate. One older officer at the depot told us that San Francisco has no climate—just the same thing from day to day. It has been quite windy since our arrival, and this is supposed to be unusual. Well, we shall see. Ha! Ha! Should you chance a trip to come here, you wont have to worry about the heat.

Received my travel money, today—a check for $118.75. It is just amazing. And we will get it again for our return trip to St. Louis. I guess we should not complain if the government wants to send us here and there via public transportation. My first day at the Depot was spent with the Transportation Section. Maybe, one of these days I may begin to understand just how it works.

August 24, 1943 San Francisco

Today proved to be quite useless, really. I just am wondering as to what this is to be about! Maybe I am just a poor little mixed up kid. Well, we will just have to see.

The Roosevelt—Churchill conference in Quebec seems to have ended in quite an exuberant array of hopeful gestures. I hope more help for China may come from this. More needs to be done to give the Japanese their comeuppance—and soon.

It is chilly, running around in my khakis! I did some purchasing, but some fitting had to be done. So it is a matter of waiting—for local delivery and for the big box to arrive from Lincoln.

August 26, 1943 San Francisco

Be sure to keep tab on all the reverse-charged telephone calls. I shall settle with you one of these days.

Much to my liking, we were just real busy, today.

Elmer Metz and I worked until just after 3 o'clock, and then we headed back to our room. At a nearby grocery, I purchased a sack of apples—about ten of them in the sack for a quarter, and good and juicy. We are munching away to our hearts' content.

Had left quite a sack of dirty clothes, and picked them up at the laundry. Everything came back just immaculate. Reasonable cost, too. So, that is good! This place is close by.

As for the ODs sent from Lincoln, it may well take up to a week's time. No real problem! Once they arrive, I shall have to have some "straps" put on shoulders of some of the shirts.

Francis Tische is stationed in Oakland, and Erma Jane has sent me his address. So, I must be getting in touch with him. It would be great were we two Wood Lakers to have a get-together!

August 27, 1943 San Francisco

This weather, here, seems to make me sleepy. I just yawn about half the time. The fog, or mist, just moves in about six in the evening, and then it seems to lift about 10:30 in the morning. As yet, it doesn't appeal to me. I think my month's stay will be enough. Ha!

Dan Mathisen's mother drove up from Los Angeles, and we all crowded in her car and went to Fisherman's Wharf and ate at the International Settlement. Dan is one of our foursome, and his mother is quite a lady. My choice was a "Chef's Special Plate"—frog's legs, prawns, shrimp, clams, scallops, and sea bass; I could hardly get around all of it, and for just $1.25. It was lively business all over—with people just everywhere. Then afterwards, we went to quite a staged show—featuring "The Gay Nineties," "The Barn," and "Show Boat." The better numbers were in the "Gay Nineties" and included a melodrama—a scream from start to finish. Ha! Ha! They dropped us off shortly after 10 o'clock. It was a great evening!

Write me at the Depot, for the mail seems to be delivered there sooner. The service to governmental institutions is better, so they say—maybe by as much as two days. It takes six or seven days, sometimes, for a letter from Lincoln to reach me—and four days just once, so far.

The hat, which you sent separately, has arrived. The other stuff, not yet. I will get it, do not worry. Then I shall be sending to you my summer khakis. Ho! Ho!

August 28, 1943 S.F.M.D. 1855 Folsom St.
San Francisco

At the depot and am trying to keep busy—but, a lag. The big box of clothes arrived. So, everything is now here. May send you a box of my khakis, but not for sure. So, Moosie, don't get in a stew if nothing arrives. Will save this big Cadwallader box—just in case.

Have tried to reach Francis by telephone, but no luck. He is always on duty and out of reach. We must have a rendezvous, and he is just across the Bay.

Earlier today, we had a practice air alert, and the sirens were sounding all over the place. We had to move quickly into the safer areas of this large system of warehouses, etc. More fun! And this came after I had a rather miserable night of it—some sort of indigestion. Maybe I have just been eating too much seafood. Maybe a frog leg, or two, was kicking! Next time I go to Fisherman's Wharf, I shall stick to the fish. Just think, to grow up in Wood Lake, we ate lots of beef—and the rarer it was, the more musical was the growling. Oh, well!

I want to see "Behind the Rising Sun," but the lines have been so long!! So, I 'll just bide my time.

Am going to buy a packet of "V-Mail"—not much space on each sheet, but each letter is to be given special priority. We shall see!

After return to my room at Tina's, I unpacked the clothes. The pants will need no pressing, but the shirts and blouses were very wrinkled, particularly the two blouses. I will need to do some pressing.

Well, it is now the 29th, and over night all the wrinkles disappeared. I hung shirts and blouses on hangers, and a magic wand was waved over them. So. Mother, I guess you did a perfect job—By Golly!

Monday, Metz and I are to go to Letterman General Hospital for three days of duty in the medical supply office. We get there by street car, and we hope this work will prove to be interesting. Both of us are looking forward to this change of pace!

Did get to see the movie last evening. If you want to see something to rile you around and around and around, see it! Whew! And, finally talked with Fran Tische, and we will spend the weekend together. He is coming here—has free time from Saturday noon until early Monday a.m. We have room for him with us. Howzabout that!!

August 3l, 1943 San Francisco

So nice and cool, here, and I nearly forget what the summer heat of the midwest is like. The flowers are so pretty, just everywhere; the grounds are so green and beautiful, and the palm trees are so different. It amuses me that some of the locals who work in the Depot complain when the sun shines and it warms up a bit. They just do not know what hot weather is. Ha! But, you will find no mosquitoes, here.

Have spent a good bit of time cross-checking stock records with warehouse counts. We have an officers' meeting this evening. It will be long and a bit boring, but we must be there to respond to the roll call. It's much better to sit by the radio and munch delicious red grapes and a juicy, crisp apple. But, at the meeting we may learn something useful—and, who knows?

September 2, 1943 San Francisco

We are now bouncing out of bed about six o'clock in the morning, for we are being asked to be at the Depot earlier. But, yesterday afternoon, when it was slow everywhere, Metz and I sneaked out to go to a shoe-repair place. We waited no more than a half hour to have the shoes resoled, and cost was $2.50 for me. I'll get another eight months of wear from my pair.

A couple days ago, while at Letterman General, I went to the dental clinic to have my teeth cleaned, and the crew worked me in without an appointment. And Don, read this well. The oral hygienist began her work and then called the Captain to come see. They both told me that the inlays were the best they had ever seen. When finished, the H.O. said: "Those inlays are polished to perfection. I have never seen anything like this that was done in California!" So, Ahem!!

Letterman receives many patients who have been on duty in the Pacific areas. In the afternoons, so many of the patients are out sunning, and several are limping, and a few have had an amputation. But, all appear to have received excellent care! One of these men told me that his hospital ship was practically as good as Letterman—as for the care he received. Too, I was impressed by the number of "family members" who were visiting.

The four of us stick quite well to lights out by about 10:30 and radios off by 11:00. We didn't make it a couple evenings ago when one of the guys came in with some pickled pigs feet. Of course, we had to chew on them, they were good, and we just delayed our bedtime. Ha! Actually, they were not the tastiest feet I have eaten. Again, Ha!

Francis is stationed at the Naval Hospital in Oakland. He plans to come over Saturday, unless some sort of emergency should cancel his liberty.

Sept. 3, 1943 San Francisco

Am observing and "working" in the Parcel Post and Biological Departments, today. I just poke around and try to make a nuisance of myself. The latter is not difficult to do!

I am getting tired of the sameness of this weather pattern, and too much fog and chill. Just give me the prairies and something other than this sameness. Could be that I need more sunshine. Last night a fit of coughing hit me, and I really whooped and whooped… Do not have a sinus flare-up, but some sort of postnasal drip really hit me. So it goes, sometimes! Maybe my brain is shrinking and all this extra fluid has gathered to fill in the space. Oh, well!

Lots on radio about the allied landings in Italy. The British Eighth is doing its work, and I hope the Italians will revolt against Badoglio. Sure would like to see Italy get out of this war—pronto! We'll soon know how effectively Italy has been "softened up." An "unconditional surrender" should come quickly.

Saw the movie, "Claudia"—excellent, with Margaret McGuire.

Sept. 5, 1943 San Francisco

A Sunday evening, and quite a bit to tell you. Francis arrived from Oakland about 4:15 yesterday afternoon, and we came to our room—to leave his kit and for me to change clothes. We then had supper—roast sirloin, and the first good beef dinner I've had for some time. We then went to see Edward Everett Horton in "Springtime for Henry." The acting was just "tops," and Horton is as funny on stage as on screen. We did enjoy it—all three hours, and not a dull moment. We were fortunate to get in—all sold out, but two cancellations had come in just before I asked for tickets. The house was packed, we were in center section and well forward, and each seat cost $2.25. We just laughed ourselves almost silly.

We got to bed about midnight, slept comfortably in my double bed, and then up in time to go to church at Trinity Episcopal. The choir was superb, the sermon was good, and we had communion. The assistant rector was Chinese, and he impressed me profoundly—and this working side by side of American and Chinese priests seemed almost prohetic.

After church, we hit a Chinese restaurant for chow mein; then to see a double feature, Edward T. Robinson in "Destroyer" and the Bumsteads "It's a Great Life." And, Moosie, you would enjoy the Bumstead film, for it is just about your style. After the movies, Francis returned to Oakland, and I to my room.

It takes so long for the mail to be moved along and delivered—a full week from Boston, and this means two weeks to receive a response. And, rarely less than five days, to and from Lincoln.

Tomorrow I am to begin a week's duty at our central warehouse. Daily schedule for me will be from 3:00 to 11:00 p.m. Well, I should gain some understanding about some of the problems to arise from the storage and care of medical supplies. And, I'm still guessing that I'll be in this military business for another two years, yet!

Sept. 6, 1943 San Francisco

One day we have feelings that we four are going to be retained, here; then, the next day we think we shall be returned to St. Louis for definitive assignment. Inklings today are that we shall return to St. Louis. Ho! Ho! Anywhere but in this fog! The midwest would be great!

We have been palletizing 42l-pound drums of alcohol, and the stacking is done with a forklift. .It seems to me that our work crew is taking forever to do it. Were I a commanding general, I would figure out a better and more efficient way to do it. But, maybe I just don't know what the score is. Ha! It wouldn't be the first time.

I am on what we call the "night shift"—from 3:00 to 11:00 p.m. One can snooze real late each morning. So, a bit of advantage, maybe. Just finished checking a 15-page requisition that had been filled on this floor, and it took me nearly three hours to do it. It proved to be quite a job! When on duty, I wander around to see that the civilians are working, for some of them like to sit and visit. So, I just nose about.

We use this double-sized type to make out requisition and shipping tickets. General notices throughout the Depot make use of this large print. It is easy to read. And, for letters, it really fills a page in a hurry, and one may think a letter is a very long one... So, don't be fooled.

Yes, I received the pants presser, and will use it when needed. Thanks for sending it. And, I must do some more nosing about.

Sept. 10, 1943 San Francisco

The war news has certainly been encouraging. Italy's surrender was expected. This seems to have come so quickly, after the successes in North Africa. The Italians have received thorough beatings. Eisenhower's appeal to them was something different, I thought—that they show their spirit has not been killed, that they sabotage all German activity in Italy, that they not scuttle their fleet, but permit the Alllies to police the Mediterranean with it, etc. I have a hunch that Hitler and Tojo are a bit unhappy. This has been a rather exciting two days, don't you think?

On duty in the Depot until about 11:30 each night, I eat my evening meal at the cafeteria. For sixty cents one can have a very good supper. When I sleep so late, a light lunch somewhere is the other meal for me each day. My Scotch blood likes the reduced expenditures for food... Ha! Ha!

A cafeteria near to our room also has good food at very reasonable price. One of my favorite lunches is vegetable soup, rice pudding, and berry pie—and at cost almost as little as at the Depot. We just can't lose!

Action here at the Depot has picked up this week, and I haven't had lots of time to sit down to write letters. We have received several orders that needed to be expedited, and these have kept me on my feet and on the prowl and on the prod. Really, it is almost refreshing to be busy and to know you are doing something useful. And, our chief officer has asked me to do some special inventorying. He must have heard that I was twice Cherry County's ciphering champion. Ha!

With all the delays to be encountered, our departures for St. Louis will probably not be before the 25th. Of course, I hope I can arrange a return via Omaha—with a day or two at home. Yes!!

Yesterday and today, the sun came out shortly after noon—just bright and warm. Hurrah!

September 13, 1943 San Francisco

Our departure from here will probably be on Monday, the 20th—much sooner than I had guessed. If I can be sent via Omaha, rather then Kansas City, you may see me on the 22nd. Colonel Smythe, our C.O., has requested that I be assigned for here, but he thinks it will be otherwise. Along with the various Depot duties, he wants me to conduct classes in military correspondence, and such, for all the "graded employees" of the depot. He also said something about my being a "training officer."

For the final week, here, I am to be in charge of our first floor—receiving, shipping, and the labor pool. This is going to be a very interesting week—one with much to learn that will be highly practical. I much like and respect our C.O. He thoroughly knows this business, and is a good person and to be admired.

Too much fog and chilliness, again. Humph! But, nice to be able to listen again to some of my favorite radio programs—such as "American Album" and "Hour of Charm."

Sept. 15, 1943 San Francisco

Will be my final letter from SF, and I may be wiring or calling. The four of us plan to leave SF on Saturday. The U.P.'s "Challenger" should get me into Omaha at 10:00 p.m., Monday. Have sent two telegrams—to reach you either at Valentine or at Wood Lake.

So many fellows are losing their lives in Italy, and the battle for that country is just beginning. I'm quite certain that we shall be well into 1945 before this can be ended—even 24 months, yet. My optimism is not high, today. And, this final week has been my best at the depot.

Gee! But I do hope my assignment will land me somewhere in the Midwest—at least not on either coast or in the deep South. Will know before long. We are to report in on the 23rd.

St. Louis

Sept. 24, 1943 St. Louis

Back at this depot, again. And what a treat to have had another three days at home. One of the better things about it is that I do not use any leave time. The fifty fellows in our class are once more here, and some of them think I pull wires to get home, going and coming. But Metz lives here in St. Louis, and he is home all the time we are here. Sometimes, if you are going to get a good break, you have to sort of arrange for it.

How wonderful to have some good, home-cooked meals, again. Eating at cafeterias and restaurants is O.K., but it just lacks the good old touch. Those juicy steaks, shoestring potatoes as only Bin can make, the fresh tomatoes, cukes, and squash straight from the garden, that chocolate cake with the fluffy frosting, and our home made caramel ice cream—Gee!, but I ate until I was miserable, really. Had to laugh, Mother, when you let me know you had expended 38 points for the steaks. It sure was worth it, as far as this soldier boy was concerned. Yessirree!!

Was sorry you had to wait so long for me in Omaha, but the train was over an hour late—as you know. One surprise for you was the picture of Mim, and it arrived in San Francisco the very morning I left. Boy, talk about close connections! She is saving a week of vacation time—to come to Lincoln to meet you. We shall take a look at Christmas, or soon after.

September 26, 1943 St. Louis

Dan Mathisen and I have a room at the "Y"—much less cost than at a hotel. We were lucky to get the room. Quite cool, here, for this corner of the country. Nice! I think the salt air in SF cleared my sinuses. I hope my head stays clear!

Woody Mills, Elmer Metz, and about 18 others already have their orders—two of them heading to N.Y. Port of Embarkation. Yes, some of us will receive overseas assignments. It becomes a matter of sweating it out, and some of us may have to wait several days. Our depot officials find things for us to do, but none of this time counts toward promotion. One must be assigned to a specific unit. This is what I am waiting for. Preferably would be that this war end before we had time to gain promotions.

We saw James Cagney and Humphrey Bogart in "Oklahoma Kid"—a good western, with lots of shooting, etc.

September 29, 1943 St. Louis

Will be eating out with Uncle Arthur, his brother, Al, and sister, Lillian, and the four Lueckes—Ray, Rose, and their two daughters, this evening. Uncle Arthur and I ate at the Statler last evening. Nice to have him here for a day or two. He is going to Springfield, Mo., to see his other brother, George, who used to practice with him in Chadron.

A few more of my class have received their orders, but I am still waiting. I putter around the Depot, but for my purposes it is a sort of dead place. Several of us are just marking time.

We went to see the lawn mower factory where Ray Luecke works. This plant is making plugs for 500-pound bombs, with special machinery obtained from the War Department. It is a busy place, and Ray's explanations were highly interesting and informative.

Dan and I now occupy a much larger and nicer room at this YMCA. Each of us has his own bed. I will no longer be bumping my head on the springs of the bunk overhead, as has been the case. Ha! Our small room had only the double bunk-bed.

Had quite a headache hit me yesterday. I had been doing a lot of close work with inventories, and I think the eye-strain had its impact. My guess is that I need to have my eyes checked, and I probably need a new prescription. We shall see. By later afternoon and off duty after three o'clock, I soon felt just fine.

As for the new pictures, I have marked the three I think are better. Pool your choices, and then we shall order as many of each as we need. It was one thing we accomplished while I was home. Then, send me the bill. This is to be on me!!

October 2, 1943 St. Louis

Still no news. But, I've been asked to check up on the janitorial services here at the Depot. So, I search for dirt on the floors and stairs, and see if I can find dust on things. Those of our class still here are doing all sort of duties.

About three time each day I go to the dispensary and have my nose sprayed and breathe in the fumes to clear my sinuses. It seems to be doing its job. The depot's surgeon and I have become somewhat chummy, and he pemits me to use this typewriter.

Those of us who remain, as yet, without orders remain somewhat perplexed. Here we are, day after day, receiving our salaries, and doing so little. There has to be some deep confusion somewhere, and it has to be up above. Oh, well! The war is progressing in the right direction.

Somebody somewhere must know what is to be done. These set-backs do distress me, for there is always such loss of life!

October 4, 1943 St. Louis

Well, yesterday was another Sunday, and I seemed to be a bit lonesome. So it is. Did attend an Episcopal communion service, and the sermon was a good one. Most Sunday evenings, I enjoy listening to Frank Munn and the All Girl Orchestra.

Saw Bette Davis and Paul Lucas in "Watch on the Rhine." This is one you do not want to miss! The acting is simply as good as any I have ever seen! No war action, but the war is always in the "background." I sat through it almost twice. It is gripping! Also very good is Wallace Beery in "Salute to the Marines."

No orders, and I am getting a bit restless. I wonder if some new units are to be formed and if we are being saved. Some day it may make sense. I am not comfortable with this uncertainty.

And, Moosie, you were worrying that you might not be able to get the extra sugar for canning. Rose Luecke and Lill Griot were concerned about this. My guess is that your needs will be met. Produce from the "victory gardens" is simply too important to our total war effort!

It does seem to me that there is a good bit of "smoke" in the air, here. Maybe I am missing that foggy air of San Francisco. But, I do not want a sinus problem to develop. I just keep on inhaling the spray. And, I get a kick from the song, "Pistol Packin' Mama."

October 5, 1943 St. Louis

Have placed a call to you, person to person (Mary Mickey), but circuits are full, and do not know how long the delay. May still get through this evening. I have news, for our orders came through, and here is the dope. My address is now 31st Medical Depot Company, Ft. Lewis, Washington.

This sort of company is to establish a medical supply depot somewhat near a front line and to issue medicines and aid materiel to forward medical stations and to the aid personnel of the various military units. Forward hospitals will turn to such depots. So, we are destined to serve overseas. Our training, as a company, will be intense and will take from three to six months. It is doubtful that a supply depot of our sort should ever be under fire. I much doubt that you will hear from me that there is so little to do. Ha!

There is another Med Dep Co to assemble at Ft. Lewis, and about four of their lieutenants are in our class. The other three from our class who will be my cohorts are Charlie Teague, from North Carolina, Russ Peterson, who hails from Minneapolis and is a typical Swede, and Ken Lane. We shall be traveling together under the same order, and will go from here to St. Paul, and then via Northern Pacific or Great Northern to Tacoma, Washington—about 15 miles from Ft. Lewis. I think we pull out tomorrow.

While in chow line at the cafeteria last evening, I met a fellow from Sidney, Nebraska, and I think his name is Ehlers. We decided to go see the stage-play, "Doughgirls." Our fifth-row seats cost $2.80, and we just laughed until our sides ached. It is a scream! The plot deals with the crowded conditions in Washington, D.C.

Willkie is to speak in St. Louis, and I should like to hear him—but no chance. I sense that certain Republicans are trying to scuttle him for 1944. We shall see.

Just visited with you on the telephone, but will mail this—just the same. Mim is saving a week of her vacation time, and I hope we can arrange a rendezvous in Lincoln. Do let her hear from you. Gee! But we seemed to get a lot said, didn't we

Thanks for forwarding the letter from Archie Wayne. You asked about the number he had put after my name—0-1547072. This is my "serial number." It is for identification purpose, and is nearly always used for overseas. It is not absolutely necessary, but does assure identity.

Two of our gang had just departed for seven-day leaves, but they are making immediate changes in plans. Some had hoped we might be assigned to new "general hospitals" being organized near some larger cities. As for me, I am not displeased. In less than six months our company should be enjoying a little boat-ride to somewhere. And, once most of our training period is over, we should be getting some leave time. So, I should be getting home for a few days—maybe to greet Mim in Lincoln.

Ft. Lewis, Washington

October 9, 1943 Tacoma, Washington

Out of St. Louis on the 6th, and to St. Paul the following morning. Between switches, I had time to eat a hearty breakfast of good pancakes. Then by Northern Pacific, and nearly two days to get here. We were greeted by dense fog. Our orders had specified that we were to have "no delays" or "leaves" en route. So, we just came right along—with quite a bit of snoozing and a lot of bridge, and Charlie Teague and I proved to be rather formidable partners—Yessirree! Our meals were pleasant pastimes and catered in the diner.

We shall have no more than a cadre when we first assemble, and so many new persons to know. We do not think we are to be a large company. But, we have at least four second lieutenants. Ha! And, we will be able to begin to count time toward promotions.

October 11, 1943 Ft. Lewis, Washington

Good to sleep on an army cot with a spring mattress, and without the motion of a train. And, we are surrounded by all things green. This is a scenic region. It has been raining most of the time since our arrival. Flowers are lovely.

Our commanding officer has not arrived, and some of the cadre. But, I am most favorably impressed by the men I've met. If this caliber of person is indication of our "make-up," then we are in for some good times.

We have a minimum of ninety days of special training and instruction ahead. It is likely that we shall be attached to an army, to set up an advanced station for medical supplies. We really do not know. We shall be busy—with much work ahead. No doubt about it!! Well, we shall see!

Our second in command is a Captain Earl Grove—very pleasant. He's from back east, maybe Pa. or Ohio, and definitely not regular army.

October 13, 1943 Ft. Lewis

For rations, we are attached to Section III of the Station Hospital, here, and we eat in the dining hall. Furnishings for our rooms come from hospital supply. We have just the minimum of furniture and necessities. Our meals are very good. Rumor is that we will be relocating soon within the camp. It will not make much difference, for our training will be quite intense.

A wonderfully clear day, and we can see Mount Rainier—quite a distance to our southeast, but looks near enough to reach out and touch. It is a beautiful peak! Could be nearly 20 miles away.

We are starting from "scratch"—as for our getting organized and for our training program. We will be pressed for time. Our commanding officer, Lt. Col. Joe N. Cole is now here, and the pace of things should pick up. No doubt about it, we are a new organization. And, we have a couple ping-pong tables, etc.

October 19, 1943 Ft. Lewis

Seems to me that I am doing nothing other than to work on training schedules. And the weather just switches from clouds and drizzle to sunshine. It just keeps us guessing. I am tired, but think it is response to just thinking about all that we must accomplish in preparations for an overseas assignment.

I need several training manuals that are somewhere in the closet of my bedroom—on a shelf, maybe in a box, even on the floor in a corner. But wherever, I need them. One, a white one, is entitled—"Army, Navy General Specifications for Packaging and Crating for Overseas Shipment." It has about six file-holes punched in it. Also, please send the pair of good fatigues—the green ones, and not the ones mended and patched.

We made a run into Olympia—a small town of about 15,000. It didn't seem to be overrun with soldiers. We went to see Ethel Waters and Rochester in "Cabin in the Sky." It is a different sort of production, but I thoroughly enjoyed it.

We still guess that we will be here about three months, to complete our initial training and preparation. I've been working on "plans" and it is 12:45 of tomorrow. Must hit the hay. Six o'clock will come too soon. And, I feel a bit lonesome and sorry for myself. Oh, well!

October 22, 1943 Ft. Lewis

We are moving to another part of this camp, so drop all reference to Section III, Station Hospital from my address. As you may guess, I am our "plans and training officer." Have the program quite well together—subjects for study and who will do the instructing and supervision. It proved to be a tedious job. Have had to requisition the manuals needed for study—a few boxes of them altogether when they arrive.

This damp and cool weather finds me in need of some warmer stuff. So, please send me my woolen underwear, the "longies"—and I also need that pair of army shoes on the closet floor. My head is hanging low with shame, for that manual on packaging and crating is here. I had it tucked beneath other notebooks. I hope you haven't spent much time looking for it. Our classes of instruction and training have been underway for a few days, now.

Haven't been to an Episcopal church service, here, but hope to make it this Sunday. Col. Cole is a member of the church, and we have talked about going to Tacoma for a service.

Well, it has been a rough two days, but did relax a bit last evening—went to see Lionel Barrymore in "Dr. Gillespie's Criminal Case." An excellent production!

Of course, I have to take my term to be Officer of the Day . This means that the checking of guards and security leaves me with few hours for good sleeping—maybe four, at the most. The men on duty wear sidearms, and so must the OD. We sure hope we never have to use these pistols. It is part of this training for overseas duty.

October 26, 1943 Ft. Lewis

So much drizzle and mist, and my sinuses are acting up—quite a bit of drainage. If I get a bit stuffed up, I'll have to rig up some sort of device for steaming.

I do so much enjoy that little radio. So often I go to sleep with it on, but no one has complained about it. Two of the stations have such good music. I keep it soft. Ho! Ho!

The rain stopped long enough for a softball game—our men versus the officers. It was a rare game—29 to 3, in favor of the EM. Ha! We poor officers—Oh, woe!

Saw the movie, "Young Ideas"—with Herbert Marshall, Mary Astor, and Susan Peter. The story was free from any war atmosphere, and several good laughs along the way. And, have I ever been reviewing training films! Some of them are proving to be very useful.

The pamphlets, fatigues, and cap arrived in A-1 shape. But, you forgot something! You didn't put in anything to eat! I feel neglected and expect a shipment real soon. Ahem!

I think I shall put my calls through "collect" from now on. Then, we shall balance our books periodically. To make a call from a pay-phone, one must have no less than about five dollars in change—quarters, dimes and nickels. If we visit longer than the minimum, then it is back to the pocket for more coins. It will be so much easier just to reverse the charges. O.K.?

Almost a year and a half that I've been in the army. And, I've seen quite a bit of the country.

October 29, 1943 Ft. Lewis

We have had a couple of clear days, with sunshine, even. The first day of clear weather, we had a six-mile training hike. It really proved to be enjoyable, and even the men said they had a good time. Much of it was along a clear stream, with trees overhead and with homes and yards and some livestock to see. Our next hike will probably be in a drizzle and fog. We shall see. And, did we have some magnificent views of Mt. Rainier. Have been told it is over 50 miles away. I will have to get a map.

Quite a bit of discomfort above my right eye. I fear this sinus problem may return. One thing for sure, I can't blame it on dust in the air.
Deliveries of airmail have been delayed for a day or two. We understand that storms over the Rockies have kept planes grounded.

You keep asking me to get another photo taken. For each day, including Saturday, we are on duty until five o'clock. With this training program to be underway, I have not found a day free from schedule. But, give me time! Have had my nose to the grindstone adjusting this coming week's schedule, and it is done. Yeah! Yeah!

October 31, 1943 Ft. Lewis

Today is Halloween. No spooks, here, that I know of. Just hope this nice weather will hold for a while. Am certain the drizzle will return before long.

Would certainly have enjoyed being at the wedding. Too, the pheasant hunting at Randolph would have been lots of fun.

Went into Tacoma to church this morning and had quite a time to find an Episcopal church. It is a nice church, but I didn't care for the minister. The people were so friendly, but not many there. I was the only service man present. Will seek out the other Episcopal church some Sunday. I had felt so at home with the church in Abilene, and maybe I became a bit spoiled. H-m-m-m-m?

We have eight new typewriters for our office. Six of them are Underwoods. I prefer Royals. Just seems to me that the action isn't quite as smooth with these Underwoods. But, who am I to be the judge?

November 2, 1943 Ft. Lewis

I do like to listen to Lowell Thomas. He is quite optimistic The conference in Moscow indicates some major happenings. Interesting to note that Badoglio had requested Victor Immanuel to resign. Italy's government hardly functions.

Went to an officers' clothing outlet store and bought my short overcoat. These "beavers" are not being made anymore, and I was fortunate to find one to fit. Rudy Kelemen, a lst Lt., says it "looks great" on me, but it makes me appear to be about as broad as a bear. It cost 29 smackeroos. This should complete any purchases for clothes.

That piece of wedding cake, from Mary Elizabeth's wedding, arrived in the Royal Baking Powder can, and it was as fresh as could be—and was it ever good! I gobbled it in a hurry and didn't put even a crumb under my pillow to sleep on. Ha!

Our mail continues to be quite irregular, and airmail seems to make no difference as to length of time to get here and to be delivered… But, it all arrives—even if eventually.

A different sort of meal served us today—made entirely from dehydrated foods. We had ham and eggs, applesauce, bean soup, tomato juice, milk, cheese, and butter. Once overseas, we may have to depend upon dehydrated foods, and our cooks must know what to do with it all. Could be more than just interesting.

Seemed to be so very busy, today. We'll have an eight-mile hike tomorrow.

November 4, 1943 Ft. Lewis

Was OD yesterday and last night. So, only about four hours of sleep. It's only nine o'clock this evening and I can hardly keep my eyes open. I'll really do some catching up on the shut-eye.

Our eight-mile hike took us to Steilecoom, near the place where the large bridge across the narrows of the Sound was blown down by the wind about three years ago. Something about its construction was faulty, and the wind from just a certain angle caused the structure to begin to sway—and it just collapsed. Some of the approaches to the bridge are still visible, and a good bit of the cement base. Remember, we saw pictures in the paper. The scenery is beautiful, and this is so different from the heat and sand we had at Barkeley and the heat at Shelby.

We've been here a month, and it hardly seems possible. We are now really functioning as a company, and with each one doing his thing. We have so many splendid NCOs. Our men are really pitching in, and we are fortunate to have them. So few of them are a bit problematic.

The sinus pressure has cleared, and what a relief! I think our stretch of clear days turned the tide. But, the rain is coming down, again, like cats and dogs!

The war news is quite favorable. The collapse of the "little Rommel line" in Italy wasn't expected. If Roosevelt's optimism is realistic, the results of the Moscow Conference should be more than just promising. Maybe things are progressing toward a lasting peace.

Will use my new picture for Christmas presents. It will probably bankrupt me to pay for the prints.

November 8, 1943 Ft. Lewis

Sunday, again, and I'd much like to go to Seattle to look up the Clarks and to have a rendezvous with Jim Tische. So, must make some plans.

Went in to town to the other Episcopal church, had communion, and the people were so friendly. The choir was about the worst I have ever heard. There were two tenors, two altos, about 8 sopranos, and no bassos. The tenors were elderly and with raspy voices, and one of them persisted in singing a bit under pitch—always flat. The altos and the sopranos were never quite on the same beat, and seemed to engage in a sort of tug-o-war. Two of the sopranos sang with much enthusiasm and kept sliding onto their tones. To me, it was just funny, and when they finished their anthem, I think I was grinning like some sort of Cheshire cat. The saving grace was their earnest sincerity. I was seated next to the central aisle, the line of march for the choir as we sang the closing hymn. One of the women had heard me sing as they recessed, and came right to me after the service. She wanted me to join the choir. No chance, because they practice Thursday evening, and we have a meeting of officers and non commissioned officers each Tuesday and Thursday evening. But, it was nice to be asked.

Was almost under the weather, yesterday. We had some sort of sausage for breakfast, and it may have brought on some sort of indigestion. The nausea never reached an upheaval, but I was put to considerable discomfort.

A heavy frost last night, and most of the flowers are now gone. The weather had cleared, and the temperature took a sharp drop. And when it clears, we do have this marvelous view of Rainier. It is almost a perfect peak. I'd enjoy a drive through Rainier National Park, for it must be very scenic and beautiful.

The news keeps promising. Hitler has to be getting a bit uneasy!

Put in a call to Lincoln, and the operator estimated a six-hour delay. So, we shall see. Gee!! I will probably cancel should there be further delay, for I do not want your telephone to ring after 9:30, your time. Again, we shall see.

November 12, 1943 Ft. Lewis

Not much done about Armistice Day. There are not enough hours in a day. Seems to me that it is get up, eat, work, eat, work, eat, work, and go back to sleep some more. If this clear weather could hold out, I think this would not be a bad place to spend a winter.

Had a ten-mile hike a couple days ago, and the men just tramped along in fine style. Yesterday, the special adventure was to perform all the antics to go through an obstacle course. One way and another, we are to get toughened to meet the challenges of the future. We'll make it. These men of ours are such good sports. I think they are, collectively, an unusual group!

Received the box, today, and have we been gobbling dream bars, nuts, etc. We turn ourselves into magicians, and just make things disappear—as if by magic. Yessirree!

November 15, 1943 Ft. Lewis

Our officers' quarters are about at they were in Camp Lee, with each chamber about ten by ten and furnished with cot, chair, table, and clothes-rack with a couple of shelves. 'Tis not ritzy, but comfortable and cozy. Each cubicle has no ceiling, other than the roof overhead. So, we share a sort of military togetherness. Each of us continues to live, somewhat, out of his footlocker.

We officers continue to eat at Hospital III, and we pay $10 for a thirty-meal ticket. The ticket is punched only when you eat. The hospital also furnishes the mess for the men, and I have not heard complaints. We are frequently treated to "field rations," and there is a logic to this.

Was again OD, so not much sleep last night. One must inspect the guards about every two hours, and this keeps them alert. This is all a part of the training and of the disciplining for overseas responsibilities. Even with this diversion, there is a sameness to each day's routine. We are engaged in sequences of classes. We officers are instructing the men—in the areas of our specializations. Some of our Noncoms are highly knowledgeable, and we make good use of them—with several doing the actual instructing.

Did much enjoy the Ritz Brothers in "Never a Dull Moment." They are, at times, quite funny.

Have reached Jim Tische via telephone, and he is coming to see me next weekend. And, have also visited with Pearl Hitchcock Clark, and she has invited me to have Thanksgiving dinner with them in Seattle. So, some special arrangements lie ahead. Nice! But, nothing is certain, for Col. Cole has some quirks about things.

An identification bracelet would be a perfect Christmas gift—just what I need. Be sure to have my serial number recorded on the underside—0-1547072. This will make it more expensive. Ha! Ha!

A recent graduate of the OCS at Camp Barkeley was assigned to the station hospital, here, and he came over to chat awhile. The final class is about to graduate, and the school is closing. He said something about "reserve commissions"—to be activated only upon assignment, with one's enlisted rank to continue in the meantime. Am not sure I have this straight, but maybe we have an oversupply of MAC officers. We do not have a shortage, here. This, I do know. Ho! Ho!

The box of Christmas cards arrived, and many thanks. I shall make good use of them. Put the cost on my bill, and we shall make our periodic settlement, and it is not far to the bank for you to go with my check. Neat, huh?

We just received notice that we are to be inspected—to see, I guess, the degree to which our training has been effective. Maybe we shall find out just what we are supposed to be. Oh, well!

November 17, 1943 Ft. Lewis

The fog is hanging around, again. I think it is entering my mind. I know it does each time I am OD. Shortage of sleep just seems to leave me out in the mist, somewhere. Could be that that is where I've been a lot of the time.

The mist has now turned to rain, and tomorrow we go on a daylight bivouac—have to set up a camp and then tear it down and move to a new site. It will be just more fun if we have to take a good soaking. We shall see.

Saw Pat O'Brien in the "Iron Major"—about Frank Cavanaugh, and a good portrayal of this football coach. With one of the camp theaters close by, I can slip over and in and out when time for a break permits.

War news not encouraging. To open Italy and the Mediterranean, the price is so costly, and we have been overly optimistic. Also, the Russians have slowed somewhat.

Mim has raved about my new picture. I am now on display. Again, thank you for sending it, all framed, etc. Keep track of the expense.

November 20, 1943 Ft. Lewis

Am waiting to listen to Lowell Thomas, and I am so sleepy. My peepers just do not want to keep open. Ha!

Had one of my headaches this morning. Maybe it was in anticipation of the booster shots we were to receive this afternoon. One was for tetanus and other for typhoid, and my right arm is just a wee bit sore.

(A p.s. added before mailing the next morning noted that I had slept from 9:30 to 9:30—around the clock!)

November 24, 1943 Ft. Lewis

Am out of airmail envelopes. So, slower mail, today. It probably won't make much difference.

We have nearly finished the box of Whitman's Samplers and also a box of chocolates sent from Rose Griot Luecke. She has been so very nice to me, and I did so much enjoy meeting all Uncle Arthur's folk in St. Louis. She also sent me a box of nuts and cookies. We put our goodies out on a counter, and sometimes on a table in our Hqs' office. It all disappears in short order.

We went on an overnight bivouac yesterday, and it was cold. We officers bedded down in two large tents—hauled out in a couple vehicles. We had cots, mattresses, and our bedrolls—along with extra blankets. I may have had three hours of restful sleep. The men put up their pup tents, with two to each tent. Their bedrolls were on the ground, and I doubt if many did much sleeping. But, this is training! We hiked the nine miles to the place, and then on foot to return.

Am OD today, and will be free to go to the Clarks for Thanksgiving. Actually, our roster, when put up, had me as OD for Thanksgiving Day. But, I made a switch and am free to be in Seattle. But I have to make the rounds tonight, and will be fortunate to have four hours of sleep. Maybe I shall just have to put my head on the table and take a quick snooze while we are eating dinner. Or, maybe my face will just fall into the gravy. Ha!

We shall be needing our birth certificates. Mine is in a stationery box, with a photo of ducks on the top. The certificate is in a "State of Nebraska" envelope. Please send it to me. The box is either in a dresser drawer, or on the shelf in my closet.

Thanks for writing to Mim. She will feel welcomed should she come to meet me in Lincoln—once this training is over and before we head overseas.

November 26, 1943 Ft. Lewis

The day after Thanksgiving, and I still feel overstuffed. As OD until after reveille, yesterday, I had delays which prevented me from catching the 8:00 bus for Tacoma. So, I took the 9:00 bus into Tacoma, a 10:00 bus to Seattle—to arrive at ll:25. Called the Clarks and followed instructions with respect to which street car and which stop for descent, and met Jean. We then buzzed right over to the house. The minute we opened the door, Pearl's little jaw just started to wag, and she never stopped talking. She is a riot, and she is a cute little thing. No problem to understand, Mother, why she was always one of your favorites. She is a chatterbox!

Jane Thurtle joined us, and we had a Lincoln reunion. There was a lot of chatter about Willards and P.E.O. Mr. Clark said he had P.E.O. and Willard stuffed down his neck for the past 36 years.
Ha! Ha! We two men couldn't get an oar in sideways. "Bud" informed me that he always thought you two "Hanna gals" were darned good musicians. Jean is a nurse, R.N., and works at Seattle General Hospital. Jane is training to become a dietitian, and had to return to work at six o'clock. We managed to get in a few games of bridge—after our return from a Swedish smorgasbord.
As for that smorgasbord—a minimum of 30 choices for hors d'oeuvres, and I filled on them. Then came the turkey dinner, and we were all in pain. So good! Mr. Clark is away most of the time as a salesman, and Pearl did not want a lot of food to be left on hand. So, we went to the smorgasbord.

I called Jim Tische, and he met me at the bus station at 10:00, and it was just a treat to see him again. Connections were right on time, and I was back in camp by 11:45, and to bed shortly after midnight. Today I feel as if on top of the world.

The box of Whitman's arrived today, and each morsel makes mighty fine chewing. And you have had such good luck hitting the pheasants at Randolph, and we shall have some more good chewing on them, when I get home. Am going to put in my bid for my two weeks' leave—to be around January 15—probably a few days later. I sure hope that Mim can get to Lincoln—if her bosses will permit her to take a week of her vacation for 1944. They insisted she use up the vacation days for 1943 before year's end. Mim has never eaten pheasant.

Well, I have been an officer, now, for six months. We second lieutenants have our eyes on the possibilities of promotions. For the five of us, three could soon be moved up to be 1st Lts. We shall see. H-m-m-m-m-m?

November 29, 1943 Ft. Lewis

Rains seem to be holding off, but it is cloudy and humid. We have about two weeks of training ahead, and no one seems to know just what lies ahead. We could be attached to a large unit to participate in some sort of maneuvers. My hunch is that we will head for overseas, but not until well into next year.

Had roast chicken for our noon meal, today, but it should have stayed in the oven longer. It was tough chewing and gave us quite a work-out. But, the pie was unusually good—basically lemon, but with shavings of orange peel and shreds of pineapple. And, the crust was flaky. These cooks do their "things" just right—most of the time.

A box of cookies from Rose Luecke. A bit of a mystery to me—all of this kindness. We have made "quick work" out of them. I shall keep her informed and thanked.

Several are requesting to have leaves for the Christmas holiday, but I'm going to hold out for after January 15. I could be left with an empty bag. I much appreciate your writing Mim. She is beginning to get excited about the possibilities of her trip to Lincoln.

To come home by train, it will take about fifty hours each way—a loss of four days. So, I'm going to check the air schedules. Reservations should be much easier to get, once we are into late January. So, will keep you posted.

Some are speculating upon an early collapse of Hitler's regime, even by early spring. This will not happen, and my guess is as good as the next.

Did see and have a visit, today, with Mother Brown. She is just one of the loveliest of persons, and did we ever review some of the events that occurred at NWU and in the Crescent House. What a treat for me! Her daughter works in one of the Pxs.

December 1, 1943 Ft. Lewis

Just keep thinking about those pheasants in the freezer! My mouth keeps watering. It will be great to be home for Bin's birthday. We can celebrate together! Just more fun, and I do so much hope that Mim can be with us. Keep writing to her. Col. Cole sees no reason which should interfere with our plans. But, orders from higher up could change everything. But the furloughs for the men and our leaves should hold OK.

Yesterday, we went through an obstacle course, with machine guns firing live bullets about 36 inches above our heads. Of course, we were crawling along on our stomachs, and then wriggling along on our backs when beneath the low-strung barbed wire. This course was about 100 yards long, and we were given no more than ten minutes to make it. We were huffing and puffing and covered with dust. One thing for sure, we did keep our heads down!

We had pan-fried chicken this evening, and it was done to a turn. We were hungry, apparently, for we licked the platters clean. Yessirree!

Doesn't seem possible that just 24 days, yet, until Christmas. And, two months from now I should be home.

I should like to know what is going on at this current conference—between Roosevelt, Stalin, Churchill, and Chiang. It has no parallel in history—that I know of. Something momentous must be in the making. The courage which our leaders are showing must be causing Hitler and his mob some profound concerns. We await announcements. One thing should be certain, that we shall make no "peace deal" with Germany. Once Germany is taken care of, there will remain Japan. It is going to be a good bit of time, yet.

Received another letter from Rose Luecke, and she addresses me as "Dear David." I have to grin, for in St. Louis, except for Uncle Arthur, all the Griots at first called me "Lt. Mickey." Finally, I put my foot down! Uncle Arthur just chuckled to his heart's content. They are grand folk. I wish I could have had more time with Uncle Arthur. I hinted to him that I didn't think it too wise to be quitting Chadron. We shall see.

Raining like the dickens, today, and we have an overnight bivouac tomorrow. We posted about fifty promotions for the men yesterday and today. We officers have had several meetings, and we had some sharp disagreements. Of course, those receiving promotions were delighted, and some of our men were openly very disappointed. But, our Table of Organization has limitations.
Several openings remain for future action. As for us officers, the Colonel will have almost sole control. We have five 2nd Lts, and the TO calls for no more than three advancements to 1st Lt. So, again, we shall just have to wait.

December 3, 1943 Ft. Lewis

We have had rain and more rain. We should be turning into ducks. We had our overnight bivouac. Temperature has not been too low, but it was a challenge to keep dry. We slept in our pup tents, and I was snug and warm. But, I seem to have come down with a cold, and am always a bit anxious about a sinus flare-up. So, I have taken a couple APC—aspirin, phenacetin, caffeine—capsules.

About time for news, and I am eager to know what Lowell Thomas has to say about the big conference.

December 6, 1943 Ft. Lewis

Yesterday was not a good day, definitely one of a different sort. I was somewhat flat on my back with a temperature of 102.4. Didn't feel well on Friday—felt a cold coming on. So, took an APC and went to bed. Felt better Saturday and went in to Tacoma to do a bit of shopping. Had supper with Charlie and Adelaide Teague, and we went to see Bob Hope in "Hold Everything." Returned to camp and signed in at 11:15.

Had planned to into town for church and communion. Got up about 7:30, felt dizzy, and went back to bed. Then got up, went to the office, and joined Rudy for dinner. But, two bites, and had to leave. Did I feel hot! My lips burned, my back ached, and I went back to bed, with temperature at 102.4. Rudy brought me two APC capsules, which I took about 8:30, and drank about a quart of water. Dozed off, and awakened about 9:30—just wringing wet and melting away. Whew! I cooled down, and at 10:00 my temperature was normal.

Well, my bed needed changing. Got that accomplished . Also, I was OD, and had informed our CQ of my illness and to keep me posted were something to need my attention. Nothing took place.

So, this morning I checked reveille, took the reports, felt no twinges of illness—but not much pep. And, temperature was normal. This was a strange illness. And, now you know the lurid details. Ha!

Glad you found the birth certificate. Must begin to address my Christmas cards.

December 8, 1943 Ft. Lewis

Two years ago, yesterday, the Japanese attacked Pearl Harbor, and the world has been upset since.

We had a fifteen-mile hike, yesterday, and I didn't seem to have any difficulties after my bout with that flu bug. Really, I was no worse for wear. Some others have really been laid up with this bug, and on sick call for three or four days—with fever, aches and pains, stiffness, etc. These longer marches may cause me to have a bit of ache in my right hip, but no problem with my feet. When I took my physical before being in this man's army, I was told my flat feet would give me trouble. Well, whatever, my feet have never been a problem. So much for medical opinion, eh?

Tomorrow, we go out for another over-night bivouac, and we have a clear day forecast. Today has actually been a dry day.

The Col. continues to be agreeable to approval of leaves and furloughs. So, my coming home after the 15th of January is still in the offing. Mim has yet to clear the air with her bosses.

December 10, 1943 Ft. Lewis

Last night's bivouac was a cold one—temperature, here, dropped to about 27. I crawled into my pup tent, with the square of tarp for its floor, and nestled into my bag and bedroll. But I could not get warm and could not get to sleep! About

2:30 in the morning I remembered having read that a person loses a lot of body heat through the top of the head. So, I wrapped my field jacket around my head, warmed up, went to sleep, and didn't awaken until nearly all others were up and at it. Well, I think I may have learned something.

Yes, I do listen to Lowell Thomas. Also, Frank Munn's program is one of my favorites; but, so many of his songs are so nostalgic and cause one to dwell upon fond memories. He is good!

It appears that I should make it home about January 19. We shall see!

December 13, 1943 Ft. Lewis

In town to church, yesterday. We have much fog and cold, and I wore my beaver coat, and is it warm! I guess I much prefer the drier air in Nebraska, for this combination of cold and high humidity seems to cut right through me.

I keep thinking about getting home—eating some of those pheasants and getting out the freezer and having some home-made ice cream. The saliva is flowing! Ha! Ha!

Was out much of yesterday afternoon driving around in a jeep. We are to have a training hike of 20 miles, and purpose was to plan the route. We are to avoid certain areas for these marches, and we have to do some angling, here and there.

We will soon be shifting to a different part of camp, and our officers' quarters are not going to be so nice. Our cubicles will be entirely open in front, not like little rooms as now. We shall be sharing the same mess with the men, but our cooks have been better at it, often, than those of the station hospital. The men may be happier with their barracks, and we shall be near one of the largest of the camp's PXs. I guess we are to be in one of the older areas of this camp.

And, Moosie, this is your 59th birthday. Have wanted to call you, but the long delay just ruled out the trying. So, when you read this, you will know I have wished you a HAPPY BIRTHDAY!

December 17, 1943 Ft. Lewis

We are now in our "new" quarters, and it took two days to make the move. Our cubicles are open to the central passage, but we have curtains that can be pulled across. So, we do have just a smidgen of privacy. Also, each of us has a small table, and this is an extra we didn't have. Our latrine is outside the building, and this will be inconvenient and a bit cold now that winter is upon us. For shaving and morning wash and brushing of teeth, we have inside sinks with mirrors. For heat, we have some coal-burning stoves, which our rotating orderlies are to keep fired up. Our pending departure brought this forced move. We are not all that happy about it, but some of us remember Camp Barkeley and then feel better about it. Ha! Ha!

Have received several Christmas packages, and would like to save them for Christmas Eve. But, most contain food. We are enjoying each other's goodies.

We are to continue with our separate officer's mess—about three companies involved. We had understood that we would share with the men, and I was personally looking forward to it. I think our company cooks do a far better job of it than those that come from the Station Hospital.

Had my hair cut, yesterday. Delmar Haught is one of our men, now a PFC after promotion, and he does our barbering. He is good at it. No one needs to go elsewhere.

Jim Tische plans to come from Seattle to Tacoma, Sunday, and we shall go to church, have lunch, and then see a movie. It will be great to see him again.

Have made my reservations to come home. Travel will be by United. Am not sure as to my hour of departure, but I'll leave Tacoma on the 17th for a night flight into Omaha—could even be arriving at 1:30 a.m. But, my guess is that my departure will be a later one, with arrival at 7:45 a.m. The trip takes about 12 hours by plane. To come by train would entail more than 50 hours. So, we gain about three days if to come by plane. I will return on the 30th. So, we can make some plans. My fare costs $174, plus tax. So, prepare ye the way! And, Mim's boss has agreed to her taking a week's vacation in January. Howzabout that!!

I'll be OD Christmas Eve, and will be making the rounds during the night. But, since I will be going no where, it really makes no difference.

The bracelet arrived, and it is beautiful—just what I want. Will be removing two or three links. It just couldn't be nicer. Thank you! And your packages of goodies, along with those from Cybo, Rose Luecke, Mrs. Hodgson, and others. Altogether, we have been nearly buried alive. We plan to have a party on Christmas Day, and it has been my job to be chair of our planning committee.

Reports are about Winston Churchill and his battle with pneumonia. Boy! We just can't do without him. I wish it were Hitler who was sick.

Am very sleepy. Was OD through last night. So, not much sleep. With a few on Christmas leaves, the rest of us find this OD business swinging around more often than usual. But my turn to be away lies ahead. So, it evens out.

December 19, 1943 Ft. Lewis

We've just had quite a change in our training procedures. As Plans and Training Officer, I have had to do a good bit of figuring and parceling out of personnel, and it has been taking a lot of time—with much communicating. All but about 12 of our men are now working with Medical and Quartermaster supply units. They are getting in on some very good experiences, and this has largely solved some problems for us. I have two men, Pfcs—Privates First Class—who are simply marvelous. All I need to do is to suggest that we have a problem to solve or a schedule to prepare, and they put their heads together and lay it out. I hope that they will receive another stripe on their sleeves come our next round of promotions.

Was in town (Tacoma) by ten this morning, and met Jim Tische at the North Coast Stages bus depot. We went to church, and then to the Winthrop Hotel for dinner. We chewed on turkey, and just visited like mad. He had the latest news from Wood Lake, and we certainly stirred up some wonderful remembrances. He and Francis are very different. He continues to work in the shipyards, and he wants to take some classes at Washington University. But, I suggested he not get involved with college work, but to work, save his money, and then hit college when this war is over. He is a great kid. We then went to a movie.

Back in camp, and I'm listening to Frank Munn and "The Hour of Charm." His singing makes me a bit homesick. Rudy, Charlie, and I are going to play some pinochle. We have had several hard fought and cut-throat sessions, and we do have fun. They are two good eggs.

Did so much appreciate Don's getting roses for me—for the birthday. Be sure to keep track of what I owe. Ha! My priority for the trip home will be only a 4, and I could get bumped. So, we must just hope that it will all work out as we want.

December 23, 1943 Ft. Lewis

Just about the same from here as for the past two or three days. The fog has been terrible. I do not know, yet, the days for my reservations to come home, but will keep you informed.

Have opened all my Christmas packages, but have left all the non food parcels unwrapped. This I shall wait until tomorrow evening—Christmas Eve. We have been sharing our good stuff!

We shall be having a big dinner, and we will be having a party with the gang of the 30th Med Depot Company. Several of our men are home on Christmas furloughs.

This $50 check should take care of what I owe. I leave the accounting up to you folks "at home."

Have been keeping my ears to the news about this pending strike of the railroad workers. My sympathies have settled with Labor, for the five brotherhoods have done all they could to get their grievances heard, and the "big wigs" have just turned their deaf ears. Too many millions have been flowing into the pockets of the few!

We've been out to the pistol range. When ODs, we have to wear a side arm. So, we should know how to use it if necessary. I'd have no problem with my old 12-gauge shotgun. We all fired our 100 shots, and my score was 79. The weapon was a 45 cal. I doubt if I could qualify to be a "marksman."

Mim writes that she is battling the flu bug.

December 24, 1943 Ft. Lewis

Here it is, Christmas Eve. Knowing that I will probably be home in late January has kept me from descending into deep doldrums!

At 10:00 I opened my packages. The sterling identification bracelet is just what I wanted. Of course, the dill pickles, jelly, little red-waxed cheese, and the fruit cake are already partially devoured. The candy from Miller and Paines, the roasted nuts, and the three linen handkerchiefs have been somewhat devoured (not the handkerchiefs—Ha!). Blanche Hawthorne, from Oshkosh, send me Lloyd Douglas's THE ROBE. From Lill Griot and the Lueckes came cashews and a box of this nice army stationery. Cybo and Pat send me a cribbage board and two decks of cards, with a little khaki packet to keep the decks in. From the Chadron Griots came the cutest little calendar. Three bars of Old Spice soap came from the Tisches. Mim sent a fruit cake, a fancy little comb and file set, and a lovely pair of pigskin gloves. From Aunt Yippee came a box of cookies, and nearly all gone.

Well, this about does it. We put our eatables out on a table, and several of the men have passed through to share in the eating. And, tomorrow we will have our big party. And, this evening it is raining cats and dogs.

Listened to Lionel Barrymore play Scrooge, the other evening. He is really "something else."And, Roosevelt's speech,, today, was quite assuring in many respects. He did sound confident.

Would be wonderful were this war to be over by next Christmas. I do not think so! But, we can always hope!

December 27, 1943 Ft. Lewis

We had a top-notch Christmas party with the 30th. Will be sending you a copy of the program which, I think, our men, Donaldson and Thirlby, put together. I don't want to lose it. The menu went right down the line—Turkey Broth, Waldorf Salad, Roast Turkey and Dressing, Mashed Potatoes and Giblet Gravy, Creamed Peas, Sweet Mixed Pickles, Cranberry Sauce and Ripe Olives, Mince Pie and Ice Cream, Coffee, Salted Nuts, and Candy.

Listed as guests were the officers and wives, including Lt. and Mrs. David H. Mickey. The wives of several of the men were also guests. Col. Cole was on leave and not present.

Am not going to make any train reservations, to be used in case my priority "4" lets me get bumped. Am just going to trust that the air schedule will work just fine.

We are all giving loud "Hurrahs"—at the news that the British Navy sunk the "Scharnhorst"!

And, now that we have settled in and put things in order, we are no longer unhappy with our new quarters. They are no better than they were, but we have just made satisfactory adjustments.

December 30, 1943 Ft. Lewis

Well, this old year has just about run its course. Last few days have been almost clear.

Have acquired two pair of G-I glasses. The have steel frames and are very sturdy. Vision with them is excellent. So, I guess the prescription is a good one.

Had sort of planned to try to call you Christmas Day, but report was that all lines were full and overloaded. Saw the movie, "Destination Tokyo"—excellent, and only one American gets killed... Some of us are going to see "Jack London," this evening.

Leo and J. Alf sent me a ball of soap with a leash, so that I can hang it around my neck. We have been having some fun with it, for it has been dubbed to be my "Ball and Chain." Really, it's pretty fancy.

Have started to read "The Robe," and it is going to be difficult to put down. It is something you will want to read, Mother, and I shall bring it home with me.

From reports which come back from the outfits where our men are deployed each day, we are in darned good shape. I am not surprised, for these men are sharp. With the action elsewhere, our company area is a pretty dead place during the daytime, especially.

January 1, 1944 Ft. Lewis

And, it is a Happy New Year to all of you. I didn't care to know that you, Moosie, are having a bout with this flu bug.

The rains have set in, again, and we would soon get soaked if out in it. For tomorrow, if this rain lets up, I will go to a nearby chapel for service. Was there last Sunday, but I had difficult to understand the chaplain—he seemed to have a bit of mush in his mouth.

War news continues to be encouraging, and I think Hitler must be starving for a victory. Once we have dealt with him in Europe, we'll have the Nips yet to deal with. So—??

We had another turkey dinner, yesterday. These cooks do their job so well.

Do not know exactly the hours of my flight, but will give you the dope. Got a Burlington timetable, and sent it to Mim—marked a couple schedules for her to take from Chicago. She has not traveled outside of New England. I have warned her to be ready to eat lots of pheasant and home made ice cream.

Some of us plan to see a movie with Frank Sinatra. From reports, he should be called "Swoonatra." Well, whatever!

January 6, 1944 Ft. Lewis

Am not going to put much in my letters, as you are noticing, for I expect to be home before long. That 20-mile hike we had three days ago really caused my right hip to protest. I've worked out the kinks with a series of twists and turns. It is not a serious problem.

Before Christmas I received a fruit cake from Massachusetts. Return address had been almost obliterated, and name of sender was not readable. So, I wrote Mim and asked if her mother had sent it. Just received her reply, and it didn't come from 148 Summit St. Well, I will need to make inquiry of her two aunt Agneses. Ho! Ho!

Our men are still working at various supply installations here in camp, and they do seem to like what they are doing. They may prefer to work rather than to take a long hike. Could be!

And tomorrow, big old 26 hits the register for me. Will celebrate with you, Bin, on the 21st.

Will be going into Tacoma, tomorrow, and should get my trip home all settled.

January 7, 1944 Ft. Lewis

In town, today, and have my ticket. Will leave Seattle at 7:00 p.m. (the 17th) and am to arrive in Omaha at 8:14 a.m. (via United), the 18th. Return to be on the 31st—to leave Omaha at 8:18 a.m. and to arrive in Seattle at 8:29 p.m. Mim will arrive the 20th via train, and it will be in the evening and not too late. She is getting so excited about her trip! I think she will have six full days to be with us.

Have finished reading "The Robe," and it is a wonderful story. I will bring it home with me and leave it with you.

Have written Aunt Bertha twice since Uncle Herbert's death. I am not surprised that she will be going east. Do you know if Hugh is going to get married?

Received your two birthday cards today. Now, I call that perfect timing!

January 9, 1944 Ft. Lewis

So many rumors flying around with reference to what our future as a company will be.

We go on a 20-mile training hike, tomorrow. With morning calisthenics and these scheduled training marches, we are supposed to become amply toughened to do well with whatever service we are to perform, and where. As Plans and Training Officer I must work all of this into the schedule, and nearly everyone blames me. Since I go on all of these "long walks," no one can complain too much.

I remain a bit uneasy that my priority "4" may not hold for my trip to Omaha, etc. But the young lady at the United office assured me that I should have no problem, for the holiday traffic is over by mid January. I sure hope she knows what she is talking about.

Some of us will be seeing "Cry Havoc" at post theater # 1 this evening. And we are to have our second Ninth Service Command Inspection tomorrow.

January 13, 1944 Ft. Lewis

My last letter before I see you. Then, Mim will arrive on the 20th, and she plans to stay a week. Since she has never traveled out of New England, she is a bit apprehensive about her long trip to Nebraska.

I'll bring my # 3 ration book which we can use as needed. Mim wrote that she would be bringing hers. So, we should not have a problem with food, eh?

This air traffic keeps me just a bit uneasy. But, to come by train would cut nearly three days from my time at home. I do not want to get "bumped."

February 1, 1944 Ft. Lewis

Am back at my table in my ceilingless cubicle, and am just reviewing those wonderful 13 days at home. Was OD this morning. So, I had to get right back into the middle of things, here. Teague covered for me while I was gone, and Rudy helped with plans and training.

This travel by plane is quite the deal. Over twelve hours from Lincoln, and back into the duties, here. Route took us to Denver, Salt Lake, Boise, Pendleton, and Seattle. So much beautiful scenery to look down upon. The mountain ranges really looked rugged, here and there, and some of the snow-covered peaks were just gorgeous. The plane moved along through the passes, and we often went through banks of clouds. Had a clear view of the Salt Lake region.

Clouds were heavy and low over Pendleton, Oregon, and we circled and circled to come down through them. Had time to get off the plane, and some people there to meet others. A rather elderly woman was so disappointed when her grandson, I think, did not arrive that she had a heart attack. Her daughter was with her, grabbed hold of her, and lowered her to the floor. I doubt if the poor soul lived…

We were just two minutes late into Seattle. A bus-ride into the city, and connections by bus to Tacoma and into camp. It was 11:30. Most of the gang greeted me, and we visited until after one o'clock. Then, up at 6:30 to check reveille, as OD. So, I am sleepy as I write this. It was pouring rain when we landed in Seattle, and it is a constant drizzle now. Also, a bit chilly.

Rudy has received his Captaincy, and Earl Grove his Majority. Each of these promotions is well deserved. We poor new second lieutenants will have to wait a few months, for time doesn't count for us until our appointment to this company. All our months of training as a class do not help. We must just grin and bear it!

Am listening to Judy Canova. And, again, what a grand time—and to have Mim with us for a week!.

February 2, 1944 Ft. Lewis

Am constantly listening for news of the action in the Marshalls. Gee! but I hope there isn't going to be a slaughter such as took place on Tarawa! Those Nips are always so darned hard to handle. It seems that the news is somewhat promising.

Went in to Tacoma, today, to make application for a passport. We are getting them, for it will simplify the getting of visas should we want to do some traveling and looking around—wherever we might be. Speculation is now that we will head for Europe. My old 85th Division has been in Africa, and is now in Italy.

By tomorrow I shall be back in the groove of things. Just must stop wishing I were back home!

February 5, 1944 Ft. Lewis

A Saturday, and plenty of rain, mist, and fog.

Saw Greer Garson and Walter Pidgeon in "Madame Curie" last evening. It is excellent. Be sure to see it. The acting is superb.

Have been thinking about my trip home. Two times, one eastbound and the other west, all except two of the passengers were in uniform. Nearly all of us in uniform had "C-4" priorities. So, I guess we who had these priorities are really keeping the airlines in business.

I was quite impressed and did much enjoy the meals on the planes. The ticket includes meals, and no tipping. The paste-board trays were more like boxes and had round openings cut for glasses and deep dishes—even little openings for the salt and peppercellars These trays rested nicely on pillows to be on our laps, and there was no danger of spilling anything. Samples of what we had to eat: for noon—lamb chop, potatoes and green beans, fruit salad, roll and butter, and a cupcake; for supper—chicken, potatoes, corn, vegetable salad, roll and butter, and blueberry "betty"; and for breakfast—scrambled eggs, sausage, and roll with butter and jelly. Of course—coffee, tea, or milk, and sugar. This certainly beats the train all to smithereens. And, I was surprised how often some people used the small "johnny." Ha!

En route, I read Agatha Christie's "Mystery at End House." This travel by plane seems to make a little jaunt of travel across half the nation.

Visited with a sailor who sat beside me, and he was a cribbage fiend and had a board with him. So, we had to have a game or six, and he won four of them.

Am adding to this on Sunday evening. Col. Cole and I went to church this morning—a small Presbyterian church in nearby Lakewood . We had passed it while on one of our longer hikes.

Small congregation, but they certainly made us feel welcome!

February 7, 1944 Ft. Lewis

Am enjoying an afternoon "off." The Col. decided we were well on top of our schedule and work. So, we have spare hours for some breathers. Nice! Have nearly finished reading "Burma Surgeon." And, did some strolling around and about—for we have a beautiful and clear day, here. Am at my table, and the window is wide open. A breath of spring is certainly in the air, here.

So, you had many good laughs at a Laurel and Hardy movie. Well, I have had many a chuckle each time I think about the problem we had when Mim arrived in Lincoln. She had told me that she would be coming in on the Burlington. So, that is where we waited through two trains for her—but no Mim. Good thing we decided to check the Rock Island, and there she was—quite worried because no one answered the telephone. In Chicago, she had a change of stations to catch the Burlington. Some kind gentleman had told her that all trains used the same depot in Lincoln; so, she hopped on the RI. The conductor just accepted her ticket. She had arrived a bit ahead of schedule, too. She had waited more than an hour before we arrived. In Boston, all trains come into the same station—from north, south, and west.

In each letter, she writes about her time in Lincoln, and what it has meant to meet you. She just raves and says it was the best vacation she ever had. But, she hasn't said a word about her arrival. Ha! Ha!

And since my return, I learned something. When I left camp to begin my trip home, I was so excited I forgot to sign out. Col. Cole noticed this, and he had Rudy forge my name. As I understand it, had the plane crashed before midnight on the 17th and were I to be killed, the government would have been released from paying certain compensations. It has something to do with being on official leave and being on the morning report for the day. I had not thought a thing about it. Howzabout that!

February 8, 1944 Ft. Lewis

Typing this time, for I can visit so much better. It sure beats my scribbling.

Rainy and foggy here today. When the sun shines, this is beautiful country. We have on a clear day such a strikingly gorgeous view of Mt. Rainier.

Bin, quit stewing about sending the ring. It is in its many packages in one, all camouflaged. I 'll tell you when—and how it is to be addressed!

Do not miss seeing Fred MacMurray and Paulette Goddard in "Standing Room, Only." It is a scream, really! What a take-off on the situation in Washington, D.C. It keeps you giggling all the time.

Several new men arrived—to bring us up to our TO. Now, it is up to me to see that they are quickly orientated and prepared to fit into our medical depot company. I and a couple noncoms will be somewhat busy with them. This will take about two weeks. Some of them are already familiar with our sort of work.

When it is not raining, we may have time to play a little baseball. When raining, we play some darts. I'm not much good at either. So it goes.

By the way, I need pronto about 18 white handkerchiefs. They are in a top drawer of my dresser. We are now getting ready to await orders, and our personal needs are to be met. I will be spending about $25—several pair of sox, at least six pair of undershirts and shorts, a green rain coat, and a pair of G.I. shoes. Expectation is that I shall be packing full my little footlocker to send home. So, be prepared—just like all good Boy Scouts!

We have nearly finished those two boxes of "Witching Hour" chocolates. Yeah! Yeah!

February 13, 1944 Fort Lewis

Two evenings ago, three of us went into Tacoma to hear Wendell Willkie speak. We purchased tickets for a banquet which preceded the speech, and we had a balcony spot with a good view of Willkie while he spoke. Col. Cole, Russ Peterson, and I agree that Willkie is a good man and ought to receive again the Republican nomination for the presidency. He is an effective speaker, and is one of the two Republicans I prefer to FDR. It is my understanding that many old-line Republicans are opposed to his renomination. He certainly knew what he was talking about!

Pete is one of us poor, little second lieutenants—except, he is a tall Swede from Minneapolis and intends to be a mortician. He doesn't hesitate to let one know what he thinks. Yup!

We had a 20-mile hike two days ago, and I was a bit tuckered out because of it. My right hip was really tuned up, and it kept me from getting a decent night's sleep. One of these days I may hit the station hospital and have it x-rayed. But, yesterday—no aches or pains. So, I doubt if there is anything wrong.

Am reading the book, "Under Cover." May join the group and go see Joan Fontaine and Orson Welles in "Jane Eyre"—in one of our post theaters.

The Col. did send in some requests for promotion, and these involved some of us 2nd Lts. But, all were rejected, for we had not had sufficient time to qualify—after all the special schooling we had received. We are at least two months short. My understanding is that we have to have six months of "duty"—!! And, we hear nothing about our future.

February 15, 1944 Ft. Lewis

Well, another Valentine's Day is behind us. Received a box of candy from the Lueckes, and such a nice note along with it. Will send the note to you. And your cards were so cute, and the one from Mim.

Really no news from here—about our move. We are not wanting to become rooted here.

My watch is not keeping accurate time. Am sending it home, and Mr. Beard down at Sartor's can check it out. It's not very old, and I've never bumped it. I do not overwind it. When it stops, I give it a little shake, and it will start to run. Then after a short time, it will stop. So, I think there is a wheel loose—er sompin.

A ten-mile jaunt coming up tomorrow. It will be no more than an afternoon stroll. Our new men may need a little toughening into it. Only a handful of them are recent inductees, however.

Saw "Broadway Rhythm"—George Murphy and Ginny Sims. It was a good film, and Charles Winninger was just excellent in his part.

February 20, 1944 Ft. Lewis

Just no news of importance, as you have gathered from my recent letters. We have no info about anything.

Went to church at a nearby chapel and enjoyed the music—a good choral number, and the soldier who sang a solo did a nice job of it.

The Don Carlos Co. is presenting "La Traviata" and "Carmen" in Tacoma tomorrow evening and Tuesday evening. Some of us plan to take in both of them. I wish "Cavalleria Rusticana" were on the slate, for it has some of my favorite music. Then, I should get to Seattle this coming week end to see the Clarks and Jim Tische.

You have been having one winter storm after the other. The weatherman was so good to us during my leave. We had it lucky, eh? Here, we have a mixture of clear and drizzle—actually a few large and fluffy snowflakes came floating down this morning.

Do see Ida Lupino and Paul Heinrich in "In Our Time." It is somewhat tragic, and takes place in Poland before the German invasion and occupation. It requires your attention.

Received a letter from Joe Hodgson. He wrote from New York, was awaiting shipping orders, and a line or two had been censored—cut out. My guess is that he said something about time and means of departure. He is classified, I think, as a skilled repairman of certain instruments.

Was OD Friday night. So, I started the weekend a bit sleepy. And, letter from Uncle Arthur indicated that his mind is not made up, about moving to Springfield.

February 23, 1944 Ft.Lewis

Well, "La Traviata" was sung in Italian and "Carmen" in French. No problem to follow along because the programs were excellent guides. For me, each was a treat. It was well after 11:30 before we returned to the company area. Col. Cole and I saw "Carmen," and when we came from the opera, the wind was blowing a fierce gale, and it was cold. I thought the bus for camp would never come.

Yesterday, we had an inspector from the Ninth Service Command. It seemed to me that all I did was to make reports as to our training and readiness. It was to have been an afternoon "off" for me, but in no way. So, we shall see what comes forth. I may just go into hiding, tomorrow afternoon. Ha!

Had meant to urge you so see "The Sullivans"—Anne Baxter and Thomas Mitchell. I'm sure you read about those five sons from Waterloo, Iowa, who all went down with the cruiser, "Juneau," during the battle of The Solomons. It is just full of humor nearly to the end, and so well done. Each American should see it.

Am OD tonight. So, not much sleep.

February 28, 1944 Ft. Lewis

Had such a pleasant time with the Clarks, Pearl and Jean. Bud was away on a selling tour. Was delayed at camp, but caught a quick bus into Tacoma and then one to Seattle. Hit the Clarks about 7:30, and dinner was waiting—ham, sweet potatoes, etc., and apple pie. This little Pearl can talk as fast and as long as any person I have known. She is a "blue streak"—if there ever was one!

Pearl and I went to the Methodist church and heard a good sermon. The choir was one of the best I've heard for months. Jean is at the hospital from seven to three each day. So, our Sunday dinner was not until about 4:30—chicken and all else to go with it. I made a pig of myself, and Pearl seemed pleased with each bite. We played a round or two of hearts, and then I had to catch the buses back to camp—almost midnight before I got into bed. It was a very nice break from the usual routine.

My old Elgin arrived, today, and I have returned Rudy's extra. Will now await return of my good watch, once it has been checked and fixed.

March 1, 1944 Ft. Lewis

We have been alerted—to be prepared to move out when so directed. We do not know to where, but we'll be ready. Now, no more fretting about staying here. Ha! It is now to be hustle and bustle.

I have just shifted into a different cubicle, or "roomette." It has an extra little shelf—just perfect for my radio. Now, with this improvement, I shall soon be vacating. Oh, well! Gracie Allen is now on, and she is always a bit daffy—maybe "cwazy," eh?

A beautiful, clear day, today. With weather such as this, I can understand why the natives are such enthusiasts about the climate. But, for me, too many clouds and too much rain.

Have dropped Pearl Clark a note. I just keep grinning, for she is such a chatterbox.

Glad you and Mim are carrying on a lively correspondence. And, be sure to see Ginger Rogers in "Tender Comrade."

March 5, 1944 Ft. Lewis

We are going to be real busy—to get all excesses disposed of and to be ready to head for a different locale. As yet, I do not know where to. Will be sending home much of my surplus.

Had to chuckle about Robert's latest romance hitting the dust. He just hasn't acquired the knack for "lamour, toujours, manour"! H-m-m-m-m?

Yes, I did so much enjoy those operas. Someday I hope to hit the Metropolitan.

And, this is another Leap Year. I remember the day that Orvie Ingalls announced at school that his father was "only twelve years old"—that he was celebrating his twelfth birthday. Yessirree!

Felt a little stuffy, and had my sinuses checked. No signs of any trouble. And, plan to hit a movie this evening, "See Here, Pvt. Hargrove."

March 8, 1944 Ft. Lewis

The mood around here is really one of hurry and scurry. Finally, I broke down and did buy the sox, field jackets, rain coat, and shoes and polish. And, each of us has acquired a standard G.I. footlocker.

Our new men seem to be about as ready as the rest of us. They proved to be a bright group, generally.

Was up until after 12:30 yesterday morning—substituted as OD. And, no time to get in a few extra snoozes. For some reason, we are beginning to feel a bit of pressure. Ho! Ho!

Do not miss Robert Walker in "See Here, Pvt. Hargrove"! I laughed until I thought I'd have a hemorrhage. It is funny!

Do not send my watch any later than Monday, the 13th—the 14th at the latest. We are guessing, more and more, that we will be heading to Europe.

March 11, 1944 Ft. Lewis

Glad to know the watch is on its way. Thank you.

You mentioned that Philomene was coming. I wish I could be there, for we always have a riot going through our "Eddie Holmes" routine. Too, we always manage to smear a little ketchup on the table cloth! Well, another day and this war will be over.

Please, Moosie, do not worry about our going overseas. We will have a definite mission to perform, and ours will not be a front-line position. We could be not too far removed, however. We are really quite excited about being alerted, for we were just marking time, here—a very dull existence. The spirits of our enlisted men have risen noticeably since we were told to get ready.

We had a "farewell party" with the 30th. It was a turkey with all the trimmings and an apple pie affair. Several wives of men and officers are still here, and they were not too jovial about our pending departure.

Col. Cole and I plan to go into Seattle for church and communion, Sunday. While there, I shall attempt to see the Clarks and Jim Tische. This will be a sort of "fond adieu."

Saw the movie, "The Purple Heart"—well written and played. But, .Moosie, not one for you to see, I think.

Should be sending, before long, a change of address card. Then you will know which direction we are heading. If it should be to New York, then I hope I'll be able to make a quick jaunt to Boston to see Mim.

Well, just five minutes before midnight. So, to bed.

March 16, 1944 Ft. Lewis

We continue to await our instructions.

Sunday, I saw Jim and the Clarks. Jim wants to get into the navy from here, and will not get home. As for the Clarks—Jean has been accepted into the Army Nurse Corps and is awaiting orders to report. Mr. Clark was home and had been ordered to bed by his doctor—blood pressure was dangerously high. He carries far too many pounds, and has had one coronary difficulty before. So, little Pearl is in quite a dither and complains of headaches. She has my concern.

Then, coming back on the bus to Tacoma, an elderly gentleman sitting beside me was puffing away on a cigar, and to his heart's content. He never noticed that he was nearly suffocating me, almost. I was really quite amused, for I have never seen one little man create such a cloud of smoke. Oh, well!

The watch is here, and many thanks. Now, I shall keep the old Elgin as reserve.

Most of the wives have departed. My plan is to fill my little Miller & Paine footlocker and send it home. Will send the key later. We are awaiting the promised cookies—yessirree! And. as usual, it is nearly midnight.

March 19, 1944 Ft. Lewis

Received the handkerchiefs, candy, and cookies. The eatables didn't last long. Here is the key to the footlocker. Now, you can open it, but I think there is another key in the top drawer of my dresser. Enclosed is the Express receipt—just in case you should need to do any checking. The two suits of tropical worsteds should be put where moths wont get to them. Will be keeping my radio, electric razor, and—of course—Mim's picture. .

The additional attire I purchased cost about $45. But, advice was to have so much and many of this and of that.

Seems to be we are pretty well caught up. So, four of us played golf—the 18 holes here in camp. It was spirited, all with clubs rented. We had not shot a golf for a long time, and we had a lot of fun. I scored a 54 and 49, and my 103 was low for the four of us. The others couldn't get over my cross-hands grip. That Teague is a character on a golf course. We sure had the laughs. And, we have been getting in some games of bridge. We are finding time to be a bit heavy on our hands.

Will have to send a package of stuff. Am listening to Frankie Carl and his orchestra.

We are being urged to use V-Mail. So, something to look in to. And, this enclosed certificate has to do with my Class E Allotment. The $90 checks should come to you, Moosie, and then you can transfer each amount to my account. Your endorsement validates each check for the bank.

Quite a gang from our company were in the nearby chapel for church this morning—the most I have ever seen. Several have been regulars, but today the number was large.

March 21, 1944 Ft. Lewis

A good chat the other evening. And, do address the package to Boston just as I have written. Insure it. Do not register it. Mim knows that you are sending me a package addressed in care of her mother and that there is an outside possibility that I may get to Boston You will receive the card that our APO will be New York. We prepared the cards on the 15th, but orders were that they not be mailed until our departure—tomorrow.

It would be wonderful were I to get to Hyde Park to be present when Mim opens that package, with the several smaller ones within to be unwrapped before she finds the ring. We shall just have to await developments. Oh, boy!!

It is now quite certain that I'll not make it home until after this mess is over. Just remember that ours is not a combat unit…

We have turned in all our furniture, and my knee is the only desk for writing this letter. Ha!

As far as I know, we have eaten all cakes and cookies down to the last crumb. Some of us may go to a movie this evening. We are ready to travel. Ho! Ho!

APO. N.Y.

March 27, 1944 APO 9826, c/o PM N.Y., N.Y.

(Camp Kilmer, N.J., was our staging area prior to our embarkation from New York.)

This address is temporary, but write me, here. We'll have another, shortly. No chance for me to make a quick run to Boston.

I am to be one of our company's censors—three of us officers, and this is proving to be quite a task. This is highly important, for no one is to give information that might possibly be of use to our enemies. We've had two sessions with the men, and they are aware of the sort of slip-ups that will have to be deleted. Most of our men do write home often. And this is going to be woefully time consuming. Also, we who censor are honor bound to say nothing to anybody as to content. Several of our men are married, and their letters are highly personal, sometimes. About six have given me their letters, rather than to put them in the box. I appreciate their trust. This is tiring business, I'm in need of some shut-eye, and I must hit my pillow—well after midnight.

March 28

Had my curly locks hacked away, today—down to my Camp Barkeley OCS length of one inch. I look like some young high schooler—with this brush cut. This short hair has become a contagion. Ha! It is very practical. Our company barber is really busy, and Haught is excellent.

March 29

Have hesitated to tell you that our troop train made a stop in Omaha . Yes, so close to home, and no one was permitted to set foot on soil. Military personnel along the platform made certain that no one attempted any sort of communication.

Lots of rain, today, but we are well accustomed to it. No one may leave our staging area or make any phone calls. An official pass will open a gate, and one has to be on "business." We are under the tightest of security restrictions.

As for mail, we are receiving letters forwarded from Ft. Lewis, and we are now receiving mail addressed to us, here.

I think that no one in the company has any fear as to what may lie ahead for us. We all hope we will soon be doing the work we have trained to do. Hitler and his mob must be obliterated!! Our job and mission is a comparatively safe one. So, do not worry! Once we are on the move, there will be quite a lapse of time before my letters will begin to arrive.

Have that old Elgin tucked away for future use, if necessary. It is again after midnight. I hope we can catch up with this censoring by tomorrow evening. Whew!

March 30, 1944 N.Y., N.Y.

Do not know just when we leave, nor just where we will go. You will be receiving a new APO number. And, I wish you a Happy Easter.

We are certainly in a whirlpool of activities, and we have really been flagging our fannies around and around. The men collectively are in great spirits, and they must be an unusual bunch.

We all know that "War is hell"! Most people throughout the world want to live in peace and be free from want. A few become driven by greed, hatred, and jealousy, and their corrupting influences lead to suffering and chaos. Today, we have this unprecedented conflict. Sometimes I think human beings are not very intelligent, for it takes such a few to make life miserable for the many. Our white race, which claims to be Christian, largely, has not left a very promising record. We've heard a lot about "Brotherly Love," but we need a new slant on things if there is hope that our side will bring the rest of the world into a new and lasting era of peace. "Uncle Joe" wants to use a labor pool of 4 ½ million Germans to rebuild the Russia they have ruined and desolated. We just keep planting the seeds from which future wars take root.

Gee, but I certainly worked myself into a preaching mood. I should search for a soap box, go find me a good corner, and give any listeners a bit of harangue. But this is close to the eve of our embarkation, and I am not just all that content. There is no doubt about it—"The Fighting 31st" will turn the tide!

Foggy and misting, and we are not getting any relief from that weather of the Puget Sound area. We may yet have to become web-footed and moss-backed!

Must do about three more hours to read letters, if I can keep awake. My admiration for our men is increasing—letter by letter!

Must get a note written to Mim. She is so much pleased to be hearing from you.

Voyage

(Victory Day in Europe brought virtual end to all censoring of letters. I had filled a notebook with all sorts of jotted reminders and turned to these to compile a 22-page single-spaced account of our experiences—entitled "Just a Bit of Travel," and this I mailed home on June 5, 1945. It also fell to me to write an "official history" of the 31st Medical Depot Company. After the war's end, with time sufficient to put it together, came a remarkable review of the company's experiences, "Supply Medics"—largely the work of one of our highly able and contributing sergeants, Ross Donaldson, of New York. These "documents" furnish the particulars which wartime security kept secreted, and they now serve to supplement the letters and to feed into the narrative.)

We departed Ft. Lewis 1200h March 22, and our long ride by train took us to Portland, through the Rockies, and via Omaha, Chicago, Erie, Buffalo, to Camp Kilmer, New Jersey—arrival at 0500h March 27. Departure from Kilmer, our staging area, came at 1900h March 30 via train to a pier on the New Jersey side of the Hudson River and to be ferried to the foot of 51st St., New York City for immediate boarding of H.M.S. "Queen Elizabeth." We sailed from New York Harbor, 1330h, March 31.

While at Kilmer, we had a potent rumor that we were to sail on the "Queen Elizabeth," but Col. Cole, in a rather authoritative way, informed us that we were to cross the Atlantic in a convoy.

Footlockers and TAT equipment, along with certain other items, had preceded us and were on board. While we awaited our orders to board, women of the Red Cross served us coffee and doughnuts. We officers, carrying our duffels and kits, were conducted onto the ship via a different gangplank from that for the EM. Our mess and billet cards told us on which deck and in which compartment we were to bunk and when we were to eat—at which hours. Our men were to be billeted in the very lowest area of the ship, forward, and far below the water line. One descended into the area by use of wall ladders which also provided descent to the two decks above. It was a long climb upward to reach the lowest deck to provide view of the ocean.

The quarters for our enlisted men was designated "E" deck, and they shared the large area with the men of the 30th. This bottom deck had been used for automobiles and large and bulky cases. The lower decks above served to house the various levels of enlisted personnel. Then came the lieutenants, captains, etc., with colonels, generals, and special passengers, such as Edward Stettinius, Under-Secretary of State, to enjoy the uppermost and airy staterooms. Nine of us lieutenants, including five from our 31st, were in a not spacious room on a level just above the decks occupied by the enlisted men. Captains were less crowded, etc. Along with its "crew," this magnificent ship sometimes transported more than 15,000 troops. For our voyage, we were not quite so many—with some being Canadian, Australian, French, and South African. A small contingent of WACS were in some of the upper staterooms, and they were strictly "off limits"!

Ship regulation required that each unit have an officer on duty among its men—concern being to guard against fire and to maintain absolute "black-out" at night. Col. Cole appointed us junior-grade officers, and a daily roster, with captains and warrant officer included, gave us the line-up. One did not leave his post until his relief appeared. Russ Peterson was my relief.

This remarkable ship simply cut through waves and swells, but it tended to roll ever so gently. Perhaps it was this motion which caused a general prevalence of seasickness. Had it not been for the general effectiveness of the ship's system to circulate air, the stench from the vomiting would have been overwhelming for our men. Fortunately, I never had a moment's sickness. But, Lt. Peterson stood his first watch and then became seasick for most of the voyage. Col. Cole would not adjust the roster, and my succeeding watches stretched to four hours.

Expectations were that our "Queen" would take four and a half days to make the crossing. Her speed enabled her to sail alone, for she could easily outdistance any submarine. Our third night out, the ship's sonar detected submarines ahead, and the crew turned the vessel sharply to the right and headed south and into warmer waters. The outward thrust of centrifugal force rolled many persons from their bunks. In an upper bunk adjacent to a wall and with head to the fore, I found myself pinned against the wall and with such force that I could not free myself. Awakened abruptly, I had the feeling that the ship was lying on its side. This sensation soon passed, and the intercom directed everyone to stay put. The crowding of the ship had caused certain companies to be "double-decked" or "double shifted"—half-time in and half-time out of staterooms. I do not remember that we lost anyone overboard. Later, of course, as we related experiences, accounts caused much laughter.

We ate twice a day, in several shifts, and our time was 8:00 a.m. and 6:00 p.m. We officers went to the dining room, were served by the ship's English waiters—all in tuxedos, and ship's china and silverware and white table cloth were order of the day. The food was excellent and the menus varied. Nice! But, the men did not fare so well. They ate from their mess kits and drank from their canteens. Several chow lines formed twice each day, and the menus seemed to be variations of ways to prepare corned beef and potatoes—and always with tea. They sat at long uncovered tables. They were in line again to rinse heir mess gear. Reference was that they traveled "poorest class." It was understood that passage over and cost of food was to be chalked up to "reverse lend-lease," etc. If so, it did not prove to be the case for us, the officers of the 31st, for the regular discount for rations was exacted throughout. But, why? Rumor would later indicate that our CO had neglected to approve the favor. Well, whatever!

The dodging of the submarines added nearly two days to our crossing, and this resulted in a lessened menu for the men. There seemed to remain a plentiful supply of potatoes. Since our company's cooks were assisting in the kitchen, a supply of potatoes slipped into the hands of our men. With salt, several of them found the raw potatoes to be tasty. Some of them were careless about letting peels lie on the floor. Stepping from the ladder to begin my watch, I hit a potato peel, slipped, and turned as I fell onto the pile of duffle bags. I lit on my back, but was to be overcome by a siege of vertigo and of such severity that I could move neither arm nor leg. I could move my eyes, but it was an equivalence of paralysis. I soon could speak, and urged the men to get the floor cleaned and dried. They had started to do some mopping when Col. Cole appeared at the foot of the ladder. He spotted me and asked me what I was doing. I told him I was lying on the duffle bags, and then attempted to tell him the cause. He ignored my explanation and ordered the men to clean the place—which, or course, they were doing. He had used his most authoritative voice, and then mounted the ladder and departed. The men were somewhat amused, and I was angry. In thirty seconds the vertigo ceased, and I was on my feet and in full form. The colonel did me a favor by rubbing me the wrong way. Ha!

Except for the detour, our trip across the Atlantic was somewhat uneventful. We overtook a large convoy and sighted another en route to the U.S., and we encountered the "Queen Mary." We would regain a bit of lost time before reaching the Firth of Clyde, Scotland.

April 6, 1944 Firth of Clyde, Scotland

It was Maundy Thursday, and we had passed through St. George's Channel and the Irish Sea and had had glimpses of the Emerald Island on our way northward. Permission to uncover and open the portholes had been granted. Prolonged cases of seasickness came quickly to terminations, including that of Lt. Peterson, and all were eager to set foot on land. At anchor within the Firth, we found ourselves surrounded by a myriad of vessels, naval and otherwise. We would debark the next day, Good Friday.

Except for raw potatoes, the "Elizabeth" had little food in reserve to offer the men for evening and breakfast. Col. Cole had directed that our men be issued a full day's "K ration"—to be eaten the next day while en route to somewhere in Great Britain. Our Catholic men proceeded immediately to eat the "meat" portions, and nearly all others followed suit. Consumption of raw potatoes continued down in the hold, and the deck again became a slippery mess—to be mopped and dried. No doubt about it, those salted raw potatoes were the tastiest food available to our men. And, some sort of breakfast lay ahead for the next day. Officers, of course, fared much better; six of us were at our table, and we left a rather generous tip for our highly attentive and efficient waiter.

April 7, 1944 England

It was Good Friday, and we had to await an assembly of ferry boats to take us ashore to the port of Gourick, which lay to the west of Glasgow. Not until nearly 5 o'clock in the afternoon had we quit the ship. We received a rollicking welcome from Scottish bagpipers. They paraded up and down for us—all in their kilts and with inimitable rhythmic and lilting steps and countermarch.

On hand to add to the welcome were a host of "pink faced Scotch girls" who "handed around doughnuts and coffee"—furnished by the Red Cross. Almost without hesitation, we boarded the train and settled into its "funny little compartments"—each to be somewhat crowded with six men and their duffles.

We journeyed up the Clyde valley to Glasgow and in silence observed the marvel of the Scottish countryside—green, neat, clean, pastoral, peaceful, many trees, garden plots, huts and homes, a natural beauty, and unmarred by war. Darkness settled in as we passed through Glasgow. The seats were comfortable, windows were closed and covered, the breeze outside had a definite chill, we had "K rations" to munch, and snoozing was rather fitful. Morning's arrival in London permitted descent for doughnuts and coffee. On board again, each received another issue of "K rations," and we proceeded to Andover in Hampshire (Hants). Trucks, procured by the RTO, awaited our arrival and carted us, on the left side of the road, to Chilbolton Camp A—a desolate appearing spot and about 12 miles from Andover. It was 3 o'clock afternoon.

Andover Junction was not far from Salisbury and Winchester, and our camp was less than two miles from the village of Crawley. Pine, cedar, and ash trees were scattered about in varied densities, and recent rains had made it muddy underfoot. The buildings were of a Nissan sort, had not been used recently, and were thoroughly filthy and in need of as much cleaning as could be given before occupation. A Quartermaster officer from a nearby station hospital was on hand with a two-day supply of "rations." We were not a happy company, it was April 8, and Easter was tomorrow.

Chilbolton

April 13, 1944 Chilbolton

Our encampment was three miles from the town of Stockbridge. The port of Southampton lay about twenty miles south, with Winchester midway between. Except for the one case, supply installations were unaware or our presence. So, nearly everything had to be initiated—even to the borrowing of vehicles from nearby American units. It just took a few days to bring some sort of order out of the chaos. "K rations" endured until a kitchen facility was readied and a chain of food-supply had been effected. At best, our situation was highly discouraging. Much time would be required to requisition and to gather our equipment—to come from all parts of England.

It was an affair of doing everything over—including the tearing out of old brick walks and the laying of new ones. Each building needed a scrubbing—from top to bottom and inside and out. The men even swept up the pine needles and disposed of them—then to wish they hadn't, for rain continued and the mud beneath was worse. Our greatest puzzlement arose because no one knew what our mission was to be. So, we fell back upon a resumption of "training"—much of which would be old stuff and to the second and third time. Emphases pointed to recognition of aircraft, passive air defense, protection against chemical attack—and to a degree that one of our sergeants noted that everything was beginning to smell like chloropicrin, waterproofing of vehicles, sanitation, physical fitness, military discipline and courtesy, orientation with respect to civil and military events, and the French language.

April 13, 1944 Chilbolton Downs

A little Anglican church near here, about two miles, in Crawley. The service reminds me so much of Holy Trinity. A church has been on this site for over a thousand years, and the "yard" and cemetery surround the structure. It is so quaint and beautiful. We had quite a group present for worship.

This countryside is just so picturesque. The green of the landscape is so deep, and the cleanliness of it all causes us Americans to stand and stare—for it seems a story is going to jump out from somewhere within pages. The quaintness of the cottages, nearly all of thatched roofs, is just fascinating. Daffodils, jonquils, etc., are in bloom everywhere, and plumb trees are beginning to burst forth. Grounds which surround buildings are meticulously clear of weeds. One sees no waste of space. The English citizen is not a person of wealth and has no margin for waste of any kind. We Americans have a lesson to learn. There is a coziness which tends to overwhelm. So many of our men have said something about a "feeling."

For the first time, we must use a money not our own. It is a matter of exchange—each turns in his American cash and receives back an equivalency in British. We just have to get used to pounds, shillings, and pence. Each item for sale, including any drink in a pub, has its cost clearly marked. The conversion is close to the following:

>   Pound ($4.03)
>   Crown ($1.00)
>   Half-crown (50 cents)
>   Florin (40 cents)
>   Shilling (20 cents)
>   Sixpence (10 cents)
>   Thruppence (5 cents)
>   Penny (2 cents)
>   Ha'penny (1 cent)

We're having fun getting used to this, but give us time! Our pay will come a la British...

We are being supplied with a British bread. For one who has never been a heavy bread-eater, I find it to be very good—perhaps, as our cooks tell us, composed of two cups white flour to each half-cup of rye and of whole wheat. I may become a converted bread-eater...

One other observation. Seems to me there are plenty of small children running around. They appear to be very sturdy! I gave a hunch that parents and elders have been scrimping to make sure the children had sufficient food. Bravo! And, gardens are everywhere—often just tucked into small corners.

April 17, 1944 Chilbolton Downs

Am using quite a bit of this V-Mail. Let me know if you find it difficult to read.

This censoring of mail is such a chore. Some of our married men are a bit touchy about it, and I don't blame them.

Do not send any cake or cookies. Crackers, cheese, and peanut butter would be better. Our food is just fine. We are so fortunate, for our company's cooks are unusually good. What they work with is not fancy, but they do so well with it. Inquiry at adjacent installations leads me to believe we are faring very well.

The little coke burner in my room is performing so well. Of course, I have figured how to get the stuff to glow and then to keep the coals alive throughout the night. The cold and humidity can really get to one, here, at night. Each day seems to bring a bit of drizzle.

Several have been doing a good bit of walking, and the people do enjoy visiting. They are plucky, but so many appear to be weary. This war has been such a long siege for them. And, I am trying to persuade myself to buy a bicycle. These English bicycles are marvels. Our heavy company bicycles are nearly impossible to pump up a hill—and these English women just cruise around us with a smirk on each face. So it will go until I make my purchase. Winchester, here I come, I think!

We are engaged in a busy training schedule—mostly review of much already covered.

April 22, 1944 Chilbolton Downs

Bought a bicycle the 19th, and paid 10.3.2.—10 pounds, 3 shillings, 2 pence—about $40.40. It is geared, very easy to pedal going up hills, and nice. Have been out for two runs—each better than 12 miles. One can really get around—just a wee jaunt into Winchester, now. The beauty of this countryside is just beyond adequate description.

We have been so dependent upon my little radio. We have had it connected in a series with a 60 watt bulb, to reduce the 230V current down to OK. One of the men in our Hqs gang knew how to do it. We regularly pick up broadcasts from

France, Germany, Netherlands, Belgium, and all of Great Britain. Now a short of some sort has developed, and it will pop off and on and off and on. So, we shall see about it.

Col. Cole, I, and others plan to attend church tomorrow in the cathedral at Winchester. This will be a different sort of service, probably, from the one we like in the small church at Crawley. But, maybe not.

April 25, 1944 Chilbolton Downs

It seems to me that we have been seeing quite an increase in number of planes overhead. These are nearly always our own (U.S. and British), but with an occasional German. These people refer to the "bloody Jerries" and enjoy shaking their fists at the German planes. Out for a stroll, I encountered a local citizen, and he used the word "bloody" with reference to the Germans. I asked him about the word's meaning, and his reply implied that it was anything and everything bad, but a word never to be used "in the presence of the ladies!" About two days later when I took my laundry to the good soul who does it for several of us, a German plane flew over as we were visiting at her door. She looked up at the plane, raised her fist and shook it, and said—"Somebody ought to shoot down that bloody Jerry!" I had to wonder if my wash lady happened to be no "lady." We have had some good chuckles over this.

The radio is back on track. I discovered a tube hidden away in my locker, and it has for the present taken care of the short-out. We are happy with its recovery from its illness.

The past three days have been just wonderful—so clear and sunny. It seems that we are able to get more accomplished when it is not cloudy and rainy. Those of us with bicycles have been doing so much traveling about. This countryside is just astoundingly clean and beautiful. There is a pastoral serenity quite beyond anything I had expected to witness or experience. The green fields are so clean. Tradition and custom seem to be so deeply entrenched. In some respect these people seem to be almost decades in the rear, but they are so genuinely friendly. They do show the strain of nearly five years of war, but do display eagerness to open a second front against the Nazis—terribly costly in lives lost as they know it will be!

No hints about any promotions for us lowly second lieutenants. Of course, about four of us should receive advancement. Col. Cole's absence on some sort of detached service may explain what we believe to be some sort of neglect. Ha! I'd much prefer to have this mess end quickly and just return home.

Do you enjoy receiving these V-Mail letters? Are they easy to read? Also, remember that your letter to an APO requires no more than six cents' postage.

May 2, 1944 Chilbolton Downs

(We had been placed under the most limiting of restrictions with respect to references in letters to place and activities, and censorship of mail limited correspondence to little other than weather, food, recreation, health, and certain observations of persons and their customs, friendliness, and well-being. It was my responsibility to inform the men of the company, and they were most cooperative—amazingly so. Each officer was his own censor, but letters were mailed unsealed. Upon reading at much later date my preserved letters, it did not surprise me to notice that some of them had been read and stamped with a subsequent date. Central censors had to have done a good bit of spot-checking of home-bound letters. We urged our men to maintain the "Q.T." when away from camp and in the local pubs.

(April 30, our Base Platoon was assigned to be on temporary duty for sixty days at nearby G-55, a general depot—at Lockerly. The medical section of this depot had been assigned a task which proved to be beyond its capacity. Into two or three large warehouses had been stored "medical supplies" to accompany the troops to engage in the cross-channel invasion and to cover estimated needs for the subsequent ninety days—including equipment for at least two advance field hospitals. These supplies were in their original packages and boxes, and were to be assembled on "skids."

(Each skid was of wood, approximately five feet by four feet, and supported by "2-by-4s" which were spaced to permit steel bands to pass beneath—two lengthwise and two sideways. A large square of heavy canvas was placed across a skid. upon which were then to be assembled in a sort of matching order boxes and cases to reach upward to no more than six feet. Each load was then closed within the folded canvas and firmly bound together by the clinched steel bands. Each skid-load could then be picked up by a crane equipped with hooks to be slipped beneath the crossed bands atop the load. Medical supplies thus assembled and wrapped were virtually weatherproof.

(Major Grove, temporarily in command of our company, assigned me, a lowly second lieutenant, to be in charge of our men at G-55. I discussed the project with the men, and at least two of our sergeants had had experiences with warehousing and knew of the procedures needed. I turned them loose, and within a day's time "things" were moving at an amazing pace. These men responded with a zeal which seemed to speak with clarity of their "delight" to be doing something to assist in the effort to turn the war against the Axis powers. A year later, when the defeats of Italy and Germany were accomplished and with censorship at end, I sent home, under the date of June 5, 1945, a review of this endeavor at G-55.

(Pressure was on, for a deadline had to be met—all of which had to do with the supplies to go in with the cross-channel movement of men and the landings on what would become known as Omaha and Utah Beaches. I had never seen a group of men waylay a task of overwhelming odds in such fashion as our men did. The sergeants got their crews organized, and by the end of the second day it was evident that they had developed an increasingly efficient system. We had to work from about 7:00 in the morning to nearly 11:30 at night. The men walked around like zombies much of the time. During the first ten days, nearly every one of the men just sort of shrunk. They were billeted in tents, about three miles away, and slept in their bed rolls on the ground. Nights were cold, and a cot was simply of no use. Breakfast was at 6 a.m., and then a combination of trucks hauled them to the depot. My quarters were the same, and I breakfasted with them. Second meal came in shifts about four in the afternoon—at the depot. Food was plentiful, well prepared, but nothing fancy. After about ten days, my job became that of a sort of liaison officer—to communicate on a daily basis between our company headquarters and our men at G-55. Major Grove, Captain Stroh, and Lt. Ryley also lent their expertises.

(The medical supplies to be in place and on board ship to go in with the invasion had been prescribed and included the equipment for an advance field hospital. The deadline to be met by us at G-55 seemed, at first, to be quite beyond the possible. The final loads of supplies were away from G-55 just two hours behind the assigned time. It was a remarkable achievement. Subsequent shipments were easily on time and to supply the stores of the medical depot established by our company at Trevières, four miles inland from Omaha Beach.

(The Advance Platoon, both sections, of our company was, as of May 7, attached to the First U.S.Army and proceeded to Dursley, in Gloucestershire, to join ranks with the 1st Medical Depot Company. Training focused upon preparation to establish initial medical supply posts upon "invasion," and change of locale took them to Whitchurch, Wales—and then to Cardiff where they boarded H.M.S. Hospital Carrier "Lady Connaught." It was May 28. The ship took position at Portsmouth, June 5. The men debarked, Utah Beach, somewhat before midnight, June 7.)

Bought my weekly ration of 2 cokes, 2 chocolate bars, 1 bar of soap, 1 package of gum, and 1 #2 can of grapefruit juice at our little company PX. Except for the soap and three sticks of gum, I had consumed all of it before bedtime.

The weather has been cool and crisp, and those of us with bicycles have been touring the vicinity. The fields and land divisions are so neatly patterned. The green is just intense. The houses are quaint and dainty and old, and wherever one looks he sees a picture to be taken. The people are so plucky, and they seem to be prepared to face any eventuality—whatever it will require to crush Hitler. They were sorely threatened, and this must never recur.

Had a long ride via jeep, yesterday—without side curtains, and it was four hours to go and four hours to return, and the breeze just chilled me through and through. I was certain I had caught a bad cold, for I couldn't stop shivering. But, I'm fine, today!

Was surprised to read that Willkie lost out in the Nebraska primary. But, I was under the impression that he had already withdrawn. He was, by far, my choice.

May 8, 1944 Chilbolton Downs

Three of us took a nice 250-mile jaunt today—nearly all through this beautiful rural scenery. We went to hold interviews regarding change from gold bars to silver. So, hold your breaths! Well, our promotions are several weeks overdue! Col. Cole is away on some sort of special service, and he has paid no attention to his responsibilities for us. We can thank Major Grove for getting this done, finally.

These nights are so chilly. To sleep at night, I keep warm by putting my bedroll on the ground; for to use a cot just invites agony because of the air circulating underneath. Ho! Ho! And, one has to wear socks to keep feet from turning into icicles.

As for what I have been doing? Well, I've been busier than ten bugs under a dishpan. One thing I have learned, that our men are an unusually capable and resourceful lot. Have they ever opened my eyes! They are simply a great crew, and I don't mean maybe. Despite near exhaustion, they have proved to be of an amazing spirit and of good humor, collectively. And, temporarily, we have no hot water for shaving and showers and are on a two-meal per day routine.

May 18, 1944 Chilbolton Downs A.P.O. 350

Have been spending my time between our camp and the men working at G-55. The more I keep tabs on the men at the depot the more I admire them. They are really a superb bunch. And they are really putting those skids together. Some days I ride my bicycle, but it takes a bit of time and most days a driver from our motor pool skoots me down and back.

We located a very nice lady to do laundry for some of us, and I was quite amused the other day. An elderly gentleman walks regularly past our camp, and I have visited with him on occasion. He uses the word "bloody" often to refer to something he does not like, or finds much to his disgust or disfavor. I asked him to explain the word to me, and he proceeded to do so. When he had finished his discourse, he added that one should never use the word "in the presence of the ladies!" Well, not far from where our laundress lives is a large bomb crater—the bomb of German origin. When I questioned her about it, she went into somewhat of a tirade, shook her fist, and proceeded with some vehemence to condemn those "bloody Jerries"! My conclusion, with a grin, was that she was, perhaps, not a "lady."

Our mail service is somewhat of a puzzlement. For three or four days, no letters from anyone. And then in will come some fourteen or fifteen. The mail always gets here, eventually. So, our service is functioning. Every once in a while a letter will have been written a month ago—was just lying in a basket somewhere. But, most letters from home arrive within a week's time. Pretty good, I think!

Nearly all of us are now sleeping out in our pup tents. Seemingly, as I gather, our "uppers" think we should become accustomed to living in "the rough"—as we expect will be our fortune once we make it to the shores of France. There will undoubtedly be much destruction of all facilities, as progress is made against the German resistance. The poor French populace will be caught between and betwixt. I just received a letter from Joe Hodgson, he is now in Italy. He had been through Naples, reputed to have been one of Italy's most beautiful cities. Joe wrote that the city was largely destroyed and in ruins. The Germans, as they retreat northward, seem to be determined to leave the Italy of yore to be almost beyond recognition. Of course, the bombing from the Americans and British leave their awful marks. Well, Mussolini's fate will soon be sealed. It will require considerably more time to deal with our "paper hanger" and the "Son of Heaven"!

We certainly depend upon my little radio. It is the only one that works, and it is in our headquarters office. The English stations give us so much music—much of it symphonic. Interruptions are frequent—to drop bits of info about the actions on land and sea. Much of the chatter has to do with the expected cross channel invasion. My hunch is that much of what is said is designed to keep our German friends confused—even purposefully misled. We shall see.

May 24, 1944 Chilbolton Downs A.P.O. 350

Nights just keep giving us the chills, but I just snuggle in my bed roll and sleep like a log. The English have furnished us with what are called "biscuits"—three square cushions per person, and these give us some added comfort for sleeping. No trouble to keep warm in my wee tent.

Do not know what our advanced platoon is up to. Some correspondence, but no one may give any sort of "information." We know what is going on at G-55. Here, at our headquarters, we have many discussions, and there is a very warm camaraderie between the men and officers. We spend free time in the afternoons at volleyball, and some good bridge games find us hard at it in the evenings. The caliber of our enlisted personnel is just amazing, and so many of them are not long out of high school.

Still no word about promotions for us three lowly lieutenants. When we do get the word, once the red tape has run its course, we will receive pay increase from date of decision. So we shall just have to wait. Some decisions on other matters just keep pending and pending and pending. I just do not understand all the procrastinating. I think too many of our superiors are fearful of being held "accountable"! But, after all, I'm just no more than a lil-ol-lieutenant who isn't supposed to know much. Humph!! But, so much and so many things just keep getting "screwed up"—and always from "above"! Oh, well, and this is the army!

Gee, and you wrote about eating strawberry shortcake. You must be trying to torture me. My mouth is watering. The two boxes of candies and cakes arrived, and they didn't last long. Boy, but those caramels just melted away. So, send some more—just any time you get the urge. We are hungry for marshmallows and olives (ripe and green and even with pimientos). As per each week, I just bought three bars of candy, a can of grapefruit juice, two packages of cookies, a bar of soap, and two little "cakes." Each of us has his "weekly ration"—available at our nearby PX.

Just a suggestion. Address my letters to Lt. David Mickey. Leave off the "2nd"—for we think it is about time!

May 27, 1944 Chilbolton Downs Saturday

Thursday, several of us peddled in to Winchester to hear a singing of Handel's "Messiah." It was sung by the Hants chorus in the marvelous, old cathedral. It was just great—full orchestra and chorus of over 250 voices. The singers sat in tiers arranged on platforms constructed above the chancel. I was just thrilled to hear such marvelous music. The contralto soloist was magnificent—such a soft, mellow voice with reserve which could just fill the cathedral. This Astra Desmond was one of the finest singers I have heard.

The nave of this cathedral must be at least twice as long as that of First Plymouth Congregational church in Lincoln, and at least double the width. We sat about midway, and I was just amazed at the acoustics. It was a packed house, and well over half were American service personnel. The basso was also unusually good—could really rumble through the runs, even to some near bellowing. But, it was the contralto who caught my fancy, and she was probably about fifty in age and a bit hefty. She sang with so much "expression," and one didn't miss a word. And, that "Hallelujah Chorus" just brought us all to our feet. Had Hitler heard it, he would have known that his cause was doomed. That chorus just seemed to sing with a defiance. It was simply a thrill, altogether!

Yes, I regularly receive my copies of "Stars and Stripes" and "Yank," and I read them. So, along with the radio, I do keep up on the news. I am also getting to be pretty good at identifying our aircraft. We see no German planes, of course. But, we do study the photos and profiles, for who knows what lies ahead for us.

No complaint about my appetite. I just seem to be hungry for each meal. Our cooks do well for us. So many "things" about this company of ours that are discouraging, and the "red tape" that seems to cause delay is, to me, just baffling. For me, a saving grace is to be found in the caliber of our enlisted men. As a group, generally, they are just "top notch"—and I haven't seen others quite like them elsewhere!

No word about promotion. Don't forget to send me about four sets of silver bars. Ho! Ho! We must live in hope!

June 1, 1994 Chilbolton Downs

Found a thruppence (a three-penny piece) along the road, yesterday. Maybe it is a good luck sign. We shall see. Maybe the promotions will come through. Ha!

The lacing on one of the volleyballs broke, and it was almost a riot to get the bladder deflated, a new lacing inserted and tightened, and then to inflate by use of a tire pump. It took some doing, with several heads giving advice. It was worth several laughs.

Mixed weather, but it is definitely warming. My shivering has just about ceased. Humidity is always high. The countryside is just so green and beautiful! We go for a spin, now and then, with our bicycles—often to seek out a different road… So many women use bicycles, and they do a lot of transporting—up hill and down hill, and here and there and everywhere. There is no use of gasoline for pleasure-driving.

Have been grinning a bit as I read about all of the speculation concerning an invasion. We, too, are wondering. But, we hear nothing. We know that utter secrecy must prevail, and we know that censorship rules out almost everything with respect to letters written to the homefolk. So many are using V-mail. If one types, he can get quite a bit on a page; but, most of the men prefer to use regular sheets and envelopes.

The hoot and cry are summoning us for volleyball. So, will close for now.

June 4, 1944 Chilbolton Downs

Well, certainly no news to relate. Nothing to report about promotions. The three of us have about lost interest. My guess, almost, is that my gold will turn to silver only as I age enough to turn gray. Oh, well!

This weather just keeps us guessing—can be warming and nice for a moment, and then a change to wind, cool, and bluster. It just keeps us guessing, with life always just that much more of a challenge.
Our mail service is becoming more and more problematic—virtually nothing for two or three days, and then sacks of it.

We are in the dark as far as an invasion of the continent is concerned. Quite a bit of talk about a "D-Day"—debarkation or disembarkation from ships and transports to land on the coast of France. We just hope that "Old Jerry" will be in for more surprises than he can handle. We keep receiving reminders that we must be thorough in our censoring of mail. It certainly takes much of my time. It has become a rare occasion when I have had to return a letter to one of our men—for rewriting.

Happen to be OD today, and this always takes time to do all the little extras—so much checking up on little routine matters. As evening approaches, we must make certain that all black-out curtains and drapes are drawn throughout the offices of our camp. Periodic checks must be made to make certain that our "guards" are at their posts and awake. Also, as "officer of the day" I must carry a pistol—my side arm. As for our lay-out, we have nothing that would give any aid or comfort to our enemy.

May get in about four hours of shut-eye, to night—will just stretch out on one of the benches in our headquarters office. Snore, snore!!

June 6, 1944 D-Day Chilbolton Downs

Well, it has begun! I was awakened, perhaps about 3:30 this a.m., from the constant drone of airplanes. It was quite evident that much was in motion—with but one conclusion to draw, that the invasion was underway. We have stayed glued to the little radio. Actually the earliest acknowledgment of the invasion came over a German radio. Then followed regular reporting via our English stations. These British just give the bare facts, and nothing more—no commentary.

The air is full of planes—British and American—going and coming. The announcements on radio have given us figures as to how many planes, how many ships, how many persons are involved in this operation. Apparently, concentration of British and French troops are to the east of the Americans—and some Polish, I understand. Occasionally is reference to "high casualties." Here, we are surrounded by this beautiful and peaceful landscape—such contrast to what is taking place in channel and on shore. Whew!! I wonder if these announcements with reference to number of planes, ships, men, etc. are given out with purpose to discourage the will of the Germans to resist. Too, we here at Chilbolton are concerned about our advance platoon—for we have understood that they are to be in the invasion to set up the first station to issue medical supplies. We shall find out, eventually. Some close friends, there; and I do not want to lose any of them!

King George is to address, via radio, the nation at nine his evening. I want to hear what he has to say. Of course, by time you read this epistle, everything will have become old news.

No doubt about it, our ETO-USA Hqs has been very busy and concentrating on "invasion." So, no one has been giving attention to such lowly matter as the promotion of three lowly shavetails from the 3lst Medical Depot Company. It has been over two months since promotions came to another medical depot company, and we are now outranked by three or four who were in our OCS class at Barkeley. Our colonel was just neglectful, and we are paying for it—as you may surmise. I am beginning to think we really have a lemon for CO—a real sour one!

Planes! Planes! Planes! And, more Planes!

June 7, 1944 Chilbolton Downs

The invasion is really on, and much in earnest. The air activity is just amazing—planes in countless numbers going and coming. Virtually, we have an umbrella of planes overhead. That "old Shickelgruber" is in for a good beating eventually. Our combined air might is just colossal.

Reports come filtering in that the beachheads have been "established"—but, at heavy cost. We shall have to wait to learn just what that means. I think most of us have been doing a lot of praying! This air traffic is night and day. I think I have been able to identify nearly all American and British aircraft.

Things are sort of tense around here, for we are certain our advanced platoon is in on these landings. Some day we shall know. We have played several games of volleyball and baseball—just to pass the time. We have scheduled some study sessions, for review; but, our hearts are not in it.

And, tomorrow is an anniversary for you, Bin and Don. Yes, I have remembered.

June 11, 1944 Chilbolton Downs

Our air activity continues. For us, the initial excitement has simmered down considerably. But, we are anxious. The British newscasts are just with the bare facts, and there is no guessing as to what might have occurred. These BBC reporters just seem so dry, but they tell us what has happened.

Our company's cooks have been turning out some of the best meals. Except for the officer's mess at Camp Lee, this comes close to the best I've had—day after day. They have to be using some rations, here and there. Their hamburgers are about as good as one can find anywhere. Of course, they are just part of the gang which makes up our company, and we have far above our share of unusually able persons. Those fellows down at G-55 just amazed me, and they met what was at first a seeming impossibility. They know how I feel about them. I so much regret that our T/O has so few promotions available. My praises do not put more stripes on their sleeves and a few more dollars in their pockets.

No info about promotions for us three lowly second lieutenants. We are wondering if our papers became lost or buried. Our colonel really neglected us. We do know that promotions for the second lieutenants in one of our sister companies were effective about April first. So it goes in this man's army! I often ponder if it would have been better had I stayed with the 85th Division. But, one thing for sure, I do much admire these British and their pluck, and this I should have missed. Bravo!

One of our noncoms just knocked on my door (I'm back in my room, for we are no longer training ourselves to become accustomed to the pup tents) to draft me for a bridge game. We have some great battles, and prolonged rivalries often continue until long after the black-out curtains have to be drawn. A wholesome camaraderie with nearly all in our company is just heart warming.

The weather has been too often cloudy and rainy, and this has been somewhat of a problem for our pilots who need to target German installations in Normandie. But today was clearer. So, let us hope our marksmanship will become much improved!

Our mail arrives irregularly. The dates of letters received are often far from being in order. I know you experience the same mixing of dates when you hear from me. I'm glad I do not know when a big sack of mail lies unattended for a few days in a corner somewhere. Oh, well! What is important is that it eventually comes through. Yes!

June 15, 1944 Chilbolton Downs

Just bought some of my weekly "rations"—some coke, Baby Ruth bars, and cookies, etc. We fare quite well.

Some clearer and warmer days. These clear skies mean that our planes can see their targets. We heard that casualties continue to run high, and these reports are sickening. No doubt about it, Adolph and his buddies are in for a real beating. The whole front of the beachhead is secure, but penetrations inland are not deep. It will take time and will be costly.

Our cooks just continue to do such a bang-up job with their meals. They have become experts at disguising. Ha!

Our mornings are busy with routine matters. Nearly each a.m. I get driven by jeep down to G-55 to make certain our men are O.K. About three of our sergeants keep close tabs on "things," and nothing slips by or around them. The men continue to skid-load medical supplies, but they are ahead of established "instructions." Once loaded and secured, a skid can be moved by forklift or crane. It is my understanding that these prepared skids are being assembled, now, in two areas—one near Southampton and the other near Portsmouth. Also, the men at G-55 were told that they were to complete for shipping medical supplies to meet demand for the first hundred days after invasion. We wonder if we shall be tearing apart most of the skids we have put together. For those skids which we knew were destined to go in early with the invasion, some of the fellows tucked in notes to the men of the advanced platoon. It will be interesting to know if these special communications were received. All such doings are good for morale.

When we get reunited, there is going to be lots of "catching up" to take place. I do so hope that none of our men became casualties!

June 19, 1944 Sunday Chilbolton Downs

Friday, while we were shaving in the latrine, Major Grove said to me, "Mickey, old boy, how would you like to run into London with me to do some purchasing and looking around—mostly looking around?" So, to London I went, and this is what I saw there.

You can make real good connections into London from all directions by train (Winchester, for us). We got to Waterloo Station about 9:45, and then just started out on foot to see what we could see. We inquired as to the nearest way to Big Ben, and a Bobbie told us to just go to the bottom, turn to the left, and cross the bridge to the right, and there we would be. So, we went down York Road, across Westminster Bridge, and there were Big Ben and the Houses of Parliament—just as one has seen them so often in pictures and movies. We just marveled at Big Ben with his four faces, and we immediately set about to set our watches by him. Surprisingly, I was accurate almost to the second. A perfect day for pictures, and we had a good look before we crossed the bridge.

We were sort of like Twain's "Innocents Abroad" and just wandered right into the Houses of Parliament. A Bobbie eyed us suspiciously, raised his finger, and proceeded to inform us that no visitors without passes could enter. We didn't press the issue, but we did let him know how disappointed we were.

Westminster Abbey is just across the street from the Houses of Parliament, with the main entrance from Victoria Street. We entered the Abbey, and it was awe-inspiring. You really felt as if you were on hallowed ground. Just inside the entrance is the tomb of Britain's "Unknown Soldier," and above it is the Congressional Medal placed there by General Pershing. We just browsed around inside the Abbey, and one can find the burial places of many of England's great notables—Shakespeare, Keats, Southey, members of the royal family, poets, doctors, scientists, etc. Chamberlain is here. We just walked around in a sort of daze and couldn't believe we were really here. Certain of the more elaborate memorials have been bricked and walled over to protect them from possible bomb damage. Only a small part of the Abbey has been touched by bombing.

Next, we went up Whitehall to Trafalgar Square and viewed there the immense pillar and statue of Lord Nelson—commemorating his great victory over Napoleon's fleet at the Battle of Trafalgar. On the way up Whitehall, we passed #10 Downey Street, Churchill's residence, but he was not around for us to greet. There are so many statues and memorials along these streets. At the base of the monument to Nelson are four immense lions, and these signify the four great naval victories won by Nelson. The square, here, is immense and serves as center for several intersections.

We took some time at this square, and then went down the Mall, up Waterloo and Regent Sts. to Jermyn and thence to the ARC Jules Officers' Club, and there we ate our dinner. It was good, and we needed a rest, for we had really been hoofing it. We made inquiries about guided tours, but none began before 2:00, and all were filled. So, we just decided to go it on our own and were on our way by 12:30. We would walk it for the afternoon.

We went to Piccadilly and thence to the Circus—a center for all sorts of dives, burlesques, etc. Gee! Talk about amusements! No difficulty to find a place of "ill repute"! It is an interesting part of the city, and should be observed. We next headed to Buckingham Palace, had to back-track along Piccadilly to Green Park, through this park and to the Palace. It has its magnificent gates, and is enclosed with its iron fence. Again, we were thrilled to be before what we had so often seen in photos and in movies. We could see into the grounds only through the gates, but we did walk clear around. At the front is the great statue of Queen Victoria, and she looks every bit THE QUEEN. The poise is wonderful, really majestic. We just looked and looked at her.

It was back up the Mall, again through Trafalgar Square, then up the Strand to Aldwyn, and on to Kingsway. Just off Kingsway is the Old Curiosity Shop—made famous by Dickens' novel. We went in, and it is a quaint little place and doing business, as usual. It is so in need of repair, and appeared to be about ready to fall apart and to tumble. Each of us purchased some etchings, and I'll be sending mine home in my footlocker. This little shoppe is most interesting, and we did much enjoy being in it. First editions of many of Dickens' works were for sale, but the prices were quite beyond the poor salary of a Second Lieutenant from the USA.

We then went around to Chancery and down to Fleet Street, and then along to Ludgate and to St. Paul's Cathedral. This is really a landmark, and into it we went. Really, it is wonderful, and it gave me a bigger thrill than did the Abbey. I don't know why, but it did. It is one thing that comers to London to not want to miss. It is just beautiful, and was damaged a little by bombing One sees a huge hole in one of its wings, but no other "great damage."

We went into the crypt where more—several—of England's notables are buried. We saw the memorial to Lord Kitchener, the Duke of Wellington's tomb and the immense funereal hearse, the tombs of Jellicoe and Beatty (leading British admirals of World War I), and tombs of many others. All members of the armed forces can see this crypt without paying, but it costs the public, in general, sixpence. It proved to be most interesting, and we just reveled in it. I bought a little packet of sixteen pictures of St. Paul's, and will send them in the footlocker. Don't hold your breaths, for it could be weeks, yet.

We trudged on down to the Tower, the Old London Tower—really a sight to behold. It has as windows for the cells just crosses—little slits through which a bit of light and air can pass. One can think of the many poor souls of the past who rotted away inside these immense walls. Around the Tower is its immense moat, another symbol of the so-called "Dark Ages." One goes down Cannon Street and Eastcheap from St. Paul's to get to the Tower, which is by the famous bridge of song and story—"London Bridge" (now called "Tower Bridge"). For us, it was a thrill to walk across it.

We could view the Thames River, up and down, and were surprised because of all the business and commerce being carried along. We pinched ourselves—to make certain we were really there.

Well, on to Tooley, Borough, Southwark, and Stamford Streets—with return to Waterloo Station and Big Ben. We looked for a place to eat—off Trafalgar Square. It was about six, and we found a brasserie—a good meal for a crown, or five shillings, or a dollar. Ha! Then, it was back down Whitehall to give Big Ben a last look, and to the RR station and train and back to camp. It was for us a wonderful day.

Along the river front are warehouses, warehouses, and more warehouses. The worst of the bombing seemed to have taken place, as targeted, right around St.

Paul's. On all sides of the Cathedral, for blocks, nearly all structures had just been leveled. The great church stands as a sort of Christian edifice in defiance against the Nazi assault! Really, it must have been a focal point for attack from the air, but suffered just one hit—but no explosion. It just stands forth, with no buildings around to hide it—only cellars and basements, but with all debris removed and cleared.

The funeral hearse of Wellington (defeated Napoleon at Waterloo) is something else. It took eighteen days to build, and it is made of iron and with much overlay of gold. His funeral procession had few equals in history. One must ponder the homage which was paid him by the British. He died in 1854. His tomb is a magnificent bit of marble. But that hearse is just almost beyond adequate description.

The little taxi cabs are everywhere—as thick as fleas on a hound's back. We never hailed one, and we noted that the drivers often appeared to be "characters." There was far more traffic in the city than we had expected. Each taxi is always marked FOR HIRE.

The city of London is very small, geographically. St. Paul's is within the city, and also the Tower. But, Big Ben, the Houses of Parliament, the Abbey, Piccadilly and Trafalgar Square are in Westminster. It was for us a wonderful day!

The people in London were smiling, somewhat, because of 's Adolph's newest weapons, the "robot-bombs," or, "pilotless planes." They came in somewhat regularly, but none of the citizenry seemed greatly alarmed—just annoyed. Of course, damage could be extensive, here and there. One gentleman said to us, "We've handled everything else he has, and we'll do him up a bit over this one." The English have Hitler's goat, no doubt; and I think they expect the lights to be back on for next Christmas. Well, that will be something to hope for, eh?

I'm sending you the map of London which we used—marking our route. You can follow our itinerary. We must have walked over twenty miles—maybe nearly twenty-five. Our feet ached and were a bit swollen. But it was a wonderful day!! Cost of a meal in London was so reasonable. Chicken seemed always available.

The pace of things for us has slowed, and our men are just cracker-jacks. We have a couple of officers who just do not know how to get along with others. Oh, well! And now for some shut-eye.

June 21, 1944 Chilbolton Downs

Am still enjoying that trip to London. In some of the shops they had for sale some rubber items—such as bands and jar rings. One proprietor told us it had been three years since he had any to sell, and he didn't know why they were suddenly available. Interesting, eh?

So many restrictions have now been lifted with reference to what may be said in letters to our "homefolks." As censor, it is much easier to scan for any "no-nos." Locations of encampments and dates of movement, or reference to expectations are to be avoided.

Several of our men understand well the German language, and we occasionally can pick up a broadcast from Germany. Claims have been that the missiles (robots) have devastated areas of England, but these are mostly fabrications to spur up morale. Four or five have fallen not far from our camp. Alarms sound about twenty seconds before arrival, and we have heard only the distant explosions. London has been the target. And the people are more and more determined to see this war through to the finish of a Nazi Germany. Londoners do head for cover, for the city in general is the target. There is little accuracy in targeting specific buildings.

No new supply of candy has arrived, and you have referred to two shipments. Also, one is due to arrive from the Boston area. The sweet stuff doesn't last long once it arrives. Our men are not only an amazingly efficient group, but they have great appetites for all special shipments from the home front. Ha! Ha! They are collectively a great crew!

We've been having some sunny and warmer weather, and the planes are coming and going regularly. There has to be lots of attention being paid to the entire front. We have been keeping track of the several American and British planes identified, and we have some classes to assist us. We have walls covered with photos—some of them large. Also, we are working on the French language. Two of our noncoms and I are directing the studies. We have a few GI manuals, and we make good use of a large portable blackboard. You should hear our nasal tones. We spend most of the time just laughing at our efforts. Fortunately, I had a year's course at Wesleyan, and another review at the University of Nebraska. We are having fun!

One of our sergeants was a major in "modern languages," and he is good.

Delayed in getting this into the mail, and a bonanza of mail arrived—several letters and two boxes of candy. Yes!

June 24, 1944 Chilbolton Downs

Not much of importance, from here. We are awaiting the fall of Cherbourg, and we cheer when we hear of the sinking of parts of Nippon's fleet.

I have no idea as to the number of planes we saw at the time of the invasion. For days the skies were full of planes—coming and going. It remains a night and day traffic. Clear and warm, today, and it seems to me that there is increased activity. Removal of the Germans from Cherbourg is going to be costly, but it must be done. Then, Rommel's "panzers" have to be targeted wherever they can be found. It will take some doing to break through from the beaches of Normandie.

The robots are really of little decisive importance—Hitler's claims are designed to bolster the morale of the German people and army.

We are playing lots of volleyball and baseball in the afternoons, and then bridge is the evening sport. I've been doing some umpiring. Fun! And how the fellows do razz the poor ump!

June 30, 1944 Chilbolton Downs

A package or two of goodies arrived, and we have been doing justice to each morsel. Everything is so fresh. Really, a marvelous job of packing!

We Americans get a bit unhappy with our British broadcasters, for they give no more than the bare facts and essentials and are so "reserved."

I have a hunch that our military leaders did not expect the Germans "to defend" and hold Cherbourg. But, they opted to stay and not to abandon. Those forces could have strengthened the lines along the beaches which have confined the Allies. News from Italy continues to be good. My old 85th is right in there with the Fifth Army as it heads up the Adriatic coast.

Some drizzly days for us, and it seems that the robots are hitting London moreso when the weather is clouded.

Have been listening to the reports and broadcasts from the Republican Convention. As you know, Willkie was my choice, and Strassen is the other good one. Bricker and Warren did not arouse my enthusiasm. As for Dewey, it is going to be difficult for me to vote for him. I would prefer FDR, and some of my Republican forebears might be turning over in their graves. Ha!

Dewey's acceptance speech was the best he has yet made. Perhaps there is some hope, but I doubt it. I do not think he can defeat FDR. Quite something that our Dwight Griswold made the nominating speech for Dewey.

Two of us lowly lieutenants and two or our sergeants have been having some marvelous bridge matches. We switch around, then added our scores, and then discovered we were running about neck and neck. We do enjoy our games, and the camaraderie is wonderful. I hope our company remains intact! In an earlier series of games, two of us outscored the others 13,350 to 6,260.

No promotion news, yet. I suppose some "brass statue" somewhere is sitting on them. It is most discouraging. We will be more than two months behind others in similar companies. Our colonel has really neglected us something fierce. Major Grove is embarrassed... Teague, Lane, and I are just a bit more than angry. But, nothing we can do about it!

Our cooks have to be about the best at work in this man's army. They just amaze me! And, our company barber is one who has found in the army a new trade ; and, he is no less than a cracker-jack. We, as a company, are fortunate to have these men.

Some of our gang become a bit roiled, now and then, because of some uncomplimentary and derisive remarks made in newspapers and "on air" anent Americans. Of course, this is the first time since 1066 that a foreign army has "occupied" England. British writers are unfair, now and then, and they do not keep antagonisms from being emphasized. No doubt about it, we "Yanks" are not angels. Oh, well! But, who knows, we may hear of wings having been sprouted.

July 2, 1944 Chilbolton Downs

The rain continues and continues—now, at least eight days of it. This has become a sunshine-forsaken island. Sometimes I wonder why it is that the British will fight so hard to keep it. Ha!

Our large water pump is on the blink, and for five days these Limey procrastinators have been promising to come to fix it. Our 40,000 gallon tank was nearly full, or we'd be hauling water. As far as I know, no one here has had a shower for six days. By tomorrow, water for cooking and drinking will be it—with minimum for personal washing. News is that a crew will be here Monday at 8:00 a.m.

Our mail is being directed, we think, to our advanced platoon, now in France—well over a week since mail from U.S. has arrived. We remain in the dark as to when we will be quitting this place.

The news keeps getting darker and darker for Hitler's cause. One must wonder about the Nazi will to hold on. Of course, the Germans do not want to consider the alternative. We have certain contacts with the army hospitals nearby, and both Allied and Nazi wounded are being cared for. The foreign soldiers have done a bit of talking. In so many cases, they were ordered to the front and with warnings that they were to advance, or be shot from the rear. Well, they had little to hope for, and the wounded, here, are so grateful that they were to become POWs. From reports which filter through to us, all the months of training came to an end in just a few minutes of action at the Normandy front. I think we have reason to be very proud of our medical personnel on action along the lines inward from the beaches.

Just reread a letter received some time ago, and you asked about my use of the initials TS. You are half right—The T does stand for "tough," but the S does not mean "situation." Ha! Ha!

Evenings continue to be good for cribbage and bridge games. Several of the men enjoy poker.

Volleyball and baseball are nearly always on the market for late afternoon and evening—if the rain lets up, and then much mud to make a game difficult. This gang of men do not sit around and twiddle their thumbs. Too, we continue with our French language, and we do much grinning during the sessions. But, we are making progress.

July 3, 1944 Chilbolton Downs

Today, I changed the color of my bars from gold to silver. The orders were written as of June 15, and since that date I have been a First Lieutenant. One of our officers had a purpose to go to a central headquarters and copies of the promotions were there. So, with more copies made, we received our notices. Well, we three new "Firsts" are pleased, but we should have had our advancements in early April. Humph!

Radio has announced that the Russians have taken Minsk. The Nazis are in retreat, and we wonder how long they can expect to hold out. We shall have to see, and it will be slow progress. The Allied command has just announced that for every robot-bomb that now lands in England, the Allied air force will proceed to destroy a German city or town. Hitler is now receiving a dose of his own sort of "war of nerves." German cities are going to be wiped out, and the people should know that the cause for it lies on Hitler's doorstep.

We are to have an eight-mile hike tomorrow, and it will be almost entirely in the mud. With all this rain, we are a muddy outfit, through and through.

But, today, a Canadian pump-repair and drilling squad has arrived, and our pump is being fixed. By tomorrow noon, we should have plenty of water. With no water for over a week for bathing, we had become a real stinky crew.

Bought some of my "rations" today—a candy bar, two cokes, a package of gum, and a bar of palmolive soap. I rarely purchase my full amount, and never any tobacco.

July 7, 1844 Chilbolton Down

We are enjoying some sunshine and some drying of the ground. We are just marking time, and no one from "higher up" tells us anything. We hear nothing from Col. Cole—wherever he is and whatever he does.

Our pump is now fixed, and water for us is flowing beautifully. Our hot showers are once again just ordinary niceties.

Those silver bars do shine so nice. So many of the men engage in a bit of horseplay—to come and then polish the bars with their sleeves. It is heart-warming to have so many of them be enthusiastic about our promotions. Two of our second lieutenants did not receive promotions. One had a former association with Col. Cole and will not receive any advancement, here. The other has sort of put himself at odds and just rubs too many people the wrong way. He, too, may not receive promotion as long as he remains with us.

We had creamed chicken for dinner last evening, and I think it was nearly the best meal we have had since arriving in England. Our cooks are just "the best"—what a crew! Several of us let them know how much we appreciate their "good works"!

Have my small footlocker packed and ready to send home—just filled with acquisitions and memorabilia to be kept for later review. Enclosed and packed full is my Gladstone.

We continue to have fun with our efforts to speak French. Many of the men are much in earnest as they participate. We should know more about many things before long. We do keep busy, and keep restudying several of our manuals and reviewing directives relative to depot installation and procedures. And, our mail is certainly being sent to our advance platoon.

From reports, the robot-bombs have been pummeling London. We have been told that American and British pilots constantly search for the launching sites. But, it is a game of cat and mouse. One thing for sure, these robots will not alter one iota the course, eventually, of this war against Germany. The German people will pay a dear price!

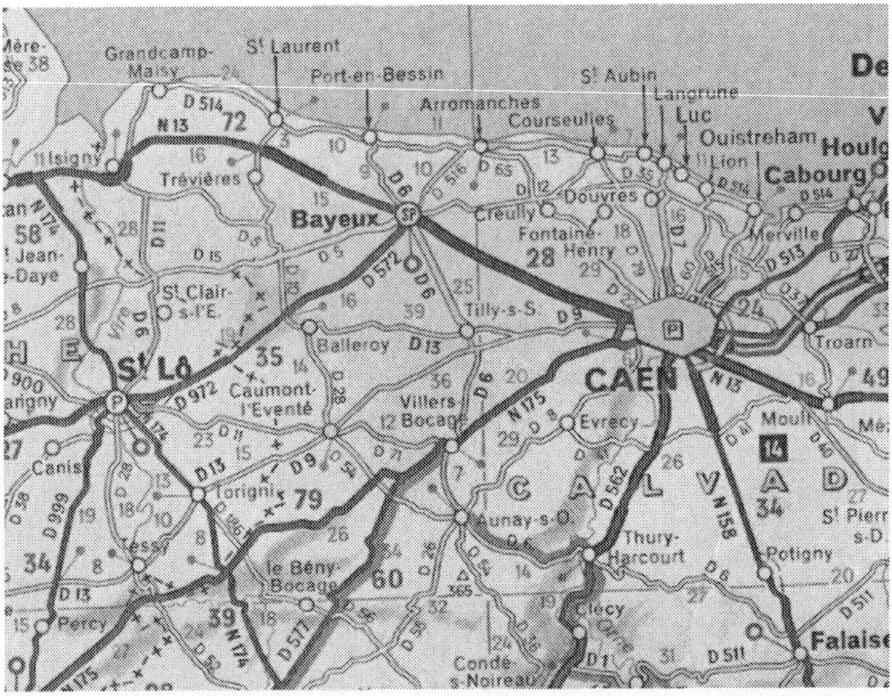
Grandcamp-Maisy
St Laurent
Port-en-Bessin
St Aubin
Arromanches
Courseulles
Langrune
Luc
Ouistreham
Lion
Cabourg
Isigny
Trévières
Bayeux
Creully
Douvres
Fontaine-Henry
Merville
St Clair-s-l'E.
St Lô
Balleroy
Tilly-s-S.
Troarn
CAEN
Caumont-l'Eventé
Villers-Bocage
Evrecy
Moult
Torigni
Aunay-s-O.
Thury-Harcourt
Potigny
Tessy
le Bény-Bocage
Percy
Clécy
Falaise
Condé-s-Noireau

Depot areas at Trevières

Treviéres

(This evening, about nine, we received a call from the RTO, Rail Transportation Officer, to tell us we were to be packed, loaded, and ready to go at 6:30 the following morning. So, we worked all night—to encase, seal, label, and be ready. It was a scramble and a night not to be forgotten. It rained like fury, and all seemed to be in a mess. We really cussed our higher-ups. It was unbelievable. The trucks arrived to take us to a nearby RR terminal. By train to Southampton, where we spent three days in a staging area. Letters, written much later, tell the story.) It was July 7th.

The three days were a godsend, for we were exhausted—and just ate and slept, and went to the movies. Every one was just pooped, and these days were wonderful. Everybody and everything seemed to be "on the ball! However, our motor pool and vehicles moved out on the second day.

July 11, we shouldered our duffle bags, marched through Southampton to the docks, and boarded the "Princess Charlotte," a former Belgian cross-channel excursion ship. We officers had our small staterooms and ate in a mess separate from the men. Our "C-rations" were warmed over. The same for the men, and they were quartered in the lower hold of the vessel. The ship dropped anchor near the Isle of Wight, and here a convoy formed. Barrage balloons were in the air—enuf of them nearly to blot out the sun.

We crossed the Channel on the 12th—saw ships, more ships, and more ships. These were of all sorts. The barrage of balloons never thinned. As we approached the shores of France, it looked as if half the merchant marine of the world had been sunk. We learned these many old vessels had been hauled in to provide breakwaters for subsequent landings, etc., at Omaha and Utah beaches. Later in the afternoon, we were transferred on to a LCT, or LCI, and were taken to a pier that extended into the shallow water. We went ashore without getting our feet wet. It was Utah Beach, and we were not overly impressed. Sand was everywhere, and nearby were a few abandoned German fortifications—all of cement in structure. Our duffles and packs were heavy, and it was hot and dusty.

Then, as instructed, we stacked our duffles—to be picked up by "transportation." We marched about four miles to a "beach-transit area ." We ate our "K rations," bedded down in the open, got some sleep—despite the light rain that fell. Some of us tried our "French" with some of the people who lived nearby. An American ammunition dump, some distance away, was in process of blowing up. We learned that no enemy action had been involved, but just carelessness. Our first night on French soil was what had become quite usual and a far cry from that experienced by our first waves of assault troops. We had no latrine facilities, except the nearby woods, and these had been long overused—each visit requiring careful stepping, if you know what I mean. Ha! No doubt about it, all rules for army sanitation had been shattered from the beginning—in this place

Of course, we were up bright and early for the 13th, were loaded into trucks, and were taken to the medical supply installation in operation by our advance sections. We had a royal reunion—with lots of hugging and back-slapping. So good to see Charley and Pete. According to them, we were to have followed much sooner than we did, but German resistance had not given way as expected. Saint Marie de Mont is the small village near to where we spent our first night, and it is not far from the medical supply station. Our "advance men" had all sorts of German souvenirs, and they had some wild tales to tell. When they went ashore during the invasion, they spent much time in their holes—dug in a hurry and often used. It was miraculous that not one of our men was to suffer any sort of battle wound. So, no Purple Hearts! We are thankful.

These men had fixed up some fancy quarters for themselves. They had received the skids we loaded at G-55, and made good use of the lumber and of the canvas. They had excellent tops above them, and things were dry and comfortable within. Beneath the cover, they had dug in to such extent that it would have taken a direct hit from above to have found them. Several of their excavations were at least five feet in depth. They were taking no chances. Such ingenuities!

As we knew, our mail had been sent to the advance platoon—including the directive to prepare to evacuate Chilbolton, etc. My packet of letters was to require a few hours to read and reread

We were just glued to our letters. As usual, we were wondering about our next move. Our advance sections had been attached to First Army, but nothing indicated that the rest of us were.

We hoped we would be functioning as a company, but no one knew.

Next day was for the French, Bastille Day—July 14, a national holiday. Orders were that our Base Platoon and headquarters were to go to Trevières, there to receive and prepare to distribute medical supplies, etc. Trucks arrived, and we journeyed through Carentan and Isigny to Trevières. We unloaded in a confined green meadow, with at least a dozen large apple trees to provide some cover. An advance section of our sister company, the 30th, was there, and they had assembled several skids of supplies delivered there. Before their departure, they gave us fair warning that 9:00 in the evening, and until about 11:30, some "Jerries" would come flying over, rather low, and that bullets would be clipping the tree tops—bullets from the planes, but more likely from the adjacent anti-aircraft unit in an adjacent field.

We put up a couple pyramidal tents for us officers, and the men scattered around the meadow's perimeter with their pup tents—with nice deep foxholes being dug. Larry Ryley and I dug ours together—deep enough and large enough for two. We were still on our "K" and "C" rations. We took nourishment and then settled down for the night. Our first aerial show started about 9:00, and we hit our holes and trenches in such fashion that an observer would have thought us to be veterans skilled in art of survival. Aftermath was that all of us proceeded to dig about a foot deeper. Ha! Our men began immediately to dig in their quarters—to resemble the patterns of our men at St. Marie de Mont.

Col. Cole had remained in England.

July 22, 1944 Trevières

Much rain and chilly. The grass of our orchard area has been virtually churned under by the trucks which have turned the area into a surface of mud. It is a mess.

Letters keep piling up, and then delivery brings them to us in bundles—I received 26 day before yesterday. It then takes some time to catch up. But, it is just great to get so much news from home and from friends and relatives. No packages from you have arrived recently; but, give the service some time. You mentioned two. So, I eagerly await their arrivals.

We have an electricity plant now working, and it is nice to have relief from the darkness. It is a bit tedious to do records while using lamps. We manage to do our mission despite the apparent confusion which seems to exist in our upper echelons. . The contradictory and confusing orders which filter down often seem to border on idiocy. We are used to this, and we just surge ahead and do what is needed to be done. The Germans were undoubtedly much confused by the garbled information they gathered with respect to time and place of the invasion, and this is one explanation as to the success for us which followed D-Day. Here, for us, we receive and store in tents or under protective canvas the medical supplies to be needed and requisitioned by the several units and the established hospitals of this area along the front.

My crew is in charge of the depot's "records"—of all goods received and then issued as requisitioned. Each item has its card, and each unit and hospital has its card. This bookkeeping is an exacting business, and my crew is simply top-notch. They do not need me. My only snooping is to make spot checks to make certain that we do have in stock certain critical items much in demand. These fellows are just remarkably efficient. With few exceptions, this is true of the men in our company—remarkable!

We have found some nearby ladies to do our laundry, and we must supply the soap. So, please send me a couple boxes of P and G laundry soap, or something of like quality. We supply both dirty clothes and soap, and the ladies give forth with the elbow grease. They do their scrubbing with brushes, and we have a supply of such in stock and "check out" as needed.

The people here are just bedraggled in appearance. They have so little—after the long German occupation. Our weekly rations of candy bars, gum, cigarettes, etc., are often shared. Not being a smoker, I never buy cigarettes, but I shall in future—to give to my French friends. The men are reaching out to the people of this town, and my favorite acquaintances are a family named Jacquet. Their son, Jean, has become the go-between. Monsieur Jacquet is a gardener, and cares for the estate of a wealthy doctor who lives across the street, but who is currently away on duty with the French forces in Brittany. Knowing that our cooks have no access to fresh vegetables and fruit, Madame Jacquet brought for our office crew a large pot of fresh garden peas and onions—deliciously prepared and cooked. She was so pleased that she could prepare something for us. Also, she brought an egg for each of us in the office—mine to be soft-boiled for breakfast. These people insist that they must share with us, and they are a proud people. If we are to give to them, then we must receive from them.

One thing is quite certain, my use of the French language is really being stretched. These people speak no English, and we who know some French do the best we can. I'm surprised that my use of the language is rapidly improving. The children just flock around each American, and they really want candy—bonbon. They will ask for cigarettes—"pour papa"; but, the little rascals will not hesitate to sneak in a puff for themselves.

So many towns and cities have been nearly pounded into the ground. One has to be thankful that we are fighting the foe on this side of the Atlantic, rather than to have awaited an attempted invasion—had Axis powers emerged victorious in Europe and Asia. So much of Italy lies in ruins. One can only contemplate with respect to the eventual destruction that will fall upon Germany before Hitler is forced to admit defeat. It will be an unconditional surrender! The people of Germany appear to have lent themselves too freely to Hitler's aggressions, and they may have to suffer certain exacting consequences. We have heard whisperings that the collaborationists in France are to be held accountable. Is my understanding that certain persons of this town have already suffered reprisals, and that some have simply absented themselves.

I had a good chuckle, yesterday, when a boy of about ten years of age asked me if my bed in the tent got wet because of the rain. He then assured me that I was to come to sleep with him should my blankets get soaked. Of course, he spoke in French, and he was so much in earnest. He asked me to come to his home, for his mother and father wanted to meet me. So, I did, and his mother told me that he was very much afraid of "les Boches"—but not at all of "les Americains"! He is a cute youngster, and he likes very much "les soldats Americains."

The Germans did not confiscate the dairy herds of these people, because they requisitioned the milk and cream for their own tables. Result, there remains somewhat of a solid supply of milk, cream, and butter. Since our supply lines may leave us short occasionally of fresh butter, these people will insist that they amply butter any slice of bread we may eat in their homes. They do not drink water, for it is not good. But the staple drink is cider, and each home has its large barrels. We have our purification units for our company, and these youngsters are somewhat perplexed to see us drink so much water. Every time I visit the Jacquets, I must down a glass of cider, and then another and another. It is definitely not a wine. The wine these people now have is that which they secreted away from the Germans, and they eagerly await the new vintages.

Jean Jacquet is, perhaps, about 18 years old, but he is small—appears to be about 11 or 12. Most of the boys, here, are not tall, and they appear to be much younger than their ages. As the boys became teenagers, many were removed to Germany to be in a sort of "labor draft." Jean's older brother, André, was one so taken, but he managed to escape from the train. He dared not get word to his parents, and they knew nothing of his fate. They knew something had happened, for German officers and soldiers entered their home to search every square inch—time after time over a period of several months. About two years later, a note was slipped under their front door with minimum information—to the effect that their son was well. (He had joined with the FFI—French Forces of the Interior and was in cooperation with the "Maquis." We shall have more to learn about him, later.)

Good flour is a luxury these people have lacked for years. Their bread is very dark and heavy and coarse. It is not good to the taste, and requires lots of chewing. I hope to sneak some flour from our cooks. One thing is certain, we cannot supply all of Trevieres with good, white American flour. Oh, well!

As for the political race for the American presidency, you will remember that I was a Willkie enthusiast. Dewey has never impressed me favorably. He will have to convince me that he has what it will take. I think that FDR has run his course, but I was pleased that the Democrats dropped Wallace and chose Senator Truman to be their candidate for the vice presidency. I fear the Republicans will again neglect our international responsibilities, just as we did after World War I... I am not persuaded that the old line Republicans will not control Dewey, should he be elected. You can certainly detect that I am not a happy Republican. Our international policies and role must be to prevent a string of events similar to that which transpired in the 1920s and 1930s and led again into this current conflict. Dewey has been a successful governor of N. Y., and I hope that the campaign will reveal that he has the substance of presidential timber. We shall see! The American people can no longer seek to withdraw into their shell and then hope that the rest of the world will just pass them by and leave them undisturbed.

Well, I have sort of climbed behind my pulpit. Mankind, generally, despairs of war and seeks after peace. Certain persons gain positions of power and seek to fulfill their selfish ambitions. Then, humanity has to pay the price. This war has become one of great length. Men have been long separated from their families—husbands from wives. The longer the conflict and the separation, the more likely suspicions mount that a "being true" has become on the wane. The costs of war are not to be measured just in terms of dollars and the dead.

Yes, I've been on a soap box. Maybe I'm in a mean mood. Before sitting down to type this, I had to straighten out a fellow officer on a matter of policy and duty. I am a bit warm "under the collar." So, tra-la-la!

Much activity overhead the past days, for the Americans did much bombing of the area of St. Lo to accomplish the break through. We are less than twenty miles away, and the concussion was great. The way across France has now been opened. We hardly know what to expect. Action began so soon after our arrival here that we had not been put on calling list, yet. Decision appears to have been made to test length of time needed to spread a "gas alert" from the front line to Cherbourg. We did not receive advance notice that klaxons would sound and the cries of gas were to be relayed to the rear. About one in the morning came the cries and the klaxons, and our guards knew not other than that is was for real. Asleep in our pyramidal, Lane and I just rolled over, reached down, and picked up and put on our gas masks. Ryley couldn't find his, panicked, upended his bed, emptied his footlocker, and then rushed out of the tent—to be confronted by Major Grove, our "gas officer," who had tested, found no gas, and was about to inform all that we were in no danger. Ryley had to be restrained, for he had left his mask in a command car and would not calm down. We had been having much rain, and mud was everywhere. Several of the pup tents were not dry, and many of the men had taken their bedrolls into the large office tents. There was a lot dashing to get to tents to retrieve masks, much slipping and falling into mud holes, and most of the dashers becoming covered with mud. Some had just climbed on tables in the offices and were holding their noses as high in the air as possible. Once we had caught our breaths, it all became hilariously funny. We have been laughing about this ever since. We did relay the alarm. Ho! Ho! Ho!

With the break through at St. Lo, the front is no longer within a few miles. So, we no longer feel in the least bit of danger. We shall continue to fill requisitions and to await further orders.

July 26, 1944 Trevières

We've been having a sort of heat wave, and it has become quite suppressive. We have not been used to this. At least the mud doesn't seem to be so deep.

I've decided to sprout a moustache. Nearly half of us are going to see if we can produce some genuinely handsome cookie dusters. Ho! Ho! We hear rumors that German morale is at low point and that the war might soon be into its final stages. It seems to me that there is little or no chance of such miraculous turn of events. We are just four miles inland from Omaha Beach… We are in no danger.

The hedge rows surround each orchard and meadow, many of which are scarcely more than an acre in area. The hedges close over runways which offer passage and in which the Germans were entrenched. The British and Americans could not put their armor to any sort of advantage in this region. Thus, to dislodge them was costly in terms of lives to be lost and wounds. The attempted revolt against Hitler failed, but my understanding is that it was an effort by Junker officers who would have ended the war before the Russians had swept over Prussia . No doubt about it, Hitler will have exacted the ultimate punishment of those who would have sought his overthrow.

Jean works away from Trevières except weekends, and he earns approximately 40 cents per day. Four of us were invited to come to Madame Jacquet's, for she had something for us. It was something special to eat, a cantaloupe—the first of the harvest from the garden. We were to be there at 4 o'clock She had it cut into four pieces. It was as sweet a melon as I've ever eaten. We just raved about it, and she was immensely pleased. As always, she had brewed coffee which was strong enough to make one's hair stand on end. We protested that she should use the produce and coffee for the family. But, she would hear nothing from us. So many of the men give their rations of sugar cubes, candy, and cigarettes to these friendly people, and it has become a sort of bartering of things for things. So far, I think we are a bit ahead of them. These people had been so suppressed. So it is, that after some four years they are free to move about, to talk as they wish, to have no fear that the slightest miscue may bring entrance of German officials into their homes. They exude new life, hope and strength. It is really an experience to see their eyes light up with each happening which gives them pleasure.

Apparently, the German officers were much feared. Many were not only cruel to the French people on occasion, but they also exacted severe punishments when displeased with their own men. We have heard many a "story," and one is caused to wonder aplenty. The children were particularly fearful of the German officer, and they were at first somewhat shy when they detected the identity of an American officer. But this has changed, and these children will cluster around us and do not hesitate to ask for bonbons, gum, sweet crackers, et cetera. To take a walk through this town is to invite a virtual parade of youngsters to follow you. The adults watch from the doorways, and the grins are from ear to ear.

Yesterday, two Frenchmen came to inquire if they could dig foxholes for any of us. They worked afternoon and evening. Our adjutant approved that they be paid $5 each, and you would have thought they had suddenly become millionaires. Lane informed them that we did not need any more holes dug. In addition, they received gratis a few packages of cigarettes and a good bit of candy for their petits enfants. We have learned that the German often required the locals to work for them, and this without pay. It is my hunch that the French may be of a mind that finally the Americans are beginning to repay the debt we have owed Lafayette—ever since the American Revolution. Oh, well!

The French are nearly overwhelmed by the vast quantity of rolling equipment which the U.S. has. When a convoy rolls through, these people just rush to their doors and windows to watch. To me, these people are more friendly and much "warmer" than the English. The English were somewhat frightened, but they were never crushed as were the people of France. The French are not fond of the British, but they do greatly admire General Montgomery. They want the Germans to suffer utter defeat.

Throughout the town, the people seek to do something for the American soldiers, and they refuse any sort of compensation. Often a man or woman will arrive with jugs of cider. On one occasion a lady informed us that she would not return were we to insist that she be paid for her cider. Jean had said the same thing. These people are again able to be themselves, and they are constantly reminding you of this.

A cute youngster, who is no more than nine years of age, has been wanting me to go with him to meet his mother and father. His name is Ferdinand Bazile. He enjoys to go for a promenade with any American, and he wants each of us to meet his parents. We call him Ferdi, and he does not hesitate to tell one that that is now his name. To meet his parents is to be welcomed with open arms and to be treated to the usual glass or two or three of cider. Ferdi is no longer timid in the presence of Americans.

News from the Russian front continues to eclipse that from this front and even from Italy. The Russians have the German "goat," and the sweep across Poland has certainly struck fear into each German heart. No doubt about it, I think—Germany will eventually suffer as complete a military defeat as we have recorded in history. Hitler's hold upon power will prevent any compromise. It will end only with unconditional surrender. An assassination of Hitler might introduce some mitigating factors. We shall just have to await the developments.

We hear so many rumors which treat of the doings of the upper brass who will do whatever is necessary to maintain their highly salaried positions. These "big boys" will pull whatever strings are available and will knife another in the back when such will gain advantage. We are winning this war, and we have some of the best strategists at work We are adjacent to what has become one of the most used roads, and the parade of command cars bearing the insignia of generals and colonels is to be likened only to the clouds of dust which rise from their passing. I guess my nose is out of joint because of our own situation.

Our CO had remained in England, and we were quite hopefully certain that we would have Major Grove moved into the position. The excellence of our total performance as a depot is attributable to the high morale of the company, and Col. Cole's absence has been quite central to this prevailing "good feeling." We had heard a rumor that Cole would be rejoining us, that he had not fit into the picture. When he realized that he was "in trouble," he informed his superiors that his depot company was in such a mess that he felt obligated to return to it—"to straighten things out." Well, this is a good example of the ways in which certain things are accomplished in this man's army. I just guess that I am too naive to believe that such "things" do regularly occur. He had the "nerve" to use his subordinate officers as the "goats" to enable him to get himself out of a tight place. We have suffered from a dirty deal, and he is again present among us.

Am not sure this is true to the fact, but a supply officer for a nearby hospital installation told us that D-Day had been scheduled for June 5. That it was delayed a day and gave the Germans more time to prepare their defenses, and that the Germans were aware of the schedule and of the points along the beach where the landings were to be concentrated. We do receive so many reports which are supposed to be the gospel truth.

I keep reminding myself of the certainty with which the French viewed their Maginot Line—that it would prevent any German invasion. Of course, their northern flank was not secured, and military disaster for France followed. This somewhat translates into the American point of view in the 1920s and 1930s, that somehow we were secure against all future aggression. The broad Atlantic was translated into a "Maginot Line" by us—for us. I know you are worrying because I have so little enthusiasm for the Republican Party's platform and for Dewey's nomination. We dare not repeat our neglects in foreign policy which followed the First War.

Madame Marie (Jacquet) just brought us more fresh eggs and a marvelous stew made of all sorts of vegetables. As special treat, she had a bowl of ripe red gooseberries—sweet as can be. These people are so desperately poor, and they seem to be so utterly pleased because of our presence. They so much want to visit with us, and they have so many questions about America. My use of the French language is rapidly improving, but they speak so rapidly and with such zest that it is very difficult to understand. We simply have to persuade them to slow up—for our sakes. But, they seem always to be so excited about their regained freedom and their camaraderie with us Americans. They absolutely refuse to accept payment for anything—the exception being for the special work done by some of the men at the depot, and this is always on a sort of contract basis.

August 3, 1944 Trevières

More rain, off and on, but with more sunshine and warmer. A nearby engineering outfit laid out for us a roadway around the inner perimeter and through our camp, and it is of crushed rock and brick. So, we no longer churn the soil into muddy messes. It is quite an improvement! The soil is much dryer, and tanks keep moving through into France… The Jerries must be hard pressed. Rumors about early end of the fighting come and go, but no one here is holding his breath.

One box has arrived, the one without olives. Those "dream bars" are so good, and they are always the first to go. We put our boxes out on the office desks, and as if by magic all just disappears quickly. I took two bars to the Jacquets, and they nibbled slowly—to stretch the taste. Madame stowed one away to await Jean's return from his work. Madame Jacquet is 62, and Monsieur is 61. She keeps bringing small bouquets of carnations, with a rose or two tucked in. Then she will bring another kettle of green beans or peas, or some eggs. The pears and cherries in the doctor's orchard are now ripe, and we get more and more of the fresh fruit. She often invites two or three to visit her home and to be treated to fruit and cider. Her home is just bare of any luxury, but she will treat us again and again.

Madame Marie now does my laundry, along with two or three others from the office. When she refused to accept any payment for the first job, I had quite an argument with her. When I told her that I would not let her do it without paying, she agreed to tell the amount. So, the next time I expected to receive an accounting. To be away from camp on some sort of mission, I left instructions with the men to pay her, etc. Sure enough, the laundry was back, so neatly done, and with the "bill"—beside each item was a zero, and beneath the column of zeros was a line with two zeros below. Later, when I accused her of tricking me, she took me firmly by the arm and then made it quite final: "You are our friend, and we do not charge our friends." Later, she told me that the Germans brought laundry for the women to do, and they never paid. There was no way for me to win this argument. The best I have been able to do is to leave two bars of bath soap—sweet smelling. Of course, we must provide "laundry soap"!

Monsieur Jacquet took me on a tour of the doctor's estate and garden and orchard—quite an establishment. Some sort of shell had struck a wing of the mansion and had left quite a hole in the wall. He had used all sorts of scrap canvas to keep out the rain, and he had used some discarded material and lumber from our depot. For our construction purposes, we do have quite an accumulation of scrap wood, etc. The people will ask if they can have it to burn in their stoves, and it never accumulates to any degree. Whatever we throw away, they will make certain to make some good use of it.

August 6, 1944 Trevières

We are having some hot, dry, and dusty days. Last evening we showed the movie, "Knickerbocker Holiday," in our mess tent. Was pretty light, and Nelson Eddy just didn't fit in very well. He is somewhat of a "ham" when it comes to acting. He shouldn't waste his talents in a picture of this caliber.

No news, as far as our operation is concerned. We are busy to keep up with the requisitions, and we receive shipments of additional medical supplies. No news of the war to startle one. We listened to a rather interesting discussion on radio, of London origin, I think. It had to do with the possibilities of a German bombing of New York City. Of course, these experts were seeking to treat of every possibility for some sort of sneak to take place. As for me, it was pretty much a matter of nonsense and waste of time. Such effort would have no impact upon the course of the war, and the Germans are eventually going to experience complete defeat.

We are having quite a time just to keep up with Madame Jacquet. Word came from her via one of our men, and she wanted me to come to the house after our noon meal. So, with office fully under control and operating with full speed ahead, I went—no more than a five-minute walk. She had three fresh pears for me, and had prepared a cup of her special coffee—mostly ersatz, but with some coffee, and as strong as could be. I sipped it through to the finish, and kept telling her how good it tasted. She is always so pleased to be complimented. None of us would ever say anything to hurt her feelings. Today, she showed me her good chinaware, and it was pretty. They had hidden it away—somewhere away from the town—to keep it from the Germans, and had just retrieved it. I wish I could accurately translate all she has to say about "les Boches"! Ha!

I thought the English homes close by Chilbolton Downs were worn and their possessions long overused; but, here it is much worse. From what the men say, the people here have much less, and that has been my observation. These people keep insisting that they must share with us, that they are indebted for restoration of their freedom, etc.

Madame Marie has taken us to task because we were not giving her any of our ODs to wash. Well, it has become a bit warm to wear gear other than khaki; but, some of us forked over a shirt or two, and she seemed satisfied. And, yesterday she was almost spinning like a top, for word had come that much of Brittany (Bretagne) had been liberated, including Rennes—the city of her birth. She is certain that her older son, André, is in Bretagne and that he has probably been there during the three years since his escape from the German "labor train." What she now expects is that he will soon come home. We shall see!

Jean has asked me about gardening in the U.S., and he is particularly wanting to know about our flowers. I told him I would have a book of American flowers sent to me—for him. So, will you go to a bookstore, or maybe a nursery, and select a good one and send it to me. Do it right away, for I do not know how long we will be here. Things could break "wide open" in the near future. Many thanks, for he will be much pleased. He can read no English, but he knows his plants.

Some more things of interest about these people. Our mess sergeant and his crew have been sharing some of the goodies that Madame has been bringing to us. So, Cohen brought to my desk a 48-pound sack of flour for her. Well, when I gave it to her, she just about swooned, and then announced that she could now make some nice things for us. My efforts to tell her that this flour was for her and some of her friends fell on deaf ears. She is incorrigible. The first thing she did was to invite three of our crew to eat crepe suzettes ("garanches"??). My turn is to be for supper tomorrow evening. My mouth is watering, for the fellows said she had gone all out, and she had made some fresh jam to spread on the suzettes. My guess is that one of our gang had supplied her with some sugar.

Yesterday one of our men found in a crate of some sort of supplies recently received a small roll of a heavy silk fabric, bright red. It was something that had been tucked in the large box., So, he left it with me. Well, I took it to Madame, and she hugged it tight and seemed nearly overwhelmed. I'm eager to see what she is going to do with it, for it is about a yard in width and maybe six feet in length. Ho! Ho! It is most interesting to note that these people will come with their wheelbarrows to cart home whatever we have discarded as waste. I know of no occasion when they have touched anything else. The children who frequent our depot do not take anything other than the candy, gum, and stuff given them. As far as I have detected, they have been carefully instructed by their parents.

August 11, 1944 Trevières

We've had quite a succession of movies—"Song of Burnadette," "For Whom the Bells Toll," "Crime Doctors Strangest Case," "Adventures of Mark Twain" (Frederick March), "The Lodger," etc. Many of the people crowd in to watch—not that they understand much of the script, but they just want to see all they can about America. "Burnadette" was a four-hour film. Particularly the children come around to observe, and then many of the parents edge in. They seem to delight to come and go—and always with smiles.

Recent successes in Brittany versus the German forces are most encouraging, and these are, I think, indicative of the eventual fate of German troops. The news from the eastern front, of Russian advances, continues to be solidly good. Eventually Hitler will be cornered, but I doubt of he will permit himself to be captured.

The second box of good stuff arrived, and it had been through a good bit of abuse—but intact. The olives are great treats for those people, and I took one of the jars to Madame Jacquet; she was much pleased, but protested—insisting that you had sent them to me, and not to her. Ha! But she didn't hesitate to keep them.

Madame keeps me supplied with flowers for my desk—carnations, roses, and gladiolas. A rust-colored peony was fully six inches in diameter and as beautiful as any I have seen. When Jacques is home on weekends, he always brings something from his mother. Most of our men have become friends with so many of the families, and it is amusing to listen to them attempt to use French words. These relationships seem to be genuine.

So many of these people are bitter toward the Germans—not necessarily the people, but with respect to the German officers and several of the men. What they have to say about the Gestapo and "les Boches" is often quite venomous. Many stories treat of entrances into homes and the taking of whatever "things" were wanted, etc. Monsieur Jacquet, and others, have told me that certain "collaborators" must bear reprisals. So far, our influences have kept actions of vengeance at minimum. But, once we depart—??? So far, some "locals" have taken leave, and no one seems to know where they are hiding. Some may not dare to return.

Monsieur Jacquet insists that we Americans understand the meaning of "égalité"—equality. He thinks we are quite different from other people. He does not like the British, for he says they are "puffed up" and have "airs of superiority." He is certain that an Englishman would never come into his "humble home" and eat with him at his table. He insists that the finest honor one can pay him is to "break bread" and eat with him and Madame in their home. Those of us invited in to share with them pay her all sorts of compliments with respect to her cooking, etc. The large garden of his employer is in full production, and she desires that we enjoy all the specialties. She must use all kinds of local herbs for seasoning. Excellent!

These people are certainly freedom-loving, and some of them feel so betrayed by their officials. Their sentiments toward the U.S. and the American people are, as yet, in no way lessened. In our "day room" (our headquarters tent) we have a large wall map which we keep coloring to show the progress of the fighting. So many of the men come in to look at it, and they insist that "unconditional surrender" must be the Allied objective. They keep speculating as to when the Allies are going to break through from the beach areas. They get so excited, speak so rapidly, and even jump about. I must slow them in their speaking—and we tell them we want to understand what they are saying. They keep complimenting me and others on our use of their language, but they are simply delighted to feel to express themselves without restraint. Ha!

You mentioned recently that a report was that the Roosevelt administration was doing much to influence the voting of the soldiers and service military in the coming election. I have not heard or seen anything of this sort. The Republicans seem to be engaging in all sorts of criticisms of the current presidency, and to me they are failing to construct a solid program of their own. They will not succeed in defeating FDR in November. I am disgusted and disheartened. It is difficult for me to comprehend the ineptness of the current Republican leadership. I shall be making application for my ballot. I understand these applications are now being processed. We shall see. I wonder what percentage of our people will actually vote, and I suspect that, as usual, it will not be all that high!

Each day, now, we have two or three truckloads of German prisoners brought over to work for us. So many of them are from Bohemia and Czechoslovakia, Ukraine, Poland, Byelorussia, and the Baltics—certainly pressed into German military service by their conquerors. Goebbels had warned them, so some have told us, that should they be captured by Americans they would be hauled away to be executed. The first group brought to us huddled together and fearfully observed our armed guards. One of our sergeants, Myron Posypanko comes from Chicago, and his grandparents came from those parts of Europe. He immediately went among these prisoners to assure them, in "tongues" they could understand, that they were not to be harmed, but that they were to come daily to work for us. To watch their expressions change was a highly moving and emotional experience.

Until about two days ago, we had no shower facility and went to a nearby air force unit, or used our helmets for water supply. We now have an eight-spout facility, and we haul our water in four 105-gallon airplane gas tanks. These tanks had been damaged, and we retrieved them from a nearby airstrip. Our facility is enclosed, but with no canvas overhead, as yet. Yesterday, we asked our prisoners if they would like to bathe before returning to their enclosure. To the last man they showered and informed some of our men this was the first shower they had had in weeks. As a group they have asked that we request they be returned to us each day to work. They seem to have become much disillusioned about the war and all they were warned to expect if ever captured by Americans. Particularly those who come from the east of Germany have told our men that they are treated much better as prisoners than they were as soldiers in their own army. Our men have given them pieces of candy. Some of them have German currency, which they want to use to pay for cigarettes. The currency is of no use to us, but some of our men do "sell" a cigarette now and then. We shall see what finally develops around here with respect to supply of cigarettes and tobacco. Not being a smoker, I have not purchased any tobacco products—except to give to my French friends.

August 18, 1944 Trevières

Ate some sausage a couple days ago, and my digestive system has been a bit on the touchy side. This is nothing new for me.

It seems to me that the children are generally undersized for their ages, and I'm sure it is a matter of nourishment. On the other hand, the people of the area are not tall. An older youth of 15 appears to be no more than 11, etc. To the contrary, they seem sufficiently energetic. We have been told by the people that the Germans would come scouting around, see some things they wanted, initial a form of requisition for the articles with instructions to take the note to the mayor's office where funds had been left for payments. Well, presentation of a notice for payment brought response that the Germans had left no funds; therefore, nothing to pay with. One thing is easily detectable, these people have very little above subsistence level, and their homes are next to barren—in most cases. As far as the eye can see, the yards are all into gardens. My guess is that many were hungry last winter. I wonder as to how the situation was elsewhere in France. Summer gardens must be flourishing everywhere.

Had opportunity to do some scouting around with Grove and Rudy in a command car, and we went west a bit, and then swung to the east and touched base with a British unit, or two—each of which had been drawing medical supplies from us. So, we sort of paid a social call. Some villages appear to have nearly escaped damage, and others must have been in a direct line of fire. We get many waves and grins from the people. The are almost woefully drab as far as their attire is concerned—old and young.

One highly interesting thing happened today, and I was fortunate to be on hand to witness it. From the group of POWs sent to work for us the days's projects required some construction and building—carpenters. One of the three selected seemed quite excited and then somewhat emotional about it. He talked rapidly and with increasing emotion, and it was evident that something had impressed him profoundly, unexpectedly, and beyond what he had expected. No doubt about it, he knew tools and their uses. He would pick up a tool, hold it at arms length, then hug it, and then use it. Momentarily, he stood and silently wept. I asked one of our noncoms who regularly works "in the shop" what the man had been talking about. Well, the gist was to this effect—for he was a carpenter by trade, a builder of houses and cabinets. He had been in the German army for 2 ½ years and had never been permitted to do other than train to use weapons and to kill. He wept when he explained that he had to become a prisoner of war before being permitted to use his tools again. Well, this fellow worked like the proverbial Trojan—all day, and begged not to be returned to the stockade for the night. I don't think he was a very good Nazi, but I think he was from Germany.

Some of these POWs are quite stoical and do only the minimum required. They are not many and do not seem to be harmonious with their comrades. My hurried observation is that they are genuinely German. They must surely realize that Hitler's cause is doomed—however long it is to take. Theirs is a sort of prevailing gloom, whereas for most of their associates there is an air of acceptance and evident hope of eventual happy return to homeland. Many of them have said they purposely surrendered—threw down their rifles and waved their arms in the air. Some hid in brush and trenches and awaited opportunity to "come across." Almost to the man, they have said they were warned to expect brutal treatment from the Americans if captured. They felt compelled to take the chance. Well, enough of this.

The Jacquets received word yesterday that their younger daughter was killed during the assault on Caen. They are simply broken hearted, but they knew this was to be verified. Those of us who go to see them feel so helpless, but they do seem to appreciate deeply our efforts to be understanding and fully sympathetic. Poor Madame, she attempts to be brave, but just can't "make it"! Monsieur just sits, shrugs his shoulders, and puffs on his pipe and says, "C'est la guerre." War is such an awful game. Somebody somewhere, in the saddle of power, decides to extend his reach and will not hesitate to sacrifice the lives and happiness of others in the quest.

Letters arrive irregularly and sometimes almost in bundles, for me. And we are wondering about a continued stay, here—always so many rumors. One of these days we shall be on the move to somewhere. Maybe it will be to Paris. We shall see.

August 23, 1944 Trevières

To a Protestant service, Sunday. The chaplain was sort of bumpy in his delivery, but his ideas and prayers were right on target. It was refreshing, and a surprisingly large group was present. My observation is that these chaplains are doing a terrific job and are central to the morale factor.

Several days, now, with no mail. It comes in large batches. We are sort of isolated from the action and movement, and so we are neglected now and then—at least, this is my feeling about the situation.

The German 7th Army has to be in dire straits. The POWs who come to work for us each day are of the general opinion that the war will not last long. Some of them remain loyal to Hitler, and one went so far as to say that Hitler had been betrayed. Most of the POWs tend to keep their silence. The ones who are German must certainly be aware of the degree to which Hitler bled dry the nations his armies overran, with the last to suffer being much of France. We shall, one of these days, hear of the treatment of Allies troops who have fallen into German hands. From what I can learn, German POWs, in our hands are well fed, receive a ration of cigarettes and candy, are paid a small monthly stipend, and have a day off each week. Our own men do not get a day off, per se. Oh, well!

We do hear and read reports which treat of the degree to which so many Germany cities have been bombed and are to be in need of nearly complete rebuilding. The men whom we receive as POWs seem quite aware of the task to rebuild which Germany will face.

A rainy season seems to have set in, and this weather has put me into a dull mood of low spirit. Four of us low-life lieutenants feel almost trapped. We fare personally very well, but we have no chance for advancement. We have heard of so many "dog-eat-dog incidents" in other companies, and some of these could make one's hair stand on end. Solution?—a quick end to the war! One's personal opinion counts for little in this organization, but the real weight depends upon the glow of gold or silver leaf and eagle, etc.

News notes that Americans are now in Paris. I guess tons of food and supplies have been marshaled for quick relief therein. We shall be hearing reports from some who have been in the city. There will be some gruesome details, I'm sure. War carves out such a difficult puzzle—a jig-saw of the worst sort, and the picture which then takes shape may not be pleasant.

On a sort of mission yesterday, three of us had a ride through this part of Normandy. This is a dairy region, and more cows than I expected to see. Inquiry of two or three of the dairymen brought similar responses—that they have made rapid recovery from the German occupation, but the Germans did little to interfere, always being need of large quantities of dairy products. We visited a cheese factory, and it was impressive to see the large numbers of cheeses ready for distribution. I wanted to buy two eight-pound cheeses, but all on hand had long been sold. We did purchase a few small sorts, and have turned them over to our cooks for use. I didn't care for the taste.

Yes, Paris has apparently been "liberated." My guess is that there will be much dancing in the streets, and even throughout the most of France. The defeat of the German 7th Army has been about as complete as any event in history, and we have heard reports about the many German officers who deserted their troops. My guess is that the cowardice within the upper echelons of Nazi leadership in France has now become on display. The French have certainly learned that a people who think they can grow complacent behind a wall of armor will pay a woeful price for their fiddler. Democratic procedures must be increasingly virile and strong, and expanding, and require the active and dutiful attention of the multitudes. I hope we Americans are learning something from this experience of the French.

We must accept the victory that is nearly ours to be opportunity for renewed beginning. Democracy is the greatest "corporation" that any peoples can hold shares in, and all upturned faces should reflect that resourcefulness and creativity which arises from freedom. We the people of U.S.A. are on trial before the world to reveal the true strength of our heart's beat. "Democracy" must be wide open. No nation can long endure, except by the will of its people. So often, historically, a peoples have been at a crossroads, and they have faltered. Here we are, today!

I need some 127 film for my little camera. My hunch is that you should send several. Just stick them in a larger box of "goodies"! My French friends are so fond of the olives, and those "dream bars" are favorites, too. Just do not send fresh eggs, for such effort will end in disaster and much evil smelling. Ha! Marshmallows are a delight for our French friends. And, I'm happy to report that the other daughter of the Jacquets has returned home. They are rejoicing, and now hope to see their son after more than two and a half years.

We have a new lieutenant, replacement for one of our captains who broke his leg in a motorcycle accident. Our cooks continue to do a remarkable job with the rations and supplies they have to work with. So much comes in cans. Advancement from the south of France, and all else, quite certainly indicates that this "Battle of France" will end shortly. We hear some rumors about our future. Even our colonel is somewhat reticent, and I seem to be getting along with him pretty well, as of now. Ha! But, he is not easy.

August 30, 1944 Trevières

Remains cloudy most of the time, with rain off and on. I'm still not much impressed with Dewey's campaign. We were encouraged to note that Rumania had dropped from any further participation in this war. Our French friends were quite excited to have Marseille liberated. And, you can send me a five-pound box of good stuff anytime you wish, and do no forget the olives—preferably the ripe greens. And, you might call to see that my application for an absentee ballot has been received. Make certain APO address is correct. Thank you!

We remain surprisingly busy. Units that depend upon us for medical supplies remain in the vicinity, along with us. We certainly will not be here much longer, but only rumors prevail. Every now and then we sort of get all shook up with a "can't wait" frame of mind. Oh, well!

Yes, it's true that many Germans escaped from the Falaise trap, or "gap" as it seemed to become. Hitler's remaining hope is becoming more and more evident, that an invasion and occupation of Germany from the west will become too costly. But, the Russians are pressing from the east, and the Germans may prefer occupation from the west. Pathetic it is, for Hitler will not bear any conscience when it comes to loss of life to sustain his regime. He will never permit himself to be taken! Before he takes his own life, he is going to receive just about everything he ever asked for.

Have been DO for a couple days, one being a substitution, or switch around with another officer. The only identity the officer of the day has is the side arm he must bear, and he must make certain that the liquor products and drugs for issue are securely "under lock and key." We are an unarmed medical depot company, and the red crosses painted on tops of all our pyramidal and storage tents are our chief protection from any sort of attack from the air. Really, we feel very safe.

Have had some good visiting with the Jacquets, and they are so content to have their daughter, Madeline (sp), home from Mayenne—her place of refuge after leaving Caen. She and Andrée had decided they both should not be in the same city, and Andrée was killed. Each visit with Madame Jacquet means that I must down another cup of that strong coffee, and I always make her happy by telling her how delicious it is. Oh, well! She demands that I bring her my laundry each week. About two days ago, her only bucket sprung a leak. I found a good galvanized pail sitting around in our area, and I gave it to her. One would have thought I gave her a million dollars. She has used the heavy silk cloth (bright red) I gave her to trim the mantle above the fire place, and along two shelves, and she makes certain that I notice.

If I understand correctly from what some of these people have told me, the Germans confiscated nearly all cooking utensils, plates, saucers, pans, pots, knives, forks, spoons, etc.—just to strip these people of nearly everything. Books were stripped from shelves, particularly everything to be used to instruct the young of their heritage, customs, etc. The Nazis intended to win this struggle and to remove from the youth sources of knowledge relative to their past. One can not conceive of a diabolical nature such as prompted the actions of Hitler and his inner circle.

The other afternoon, Madeline had made a peach tart for me, but the crust was unusually tough. She said it was "tres dure"—and made apology. I assured them that my teeth were sharp and that my jaw was strong. We had a good laugh. They seem to get a kick from my sense of humor. Ho! Ho! Madame is just full of questions about life in the USA. She knows she will never visit our country, but she certainly hopes that Jean will. Monsieur gave me another bouquet for my desk—a red rose, a yellow rose, two red carnations, and a pink carnation. Also, he handed me a large bunch of grapes (raisins)—the first to be ripe. I put them in a dish on my desk, and my office gang soon made them disappear. They were very sweet.

An American transport plane crashed just beside our depot—all killed. Flying in a formation, one plane's wing clipped the tail of another, which then plummeted. It became an awful pile of rubble, and with pieces of human flesh lying about. The sanitation crew asked that we not assist them, for they followed very exact procedures—with much documentation and photography. If not bounced free, most everything was burned and charred. Not a happy sight!

Some American political aspirants make issue of the fact that FDR has sent American boys to fight on foreign soil. I have seen the nearly ruined cities of England and some of the shattered walls here in France. We have been spared this in the US—no rubbled cities, no great problem of reconstruction because of artillery and of bombs from above. Fortunately, we did not wait to be bombarded by a foe who had reached our borders.

Just received your letter, with the notice of Merlin Stackhouse's death. He must have been killed not far from here. I must write his mother. He was the apple of her eye, and it is going to be a difficult letter to write. Such wonderful memories of my two years at Oshkosh. Oh, what a table she did provide for us who ate there!

As for the political race at home—Wallace was not a popular figure, and Truman was both U.S. senator and from the central west. So, there seemed to be a possibility to strengthen the Democratic ticket and to continue Roosevelt in his role as Commander in Chief. Unless Dewey can offer "something" clear, simple, and workable—particularly with respect to foreign policy, then forget about him.

Our CO is very "rank conscious," and he never lets us forget that he is the "captain of this ship." He just needs to get off his high horse. He just puts on a demeanor that lets you know his decisions, once given, are FINAL. Well, our atmosphere became so frigid that he was forced to call a meeting of his officers. We all knew he had had a long experience in the supply business, but he simply lacked tact in getting along with inferiors. So many men in the company, particularly my office crew, complained about his attitude—of never making known any satisfaction on his part and of always seeming to be on the prowl to detect errors and to find opportunity to point to somebody's shortcomings. One of our 2nd lieutenants had asked for and had received a reassignment, and one or our captains had requested a transfer. Our colonel was aware that any more requests for reassignment would probably bring on some sort of inquiry, for we have no more than a dozen officers in our T/O. His opening question to us was of this nature—"What's going on? What's the matter?"

Well, we sat in silence, and there was scarcely more than some hemming and hawing. It seemed that this was going to be the extent of it. I had a hunch that he was waiting for opportunity to give us a sort of general dressing down as he might choose. So, I requested permission to speak. Gist of it all was to point to the general excellence of quality of our men, to their long hours of work and to the extent of their accomplishment in handling and storage of medical supplies, and to their sustained morale and to the fact that we had not had one case of discipline to lead to so much as a threat of a court-martial. Other units near to us had had their share of difficulties, but we had been spared. My suggestion to Colonel Cole was that it was time for him to tell our men of his satisfaction with their performance, that they deserved his praise. As was his usual response to suggestion, he said nothing. He dismissed us without further to do.

Well, later in the afternoon, he asked our bugler to blow for an assembly. He then put the men "at ease" and proceeded to pay them their well-deserved high compliment. They were highly pleased. I do not know what sort of dog-house I may now be in, but time will probably tell.

Another French lady gave me two fresh eggs last evening. She is about 50, I guess, and has a daughter, Theresa, who is about 14. An older daughter has not been home for nearly eight months and is recovering from wounds received during a bombardment. Madame Bazile wished to go see her daughter, a distance of about twenty miles. They had one bicycle, and Theresa asked me if she could borrow mine. I was not happy to lend it, but these people have so little, and this trip meant a great deal to Madame B. So, I didn't have the heart to refuse. The bicycle "came home" in fine shape, with just a wee bit of air needed in the front tire.

September 4, 1944 Trevières

Things are not pressing as far as the depot's operation is concerned. A visit to the Jacquets turned to discussion of possibility of early end of this war in Europe. They seem so often to have battle news that is about two days ahead of what we hear over our own "grape vines" and what is reported on our service radio. My suspicion is that this is the way our strategists want it—to give, under no circumstances, any useful information to our foe. The recent Canadian successes at Dieppe avenge the earlier disaster experienced there. Good news!

As for my Christmas present, consider only something to eat, for there is no other material thing that I need. It gives me so much pleasure to share goodies with these people. We shall be long gone from here, soon, however. Better to plan to just save up for my return from this war, and we'll just celebrate and really blow it. Ha!

You say that my letters arrive in bunches, too. It has to be the way the system works. Our mail orderly keeps telling us that he receives only what is placed in our "square." I have only a guess as to the number of sorting points a letter must pass.

Again, let me assure you that I am not aware of any particular effort to influence the "soldier vote" to go for FDR. I should think the electorate is quite fed up from the constant Republican harping upon Democratic faults, with so little offered positively as alternative. Well, we shall see. As you know, Willkie was my man. I do not expect him to break from "the Party," but he has to be a disappointed man. The "old line" wants none of his liberal progressivism. We have plenty of time for good things to develop before election day.

Got my hair cut the other day, and I look like a real "podunk." Had quite a bit taken off the top, and now we shall have the fun of watching it grow longer.

Will run up and chat a bit with the Jacquets. The men of our depot have made so many friends in this town—quite remarkably so, I think. When we depart, there are going to be some tears shed.

The more I visit with the Jacquets, the more I am aware of the story they have to tell. Some of it is almost as fiction, and I'm certain that family after family has much the same to relate.

September 7, 1944 Trevières

Have been filling in some more as Officer of the Day and as Duty Officer. The rain keeps pelting us, and this damp atmosphere seems to creep into the very marrow of our bones. It soon will be about nine months since I've been home. This war is going to last for some time, and there remain so many pockets of German resistance and several cities will require lots of action to root out the Nazis. Some ports remain targets, and the defenses along the Rhine will be difficult for our side to overcome.

You have written relative to reports about the amount of drinking in the American army. We have our share of "bottle babies," but our local problem centers in about five of the men and about two of the officers. The Germans seized the wines and brandies and cognacs which they found stored in homes, cellars, barns, etc. Of course, as Americans overrun these places, it all passes to the new victors. We have been next to some pretty wild celebrations. The German retreat was such that there was virtually no chance to cart the special fluids along.

Madame Jacquet is simply unable to cease grieving over the loss of her daughter, Andrée. The daughter, Madeline, who fled from Caen, hid in hay lofts, dug into hay stacks, moved from place to place only at night, and was constantly in fear of being apprehended and sent to Germany as a laborer—and to be much abused. She reached Mayenne and had friends there to assist her. When she reached home, a few days ago, she seemed much changed—according to her mother. My observation is that a loosening up of her old spirit is setting in. The people in these more rural areas of France have not suffered the severe deprivations that the people of the cities have had to endure—if I can learn of the realities.

We continue to furnish medical supplies for many units, and it seems that the action saves up for certain hours. Then, we will have a stretch of relative calm. As a whole, our gang is just tops. Of course, we have our lemons—but very few!

Took Madame four oranges, and she almost let out a shriek. We then sat down to drink some cider, when she let out a gasp. I had noticed a head pass along the window sill. In came their older son, André, and it was a dramatic homecoming. It was a combination of crying and laughing, of hugging and holding at arm's length, and of just standing with arms overhead. I felt like a fifth wheel and attempted to excuse myself. But, they would have none of my departure.

André appeared to be clothed in muddy attire. He was covered with dust and had been in the rain off and on. They were so excited, they talked so fast, they jumped about, and they kept grabbing me at the shoulders. He had most recently been with the Maquis and had been weeding out the pockets of German strongholds. He had worked along with several Americans, and I think he had spent much time in Brittany and the Vendée. When he learned of his sister's death, a long silence followed. His hatred of the Germans is profound, I'm sure. He referred to the certainty of unconditional surrender. He would not deal gently with the collaborators. Time for chow had come, and he insisted I promise to return. I suggested he come see our depot.

September 9, 1944 Trevières

Things have slowed much for us, but some highly interesting occurrences, methinks. Our men, collectively, must be of the most able and of the most determined to do well their work. By strokes of luck they were assigned to this company, and I am delighted. We know where we are going to go from here. (It was to be to Paris.)

About ten days ago, an American soldier came into the office. He visited with the fellows, and he seemed to be a bit dazed. He wanted a "Coleman stove" and three litters. We had a much used "burner" that just needed cleaning, and several litters were in "salvage and needed no more than minor repair. Three days later, he returned for medical supplies, and I noticed he was wearing corporal's stripes. Five days later, he returned with a bona fide requisition, and he was sporting silver bars—had received a field promotion to a first lieutenant. He had fit in well with our office gang, and we had a celebration for him. He acted like a kid with a new toy, and he then paid my office crew a high compliment. He had been into many supply offices and had to work with several crews, but he had found our men to be the most congenial and least grouchy. We would see him again a time or two, and then no more. We did not really know who he was!

Have done considerably more visiting with André Jacquet. He is one fine person. When he escaped from the "labor train" to Germany, he fled into the interior and joined with eight others. They had, for use to defend themselves, if necessary, one "tommy gun," two revolvers, and a long whip with some sort of metal apparatus on its tip. The Nazis used bloodhounds in attempt to track them, and they learned to use this whip so as to severely cut the dogs and to drive them away. They had narrow escapes, but eventually found "security" with groups of the Maquis. They succeeded, of course, in building up their arsenal. He did not refer to numbers of "victims" who fell from their attacks. He escaped the "labor draft" for Germany, but said he would be willing to be drafted to work in the U.S.

André is 21 and is much larger than Jean. One can easily see they are brothers. When the French laid down their arms in 1940, one of the conditions was that they would not take up arms versus the Germans. The younger French did not feel bound by this agreement. So, the Maquis and F.F.I. are full of the youth of France. They detest those who collaborated. I do not attempt to guess as to what reprisals will take place—here and there in this proud nation.

News is that Ernie Pyle is "going home." After 29 months, he needs rest. He, as reported, does not want to see another dead American soldier, to smell again the stench of death, and to hear another "big gun boom." I wonder if we will again see the likes of him.

From time to time we have had people come to our office (tent) in search of some sort of medical help. They expect to find a doctor, and are surprised when we tell them that no doctor is present. They see the large red crosses on our office and storage tents. We have had some fascinating "things" happen, and two or three were just typical.

Just after lunch, one day, a man brought his son, and they had come some distance. The lad had sores all over his legs and arms and upper body—mostly from constant scratching. We took a good look, and detected that he had been repeatedly attacked by chiggers. We gave the youngster a sponge bath and then generously applied a sulphur ointment. We explained to the man and the boy that the scratching had to stop. We gave a supply of ointment, with instructions to return in three days. Our "first aid" worked a miracle, and the boy was almost back to normal.

A more severe case faced us when a man brought in his son whose arm was swollen up to the elbow. The man showed us his left hand, with two fingers missing.

He feared for his son's arm, and was openly disappointed because we had no doctor. Well, we sort of poked around, and it was Donaldson or Rodenhaver who detected what appeared to be whitish in the meaty area at the base of the thumb. Well, we made an incision, and it was the seat of the infection—a sliver of wood had become somewhat encapsulated in a sac of puss. This we removed, and one could put the tip of his index finger into the cavity. A good painting with Merthiolate followed. We put on a sort of loose bandage, gave the man about a half roll of gauze along with a small bottle of medication, and asked him to bring his son back in three days. Well, it was six days, and the boy's arm was virtually well. The man brought us eight eggs, and he kept repeating that we had saved his son's arm.

A similar case was that of an older youth, perhaps 15 years old, who had a much swollen middle finger of is right hand, and it was ripe from some sort of infection. It needed a physician's attention, and he was more than mildly discouraged. I was certain some sort of surgery was needed, but no doctor. We sat him on a bench, dropped a scalpel in a bottle of alcohol, and then proceeded to make an incision. The young man was almost in panic at sight of the blade, for he thought we were going to remove his finger. Well, we assured him that we simply had to find the source of his problem. (In all of these situations our use of the French language was taxed to the limit!) This was another case of a splinter and sac of puss. Again, it was a swabbing with Merthiolate, a good bit of smarting, some fancy jigging, and a quick recovery. Three days later he returned with his mother who praised us for saving her son's finger, and she wished to know the cost of our services. One of us said, "Oh, a million francs!" She threw her hands into the air and then burst into laughter. We had made a friend for life, I think.

About two days ago, while trudging up the hill to see the Jacquets, a one-horse cart passed me. As it went by, the driver let out a yell that nearly took my breath away. Leaning out the side and looking back at me was this kid. He had a highly effective "whoop and holler"!

André Jacquet departed today, to enlist in a sort of "new" French army. He is a mechanic by training and skill. He enjoyed to tell of some of his experiences with the Germans who had impressed him earlier into servicing some of their vehicles. He knew how "to fix" something—to malfunction after a few miles. He kept telling them that he was the "worst mechanic in France." From what he told me, he has had very fine relationships with Americans. I hope nothing will happen to

André. He would much like to visit "America." I shall be writing to him while we are elsewhere in France.

September 10, 1944 Trevières

I need some 127 films, and a couple five-pound boxes of goodies. Ripe olives and almond bars are favorites, here. Must make certain to go chat a while with Madame, Monsieur, and Madeline. They are certain that I like to sip that terrible coffee, and I just play the game to keep them happy. Monsieur Jacquet so much enjoys his pipe, and I have been able to find a couple tins of smoking tobacco for him. Our mail orderly picked them up somewhere.

A box from Lincoln arrived—toffee, chocolate-covered peanuts, peppermint candies, etc. Took part of the goodies to Madame Jacquet. She just about goes into a spiral, and then protests that these are meant for me. We have our routine down pretty pat. Ho! Ho!

Had opportunity to take in quite a journey—to see some of the nearby battle sites. Well, some of these towns have few structures standing and without damage. So much devastation from planes and cannonades, and citizens are continuing to find the dead. A few bulldozers are in use.
Little flags often mark the places where bodies have been found. Oh, the sacrifices which man makes upon the altar of Mars!

The catalogues which had many pictures of flowers arrived, and Jean was delighted to have them. He was particularly impressed with the dahlias. His father was just about carried away.

Yes, the cider we drink is apple cider, made from the juice of a sort of crab apple. The apples are very juicy, green, and not sweet—no good for eating. The people never drink water, but this cider is downed with each meal, and often in between. These orchards abound, and this cider must be the major marketable product of much of Normandie. They drink it room temperature.
You visit a home, and immediately out comes the cider. It is a far cry from wine. But, it has "worked" enough to free it of contamination. The water is not to be downed—except that which we purify in our own camp. Our purification units are running a while each day, and much of the mineral is also extracted.

André had returned for a few days, and Jacquets asked me to have noon meal with them. It was very nice—roast pork, fresh brown bread, potatoes, fresh butter, and a sort of rice pudding. We then played a card game, and they almost stood and cheered when I shuffled the deck—with my reverse "whir-r-r-ring." Andre practiced and practiced, and he was catching the technique.

September 12, 1944 Trevières

(This would be the last letter to be mailed from this locale. We were in process of making a move to Paris, and new APO would be 887. Some of our advance party had returned to assist in the closing down and to lead our small convoy into the big city. They had brought quite a supply of French perfumes, and there is quite a story to be told about the findings found stashed away by the Germans in the warehouses we were to occupy in the suburb of Pantin.)

Am sending to you some bottles of Bagatel and Tosca. Once into the city, I hope to find for you some Chanel #5. Also enclosed is one of those hard steel German razors, and we can give it to Lee Jouvenat.

We are quite busy—in the process of getting away from here. Another company is taking over. Have told Madame Jaquet that tomorrow will be my last time for coffee. I have a last sack of candy for her and Madeline. So much I wish to tell you about this family, but my typewriter is loaded for our next place. So, must be brief. Their long concern about André is quite a story, and they were so long without word from him, other than a note that he was OK. That I just happened to be present when he returned was to be an experience to be remembered. André and I had some long visits, and he simply had to slow his pace of speaking—so that I could more easily understand. He had narrow escapes while with the Maquis and with the F.F.I. He will now enter into some sort of service with the French army. He has no love for the Germans.

These people are so poor, but they are rich in spirit. There is no way I can adequately repay them for their many kindnesses to me. We are just kindred in so many respects. We have visited about Hitler and what his fate should be. André is certain that Hitler will never permit himself to be captured, that he will take the coward's way out—suicide. Well, we shall see, eh? Our men have had such interesting friendships with the people of this town.

Am looking forward to this evening's movie—Mae West and Victor Moore in "The Heat's On." We'll have a full a full house—a tent full, with half of them being townsfolk. These people seem fascinated with anything and everything American. They have been through so much agony, and they are seeking to be free from it.

I learned of the cemetery of Merlin Stackhouse's burial, and it was about seven miles from here. Fred Stroh, one of our captains, and I were on a sort of mission, and we visited the cemetery. I was temporarily nearly overcome with mixed emotions of grief and anger. To see his dog tag affixed to that white cross moved me to tears, and it was a bit difficult to tell Stroh of my two years at Oshkosh and Garden County High School, and of our eating at the Stackhouses, etc. To see these many rows of white crosses, each with an identifying dog tag, was nearly overwhelming. I shall be writing Mrs. Stackhouse, and I hope she will find comfort from my having been at his grave.

Well, all of this is sort of pressing me to become a philosophic "Old Dodo." This business of war is just not my cup of tea. Those who lust after power and control do not hesitate to plant these fields of white crosses. I need to get to the movie.

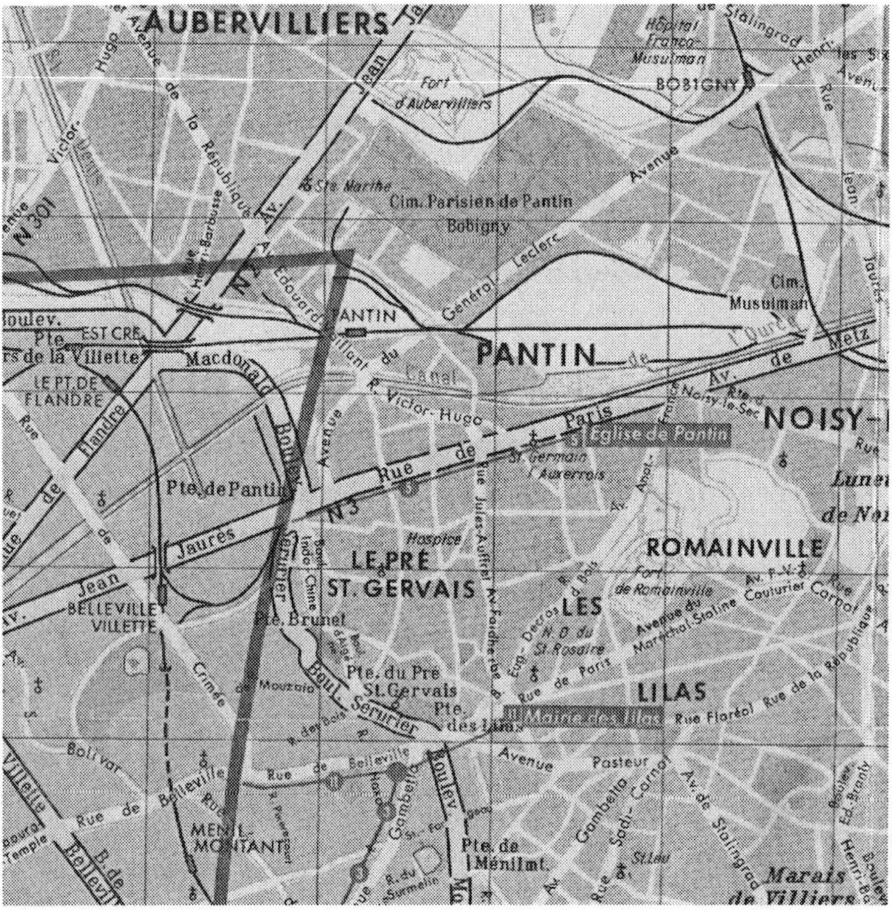
AUBERVILLIERS
Fort d'Aubervilliers
Hôpital Franco-Musulman
BOBIGNY
Cim. Parisien de Pantin Bobigny
Cim. Musulman
PANTIN
Canal
NOISY-
Eglise de Pantin
ROMAINVILLE
Fort de Romainville
LE PRÉ ST. GERVAIS
Hospice
LES LILAS
Mairie des Lilas
Pte. de Pantin
LE PT. DE FLANDRE
BELLEVILLE VILLETTE
Pte. Brunet
Pte. du Pré St. Gervais
Pte. des Lilas
MENIL-MONTANT
Pte. de Ménilmt.
Marais de Villiers

Warehouses in Pantin, suburb of northeastern Paris

Pantin (Paris)

Pantin (Paris) September 17, 1944

(We were still under strict censorship and were not to make reference to location. It was almost a matter of "speaking in riddles." However, within a matter of ten days, we could let family and friends know we were in Paris. We were, of course, no where near "a front.")

We read Ernie Pyle's articles in "Stars and Stripes," and he certainly kept his finger on the pulse beats of our troops and of the people. We expect most of the "shackles" to be lifted. He just ran out of energy—near collapse from sheer exhaustion.

The American Red Cross has done many remarkable things for the men, and nearly all without fanfare. Money was loaned when needed, information about family at home was gathered and given, flowers for special occasions were purchased and delivered, the "donut wagons" have been often right behind "the front," and the people of "the Cross" have so often been good listeners when the men have wanted "to have an ear." Each Red Cross center has often become a sort of haven and retreat—often overcrowded.

My final visit or two with André Jacquet was spent with his attempting to get me to improve my French. He kept telling me that I was one of the few Americans he had met who could speak his language, and he wanted me to improve. Truly, he is a most remarkable young man, and he is so ambitious for the future of his country. When we get settled next and my typewriter is again available, I hope to have time to tell you more about these people of Trevières.

Paris

September 24, 1944 Paris (Pantin)

My stomach has been giving me trouble the past day or two—just some sort of bug, I think. It is just that nausea and vomiting strike me if I eat anything. If it doesn't clear up, soon, I shall see a doctor. Oh, well!

André Jacquet wants to become an airplane mechanic, but he first wants to take pilot's training. He is no longer obligated to return to the F.F.I., or to assist the Maquis. He is quite an ambitious young man and desires to move beyond Trevières. Jean will be content, I think, to become caretaker of some estate. I must keep in touch with this family.

The perfumes and colognes you will be receiving are just samplings from the loot we found in these two warehouses. The Germans had confiscated all they could lay their hands on and had stamped each bottle as reserved for the WEHRMACHT. And, the same for stacks of canned Polish hams. I think there are thousands of unbroken cases and boxes. We need to clear space to store our medical supplies. The people whom we shall be employing will probably share in the eventual distributions of the stuff. This had to have been the central point of concentration for this loot which the German systematically seized. We have the best of French wines, brandies, liquors, champagnes, etc.—just unbelievable.

News is that the Allies have pierced the so-called Siegfried Line. So, we are making progress.

It is strange to be sleeping under a solid roof, again. The comfort of this thick mattress is almost more than I can endure. The first two nights in my hotel room were virtually without sound sleep. We officers are in the city, and the men are in a large school near the warehouses. We are becoming experts at the use of the subway, the "Metro."

We have received no mail for six days—letters from home. But, it will be coming through with regularity, soon. I am OD through today and tonight, and I will get little sleep. We do have so much to keep track of, and we are divided into day and night crews. The men have been exploring this great city, and they have taken to the Metro. From their reports, the city is full of wolves—the two-legged variety who wear skirts. They are of the solicitous sort.

Our company would be a much happier group were we not saddled with our CO—one who wears a silver oak leaf. This poor man has had some disillusionment in his past, and there is a psychological pinch which often limits his capacity to be an effective leader. I do feel sorry for him, and he is nearly always alone. He seems to be at a loss when he seeks to be friendly. An occasional game of bridge does seem to melt the ice, now and then. Of course, nearly everything we do as a company is done "over his signature."

Here is a little rhyme that may bring on a grin, and it eased my nausea—
Little Miss Muffet decided to rough it
In a cabin quite old and medieval.
A soldier espied her and filled her with cider,
And now she's the forest's prime evil.

September 24, 1944 Paris

We may now tell you that we are in Paris, and there seems to be a considerable easing of much that has been with respect to what may be written home. We keep pinching ourselves—that we are stationed in this great city. We are to be the central medical supply depot for so much of northern France. We have so many establishments to serve, and we are busy. And the people of Pantin, this suburb on the northeastern edge of the city, had really made us feel welcome. The mayor of Pantin presented each of us officers with six bottles of red wine, and he placed in the company kitchen a ll0-gallon barrel of red wine. The people, locally, have gone all out to make us feel welcome. Several of the men and women are seeking employment with us. So, it is more than just a game for people to play.

Yes, it would be suicidal for the German to resort to poisonous gas in effort to halt an eastern advance of the Allied forces. The Allies are so much better equipped to pour it on. The German Luftwaffe is increasingly of little effectiveness. So, do not fear that we are in danger of a gas attack. You remember we had our scare on the beach, and it was all due to lack of communication, and we have had many a good laugh about it.

I do not look for any sort of armistice to be negotiated. It seems to me that a responsible government of Germany is virtually of the past. We will just have to wait and see. Much talk floating about with respect to the length of time that American troops will be retained to prevail over a defeated Germany. Have a hunch that many of us will be over here for nearly a year, yet. As a medical supply unit, we may be around as long as American troops are on duty. We hear so many rumors, and most of them seem always to come from "above." I often wonder about our "top brass"! Hitler will never toss his cap into the ring!

The two little books of flowers arrived today, and I shall have to mail them to the Jacquets. Jean and Monsieur will pour over them with much enthusiasm.

We are trying desperately to get our routines established, and we can hardly keep up with demand for issues of medical supplies. It has been bedlam from the beginning. I keep having trouble with this indigestion, and must steer clear of anything that has any semblance of grease. I may just stop eating at the officer's club in the city—evenings. And, the hotel clerk is right on the ball when it comes to buzzing me at 6:45 each morning. We junior grade officers are soon to be moved from this very nice hotel (The Ambassador). We are to move to a smaller hotel, The Louvois, which is not far from La Place de l'Opera. It will be comfortable, and Pete and I shall share a room, I think.

Our two warehouses in Pantin are as modern as anything I saw in the U.S. We really lucked out to get this assignment. I hope our colonel was able to pull a string or two, for he needs to be able to claim credit for something. We heard via a grape vine that our performance at Trevieres gained us this assignment. One thing for certain, we are no longer in tents and we do not have any fox holes to dive in to should need arise. We are going to be leading a "rugged life"—here in "Gai Paree"!

While riding the subway into town a couple evenings ago, I struck up conversation with a man who spoke English to about the same degree that I speak French. We agreed to meet this evening for further exchange. His wife will be with him, and I do not believe she speaks much English. And Charley Teague has made the acquaintance of a gentleman—to whom he gave a ride and who wants him and a fellow officer to come to his home on October 1 for an evening meal. This man's wife will be home, then, and they wish to have us come. Charley said that the man spoke very good English. So, it seems we are going to be meeting people who want to know Americans.

We hear many accounts which treat of the heavy toll taken of Germans in the area of Paris. So many of the members of the F.F.I. were younger men, 18 to 20 years of age. From what we have been told, many of the Germans were not able "to get out." They had pretty well nestled in, for they expected to maintain quite a lengthy stay in the city. The young men who joined the F.F.I. became almost gangster-like in their behavior. They moved swiftly to take heavy toll on the Germans, and the city became something more than just liberated. From what I can detect, "things" are much calmed down, now, and order largely prevails. As I have walked about the city, I have never felt threatened or uneasy.

Our noncoms have occupied a large residence, separate from the school, and they have employed two women to clean for them. From all reports, everyone is just delighted. We have women who clean our various depot offices. For them to have income must be very nice. They certainly do try to please. The men who have gained employment with us are also much in earnest to please. We are constantly giving them "things"—including some of the wine. As far as I have detected, our employees have not been light-fingered. Of course, I could be wrong. My job remains to preside over our accounting and records, and my work within the warehouses is to make a spot check, here and there, of critical items. Litters and blankets seem often to be at premium. Too, we must make certain that drugs, gold and silver, and such are always "under lock and key."

September 30, 1944 Paris

Have been able to see much of France—from Cherbourg, throughout Normandie and the beach areas, and into Paris. Of the larger towns the most completely destroyed by the action, St. Lo and Caen were virtually erased—except as to be preserved in memory. Our two large warehouses, here in Pantin, along with the office facilities, are as modern as anything we worked in at St. Louis and San Francisco. We are adjacent to a canal, and some barges are of use. The two or three cranes are working, but need attention to keep them running.

These people were forced to get along on so little. I rarely chew any gum or eat any candy—just prefer to pass it out. I continue to buy my ration of cigarettes, and then pass them around. The youngsters are boldly not bashful when they approach, and they come with hands out and open. One of the women working for us very seriously told me that the children were much afraid of the German soldiers, but that they love "beaucoup, beaucoup" the Americans. They know how to play their game. Ho! Ho!

The Scheys, Georges and Yvette, have an interesting story to tell. By training he was a "wireless engineer"—for work with and in radio. The Germans would not permit him to practice his trade. Not long after the Nazi occupation of Paris, he chanced upon a shoe shop which had been abandoned. Its proprietor was Jewish and had fled to southern France. The Scheys did not know him, but simply took over. Georges knew nothing of shoe repair, but he learned and ran the store until the owner returned to Paris—just three days ago, and delighted to find his shop in fine order and ready for him. Schey will soon be employed in the French radio service.

Georges is so eager to improve his English, and I need to work on my French. So, we are working on each other. He told me of the French-American entrance into Paris, and he was nearly overcome with emotion. Tears just streamed down Yvette's face. He thinks the Americans are, in spirit, much like the French. He was certain that the Nazis never expected to be forced to give up the city, that all the German orders were indicative of long duration. The French want to laugh "at the drop of a hat," and they seem always to find something amusing in their relations with us Americans.

A Madame Bocquet, a friend of the Scheys, had just returned after more than a year's absence, and she told me in all seriousness that she had found the city "reborn." Her barrage was well beyond my capacity to comprehend, but this made no difference. She had to have her say, and my ears were American and she would fill them to the brim. She had some apples in some sort of bag, gave me one of them, and then darted away—still talking and with both arms in the air.

I was impressed.

Until today, I have been fighting some sort of cold. I take an APC now and then, but the darned things make me so sleepy. It must be the caffeine. The blowing seems to be a thing of the past, but my nose has been a bit reddish and sore. Can't say that this has helped by disposition.

Went to a USO show, and it was excellent—just mighty good entertainment for about 3 ½ hours. One of the most impressive acts was a danseuse on a rope, "Tosca du Lac"; her maneuvers were smooth and graceful. Much color in the lighting, with constant change. Fred Estaire was the chief attraction, and he was good. Lots of footwork, and his accordionist was particularly good. A quintette of three guitars, a drummer, and a clarinet could really put out the rythme. Pete got tickets for several of us, and it was a great evening, and no more than a ten-minute walk to my hotel. Subway ride back to Pantin for the men took no more than fifteen minutes.

Those of us in the Ambassador Hotel have been notified that we are to move to a smaller one, the Louvois. Our "uppers" got their heads together and decided our British friends should have these more spacious accommodations. As we have surmised, a couple generals made a decision "over their mugs of beer." Of course, we don't know, but we were given just twenty-four hours to relocate.

The Scheys live in a fifth-floor apartment—meagerly furnished, but in good taste. They had no coal last winter, and very little gas or oil. They were permitted no wastage. At most, they had electricity a half-hour in the morning and an hour in the evening. Food became their most taxing difficulty, and it was particularly stressful up to the liberation of the city. The Scheys used their pantry for a pigeon loft—with entrances cut through the wall, and the squabs were often their only source of meat. They told me the Germans never molested them in their homes, the French citizenry, but the Nazis requisitioned and acquired everything to such degree that the people could find little. It was subtle!

October 1, 1944 Paris

Was OD yesterday and through the night, and we were busy. Had a caravan of trucks to unload and there was little chance to take a break. So, I shall be ready to return to my room for a bit of shut eye. This poem was left on my desk a short time back, and you will get a chuckle from it.

> When bugles sound their final notes and bombs explode no more,
>   And we return to what we did before we went to war,
> The sudden shift of status in the ladder of success
>   May make some worthy gentleman feel like an awful mess.
>
> Just think of some poor captain, minus all his silver bars,
>   Standing up behind some counter, selling peanuts and cigars.

> And think of all the majors, with their oak leaves far behind,
>> And the uniforms they're wearing are the Western Union kind.
>
> Shed a tear for some poor colonel, if he doesn't feel himself;
>> Jerking sodas isn't easy when your eagles are on the shelf;
> 'Tis a bitter pill to swallow, 'tis a matter for despair,
>> Being messengers and clerks again is a mighty cross to bear.
>
> So, be kind to working people that you meet where e'er you go,
>> For the guy that's washing dishes may have been your old C.O.

Louisette is one of the French women who is working for us in my office, and she does some typing of record cards and helps to keep tabs on issues, invoices, etc. She asked me to mail a letter for her—to a friend who lives in New York. She asked me to approve its content and to mail it postage free. This I did, with a note attached. It is rather pathetic in spots, and I made a copy for myself—enclosed herewith, along with the poem:—

> Perhaps have you forgot your frence friend Louisette? But your friend think always to you. What are you become since those long years? I'm become married and I've left Pantin. Now I'm living in a little town near Pantin. It is also a suburb of Paris. I work on a calculating machine since I've left school. I like this work well. My machine is made in U.S.A.
>
> Now we are delivered. You can imagine how we are happy. The German soldiers were so bad for we! In the town where I live they have killed twelve personnes. They have cut their heads and their eyes. We were hungry since 4 years. The Boches had bought all the things when they were arriving. They said to wee "You must to work always for wee." They have taken my brother Marcel wich is 22 years old and my husband wich is 30 years old for work in Germania. They were very hun-happy here. Also my husband had saved her and he is returned at home after only three months. But my poor brother cannot to saved her. He is returned home only after 1 year and 6 months and now he is very ill. He is in hospital since of 5 months. My parents are desolate. All the men wich are returning of Germania are ill because they were unhappy. In Germania it is hard labour for all the French people. But now our dear old Paris is liberated by the FFI and near all of France is liberated by the

American soldiers. The French people is very grateful to the American women because they have send their boys in our land for the liberation of us. I send you all my love for this.

Your people is a people of good friends. I speak with pleasure to the American soldiers. They kiss our children and give to them chocolate. Also our children love very much the soldier. When a carriage stop there are ten or twelve around and they laugh all. I have no children but now I will be very pleased to have one or two because I think to have soon milk and sugar. We have not had since 4 years. Also the poor children are almost ill all.

The 25 Aout (August) the American soldiers were arrived in Paris. Also it was the joy. We have danced in road and we have made flags for put at the window. But we are very poor because we had not cloth for it. Also, we have coloured old rags and we have make beautiful flags—American, French, Russian, and English. It was very beautiful, all the windows were with flags, and all the people were crying of joyce.

My husband was FFI. Since the 15August he was in war with the German. We were very afraid in my town because the German were cross. They drank all the day and after they took machingun and grenade and they kill all the people wich was in the road. They have killed 3 boys of twelve years old and after they have burnt their houses. While all the nights they were burning mills and the houses in wich were the store of food. It was always explosion. We were very afraid. I don't sleep and I have spent all the nights at my window for to see the red sky.

Now we are quiet with your good soldiers in our town. There are large barracks for the soldiers near of my house and they visit our churchs and museums.

Now my dear I must leave you. I hope that you will ask to my letter soon because I shall be very glad to correspond with you again. With much love from you friend, Louisette.

Well, as you read this letter it becomes quite clear that these people, at best or worse, were drawn through one knot hole after another. Must get this in the mail.

October 3, 1944 Paris

Very bright day, today—with warming sun. The chestnut trees have produced an immense crop, and they will be gathered for eventual roasting.

Have been having a sinus flare up, and hope the drainage keeps on the flow. So far, so good.

We have been so busy. This depot has become an increasingly large institution, and I wonder now and then if we are going to be able to handle it without additional personnel. It is "big time" and always full speed ahead. A couple days stretched into about twenty hours of activity, and I didn't get to my hotel room—just got in about four hours of sleep on a cot. Whew!

Pete and I have a nice room in the Hotel Louvois, not far from Place de l'Opera. I hope we will be able to be here for the duration. It is such a nuisance to have to move.

As for the depot, French draymen—with their carts and mules, and some horses—are all over the place. As I understand, their services are chalked up to "reverse lend-lease"—supposedly being paid something by the French government. These men, along with the women in our offices, seem to be quite content; so, I think they must be receiving some income.

The Scheys want to take me sight seeing, and they also know Charley Teague. So, we are going to attempt an afternoon "off." We must avoid the days that either of us is Officer of the Day.

October 6, 1944 Paris

Yesterday, Charley and I did some promenading to see some of this magnificent city, but lots else going on—to be dealt with later. The Scheys were our guides. We visited Notre Dame, and I couldn't help thinking about Hugo's "Hunchback of Notre Dame" and could just see him running along all the balconies. We also visited the Cathedral of the Sacré Coeur, completed in 1914. It is of much fame, also, and had many of its windows blasted out by an American bomb which fell close by. Our problem was that the rain just poured all day.

Last evening we celebrated the anniversary of the order which established our company—the 31st Medical Depot. It turned into a sort of brawl. The mayor of Pantin gave us a hundred gallons of red wine, and we tapped our resources for cases of cognac and rum. Also, we had our supply of German loot—canned sardines, canned hams, pickles, chocolate, raspberry jam, canned cookies, some minced ham, etc.—a real smorgasbord. Our cooks did a superb job of putting it together and laying it out. The WACs who were our guests just had fits, and they were almost furious: "Where did you get all this food?" Many of our French help were present, and did they stuff—into themselves and into their pockets.

One of our sergeants can jitterbug like a professional, and he found a WAC who could keep up with him. They put on quite an exhibition, and did we have fun. They had to use a recording, for the orchestra which had agreed to come did not show. Our French guests just about went crazy watching them and didn't want them to stop.

The French tell us that the German soldier was always so very neat and clean, rarely out of dress uniform when in public, and always formal and "stiff." As for the "Yank," he often appears in public in his "work clothes"—his fatigues, with leggings and helmet. But, the order is just now out that we are to wear our "Class A" uniforms—with blouses, etc. So, maybe attire in public will change.

The Scheys live five stories up, and they observed much from their balcony. They had to be very careful while attempting to watch. They showed us where French men and older youth were lined up and executed. The bullets after passing through the bodies of victims often nicked the walls behind. Some of the women who work in our office have referred to the Germans as being like "machines"—not human beings. The Nazi, as a follower of Hitler, seemed indifferent to human suffering. Some of these people want no mercy to be shown Germany, that the nation be conquered piecemeal and then occupied for many years—that the power of the Junkers of Prussia be broken, shattered, irretrievably dissolved for all time.

Georges, the other evening, was somewhat overcome with emotion when he told me of their being able to laugh again. He said that they rarely laughed during the German occupation. When passing a German soldier on the street, they never dared smile—for fear that a smile would be regarded as solicitous and be cause for arrest, etc. "Now," he says, "we can laugh, be gay, and begin to live again. We go out on the street, and all the American smile at us, we smile at them, and everyone is happy!" Several people at the depot have also made similar references.

October 8, 1944 Paris

Enclosed is this carte postale which shows our warehouse complex. Now you can have a good idea as to our situation. This is really quite a place!

Yes, we have been following the political campaign. Dewey does seem to be turning up the heat, and FDR has come to the defense of his little dog, Fala.

Charley Teague and I went to visit a new friend of his, a Monsieur Rivet. He gave this man a lift one day into Paris shortly after we arrived, and Rivet had invited Charley for dinner. Charley told him about me, that I spoke French, etc. Well, we went to the Rivet apartment, but no one was home. We checked with the people who lived one floor down, on the fifth, to see if they knew of Rivet's whereabouts. They knew nothing, but insisted that we spend the evening with them. Their apartment was so nicely furnished, and they had a grand piano. I was coaxed to play a bit, and then their daughter did very well with some of Chopin and Debussy. They served us some Benedictine liqueur—prepared by monks who have never disclosed the formula and process so it could be "made" outside the monasteries. Their name is something like Billot??

Well, we have been under a good bit of stress here at the depot. We have been putting in long hours, but all has been kept "up to date." We needed some help, and our CO saw an opportunity to make something of it for himself. An old buddy of his, from their associations while in the WPA and CCC administrative work during the depression years, was CO of another Medical Depot Company and with rank of major. This company arrived on the scene, and Cole proposed to combine the two companies with a special T/O—one in which five of the seven key positions for promotion were to fall to the joining company's officers. Well, here are my thoughts at the moment, and I hope you can understand my forlorn despair:—

> Well, I do not have a soul left tonight. We officers have been insulted by our commanding officer as few people have the "honor" to be insulted. It is almost more than a person's self-esteem can palate. It is a case of the old WPA and CCC cliques reforming their ranks.

Selfishness has come into its own, and I have an example of it that will sicken me until the day I die. We have been slapped in the face after having made a record over here comparable by no other depot company. I'm without proper word to express my indignation. It is hard .

While in England, our base platoon, in its activities at a major medical depot there, carried on in a supply assembling program—the dimensions of which were staggering. We met the deadline, and completely outshone the other company which couldn't handle it. Our activities there brought for the company a letter of special commendation from the Chief Surgeon.

Our advance platoon, which landed in Normandie on D-2, carried on in as trying circumstances as any supply installation, and received special commendation from a ranking general of First Army. The men successfully operated under the most adverse conditions.

Then, when we were re-united and became a large medical supply distribution point, our record was again of the highest caliber. This last endeavor, as well as the other two, was carried on and highly successful without the presence of our commanding officer, who was on detached service in a higher headquarters where he was plugging for some more prestigious office than that of CO of a medical depot company. It was our record which brought to us this Paris assignment, a real prize, and it gained us another letter of commendation.

We get to Paris, and we accomplish our purpose. Our CO, our colonel has no headaches. We end up, as a company, doing the work of virtually two. We worked to make things happen, and they did. He then asked us officers to make recommendations to enlarge the company, even to a doubling in size. Of course, we saw possibilities of several promotions with a new T/O., headed by a full colonel. After a few days, this other medical depot company arrives on the scene, and its CO is one of Cole's old buddies. The Colonel then made his allotments

In five of seven central positions, officers of the second company were to be placed over ours. Cole was working to buy their loyalties, and he was wiping his feet on most of us. Our Major Grove was left jobless, and he is well liked by the men and popular, and our CO is jealous of him; our "warehouse officer" is to be of secondary place; our "motor officer" is now to be replaced; I shall be replaced as head of stock-control and accounting; our "inventory officer" will become just an assistant, etc. Our adjutant and our officer in charge of shipping are the two to be left in place. Cole wishes to solidify his own prospective position at the expense of several of his own officers. We are incensed and indignant. Several of our men are much concerned about what appears to be happening.

We have refused to be "Yes-men" to Cole, and he is going to get even with us. He is incompetent, small, selfish, unworthy, and I hope not long to remain in command, here. We officers shall seek a suitable means to remedy this situation. I have never before wished for misfortune to descend upon anyone's head, but something must happen, and soon. I shouldn't be writing this to you, but I want to write about this and to get it for the record. You will know of the eventualities.

I was so sorry to hear of Wendell Willkie's death. He was my choice for the presidency. He is now gone. He was too straight-forward in his speaking, and he would not cater to the politicians who would run the Republican Party. My ballot has not arrived, and I shall be using the Federal ballot.

October13, 1944 Paris

With this sinus drainage, loss of appetite due to our stress and strain, and being just out of good humor, I have lost about fifteen pounds. Actually, it would do me good to lose another ten. We shall see. But, do not get me wrong; there is nothing the matter with me that recovery of good humor will not cure. Ha! We are definitely not going to have to eat any dirt around here, for our little tug of war has been resolved. And, today is a Friday. So, what could be better?

We junior officers had to put our cards on the table, and we did it discretely. We put in requests for transfer—dated the 11th. We were joined by a couple others, and nine of us sort of joined hands. We employed the same statement to give reason for the request—that there was an excess of commissioned officer personnel and that the undersigned felt he could serve his country far more efficiently if reassigned to another organization within the Medical Department. Each letter was addressed to The Commanding General, European Theater of Operations, APO # 887, U. S. Army (Through Channels).

There was no doubt in my mind that we were being "sold down a river", and we knew we were in the affair together. Our letters reached Cole's desk, and he began to make the rounds—with the major and one of the captains of the other company. They must have come to my office soon, and I said only that something had to be much out of focus when a lieutenant colonel, a major, and a captain found it necessary to come to the office of a first lieutenant "to seek advice." I made no accusations, but I did note that our CO had created a problem. The requests had been put on the colonel's desk,, and he had to forward them—with or without his approval.

Yesterday, Teague and I had the afternoon free, and we were in the city—again to see more of the city. We missed a meeting which Colonel Cole called—particularly after he had threatened Russ Peterson with court-martial and reclassification. The seven officers present, who had also submitted letters, sat silently and refused to answer questions. Cole knew that were those letters to be forwarded, the IGD would order an investigation. He had no other choice—but to throw his whole plan into the adjacent canal. A following announcement was to the effect that the other company had been assigned to observe our operation and our methods—particularly their officers and non-coms, and that they were soon to be assigned elsewhere. It was weird.

Some of our non-coms had become much troubled by all that was going on. My office crew had sort of descended into a doldrums of despair and had become much dispirited... When I assured them that we would be returning to normal, how quickly the grins did return. This turned out to be quite an experience, and I think our colonel took quite a beating. Our morale was crumbling around our heads, and it was an agonizing affair. We shall see what the future holds for us, and there is no place for our CO to go. But, our discomfort has been almost as nothing when compared to situations faced by the men along the fronts. I can only guess as to what Col. Cole had to say to inform this visiting major about the collapse of their plans.

Well, to more pleasant matters. You will be receiving some more perfumes—Gurlain, Tabou, Schiaparelli, and lots of Tosca. We found hundreds of bottles of Tosca stored away in our warehouse; so, you will receive bottles enough to give some to all relatives, and even some neighbors. You just would find it all to be almost unbelievable. We have given Tosca to the women who are working for us, and they tell us that it is very good perfume. Well, we must thank the Germans for gathering it for us.

Boy, how the air has cleared around here. The water finally went over the dam, and we have our feet back on the ground. Have also purchased some of Lantell's "Massingale" and Dorsay's "Milford" and "Trophee." So many of us are just carried away with this perfume business. I think we must find some other things to spend our money on and for, etc. Ha! Ha!

Pete and I have been chewing over this problem, as it developed with the colonel. In our hotel room, it is all we can talk about. But, we won!

October 14, 1944 Paris

Your letter of the 6th arrived today. Not bad! I've been trying to catch up on my correspondence—but have not had quite enough time. It is 8:20 in the evening, and I am just a bit tuckered out. There is no doubt about it, we have the best gang of men in our company—and the ones in my office are just tops. They can really get their work done—so quickly and accurately. I doubt if our colonel will attempt to pull such a dumb trick again, and our men just roll their eyes in wonder and disbelief. So it has been.

Most of the Paris movies are now open, and "The Great Dictator" is to open tomorrow, and I want to see it. It will be in French, of course, but it will be fun to watch the people's react to it. Several of us plan to go, but we are told that there will be lines to wait out. So, some of us will just bide our times.

Plan to go over to the Scheys tomorrow evening. Then Wednesday, Charley and I are invited to the Rivets for dinner in the evening. When these French put on a dinner, it is usually about a seven-course affair, and we are at the table for about three hours. We shall see. Will be a very nice time for us, and I think Madame Rivet and their children are to be home. Pete and I just drank some of Volnay's vin rouge, and it is not bad. Paris water is purified and OK to drink. The French always drink wine with their meals.

You asked how it was that I knew where Merlin Stackhouse was buried. I was certain that he probably was slain in the action near St. Lo, and that he would have been buried in one of two places. Stroh and I just happened to choose the right one, and there was an enclosed registry of names and grave locations. The cemetery is at La Cambe.

War news seems to be stepping up somewhat. Czechoslovakia and Austria are yet to be liberated and Norway and Denmark are underway. The Russians are driving into East Prussia. I do not expect Hitler to make a play for an armistice.

Paris is a lovely city, and it is a pleasure to walk about here and there. There are so many beautiful parks, and they are so well kept. I just haven't had as much time "off" as I need. The weather has been great the past two days, and I have managed to get beyond my doldrums. The mental strain because of the mess within the depot operation was exhausting, in a way. I'm sleeping much better at night. Some of us really enjoy the beauty of this city. Others much prefer the beauties of the city. Oh, well!

One of the sergeants in my office looked me in the eye and said: "We depended and relied upon our officers to straighten things out for us, and you didn't let us down!" He just made me feel so very "good" about it. Things are truly back to normal for us, and our feet are "on the ground."

While yet in Trevières, some of us visited Bayeux, a city virtually untouched by the war. It was here that I purchased the three or four yards of fancy veiling—all for your uses. The pairs of wooden shoes were also acquired there, and here they are called "sabots," and it is from sabot that we get our word "sabotage." Howzaboutthat?

October 19, 1944 Paris

We have been almost desperately busy. It has been a grind, and I hope things slacken a bit. It rains nearly every day, and we have had enough for all of western Europe, I think.

Radio said, today, that we have landed in the Philippines. Well, MacArthur has returned, as he said he would.

Went to a style show, yesterday, with the Scheys. They were showing fall and winter dresses and coats. The mannequins were cute. A friend of the Scheys, Madleine, is one of the sellers, and she invited them and me. She had seats for us front and center. There were several "small shop" buyers there, and something took place that I was not aware of—until well along during the showing. They thought I was probably an American designer or clothier for women. So, many of the buyers were watching closely my reactions. Madame Marcelle Alix Tizeau was owner of the "shoppe"—I guess. Many of the garments were priced at 16,000 francs, in each case a few times my monthly income. Ha! Yvette and I sort of consulted each other, and I then wrote down the number of each display that seemed among the best. Some of the buyers were watching me like hawks, and they were making note of my reactions. It was a lovely display, and I thoroughly enjoyed it.

Will soon be sending you some fancy perfumes—stuff we buy for no more than one-fourth of the cost in the U.S. Several of us have sort of gone off our rockers over this perfume. The Germans had stockpiled cases of the Tosca, and when you receive it, just give a bottle to each relative and friend. Some of the other brands to be purchased are Lanvin, Worth, Lantelle, Guerlain, Schiaperelli, Dorsay, Lucien le Long, Lancome,etc. And we have loads of "eau de colognes." Whew! So, be prepared. All of you will soon be able to smell so nice!!

Was so tired yesterday evening that I was in bed about 7:30. But, Teague came in, and he, Pete, and I began to sample fruit cakes, sardines, etc—from boxes that had arrived "from home." Then in came a fellow lieutenant who had been in OCS with us at Camp Barkeley, and he had two bottles of Piper-Heidzick (sp) champagne. We did a lot or reminiscing. I went to sleep along the way and roused enough to know the party was over and guests had departed. Some deal, eh?

We are back to normal at the depot, but we could use about 100 more men and 4 officers. But, we are just putting in the hours to get each day's work done. The time passes quickly, and the men want it that way. Our NCOs were really upset when it appeared that we were to be united with this other company, and the colonel was about to play favorites in effort to buy loyalty. It is "something" to observe the upswing in mood and spirit. We officers stood our ground, and it has paid dividends—as far as company morale is concerned.

One of our men engaged in a bit of "black marketing" of some of the perfumes, and it required some investigating and disciplining. We had a small trial—with a fine assessed and some "grounding" and loss of certain privileges for a while. No problem to arise if the Tosca is given away; but, to attempt to sell it is a "NO-NO."

Evening before last, Charley and I had dinner with the Rivets. What a great time and good. We arrived about 7:45 and were served with a "vin naturel"—positively one of the best elixirs I have ever tasted. We had about four rounds of it before we went to the dining room. First came a thick soup—pottage; and then followed roast pork, peas, potatoes, mushrooms, etc., with our being pressed to have seconds and thirds. Then came a sort of head cheese, a pudding that was coffee-flavored, and a cake—always urged to have more. Two kinds of wine and finally champagne—to be followed with an armagnac, which was to settle our stomachs. About 10:45, we retired to the living room—to receive a shot of something strong enough to run an automobile. It was genuine "fire water." We departed for the Louvois just before midnight, and we had had quite an evening. They didn't want us to leave, but we had to be at the depot by 7:30, and it would take us over a half-hour to walk to our hotel.

Am keeping my ear glued to the political campaign, but still do not see Dewey as winning—but I think he is gaining ground, for he is certainly on the attack… And as for this war against Adolf, it is going to drag on for months, yet—could be for many, many months. He will not surrender, and Germany will have to be occupied yard by yard—is my guess.

October 27, 1944 Paris

Our hotel had a bit of hot water, and it was almost more than we could handle. The posted notice was to bathe during a certain hour, and to make it a quick shower. Sponge bathing with cold water is not all such might be cracked up to be, and we just splash on some extra cologne and Kolnisch Wasser. Ha! And, so it goes, usually.

Have been eating most of my evening meals at the depot, and our cooks do a better job than the ones at the officer's mess here in the city. Our men are fortunate. For dessert yesterday, one of our bakers prepared a pineapple pie, and it was unusually good. And, a butterscotch pie is also a specialty, and no pieces ever go begging. Keep telling my office gang that they should "butter up" their cooks and keep them happy.

We have been pushed to the limit with requisitions, but the night shifts seem to keep all orders caught up. We have a system to keep "back-orders" flowing into the corrals, and we seem to be the only supply company that does it—from what some of the men tell me. We also hear reports about the "black market" which thrives in Paris—particular with respect to gasoline and cigarettes. Rumor hints that a ring of American officers are within the inner circle. I do not know for sure, but rumors so often prove to be quite true.

Certain French laborers are threatening to strike for shorter hours and higher pay, and some here at our depot are complaining about their hours and wages. Our own men are on the job often from 16 to 18 hours a day, and often each day of the week. I sometimes think it is not difficult to understand the ease with which the Germans overran these people. There is an apathy that undermines a desire to push when things need extra effort, and I wonder if this "national socialism" has anything to do with this. With a war to be concluded, this sort of attitude quite thoroughly disgusts me. So far, no problems here.

Yes, I think I shall have my sweet little old American self photographed. So, be prepared. I guess we should have something to remember me by as I was in "Gai Paree"—wherever.

We understand that the U.S. government is going to slap a tariff on perfume sent home by the soldiers. Our perfume importers and marketers must have something to do with this, and I am furious. Report, if so, will mean that what is to be invested in this perfume by soldiers and their families will practically double. All of my loot is now underway and will escape any tariff. But, I am just outraged at the prospective unfairness of it. This special tariff might provide funds to pay for a second monument erected to "un soldat inconnu."

Pete, Charley, and I have been able to do some wandering throughout this marvelous city—to stroll about, here and there, and to see more of Notre Dame, the Eiffel Tower, the Trocadero—and so much else. We were at the Rivet's evening before last. Monsieur Rivet speaks English about as I speak French, but he is more fluent. Madame speaks no English, but she understands her husband's English. Their apartment complex, six stories high and two apartments to each level, is one of the several properties which Rivet either owns or manages. They are sort of "upper crust" and would never frequent a "dive." We have been invited to come to the apartment to dance, and we should have a good time.

The family who lives in the apartment below had a big wedding a day or two ago. Their son, the groom, is an engineer, 24 years old, and fought for nearly two years with the Maquis in southern and western France. He will be heading to the

French Sudan in Africa. From what I understand, he had experiences similar to those of André Jacquet.

Am OD today and through tonight. So, little sleep for me. Our night crew is really on the ball. I wander around to visit with the crews. We seem to do all our "catching up" at night, and I sort of enjoy the activity. But, I shall be sleepy tomorrow.

News of a big naval victory over the Japs in the Pacific has us exhilarated. It means we have lost many men, but it is the necessary means to the end of the war and the victory which we seek. I hope these "Sons of Heaven" are increasingly prepared to meet their "Sun God"!

Those fancy-handled and steel-bladed letter openers were just more of the unusual loot which our German predecessors had stockpiled into the warehouse. They are pretty fancy, and just pass them around to relatives and friends. We found boxes of them.

Keep the dream bars coming. The French just love them, and they just disappear as if by magic.

Left some of the last batch in the hotel room for the ladies who do our cleaning, and did I hear about it. Ha! The olives and jam are also favorites of the women who help us in the office at the depot. So, your special war effort is well appreciated.

October 31, 1944 Paris

Here it is Hallowe'en, and tomorrow is All Saints Day. I have come down with another cold, and am doing a lot of dripping. As long as things keep flowing, it is not bad. Have a little steamer at the office, and I use it off an on during the day and during the night when I was OD. Two nights ago we spent most of the time unloading box cars loaded with goods for issue. It was dusty work and this brought on this drainage of the sinuses. At least, that is what I choose to think. Ha!

A box arrived with more dream bars, olives, jam, etc. It all will not last long. Have sent you quite a store of letter openers and my final shipment of Tosca—along with some fancy straight-edge razors.

Pete is a Minneapolis Swede and I am a Nebraska Sandbur, and we do hit it off in good harmony. He is a mortician, and he and an older brother have a large, modern funeral home. Charley hails from Hickory, N.C., and is a distributor of Pepsi Cola and will probably own the business soon after he gets out of this man's army. We spend our free time together. They are married, and they tell me that I should be. So, we make a jolly threesome.

Yes, I still mourn Willkie's death, and remain of the opinion that he would have been a great president. Dewey is swinging hard, but my hunch is that FDR will win again—perhaps by his narrowest margin.

So, you were flabbergasted by all those decks of playing cards. My guess is that they are of German make, and we found several large boxes of them in the warehouse. Pass some of them around. They are a little off size, but no problem to use them.

The little Eiffel Tower I shall be sending you is a gift from Madame Schey—to you, Mother. Those fine-toothed combs are what people here and in Germany must use to get rid of head lice and cooties. A person with real fine hair might be able to use such a comb, but it takes some pulling when hair is normal. Nonetheless, they would comb out the lice.

Pete, Charley, and I were to the Rivet's last evening, and we had all sorts of sandwiches and other good things to eat. This turned out to be quite a party—about thirteen present, with about three young women and two young men about the age of Nicole—late teenagers. After our round of food and tea and lemonade, we went into the living room to dance. Jean Pierre, the Rivet's son is eleven, about eight years younger than Nicole. One of the girls told me that Madame Rivet liked to waltz, they had radio which could be tuned in to find waltz music, and I then asked Madame to waltz with me. We couldn't glide too well on the carpet, but we did our turning and reversing, etc. She seemed to be very pleased. We did have just lots of fun.

Well, about ll:45 we three decided we should head for our hotel—nearly a 40 minute walk, for the Metro was no longer running that late. Well, they were aghast, for we were to eat again—more sandwiches and cheese were being prepared by a maid, and this to come after a couple more dance numbers. Not until nearly two o'clock did we finally insist that we had to leave. Our get away came at 2:30. They protested and then insisted that we were to return the following Saturday evening for another party. Monsieur Rivet explained to us that they dared not have any sort of gatherings and parties during the German occupation, and that they were just delighted—"enchanted"—to have us as guests, to be free once again to have parties and to feast. Of course, with hallowe'en and All Saints Day, it is a holiday time, and they were not quite persuaded that we had to work both days—that our work did not stop at the depot because of a holiday.

And you will find in my next shipment several straight-edged razors—pretty fancy, and I have some uncles who will appreciate having one or two of them. The last of my Tosca will come with the razors.

November 2, 1944 Paris

Another Thursday has rolled around, and it is usually my day to have an afternoon "off." Pete and I hope to do a bit of Christmas shopping, but prices are so high for us—once we have to figure in the devalued franc, and inflation is running "hog wild." We understand that the franc is to be "stabilized." We shall see.

The British seem to be zeroing in on Antwerp. These efforts to dislodge the Germans are so costly in lives. Had our supply lines been able to keep up with Patton after the break through at St. Lo, etc., so that he didn't have to halt his advances because of lack of everything, the Nazis would have had no chance to reform their lines of defense. Now, the probing for weak spots is before us again.

We have been so darned busy—some requests for certain supplies and medicines coming in from Switzerland, even. We respond to requisitions from the British, Dutch, and French, and any questions can be answered by telephone calls to our theater surgeon's office, here in the city. So, we have few delays. This army "system" seem so often to be cumbersome, but it does function.

It is getting chilly, and the fuel shortage is severe. Our hotel room is cold, and we spend little time in it, and then it is to get under the covers and sleep. We do lots of nibbling on stuff sent from home, and we have a good bit of the loot from the warehouse—thanks to our German predecessors. On occasion, we leave a few dainties for our housemaids, but they never touch things that are not put out for them.

Am to go to Scheys tomorrow evening, but they don't have good sense when it comes to a respect for our working hours—and Sundays, too. It has become a matter of just making quick departures when schedule so demands. Ho! Ho!

I may buy a little more of Chanel # 5 and Lanvin's "Scandal," and my French friends consider Chanel to be a rather second-rate perfume. We hear, now, that there will be no special U.S. tariff applied to perfume. Again, we shall see, eh?

November 5, 1944 Paris

Sunday, again. I dashed over to the American Cathedral (Episcopalian) for a service supposedly for us in the military services—communion and a bishop from an Ohio diocese to preside and speak. It was an impressive service, and quite a turn out. We closely followed the prayer book.

We do seem to be engaging in a major drive at the eastern front, but not much information. For some reason, I'm not optimistic that we shall have any startling success.

Yes, our problem with the colonel is now behind us, and our men are in a good mood—snappy salutes and much grinning. They just were dead set against any kind of "union" with another company. All of us are putting in longer hours, day by day, but everyone knows just where he stands, and this is good for morale.

Am hoping to go to the Paris Opera. Pete is our contact person, and he tells us that tickets will cost equivalent of $1.80. We do enjoy the USO shows—just fun to watch the routines and to relax.

Charley and I were invited to visit the Billots, the family just below the Rivets. Their daughter, about 17, plays the piano, and she wanted us to show her how to jitterbug and boogie woogie. We were not very good at it—Ha! They served us some Benedictine liquor—made by the monks in the abbeys, and the process is known only to them. It is unusual and delicious.

For our walk to the hotel, we had a full moon to light the streets. We just strolled for well over an hour—past Notre Dame, the Conciergerie—in which Louis XVI and Marie Antionette were imprisoned prior to their excutions, the Ile de Paris and across the Seine River, and via La Place de la Carousal, La Place de l'Opera, and to our hotel. Pete is OD at the depot, and Charley and I then visited for about an hour and a half. We do not agree on American politics, for he is a North Carolina Democrat. Ha! We both expect FDR will win again.

Some mice got into my desk drawers the other night at the depot, and did they ever make a mess of things—just ruined candy bars and cigarettes, all of which I was going to hand around to the women who type for us in our office. I regularly purchase my seven packets of cigarettes each week—just to have them to give away. I guess, on the black market, a package of cigarettes will bring more than 150 francs—more than three dollars. We are urged not to give out packages, but to offer just cigarettes separately. So, we do attempt to keep the black-marketeers from making their windfalls.

November 7, 1944 Paris

The last USO show we saw was a good one—many pretty girls, good acts, and many laughs. Pete, Charley, and I have been eating several of our evening meals in our hotel rooms—just to munch on stuff we have saved from packages from home and from our depot findings that the Germans laid in for us.

These cold water shaves we must put up with each morning are just a bit bracing. We have no alternative. When I am inclined to complain, I just ponder the plight of the men at the fronts, and this persuades me that I have so little to harp about. I did sneak in a "hot" shower at the depot about two afternoons ago—but, "hot" means that the chill was off! So it goes!

More rain and more rain. And, I continue to have "spells" with my stomach. It is indigestion from something, and could have been some of Hershey's almond bars. This last one was a hum-dinger. By noon I was hoping I could die, and then I was fearful that I would! No relief, and about 2:30 "things" really came to a head, and Vesuvius erupted. My conclusion is that I must not eat chocolate. By 3:30, I felt like a new person, although sort of as if I had been put through a wringer. All is well this evening.

We have had some new men transferred into our outfit, and one of them wrote home about his impressions. His letter was quite revealing, and I couldn't resist copying some of what he had to say:—

> I arrived with six other men.... We were shown our rooms and beds and told to report to the adjutant in the morning.... He assigned me to

work with the carpenters.... I know how to handle tools.... This outfit came over with the men on D-day and it is one of the best medical depot companies in the army. It is the main one, and that is why it is in Paris....The men here are swell. It is quite different from a replacement outfit. Every one here is friendly because they have been together a long time and so far every one has received me as one of their family.... The chow is excellent here. We eat at a table like people.... You don't have to come in a formation.... I have a pass to go out every night and we get one day a week off.... I expect to register at the red cross for a sight seeing tour of Paris.... I work with the Sergeant who is in charge of the carpenters.... an older man 38 years old, and he took me right to the supply room and I already have a BLOUSE.... the supply sergeant took a list of all the things that I need. So, pretty soon I will be able to get dressed.... In Paris, you have to wear tie, blouse, no leggins, and OD cap, just the same way we dressed in the states. Boy, I can't wait to get dressed. We even have a laundry service here.... Oh, yes, the mail gets here seven and eight days from the states.

We still must censor the mail. This was one fascinating letter to check out.

November 15, 1944 Paris

Have been to see some operas—with Pete, and he is the one who manages to get the tickets. Gounod's "Romeo and Juliet" was wonderful—with the singing and staging being superb. The tenor and soprano were marvelous. The tenor, Lucciani, was as fine a singer as I have heard. We saw "Samson and Delilah," but it was not as good—Delilah was pretty buxom, and Samson was pretty weak. But, the scenery and lighting effects on this performance were unusual. We paid 90 francs for each performance, and it was a joy to see and hear them. The Paris Opera is a beautiful building, and about five minutes away from our hotel.

Well, not much surprised at the outcome of the election, and not disappointed, really. Dewey delivered some good punches, but his was largely a campaign of criticism and just didn't cut the mustard.

Our hotel room is always cold, and we just hop into bed to keep warm. And, we remain so busy at the depot, for we must serve so many hospitals and company and unit aid crews. We do seem to know whether we are going or coming, however. Ha!

Charley, Pete, and I were at the Rivet's for supper last night—always wine, champagne, and marvelous food. We always take a few bottles from our large company store, and they have ceased protesting. One just has to see to believe the store of wines, etc., laid away in our warehouse by our German "friends."

A very nice letter from Rose Luecke to tell me of the recent visit by Uncle Arthur and Aunt Florence. She refers to Uncle Arthur as "Bud" and had this to say of him: "He never speaks about any one with much enthusiasm. But when he talked of you, one would have thought he were speaking of his own son. He spoke so often of you." As you know, J. Arthur and I always did sort of click. Eh?

Well, I have been involved in another imbroglio, and this time with some top brass from our theater surgeon's office. It involves our handling of "back orders." We seek, through our regular reports, to maintain the respective levels of supply for all items which we issue. Our stock records keep track of each item—quantities received from our suppliers and issues to our hospitals and all medical-aid units. Each item has its stock number and its card,, and it takes lots of work to record each issue on the stock card and on the requisition, etc. Each unit ordinarily receives what it requests, and any shortage is placed on "back order"—to be filled as soon as ample supply comes in and ready to be picked up with the following requisition. It was not supposed to be necessary that a unit again requisition. To handle these back orders, to make certain they were not overlooked and left unfilled, our theater surgeon's office had handed down a complicated and very time-consuming procedure, with additional paper-work and files. The gang in my office, who kept all the records, developed a process of accounting which involved no additional paper work and time, and it was working to perfection. Report reached our theater surgeon's office that our depot was the only supply outfit in the Paris area efficiently taking care of items placed on "back order." So, out from that office came three "colonels" to offer us a compliment, only to find that we were ignoring their "prescribed system."

They would not note that we were the one depot getting the job done; they proceeded to "chew out" Colonel Cole; they called me in to account for our "deviation." Forewarned, Thirlby and I had prepared a stock record card upon which we demonstrated the thoroughness of our men's record-keeping, which involved some use of red ink to show requisitions on "back order" and to be immediately filled upon supply's arrival—all without the additional man or two to take care of things the prescribed way. I was told that a decision would be given within a day or two. What irked me was that Cole said nothing to support us. After our visiting "upper crust" departed, Colonel Cole implied that he had been much embarrassed. I was inwardly madder than the proverbial hatter, and asked him if he wished to order us to take care of "back orders" as prescribed—but, that the process would require about two additional men to handle the additional book work. He paused, and then said, "No."

Well, we waited for three days for word to descend from the theater surgeon's office. When it came, we were told that requisitioned items not in supply were now to be reordered, that no more would shortages be placed on "Back Order." As for me and the men in our "records office," we had won a double-headed victory—we had apparently proved the prescribed procedure to be cumbersome and not necessary for efficient service, and we had forced a lifting of the burden of keeping track of "back orders." Red ink was now to disappear from our stock-record cards. Did we do some celebrating in the office!

I am scribbling this while in bed, just trying to keep warm. There is no coal available for these hotels—at least, that is what we are told.

November 20, 1944

A Monday, today. I have been involved in an investigation with respect to a selling of some of our "goods" in the "black market." Something like $200 in value is involved, and we are so busy that it really irks me to have to give this sort of problem the time it requires. Thank heavens!—my office crew doesn't need me around to keep the records of all this movement of wares in and out. It is interesting to note that most of our bicycles have disappeared. Ha! I had mine chained to a post under cover, nearby our office; and, one morning, just the front wheel was there—the only part chained to the post. Well, I had not used it for more than two weeks. The subway is so efficient, and practically nothing of interest to see in Pantin.

We are all hoping for an early German collapse, but I do not think it will happen. The lack of coal continues, but I understand the food situation is easing. Nevertheless, this is going to be a rough winter for the people. As I observe these people, particularly those employed at our depot, I have drawn some contradicting conclusions. Some seem to have initiative and ambition; but, so many do not—they seem to lack "push" and desire to improve their "status," particularly if it requires effort from themselves. There seems to be a sort of general acceptance of a sort of "comme-ci comme-ca" attitude. I didn't sense this in Great Britain, where there was "defiance" and not an "acceptance." On the other hand, that English Channel was just too deep and too wide for invasion—not since 1066. On the other hand, there is a sort of American "occupation" of Great Britain during this war. Ha!

Well, skies remain overcast, but no rain for several days. Sure hope that this drying weather will enable Patton and his tanks to be more effective.

Received on the 18th your letter written after FDR's re-election, and I know how disappointed you were. Had to laugh, Mother, at your reference to the "Damned Election." Well, I repeat—that I am not discouraged. Pete, Charley, and I have been mulling over the election, and Pete and I outvoted Charley two to one. Ha! We have done a good bit of chuckling.

Col. Cole and I went to the American Cathedral, yesterday, for communion. I understand it is really named "Church of the Holy Trinity"—as translated into English. It was so nice, and in English.

Monsieur Rivet has asked Charley and me to eat our Thanksgiving dinner with them, but I think we shall be with the company. There are so many places we want to see—particularly to go to Versailles. And, we remain so busy at the depot, for we are so central and we serve so many hospitals and organizations. A sixteen-to eighteen-hour day is not unusual for us. We officers and several of the NCOs work with both the day and night crews—that is, we just often overlap, now and then.

November 23, 1944 Paris Thanksgiving Day

Am much taken by one of Sgt. Dick Wingert's "Hubert" cartoons—A medical captain is examining a fellow up for discharge, but has to tell the lieutenant who is assisting him: "We'll have to keep him in the Army—he's no longer fit for civilian life." I guess this caught my fancy because my sinus problem has really taken hold, and I feel quite unfit for anything. Have been doing more steaming, and sure hope the pressure will ease. Seems to me that we have such high humidity.

Just seems to me that the needs for medical supplies has almost skyrocketed, for my office-gang can hardly keep up with the paper work. It is the same throughout the depot. Do not expect me to send any more perfume, and I haven't had time to look for different kinds, anyway.

Pete is OD this evening. Our cooks really did a grand job to prepare our dinner for today—the turkeys just roasted to perfection, and everything else so well prepared and seasoned. I am wondering about the men at the front lines! We are so fortunate to be where we are. I am a bit perturbed because of the strikes going on in the U.S.—at this time when so much is at stake over here and in the Pacific; but, on the other hand, we have business executives who are only too eager to take advantage of their employees.

November 28, 1944 Paris

My sinuses are really giving me trouble, and I have really increased my steaming. Am on regular cod liver oil tablets and something now and then to ease the headache. And, those special vitamin pills you sent are now on my daily menu. So, we shall survive! It is just uncomfortable. Have started this at my desk, but will have to pick it up later—business and work call.

Two evenings ago, Pete, Charley and I were at the Rivet's—just another of those grand evenings we have with these remarkable people. They seem to want us to come to share their hospitality about once very two weeks, and they appear to be somewhat offended if we do not readily accept.

We take a few bottles of something each time, now—with nearly each bottle stamped as reserved for the German WEHRMACHT. An interesting part of this story is that truckloads of this loot, and I mean hundreds and hundreds of cases, were turned over to the city of Paris for "relief"—but with much of it having made way into the city's "black market." The Rivets know we do not buy our bottles "au marche` noir." We do lots of chuckling about this.

I'm usually up by six each morning, then catch the Metro to Pantin to have breakfast at the company dining hall, and am at my desk by 7:45. From then on, it is "high gear" for all over the place. After return from work last evening, I went to see the Scheys, for they had left a message at the hotel for me to come over. They plan to have a Christmas dinner with five other families in their apartment building and want Charley and me to join them. The Scheys have no children. I told them that we would join them, but on one condition—that we furnish a minimum of eight bottles of wine and some of the liquor. Our "private stock" being ample and George and Yvette had heard us talk about the loot, they readily agreed. So, we shall see what happens. Of course, war developments could change all plans. Pete, Charley, and I are pretty close to being teetotalers, but we do find much pleasure in the sharing of our plentiful supply of bottles. Ha!

Have scribbled nearly all of this in bed, and all the steaming is beginning to have its desired affect. Once the draining began, the pressure eased. Maybe the vitamin pills Bin sent will also help. I think today may be a turning point.

December 1, 1944 Paris

Am feeling about 100% better. The cod liver and vitamin pills must be having an impact, and there are two or three things that I am not eating—stuff that has been fried. The steaming has eased the sinus pressure. But, had my stomach problem not eased, I was about ready to go in for a morning's "sick call."

The mail has been so irregular. I received over twenty letters today, and they had postage dates ranging from October 23 to November 25. But, the mail does come through!

So many more units are now turning to us for their medical supplies, blankets, litters, etc. We are finding, now and then, that several of us must be "on deck" for a minimum of 16 hours per day. Most of the men are on half-day shifts, but officers and key NCOs must see their daily responsibilities completed. Sometimes, but not often, our social calendars have to be adjusted. Oh, well!

The soap, etc., arrived. Was sorry to know that two bottles of the German kolnisch wasser were broken, but sometimes these packages get pretty well crunched. What amazes me is that so little of contents is ever really damaged—just bruised a little, maybe.

We recommended five of our NCOs for direct commissions, as we were asked to do. So many of our gang would make very fine officers. The five seemed to be pleased and flattered, but I doubt if any will make application. We have a few "dead ends" in our outfit—officers and men, but only a few. Generally, throughout, morale is high for us. We hear so many reports about strife in other companies, so often told our men by those who come to pick up their requisitions, that our better men just want to stay put. Of course, transfers out would give us opportunity to promote some of our highly deserving men. Central desire is that this war might end abruptly—but, little chance for such.

Do keep the dream bars and other goodies a-coming, and send me a large can of Calox tooth powder—can't seem to find any of it here.

Our hotel rooms remain without heat—just no coal. We use wooden crates and broken lumber for our little stoves in our offices, but just enough to take the chill away. Do not know what we would have to do were the thermometer to plummet, really! No one runs around in other than our heavier clothing—under and over.

December 5, 1944 Paris

Am OD, and the typewriter is handy and to be put to good use. Have just completed my rounds to make certain all is in order, and that the guards are at their posts, etc. All is well on this front.

Charley and have been to the Rivet's to play bridge. Several of us went to see the operetta "Rose Marie," and it was delightful. Ahead in near future will be a Russian opera and the Folies—"Folie Bergere." We are wanting to see the "Ballet" and more of the Opera Comique. Pete gets the tickets, and we go if time and work permit. And, I managed to squeeze in a couple hours with the Scheys. Many of our men go to these performances.

I have become a regular pill-taker—cod liver and vitamins. Am steaming regularly, and my contraption is working—for I do feel just so much better, and with much more pep.

The value of the franc has crumbled to about ½ cent, and we are paid on the former exchange basis of 2 cents. So, if we purchase anything, we pay through an inflated nose. It is discouraging when we see something we want. I am looking for French Christmas cards, but the cost will force me to send about half as many as I had planned. My cards will arrive a bit late!

We Americans are the only foreign troops who pay to ride on the Metro. The Germans rode free, and it is my understanding that the English, Dutch, Poles, etc., do not pay to ride the subway. But, we of the U.S. seem to be willing to be clipped on every turn. Each of us just purchases a supply of tokens.

Received the pamphlet of Christmas carols, and the Rivets will enjoy hearing them. They are fond of music. Next visit for Charley and me is to be for dinner, and we will have quite a feast. We fill our musette bags with wine whenever we go, and we will be there until after midnight—with the long walk back to our hotel. But, it is just great!

Well, it seems to me that Hitler has been able to play his game unusually well, and his western lines seem to be quite formidable. I fear that cost of Allied lives will be much greater than for the taking and breaking out of Normandie. He must have rallied the support of the German people, for I think they have lost any hope of leniency. They hope that some sort of peace can be negotiated, before being forced to accept an unconditional surrender. And I am a bit perturbed, too, because of so much of supplies and goods falling into the French "blackmarket"! We see so many privately owned French cars racing throughout the city, and it is amazing. No doubt about it, much of the gasoline to fuel them has to be funneled somehow from our American supply and should be used only by our military vehicles. Maybe I am just feeling a bit belligerent this evening—having to be OD. Ho! Ho!

Will make another "round" to check on things, and then will crawl into my coveralls and attempt to get a wink or two on the couch in the office. Our night crew is quite busy—lots of requisitions to be filled and the items placed in the pens for "pick up." My "records" crew works only the day shift, but occasionally a little "night work" is needed to catch up.

December 12, 1944 Paris

Our pace continues to keep our noses to the grindstone, and it seems that I must keep an eye on too many things. But, my evenings remain largely open and free.

The French version of "Rose Marie" sort of amused me, for more than two-thirds of it takes place in France—of course. It was a colorful production. A couple evenings ago we saw the Russian opera—Mussorgsky's "Boris Godunov," and the music and orchestration was highly impressive. We have been recently to the Rivet's and to the Schey's. Tomorrow evening we are slated to see the "Folies Bergeres"—always a bit risque, here and there, but one hasn't been to Paris, really, unless he has seen the "Folies."

Have been OD, again, and this usually keeps me awake most of the night; but, this one was not so demanding.

Finally found some Tabu—this perfume is supposed to be quite intriguing, but the prices are so inflated! And, quite an assortment of ear rings—to be sent for general distribution. Get ready!

Was to church, Sunday morning, and it was a good sermon and well worth the going. Then, a return to the hotel and to read that there would be hot water for the evening. Had to run to the depot to check on a matter; and then, when back to the hotel I had a bit of soaking in nice, warm water. What a luxury!

Several packages have arrived, and I shall have so much food to share over the Christmas holiday. I think our letters are being sidetracked in order to get the packages through. We shall see what happens. I still have greeting cards to buy, and my mailings are going to be late.

December 14, 1944 Paris

Sunday—Pete, Charley, and I were again to the Rivet's for supper. We were there until about 2:00 a.m. They never want us to leave, and Nicole and Jean Pierre are just as bad as their parents. They seem to be oblivious to the fact that we must arise early and be at the depot for a full day's work. Ho! Ho! They do like us, and I think it is because neither of us is at all sophisticated—we are just ourselves, and they do make us feel so much at home.

Had to laugh when you wrote that everyone likes the "Shocking" perfume. Maybe that is why it is named such. We had so many boxes of the "Tosca" in our warehouse, and the Germans must have really latched on to an entire factory's supply. All of our men are about finished with this perfume business—so much has been sent home.

We took in another show, "The Male Animal"—put on by army personnel and the Red Cross. It was one of the funniest plays I have seen, and I laughed until my sides ached. I was just "a scream."

Did buy some Christmas cards and must now get them addressed—about thirty of them. Our daytime hours have been so completely taken with obligations here at the depot; and, now, we have this German offensive that is underway, and we do not know what it will amount to. But, it could push the Allies to the limit. We will be much busier, for sure, if it amounts to a lot. Now, we shall see!

My Christmas packages are arriving with every thing intact. It is just wonderful. I do hope mine reach you in as good condition. The razors are for the uncles and for Mr. E. Some of those handles are so ornate. I shall stick to my safeties, for those long blades would take off a nose or a chin. Ha!

Your letter of the 1st arrived today, along with others mailed much earlier. Yes, our letters arrive somewhat mixed around, but all get here. The system is working. Have not received the $100 money order; but, it will yet arrive. I just want to have some extra cash for some Christmas buying, here—and, we will have New Year's ahead, and the French do celebrate it.

Charley and I are taking Monsieur Rivet to have evening dinner with us at the central officer's mess, and we hope the meal will be a good one. We are slated to go to the Rivet's New Year's Eve. Madame Rivet, Nicole, and Jean Pierre are out of the city visiting relatives.

I continue to think about these operas I've seen—the excellence of the staging and lighting. Pete gets us such good tickets, but the performances are much better to watch when we do not sit too far forward. The music is just superb.

December 16, 1944 Paris

Am OD and in the depot office pounding away on this typewriter. Will soon be making my rounds, and then will settle down on a cot for a few hours of sleep, I hope. This cot is not as comfortable as my mattress at the hotel, but I well remember the many times in this man's army when a cot would have been a luxury. And, the rain has been plaguing us, again—almost endlessly, and prediction is that it is going to continue for several days.

We do keep busy. It is up by 6:30, a company truck picks us up to have us at depot mess hall for breakfast, and I am usually at my desk by 7:45. Often, it is a twelve-hour day at the depot. We could use more military personnel, but no chance for other than replacements. I am just amazed, day after day, the way in which our men get their work done. They are remarkable, and so little chance for promotions because our T/O is complete.

Last evening I had another round with my stomach. I think I must avoid any greasy stuff. We had some sauerkraut simmered in bacon grease, and it was excellent. But, it is probably what did the job on me. Came back to the hotel about 8:30 and went to bed, but it was back up and then down again—most uncomfortable. Pete came in and also went to bed. Then, just after midnight the phone rang, and Capt. Stroh wanted us to come to his room, but Pete said we were going to stay in bed. About five minutes later, a knock at the door, and in came Stroh, Col. Cole and about two others. They were a bit high and talking a bit loud. Another fit of nausea hit me, and I became about as green as the bed spread. They took one look at me and then straight way departed. About a half hour later, the colonel called to see how I was and suggested that I stay in bed until noon.

Well, I had about four hours of good sleep, awakened at the usual time, felt much better, and boarded the transportation for the depot.

The package with the wooly pajamas has not arrived, nor has the letter with the $100 money order. We must give all this mail the time it requires. It will come through. Our mail orderly is one of the grandest fellows we have in the company and certainly ought to have one promotion after the other. He is from Cincinnati.

December 19, 1944 Paris

The money order arrived, and it took such a long, long time. Its sack of mail must have been buried somewhere under a stack of others. Now we can rest on our oars. The postal service always comes through, and we just have to give it time. I think that all these Christmas packages are receiving priority.

We are really about packaged to the limit. Charley has received eight fruit cakes, to date. And with all that we are collectively getting, our depot personnel are having quite a time. Hard candy and candy bars are every where, and all sorts of licorice and cookies. We've learned to keep most of it under cover—just to keep it from disappearing overnight, actually. We share, too, with the women who clean our hotel rooms. We'll be toting a few of the specialties to the Rivets, Scheys, etc.

There seems to be some sort of a cigarette shortage, and most of our men are smokers. We have many explanations for it, but my hunch is that there has been a sizable funneling into the black market. Who knows! Some think it is the priority of the Christmas mail, but these mountains of cigarette cartons have nothing to do with the postal service.

For Christmas Eve, Charley and I have been invited to the Scheys. Four or five other families will be involved, and we shall have quite an evening—an all night affair, no doubt. They will not hear of our departing until we finally persuade then to realize that we have a full day's work at the depot—and, particularly with this German offensive facing us.

We are certainly much disturbed by VonRunstedt's offensive, and this cloudy, rainy weather has been to his advantage. It is advancing, and the cost is going to be so great. It will run its course, and final reckoning can only add to the stern terms of an eventual German surrender. The ground loss will have to be retaken, but the loss of lives is to be increasingly sickening. We are beginning to receive all sorts of emergency requests at the depot. It is going to be a twenty-four-hour press for medical supplies, litters, blankets, and all else. Well, our plans for Christmas Eve and for Christmas Day can quickly go for naught. This can be very serious—and particularly if prolonged. We'll just have to wait and see! The immediate future is not encouraging.

December 24, 1944 Paris

Here it is, Christmas Eve, and lots has happened in the past two or three days. We finally have had a clear day, and our planes have been able to begin to blast away at VonRunstedt's army. That offensive has made too much headway, and maybe our planes can now slow it down, etc.

The cost in lives is just sickening. We have our problems here at the depot, but they are nothing compared to the tasks which rest upon the men at the fronts.

Well, today we had to change our billets—those of us below the rank of major. The "uppers" must have decided that they wanted our nice rooms here at the Louvois; so, we of the lower rungs on the ladder had to move. Pete and I found some rooms at a small, but nice hotel, just about half way to the depot from Place de l"Opera. So, via the Metro, we shall not have to leave for the depot quite as early. One must search for a "silver lining"—wherever it may be.

Our Christmas boxes seem to have arrived, and we have been eating most of our suppers in our hotel rooms—Pete, Charley, and I... When we pool our "goodies" from home, we have some excellent meals. We have shared much with the workers at the depot and with our maids here at the hotel.

My last letter from you was dated December 2. Christmas boxes, and some cards, came through, but real "letters" have not fared so well. We shall get everything, eventually. It is a puzzlement!

Did manage to get away from the depot at mid afternoon, about two days ago, and just spent the time wandering about the city to take a look at the windows of the stores. All of the decorations were so pretty, and my mind certainly took me back to Christmases at home, and even to the ones at Wood Lake. How clear in memory were the programs at the little old church, the excitement of Santa Claus, and the mystery that enshrouded him. For so many years I had not thought of the little red fire engine, the blue hand truck with red wheels, the funny little dog on the squeaky wheels, the jumping frogs, and the brick building blocks which, by the way, provided me with the evidences I needed to detect for sure just who Santa Claus really was. Ha! Then, there was my little old flat gray elephant and the Raggedy Ann doll with the funny yellow yarn for hair. Our long stockings were always to be filled full of candy and nuts, with an orange or apple thrown in for good measure. I found myself hoping, almost pleading, that time could somehow be turned back to twenty years ago. And, Bin, you were four years older, wised up to it all, and played along just to keep me "in the game"!

Well, I went to church this morning, the American Church of Paris, a Union Protestant church, and an army chaplain delivered a very fitting message. During the service we sang the old carols—among them being "Oh, Come All Ye Faithful," "The First Noel," "Hark, the Herald Angels Sing," and "Silent Night, Holy Night." Most of the congregation were military personnel, and I could not help but notice how many of us were wiping our eyes. For sure, many a tongue was stuck in a throat. Somehow, the singing of these wonderful, old songs was almost too much for us. Yes, we were certainly wishing for "Peace on earth" and "Good Will among Men"! I then had some time to gather my thoughts as I rode the Metro to the depot.

Next to our final night in the Louvois, we were treated to more hot water and some soaking baths. Some coal must have made its way into the city. Maybe the management just wanted us poor low-grade officers to regret our having to change abodes. Oh, well—such is life, sometimes, in this man's army.

We needed to cancel our going to the Scheys for this evening—just too may demands for all needed to respond to this German offensive. I took four bottles of wine for the party, and told Georges and Yvette it was a Christmas gift from "Les Boches." The had a good laugh, but did seem to be much disappointed because of our absence. The people of Paris seem to be of the happiest for this Christmas season, for they were denied its enjoyment for four years.

Four or five of us went to see the movie, "Saratoga Trunk." I slept through about half of it, for these long hours, each day, have taken toll on my capacity to keep awake. Our noses must be to the grind stone for about 12 hours, from 7:30 to 7:30 each day. But, we are so very fortunate to be here in this remarkable city.

December 26, 1944 Paris

To be sure, yesterday we had turkey and all the trimmings—starting about 2:30 in the afternoon. Present with us as special guests were thirteen little orphan girls, along with the Sister who looked after them. How those little rascals did enjoy their food—just seemed to eat and eat and eat. Several of the men of the company had organized the program which culminated with the giving of gifts to the girls—each to receive a new doll and a book of stories (in French). Each of these youngsters simply went into a fit of jumping up and down, of hugging her doll, of nearly running in circles, and of joining the others to crowd around the Sister to show her their prizes. This nun covered her face with her hands and just wept unashamedly—then to tell us that these children had never had dolls to claim as their own, and particularly NEW ones! All of us had been contributing to a slush fund for our "Christmas Party," and there had to have been some recreational funds used, for those dolls and books must have cost a handsome bit. This, to me, was just another evidence which discloses the unusual quality of the men of our company.

My spirits had been pretty low, but this party with these youngsters put me back into a high gear. These little tots were just ecstatic, and all our hearts were just warmed—through and through.

I shall never forget this.

Had kept back three or four special boxes to open Christmas morning, and as I opened each I just became more and more homesick. The party with those little girls pulled me out of the doldrums, or I would have been "down in the dumps" all day. I guess I just have more than my share of wonderful memories. Family must have something to do with it, do you suppose?

Much to my pleasant surprise, Col. Cole presented to us OFFICERS AND MEN OF DEPOT M-407 his greetings for "a very Happy Christmas and a Joyful New Year." He well summed up the accomplishments of the company and concluded with this: "Thanks to your loyal cooperation, Depot-407 is known as the Central Medical Depot of France, and enjoys an enviable reputation."

The weather remains clear and with sunshine. Our airforce is now giving those Jerries a good blasting. It is time for the weatherman to give us the nod. Reports after the 16th of the German advances were just so discouraging, and I was tempted to give our Good Lord a piece of my mind. But, I think "Providence" is now going to favor us. VonRunstedt's western push was so full of dire potentialities. Now, I think the tables are turning. Hitler and his gang just do not fit in to our thoughts of Christmas, Santa Claus, and Good Will! Yes, I think our Nazi friends are in for a thorough mauling, eventually, but the cost will be heavy—just not the happiest of thoughts for this day after Christmas.

December 30, 1944 Paris

Have been receiving letters each day. So, I think that the mail system is now back to normal. It is so nice to be receiving mail regularly, again. I received another Christmas box, today, and none of its contents was perishable. So, all was just fine. If my count is accurate, at least 16 arrived for me. We shared our Christmas boxes with our depot help, and particularly the five women who do typing for us in the records office. These women are just as sweet as they can be—Madames T. LaRoche, Olga Sheehan, Louise Peemans, C. Olier, and A. Chasseur. They wrote me a note of thanks, which I have translated to read—

> We do not wish to begin this Year, 1945, without coming to offer our very sincere and affectionate wishes.
>
> We hope that you will interpret among our American comrades, employed in your service, to transmit to them, with our friendship, our wishes for a prompt return to their families.
>
> Think, Dear Lt., of our entire and affectionate devotion.

It was the meaning behind this letter that makes it something I want to keep.

This German offensive has really increased demand for all sorts of medical supplies, and we have really been pressed to keep up. Trucks and every type of vehicle just come and go in never ending stream. I do not think that the Germans have crossed the border back into France. My hunch is that Eisenhower is playing his game very carefully, and that Von Runstedt will rue the day he ever launched his campaign. This depletion of the German forces will leave them much more vulnerable to an Allied counter offensive.

Out hotel rooms are so chilly, where Pete and I are located. When we hit our rooms, it is into bed as soon as we can—just to keep warm. When we get up each morning, there is no wasting of time to take our cold shaves, and to get out of here. It must be agreeing with us, for we remain remarkably healthy. Ha! Ha! I just remind myself of the men at the front and then consider us to be so very lucky!

So many funny cartoons and items appear in "Stars and Stripes." One cartoon, "Hubert"—by Stg. Dick Wingert, shows two American soldiers retreating from German territory, and one of them has had the seat of his britches chewed out by a dachshund. And we have so many laughs coming for us in "Hash Marks"—

> With graceful feet a maiden sweet
>   Was tripping the light fantastic.
> She suddenly tore for the powder room door,
>   You can't trust this wartime elastic.

We have just heard about the draftee who claimed exemption on ground of bad eyesight, and he brought his wife along as evidence.

We heard a couple of chaplains chuckling over this incident. An OD, making his rounds, surprised one of the sentries by asking him quickly for the 10th General Order. The sentry was startled and replied, "Thou shalt not covet thy neighbor's wife."

Draft joke: "I got my classification today," said a middle aged businessman—"I'm in Class 5B: Baldness, Bridgework, Bifocals, Bay window and Bunions."

And, there was this unsigned verse: Mary had a little limb.

> In fact, she sported two.
> And every time she took a swim,

The soldiers cried, "Woo-wooo!"

And, somebody had this afterthought—"Courtship makes a man spoon, and matrimony makes him fork over."

And, there was "Up Front With Mauldin," with two soldiers looking down upon a beautiful village, and with Mauldin noting: "It's either enemy or off limits."

January 1, 1945 Paris

And a Happy New Year's Day to you! The news from the "bulge" continues to be good, and we are beginning to feel much encouraged. The fighting remains fierce, and we are so very busy to keep up with all the demands for medical supplies. Two or three days ago we had an interesting experience because of shortage of blankets. Regular shipments have been coming in from our supply stations in England, but our supply here, in M-407, had been gradually reduced because of increasing demands from our field hospitals, etc. To keep up with all the posting of the stock record cards, my crew has been working overtime, and fatigue was, on occasion, a bit of a problem.

So, here is what happened. In posting an issue of 500 blankets for emergency purposes to be delivered to three or four field emergency stations, etc., one of the gang tallied the figure as a shipment received. When the central surgeon's office called to see if we had supply for a large emergency run of blankets, the stock record showed a few more than 1,000. I had been checking on another matter in our warehouse and had passed by the area where we stored the blankets, and there was just one bale of them. I returned to the office about a minute after the call from the central surgeon's office (in Paris). Apprised of the situation, and informed that a couple trucks were to be dispatched to pick up the blankets, I called the Surgeon's Office and informed the officer who had place the order that we had no blankets, that the trucks need not be sent, and that an emergency order be dispatched to England to send emergency shipments of blankets by air. The trucks were on their way and not halted, and it had become a serious problem. We would have a minimum of four hours to be able to meet the emergency, and a regular shipment of blankets was due to arrive the following day.

Well, the posting error had created quite a crisis, and the fact that our men had been pressed to a condition of sheer exhaustion seemed to be ignored by our "higher ups." Actually, a shortage of blankets was only minimal in two or three forward stations—as we were to be informed. This posting of stock-record cards is skilled business, and my crew is collectively unusually able. So, we shall see what repercussions come from this.

Well into the afternoon, here, and you must know of our party last night at the Rivet's. Charley and I had a gala time of it. We were at the table from 9:00 to 11:30. We had pottage, bread, roast chicken and rice, sanglier (wild boar, the first time I had ever eaten it—delicious), salad, cheeses, cake, wine, champagne, Benedictine, sweet vermouth—just the whole shooting match, and then some. Charley and I were nearly on the verge of floundering, really.

We then retired to the living room for chatting, to play the piano, to listen to the radio hail in the New Year, to toast each other, to kiss each other on one cheek and then on the other, and always to wish one an "heureuse et bonne annee!" Our group was composed of Madame Rivet, Nicole, Arlette, Andree, and Denise—and of Monsieur Rivet, Jean Pierre, Charley and me. Then Monsieur Rivet informed us that we were to go to the Billot's, one floor below. Here we were to spend the rest of the New Year's celebration. With us went six cakes, four more bottles of champagne, sandwiches, etc. The Billots were at home in force—the in-laws of their son and the family. Charley and I looked at each other, and we knew we would have no sleep before heading back to the depot for our day's work. We were right on target.

The Billot's son had been with the F.F.I. (French Forces of the Interior) for nearly a year—in effort to keep the German off balance in rural France. After the freeing of Paris, he returned home, was married, and he and his wife headed toward North Africa where he was to engage in a training program to prepare him to enter into an engineering program. At Marseille he became ill and had to return to Paris for treatment. He was temporarily nearly blind, but treatments cleared his vision. The daughter-in-law's family were there—name of Bodens; included were three sisters, a brother, and a French naval officer who was fiancé of one of the sisters. Altogether, it was quite a crowd.

After all the introductions, after which no one really could remember the names, we settled down to more champagne, more playing of the piano, more dancing, more eating of cake and ice cream—and more rounds, one after the other. It was just a stuffing process which seemed to have no end, and every one continuously in a mood to continue the celebration. So, after bidding each a fond farewell, etc.,

Charley and I caught the Metro (about 6:30 in the morning), and were at the depot for a breakfast and to be on duty about 7:45—he with "Shipping" and I with "Records." Well, we had had a night of it, and it was all fun—but were we pooped. Fortunately, it was a very slow day at the depot, and my poor eyes kept closing about half the time.

While at the Rivets, Madame Rivet wanted to know my birthday. I told her that January 7 was the day and that I would be 27. So, she straightway informed me that we were to have a party, that I was to spend the evening with them, etc. At my insistence, we whittled the program to an evening of bridge, with no more than a birthday cake. So, we shall see—provided I am not tied down at the depot.

Well, to add it all together, Charley and I have become, practically, members of this Rivet family. They knew we had been forced to change our hotel locale. When I told Monsieur Rivet our new address, he just had a fit, and insisted that he was going to find a better apartment for Pete and me. They just insist that we are to be comfortably billeted, and it made no difference that we would be spending little time in our rooms. These people are going to do everything they can to make our stay in Paris as comfortable as possible and as pleasant as possible. Yes, we had quite a New Year's Eve—in PARIS!

January 3, 1945 Paris

Just must say again what a marvelous time we had New Year's Eve with the Rivets and Billots.

Charley and I are most fortunate to have these people as our friends. Particularly the Rivets insist that we speak French, and they attempt to use their English. WE are on some sort of a par with the exchange. We just have the best time!

Our busy time, here, continues, for the demand for medical supplies from the "bulge" does not slacken. Von Runstedt has been slowed to a walk, but the struggle remains a fierce one. There is no indication that this struggle is going to be other than a long one—certainly well into the summer, and I hope I am a pessimist. Whatever happens here, we have those Japs to deal with.

Your letters indicate that the perfume arrived, etc., and I am pleased. That brooch was such a pretty thing, but a bit expensive. I found it in a little side-street shop, and shall be on the look for a couple more. "Things" are somewhat less expensive in the back-street shops. One just needs the time to wander around and to search—and this I do not seem to have. So it goes!

Charley and I plan to go to the central officers' mess this evening, and then to go to a show. It is a musical—the Glen Miller orchestra. We still do not know just what happened to him, but he undoubtedly went down into the sea and is lost. But, the band is carrying on, and we look forward to hearing the program.

January 5, 1945 Paris

Am OD today, and thus am at the typewriter this evening. Received 21 letters today, and the dates ranged from November 16 to December 24. Now isn't that some spread! But how grand and wonderful to have them and to have the fun to read them over and over.

Indications are that our German friends are now taking quite a beating on the perimeters of the "bulge," and this is as it should be.

Pete and I are in process of changing our billlets, and we shall be together in a nice apartment. I have a hunch that Monsieur Rivet had a hand in this. I just wonder if all the rental gets figured in to "reverse lend-lease." I know that no money has come from my pocket for these billeting arrangements. Ho! Ho!

Well, I must make my rounds. WE have heard a rumor or two about our company. Humph!

January 8, 1945 Paris

Some developments that are encouraging to my beleaguered spirits, and details should be made more evident later. We have been so pressed at this depot to get everything done on time—just to keep up, and it has become quite exhausting. Relief may be just around the corner.

As you know, yesterday was my birthday, and we had a party at the Rivet's. Madame had made three cakes for me, and they were simply delicious. Then, there were three bottles of champagne and some Benedictine, and we had brought several bottles of the good stuff with us from our store at the depot. We spent the evening in singing, playing the piano, playing some card games, and just visiting. Charley, Pete, and I didn't get away until well after midnight. We just cannot get away, for they keep insisting that we stay. We do have such good times with them.

Monsieur Rivet showed us, again, the three or four bullet nicks made by the bullets fired by German soldiers toward their balcony. Boulevard St. Michel runs along one of the great parks of Paris, and one can look across to the park from the balcony. From the balconies of this large apartment building, 141 Boulevard St. Michel, the residents hardly dared to go out upon their balconies or to be seen peering from the doorways leading to the balconies, for German soldiers below might fire at them. He made it very clear that they were just delighted to entertain guests in their home—as before the German occupation, and that they wanted us to come as often as possible. We just act ourselves and fully enjoy all the fun. We just seem to fit in!

One of the cakes was a "gateau de pomme," a real speciality. Inserted beneath the frosting, and supposedly hidden, was a little china crown. As the cake was cut and served, the person to receive the crown was to be "king for the evening." Then, as they drink the champagne, each time the "king" drinks they all raise their glasses and sing "Le Roi boit"! Well, for sure the crown was in my piece of cake, and we sipped champagne each time "the king" drank from his glass. It was just crazy, and did we have a good time. We are supposed to return on the 20th for another party. But, we are not sure that we shall be able to keep the engagement. There is a big question mark.

Well, the apartment which Pete and I share is only about a 25-minute walk from the Rivet's. This was our third night in it, and it is quite a contrast to the small rooms we had in the little hotel—not too far from the depot. But, it is not any warmer.

Am going to search for some of Guerlain's "Shalimar" perfume. Some of the other guests at the New Year's Party told us it was just one of the best. So, we shall see. If it is too expensive, you may just have to get along without any. Ho! Ho! Ho!

My sinus trouble seems to have cleared completely, and I continue to take the vitamin and CLO pills. Has been such a relief to be free from the headaches. Or, maybe it has been the goodies to be eaten that came in the 19 boxes I received for

Christmas. Ha! So much of the stuff we shared at the depot, but my share was reserved for me. And, I had my helpings from other boxes. Oh, well!

January 11, 1945 Paris

The war news is getting brighter, for it is going less well for the Germans. Seems to me that Von Runstedt has now expended the bulk of the Nazi reserve, and the final showdown with the Nazis may not be as lengthy as it seemed so certain to be. But, no way to make an accurate estimate of what is in store.

We have about ten inches of snow, and it is so white and clean outside. The women in our office tell us that this is unusual—to have so much at one time. We shall have to see what the future holds, weatherwise. This has to have made conditions at the front—of the "bulge" and elsewhere—just more and more miserable. We, here in the city, have it snuggly and warm, comparatively.

Am hoping to have time tomorrow afternoon to engage in a small shopping spree, and this will be the "last time" to have "things" so handy. But, prices are so inflated that it is hard on a poor little 1st lieutenant's pocketbook.

January 14, 1945 Paris

Yes, the Germans dropped a few bombs on Paris when they opened their drive on December 16. I happened to be OD that evening, and the explosions were audible—but nothing near to us. One damaged St. Lazare Station (RR)—not too far from Place de l'Opera, close to the hotel in which we used to be billeted. Am sending you copies of issues of "Yank" and these will give you the details. The outright butchery of American soldiers, captured in the early phases of the drive, was most damnable and just fiendish. Reports of these actions infuriated our troops, and this fury was among the factors eventually to spell doom to the German offensive. Hitler will find himself backed into a corner from which his only escape will be via suicide.

For us at our depot, there has been no let up, and we are all nearly exhausted. We may be relieved in the near future.

To gain a little respite from the pressure, for the men of our records office, I had them come to Pete's and my apartment for a party—last evening. We officers had received quite handsome supplies of the French wines and liquors found in our warehouses—as stored away by our German predecessors, but the men had not openly shared in the cache. There were also the canned Polish hams, Dutch cheeses, and Belgian sweetbreads—but the most of it had gone for the purposes of "French relief," with the bulk of it, I fear, having oozed into the Parisian "black market." Well, whatever!

But, for our party, I used mostly what I had received from home—sardines, rye krisp, olives, fruit cakes, jams, etc.—along with some excellent French bread. We had quite a meal, and they did seem to enjoy it and all the camaraderie. They are the grandest bunch of fellows, and I wish I could do much more for them. They have worked so harmoniously—always free from any friction. They used the subway to arrive, but I arranged for a company truck to come for them at 12:30 to scoot them to their billets near the depot in Pantin. We spent the evening just visiting, joking, laughing, eating, sipping, etc. Pete and I washed the dishes and cleaned up after their departure. For me it was a special evening. Everyone enjoyed the champagne and good wines. We knew everyone had to be "on deck" later in the morning. Ha!

For tomorrow evening, Colonel Cole has asked me to present to a gathering of various representatives from the several supply depots of the Paris area a discussion of our techniques, problems, etc., with respect to receiving, storing, and issuing medical supplies. He should be doing it, but he has picked on me. Oh, well! It has taken a bit of time to put the "thing" together, and I trust I will make sense.

January 18, 1945 Paris

Well, that meeting on the 15th had some generals in the gathering, and nearly all were officers. My presentation was of two single-spaced pages and did not take long. Title was "Medical Supply, Seine Section." Opening paragraphs were:

> The first fundamental principle of good depot operation is "speed of movement." The issue of medical supply must be geared to operate in advance of demand—supplies of this service are vital only when they are available when needed. Medical supply, if too late, is lost to ineffectiveness.
>
> Few requisitioning agencies fully realize the delays encountered in sustaining this principle of speed when errors exist in the preparation of a requisition. Fortunately—or unfortunately, requisitions for medical supplies and items, though they be erroneously and inadequately pre-

pared, must be filled without delay; the expediency of the need will often overshadow the time to be involved in the re-preparation of the requisition.

I then noted that shortage of supply generally found the items placed on "back order," a procedure which we had dispensed with—the procedure being to "re-order." Exception to this would occur only when advance instruction had been received from the Office of the Surgeon, Seine Section. Most of my message simply stressed the careful use of our catalogue of items and their identifying stock-record numbers.

Personal likes and dislikes lie behind so many decisions made in upper brackets, and it can become a sorry, rotten system. You will understand a bit of what I mean when you read my next letter.

Dijon

January 21, 1945 France

You will note that I do not write from Paris. Three possible explanations for our departure from Pantin—the first, that companies such as ours are never to be left too long in any particular locale; the second, that the problems with the blankets may have been reason for decision to move us; and third, that we were to have received a special citation and award for our highly successful operation of M-407, which citation might have gained for Lt.Col. Cole a promotion to full colonel, and that he, impatient for the citations, etc., went into the office of the Seine Surgeon, pounded on a desk or two, and made such scene that "they" decided to get rid of him and us. It may well have been a combination of all three—and, who knows? Oh, well!

(We had moved—lock, stock, and barrel—to the charming provincial city of Dijon. We were again under restriction with reference to our location. Our advance platoon, with Charley and Pete, remained temporarily at M-407 to assist the company that replaced us—to adjust to the quirks of running the place.)

Our APO is now 667, and it is not Gay Paree! Lots of snow, here, but we are not out in it. Our food is good, my feet are dry and warm, and we are so much more comfortable than the men at the fronts. Our second evening, here, last evening, we saw Joan Davis in "Kansas City Kitty." It was silly, and Bob Crosby was in it. As an actor, I could do better. Ha!

We are to assist in a depot operation, but we could be here only temporarily. Our search for billets for the men and officers has proved difficult, and we are just sort of camping out all over the premises. One thing, for sure—we are not very busy, and what a relief from the pressures we were under while in Paris. We were just about ready to collapse from sheer extra hours in response to demands.

Paris was a beautiful place, and I hope to have time to return for about a week's leave. I could enjoy this city. During the many months we were there, my work permitted me to take no more than about two afternoons, and maybe parts of three afternoons, to browse about and to see the city. Should work and time permit, I want to return to visit, and I have three places I could stay. The Rivet's will be my choice, for they would be the least inconvenienced by my presence. The Billots and the Scheys are not very roomy, but I would be welcome.

Must make a date with our company barber, for my hair is long enough to disguise me. Ha! We do have good shower facilities, here, and this is one very positive improvement—except for that apartment in which Pete and I had less than two weeks of luxurious comfort. We are living from our foot lockers, suitcases, and shaving kits.

I do not understand Hitler's logic or motive to continue this struggle—except that the man is insane and cannot comprehend reality. His world has to be one of dreams. This struggle may have to continue until nearly all of Germany is ground into dust.

Well, much snow falling, here, but it is not cold. Much melting, underfoot.

January 23, 1945 France (Dijon)

The snow continues to fall abundantly, just several inches each day. Well, spring may come early this year in France.

I have been limping around, for I skinned my shin when I slipped from the running board of a jeep. I should apply for the purple heart. Ha!

Have been hoping that we could deliver a stunning blow to Hitler, but the weather is not in our favor. MacArthur may finish with the Japs before we can wind things down or up, here. We shall see.

We have been without mail since leaving Paris, and this does not keep me in a happy mood. It just seems as if so many things are SNAFU.

We are still trying to get billeted, but so few accommodations available, here. We are supposed to assist in the operation of this supply center, but we seem to be "surplus." But, one thing is certain, we are getting a much needed rest. For some reason, my stomach has been giving me some trouble, and it must be that the microbes in the water are of a new breed. Whatever the cause, I seemed to crave salt, and have downed two or three glasses of salted water. Now, we shall see what happens.

Am much interested in this meeting of the "Big Three." Perhaps they can come up with an effective plan to put Hitler out of the game—sooner than I think possible. The Russian pressures from the east are impressive, but the hard core will be difficult to penetrate, I fear.

I am OD for this evening and through tomorrow morning. Haven't had my hair cut, yet, and it would be appropriate were I to find a violin. But, one of these days!

Sleepiness is closing in on me. There is really nothing for me to do. For one of the very few times in my life I may be bored. Ha! And, today is your birthday, Bin!

January 25, 1945 France (Dijon)

Rudy is sitting here on a table looking at me and he reminds me of a monkey—just one that came fresh from the zoo. Ha! One would never realize it, but he is human. I'm just recording this for future impression of him that I might want to recall. He is reading this over my shoulder, and he should appreciate my reference to the primates—because that is even paying him a compliment. He has dark brown Hungarian eyes, and from their glare I'm certain he is already plotting to get even with me for the slander. But, he is a good egg and a fine fellow, but much in need of considerable reforming—quite beyond the capabilities of mankind. (Kelemen was one of our captains.)

No news to report from here, none at all. Snow continues to fall each day. We may see a movie this evening, one with Bob Hope in it.

Am billeted in a small hotel, and it has hot water. So, some of us enjoy this bit of luxury. As I recall, I hadn't had a warm bath in Paris for more than a week before our departure.

A full colonel, whom I had not seen before, just walked in, cornered our CO, who was paying us a visit, and royally chewed him out. What this was all about, I do not know. I have had a hunch for months that our CO suffers from an inferiority complex. For some reason, many of these "superiors" do not scare me, and I shall likely get out of this man's army still a lowly "First Lieutenant." Oh, well!

January 27, 1945 France (Dijon)

Just not much of news to come from this neck of the woods. We have so little to do, but the rest and relaxation have been "Godsends" really! That Paris operation was accomplished despite certain interferences from "above"—all of which we simply had to work around to get the job done efficiently and in good time. A sort of "politics" probably accounted for our departure, and we turned the depot over to a company without practical experience. On the other hand, Paris had become somewhat remote from the developing centers of action, and these supply depots will need to be much more "forward."

Report notes that the Russians are within ninety miles of Berlin. Successes on Hitler's eastern front may well hurry things along for us here on the west. I doubt that "'lil' Adolf" will permit himself to be taken alive. We shall see!

Did get to see, last evening, Bob Hope and Patricia Mayo in "The Princess and the Pirate." Two nights ago the place was filled to SRO. This show is one to have one just laugh himself silly. It is wonderful. Now, I want to see the movie which treats of the life of George Gershwin, and the music should be just great. I'll have to get in line early enough to make it in for the first showing, and this means, for us, that we have to go without supper. Oh, hasn't this army life become just too rugged for words? Ho! Ho!

We still await letters from home. But, they will catch up with us. I am eager to know if the packages sent to you were tampered with, damaged in any way, etc. Some of the fellows had heard from home that contents had been inspected and revenue assessed.

Was invited to sit in on a special meeting, yesterday, and it lasted for nearly four hours. I did not come away disillusioned, enlightened, enheartened or disheartened, or anything. I came away with one conclusion—that one's rank in this man's army is no indication of his intellect, capabilities, or righteous intent.

More snow is falling, and indication is that it will be heavy and deep.

January 29, 1945 France (Dijon)

Some letters arrived, today. So, the postal service has finally discovered where we are. Nice!

Indications are that we are not to remain here long. All of us have appreciated this rest and relief from the many pressures that were upon us in Paris. My crew which had maintained the stock records so thoroughly and well have made the most of this restful relief, here. They felt quite relieved when we departed from Pantin. They just did their work and never complained to me. But, we now admit that life, here, is somewhat monotonous, and we prefer more activities. But, this rest has done all of us so much good.

Saw "Rhapsody in Blue"—story of life of George Gershwin. I didn't know that Paul Whiteman and Oscar Levant had been so closely associated with him. Another movie we saw, here, was "The Conspirators," with Paul Henreid and Hedy LaMarr. For a change, Charles Greenstreet did not play the role of a villain.

We eat at an officer's mess, with all food prepared by a French staff. It is excellent and tastefully prepared. Our company cooks take care of the men, and they continue to do an unusually excellent job. I would have no complaint were we officers to eat at our company's mess.

Snow continues to fall. I haven't been to a Sunday morning worship service since well before our departure from Paris. There is a chaplain at a nearby station hospital, and some of us are going to get back into the groove.

We are really enjoying our rest. Paris is a fascinating city, but we had so little spare time to enjoy it. I didn't realize how much the men felt the pressure of the work at the depot. They have certainly been telling me some "things" that had escaped my attention. Just admire them more and more each day. But, we have next to nothing to do here. Strange—that we were sent here. For whatever reasons, we were ousted from M-407! Well, it had become a nightmare for us.

Before our departure from Paris, I had time to run to tell Rivets and Billots of our imminent exit from Paris and that we were to come to this provincial city. Billots gave me the name and address of some friends who live here, and I have yet to make their acquaintance—my first effort brought no response at the door.

January 30, 1945 France (Dijon)

We have certainly been enjoying this rest. I don't think most of has had any idea as to the extent of our weariness. And, today I received 34 letters, and others gained accordingly. What uplift to our morale! One of my letters was from Mrs. Dutton of Oshkosh, and she wrote of the comfort which my letter had given to Mrs. Stackhouse. She urged me to write again. So, this I shall do—just to be chatty and to dwell upon the many happy memories which we share of while I taught there. And, with time on my hands, I am in process to answer these many letters. We shall see what happens, eh?

Yes, I am sure that all my Christmas packages arrived—23 or 24 of them. The last to arrive were from the Lueckes of St. Louis. I do not know how many persons, here, enjoyed the contents. We did so much sharing.

No doubt about it, the Germans are about to find themselves in dire circumstances. We, from this side, are surely to open an offensive, soon. Maybe we can finish this European war by July, and I must admit that my optimism is growing.

You have referred to the blood-donation drives in Lincoln, and elsewhere. This is so very important. We keep hearing of the saving of lives because of the blood on hand to be given to our wounded. Seems to me that one of the miracles of this entire effort has been the availability of this supply of blood. It has been amazing, really! Many men are going to come home because of having been saved by a gift of blood.

Snow is flying again, today, and it causes us no inconvenience. I have been avoiding nearly all starchy foods and for several days have been free from any stomach problem. I must lack an enzyme or two. Too, things that are fried may not suit too well the workings of my innards. And, I have been sleeping until about 7:30 each morning, and this could be making a difference. No doubt about it, I was "on edge" before we left Paris, but my sense of humor is now returned. I do feel much better!

January 31, 1945 France (Dijon)

Have had time to catch up on my correspondence, and to such extent that I had to have our mail orderly buy a packet of envelopes for me, and with airmail stamps.

You have read from time to time my reference to the crew who are in our stock-records office. They are, for me, just a joy to have around—just a grand lot! So, I think I should tell you a bit about each of them.

Bill Thirlby is a Tech-Sergeant, and he is my Chief Clerk. He was born in England, has most of the more admirable English traits, and is one of the most dependable individuals I have ever known. He has kept my woes at a minimum. He is one in a million. Some of the gang have dubbed him to be "Hairless Joe," for he has no more than a fringe of hair around his head above his ears. He came to the States in 1927, is now a citizen, and is wholly American. His home is in New York.

Staff Sergeant Art Sell comes from a line of hotel proprietors in North Dakota. You'll not find a better "editor" of medical department requisitions in this entire army of ours. He has a line of chatter which lasts from "start to finish" and a keen sense of humor, and he is a most reliable whiz sort of kid. He can become a bit grouchy when he goes too long without sleep. I think he enjoyed Gay Paree.

Ross Donaldson has rank of sergeant and is our Chief Stock Records Clerk. Formerly from Indiana, but now a resident of Massachusetts, he is a real "crackerjack" and is chiefly responsible for having worked out our accounting system with respect to the stock-record cards. He is well versed in current literature and art, and he reads during his spare moments. I have not been able to discern his philosophy of life, but maybe I shouldn't try.

Sergeant John Rodenhaver seems often to be the center of attention of the crew, and he bears the most watching. He handles the voucher files and does the cross-referencing. He makes certain that our records are up to date. We call him "Von Kopf" and with the handle of "Fritzgerald," and both names fit him. He is a Pennsylvanian from Chambersburg and is of a long line of Dutch and Irish ancestry. He and I share a "love of history."

Darrell Frederick is also a sergeant and is one who makes certain the stock records are accurate and up to date. He does much of the recording and is as dependable as they come. I do not know what he did before he came into the army, but he is the most even-tempered person I have ever known. He is never ruffled, always has a smile, and never hesitates to give a helping hand. He comes from Iowa and is, therefore, from good, old mid western stock.

Larry Quinn is a corporal and also a stock-records clerk. He comes, as one should guess, from a long line from old Erin. His big brown eyes appear most handsomely in photographs, of which he had many taken in Paris—often because of his wife's requests. Few men in this army have managed to keep themselves as well groomed as he has. His "record keeping" is just as neat. He is as reliable as he is neatly groomed.

Corporal Charles Murphy is the pet of the entire office. With the exception of Thirlby, he tops all of us by several years. He is as Irish as is his name. His dry humor keeps us continuously in a sort of uproar. When the going became tough, he was the one who most often brightened the atmosphere. He was always at the stock-record table, and his backward slanting numerals made me a bit dizzy, at first. They were neat on the cards, and he was a whiz at mathematics. He also comes from Michigan.

Leslie Hayes, Pfc, is an "acting corporal" and is our prize typist. There is not a job in the office that he doesn't know and doesn't do well. He is a genius when it comes to turning out our "shipping tickets." I nicknamed him "Rutherford"—after one of our Presidents, and the name has stuck. He comes from Florida, and he does seem to enjoy to protest against all of this snow and cold.

Last is Ken Sebade, Pfc. For us, he is a jack-of-all-trades. He posts and does everything else—and just sort of floats about to pinch hit where needed. His work is always nigh to perfection—just one of the most capable young men I have ever known. He came to us at Paris, his home is now in Washington, and his father used to live in Kearney, Nebraska. He may have relatives who live in our State. He is a cheerful "rascal"—one whom I fear we have often overworked.

Well, you may easily surmise that I am immensely proud of my crew. They have done the work of twice their number. Their set of records was virtually flawless. Yes, a few errors now and then, but a remarkably fine performance. I could not be prouder. For me, it is always a pleasure to be in their midst.

February 2, 1945 France (Dijon)

Letters have poured in, and in the past three deliveries I have received about eighty. I had written more than forty letters in the past ten days, and now I am again much in the arrears. Am going to hit the shower this evening, for it is so handy, here. Then, before hitting the sack, I shall put about ten letters on their ways. So many of these letters have greetings for Christmas. So, it has been just as if I had a bit of Christmas again.

You will have fun reading this scribbling, but our typewriters are again packed away.

This has been a second day without snow and drizzle, but we just must slop around wherever we go. These clear days give our pilots and bombing crews opportunities to make life miserable for the Germans. Each day of open skies will shorten this war accordingly, here, and then we may still have those Japs to finish off in the Pacific. But, so much yet to be accomplished, and who knows for how long!

We had fresh eggs for breakfast—about the second time of such for us since hitting the continent. We have had to endure the powdered variety—"yellow death" as known. But, one has to be nearly amazed at what our company's cooks do with the stuff for the men.

Have written the Rivets, and I am betting that they will get several chuckles from my "French." Will be sending notes, also, to the Billots and the Scheys.

Our CO did not accompany us, but remained in Paris—but, he paid us a visit. And, Charley, as the officer in charge of our advance platoon, has received his captaincy. He fully deserves the promotion, and this now fills our T/O.

Yes, to read and reread all of my letters has left me a little groggy. Not bad!!

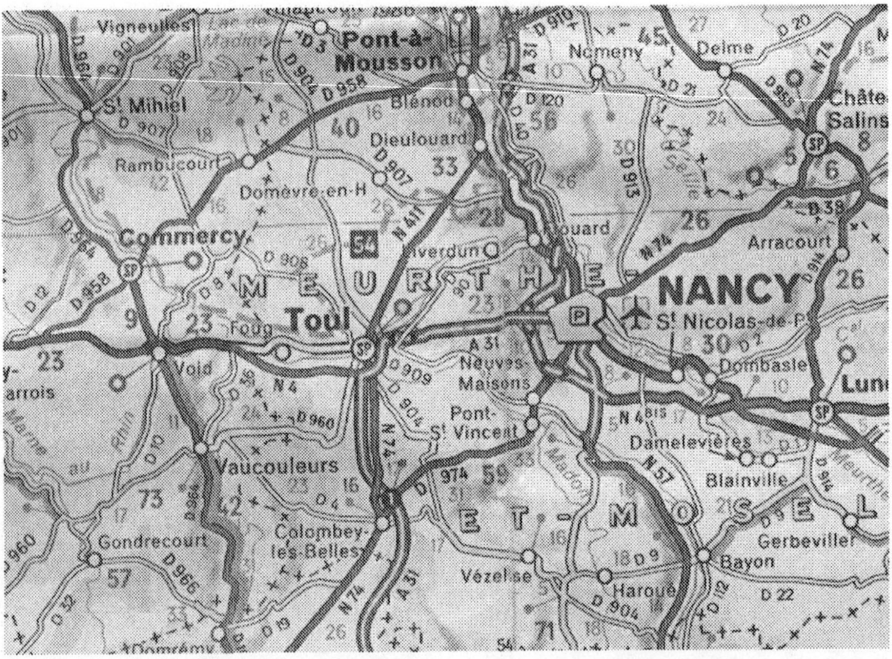
Vigneulles
Pont-à-Mousson
Nomeny
Delme
St Mihiel
Blénod
Château-Salins
Dieulouard
Rambucourt
Domèvre-en-H
Commercy
Liverdun
Arracourt
NANCY
MEURTHE
Toul
Foug
St Nicolas-de-P
Void
Neuves-Maisons
Dombasle
Pont-St Vincent
Dameleviéres
Vaucouleurs
Blainville
Colombey-les-Belles
Gerbeviller
Gondrecourt
Bayon
Vézelise
Haroué

Central street of Foug and the depot's sprawling warehouse.

Foug

February 4, 1945 France

(Our jaunt from Dijon was of short distance to the smallish town of Foug—close to Toul, which is just to the west of Nancy, which is not far to the south of Metz. We were to the west of Strasbourg. This area in northeastern France is Lorraine. For the storage of medical supplies we had an abandoned "usine"—which may have been a cement, or tile factory of several ground-level rooms and chambers, but used by the Germans as place to keep hay and grain for their horses. Our office would be in the waiting room of a nearby and also abandoned railroad station, all of which proved to be our most accommodating quarters. The main street of the town stretched from the station directly uphill for several blocks, with homes and businesses on either side. The family with whom I would have a room lived about a fourth of the way up the hill. It was here that my best stroke of good fortune became reality. Dame Fortune was really smiling on me! The Baudin family proved to be a treasure: Monsieur Gilbert, Madame Irene, Monique—daughter, about seventeen years old, and Jean-Francois—son of no more years than two.)

Am feeling fine, and my sinus problem seems of the past. Also, no stomach problem, and you need not send me any more vitamin and CLO tablets.

Have a room in the home of a lovely family, and no one speaks English. So, my French is going to be used all the time. Good! My bed has a most comfortable mattress, and I shall be between white sheets. It has been pretty cold, here, and last night Madame Baudin had placed a hot water bottle, a metal one, in the bed, and my feet just didn't have to warm up any cold sheets. This is living in luxury! The bottle is again in my bed. Howzaboutthat!

It is now 11:25 p.m. I had supper with the Baudins, right here, and such a marvelous meal. We had sanglier, wild boar, and excellent—along with white and red wines, their good brown bread, etc. They do not have bleached flour again and as yet, but this dark flour is full of nourishment, I'm sure. It may be part of the means whereby these people so ably survived the long German occupation. But, my use of the French language has been getting quite a workout, and I even find myself thinking in the French a phrase here and a phrase there. They keep encouraging me by telling me that I speak it well. Of course, they are fibbing through their teeth. Ho! Ho! But, it has been much to my advantage to speak the language, even though not well—by any means,

At supper, tonight, I was so amused. Their little boy is about two, and his father poured about an inch of wine in his glass. The little rascal raised it up, made each of us clink glasses with him, and then looked at me and said "Kang-kang"! His father had told him I was an AmeriCAN, and he was addressing me by name. He just tickled the fool out of me, and all of us just had to laugh with much delight. I feel so "at home," here. We finished the meal with a bit of cognac, and more toasts. Then, so many questions about me, my home, my people, and America. I finally had to climb the stairs for bed—and to scribble on clip-board the beginnings of this letter which I must finish tomorrow.

◆ ◆ ◆

Slept like a log. Had oatmeal and grapefruit juice for breakfast, and I may have eaten too much freshly baked "French bread." This is beautiful country, here. News is that Manila is again ours. MacArthur is very much in control, I think. We are eager for spring.

February 7, 1945 France (Foug)

Pete, Charley and the platoon are now with us, and we are all together, again. Nice! They are just in time to help clean up our warehouse—so much to be done before our items can be properly stored and arranged for issue. Many truck loads of stuff were here, and we are hard pressed to clean the place and to prepare it for the requisitions which will soon be pouring in. We shall be ready! My office crew quickly cleaned the station, and with our files in order, we are just about ready to start over with a new set of stock-record cards. More fun! Do not make a guess, even, as to how busy we may be, but we will be issuing to many hospitals, military units, and even to some French installations. It is my understanding that a sort of "reverse lend-lease" enters into all of this—including the French government's reimbursing our hosts for our rooms, etc. A Madame Beck cooks for us officers in her home, and we eat in her dining room, and I know she gets her supplies via our mess—and is our food ever good! But, she works day in and day out to lay out our three meals per day. My understanding is that she is to receive payment for her time and work from the French government.

This Baudin family is just wonderful. Last evening, Monsieur and I had lengthy discussions about so many aspects of life in the USA and in France. My French is being pushed to some sort of limit, and it is becoming much easier. How could I have been so wise as to have studied this language in college—rather than German or Spanish! The people of this town just go out of their ways to be friendly—even more than the people of Trevieres. I hope none of us ever does anything to betray their trust.

Monsieur Baudin is a notaire. Our word close to it is "notary"; but, I think the French "notaire" is more akin to our "lawyer"—somewhat more as if we were to combine the two. Baudin has many clients, and his office is downstairs in what would have been a dining room. He is also the Mayor of Foug and most people address him as "Maitre." I do not know if this is because he is mayor or because he is a notaire. One of these days I shall find out. Ha! His secretary is a Monsieur Chenot, and Charley has a room in his home. Monique does a lot of typing, etc., to assist her father, and she is about seventeen years old. Yes, this is a busy residence, and a very important one. By chance, it fell to my lot to be roomed here, and I could not have been more fortunate.

Foug is a typical small town. If something happens, everyone knows about it within a few minutes. I haven't had time to learn about the experiences these folk had with the Germans, but am sure that some of "it" will be told to me.

Fred Stroh, one of our captains, is rooming temporarily with a family, and he and I are to be guests there for dinner this evening. He told them that I spoke French, and so this bit of a dividend has come my way. These people have a piano. The man plays the violin, and the son is also musical. So, we should have an interesting evening. Stroh gave me warning that they intend to put me "at the piano"—for whatever should be forthcoming. Well, it has been a long time since this sort of challenge has been before me. They'll need cotton in their ears!

Too, I have learned that some of these people like to play bridge. Chenot is one of them, and Charley is an enthusiast for bridge. They have heard of "contract bridge," but have not played it—just what we call "auction." So, my guess is that some evenings will find us at the table.

And, they have a hunting club which seeks out the wild boars, the sangliers, in the forests which cover so much of this locale. Baudin is a member of this group, and he has asked me to join them this Sunday. Once I know what this is all about, you shall have a full report. Ho! Ho! Others of us may well be invited. So, we shall see. I think they hunt only with shot guns—no rifles to be involved. Baudin told me that he would furnish me with gun and shells.

February 8, 1945 France (Foug)

No change in the news of the war, and we haven't picked up much steam at the depot. So, what I have to write about is this dinner which Stroh and had at the Guébourg's last evening. This was an evening quite away from any I have had before. Onset came a bit after 7:30—almost 8:00.

First came an aperitif—to whet our appetites, a sweet vermouth; then the thick pottage, a sort of creme of mixed vegetables; then a liver cheese which we spread on some warm, home-made bread—altogether delicious; then came roasted chicken with pomme de terre (potato—mashed and seasoned). Well, we were pressed to have seconds, and even thirds—and we put but one thing at a time on our plate, as we moved from one course to the next. Throughout there is before us our wine glasses, and the red wine kept pouring in should we so much as dare to sip to below the middle of the glass. The dessert bears explanation.

One finds in abundance, here, plum trees—much like the ones which grow in our Sandhills out on the hillsides. The name of the plum is "mirabelle"—and they may cook it with other fruit to make a sort of conserve, or they may make of it a preserve by itself, or they make it into a jam—to be call "confiture," or they let the juice just ferment into a sort of clear white fire-water which they refer to as "mirabelle." Let me tell you, but this "mirabelle" takes some getting used to—and I don't mean maybe.

Well, our dessert was a mirabelle pudding. Madame had placed six ripe mirabelles in a dish of sufficient depth, and poured over them was a mirabelle sauce above which was a deep custard—all to be beneath whipped egg whites, to which had been added a taste of mirabelle. Stroh and I had similar experiences with this, for with the first mouthful our breath stopped, our nostrils dilated, our eyes bulged, and our ears wiggled. Our hosts and their son just went after theirs as if nothing unusual was happening—just a matter of gobbling it. Maybe this requires some sort of breath control, and Stroh and I made quick recoveries and then proceeded to enjoy it. And after this came three tarts for each of us—one which had a custard flavor, one which was of apple, and the third which may have been immersed in mirabelle.

From the table we went to the living room and piano. Monsieur got out his violin, Claude—son of about sixteen years of age—tooted on some sort of piccolo, and I attempted to do some improvising on the piano. They insisted often that I play some American songs, of which I hammered out a few. Poor Fred had to listen to all of it. Madame was always bouncing around as if entirely enthralled by all that was going on—musically. And, in addition, singing had to accompany nearly everything, even if it were no more than full-blown "tra-la-la-tra-la-la"!

Then, we engaged in one game after another, and things just kept getting more and more hilarious. I had previously experienced nothing quite the equal to this. And, before I departed for my five-minute walk to the Baudin's, with key in pocket to get in the front door, out came the bottle of mirabelle for one final sip to end the party. They have little "shot glasses" for this, and it is supposed to be a down-the-hatch procedure—no sipping. I managed to survive, and the time had reached 12:15. This mirabelle could be used quite effectively for embalming purposes, for I think it would be a preservative of the most effective sort.

Monsieur Guébourg is one of the town's butchers, and he has a meat market. They are definitely leading citizens, and they live in the part of the town which lies adjacent to the old "usine" and along the railroad tracks—not in the "upper part" of the city. I asked him if it were difficult to get along with the Germans. He told me that German officers had come to their home, requisitioned and "borrowed" their better dishes and silverware—with promise to return or pay for, etc. Of course, nothing was paid for or returned. This apparently happened throughout the town, but not to all families. I intend to asked M. Baudin about it.

His name is René, and hers is Georgette. He is tall and slim, and she is somewhat pudgy and not tall. They are quite a pair, and Claude is an evident mixture of the two. He enjoys being at the piano—just to chord it all out with vigor.

Well, it was quite an evening. I shall need to hit the hay early this evening. Whew!

February 10, 1945 France (Foug)

Some sunshine for us, today, and it is very nice to see the sun.

All of this humidity seems to have hit my head, for sinuses are acting up. Mild headache has persisted, and I'm rigging up my steaming apparatus. So, we shall keep this under control.

Have been playing some chess with M. Baudin, and he has taken me for a cleaning each time. I can see that my skill at the game must improve by leaps and bounds. One does not hurry in this game, and his last victory took more than two hours to corner me—"check mate". He bests me at checkers, and we played another game called "Loup et Mouton"—"Wolf and Lamb." And, as always, I came out the loser. I then persuaded him to play our game of "Old Cat," and this time I outscored him 15 to 1, and he was certain that was tricking him. Ha! And, I could not convince him otherwise. I think he is accustomed to winning. Oh, well!

Tomorrow, we are to go hunting—for the sangliers, the wild boars. Charley will be going with us, and we depart from the town about 9:30 a.m. and walk out into the woods for the hunt. We will return for supper at the Baudin's—by seven o'clock. He will furnish us with our shot guns and shells. Rifles or carbines are never to be used for this sort of hunting.

Mail service is again very irregular—often several days without any letters. Keep asking Ira Moyer, our mail orderly, why this is. He just grins and shrugs his shoulders. He is a most charming rascal—comes from Cleveland, Ohio.

News with respect to the war continues to be highly encouraging. Nazism is going to reap its eventual harvest—a rather complete leveling of Germany. Hitler maintains his control, and the people will have to pay heavier and heavier penalties.

Our work at this installation continues to be to get everything into full operation. The cleaning of the warehouse chambers has really taken a lot of doing. But, order has come from the chaos. So much "junk" that might be of some use has been shuttled into about two rooms, and we shall see what all is to be worth.

February 12, 1945 France (Foug)

Must tell you about our hunt for the sanglier, yesterday. We left town about 8:30 and walked at least four miles to the heavily forested area selected for the hunt. Those who have the shot guns are the "chasseurs"—the hunters. We were positioned at various points along the pathways that were hopefully to be taken by the rousted out animals. Quite a host of older boys and some men were to move about through the woods and were to roust out the animals, and these people are called "traquers." I never saw one of the beasts, but Charley did and took a shot—but without success. When a traquer spots a sanglier, he gives a sort of whistled signal, and this will alert all the chasseurs.

Nearly two hours taken for lunch. Charley and I had hit our cooks for some American cheese, and we had canned sardines, rye krisp, and several packets of cigarettes to be passed around. We also had several candy bars apiece—all to be shared. Neither of us smokes, but these French are all smokers. Baudin had furnished us with wine, and we had two hard boiled eggs each. Also, Madame Baudin had cooked us "chaussons aux pommes"—little apple slippers or turnovers. Our cigarettes and candy bars disappeared as if by magic, and we shared in some French delicacies—to our delight. Each man had his small bottle of mirabelle, and several had thermos bottles of coffee. They mix the two and seem to make a lip-smacking elixir of the combination. Charley and I did our best to keep up with them, but this mixing of coffee and mirabelle provides a drink that, for us, takes some real effort to get used to. I do not care much for coffee, particularly as strong as the French like it, and the mirabelle is difficult—and the combination is worse. The supply of genuine coffee is yet much limited, and this "coffee" is made from a sort of chicory, I think—and mixed with charred grain. The cold weather seems to prompt one to need all sorts of bolstering, and these fellows know exactly the extent of their needs.

We were the welcomed guests of the entire group—about thirty, altogether. Each greeted us, and always with that firm handshake which is a French gesture of friendship. It rained most of the time—just a drizzle, but this did not dampen any spirits. Several of the men had their dogs along, and these friendly creatures let you know that they expected to share when it came to the eating. Out in the woods and along the trails, the dogs heel close beside their masters. This whole affair is organized, and the safety of each person is of prime importance in all procedures. Baudins had invited us to have supper with them, and it turned into a most tasty meal—with sanglier as the chief feature of the menu. It was a delightful repast. Charley brought a bottle of Madeira wine from his personal supply taken from our Paris loot and brought from Pantin; and I fished out some champagne, from my "reserve." Monsieur Baudin protested our furnishing of this drink, but soon changed his tune when we explained to him that it had come by way of the Germans. It had taken three trucks to haul our loot from Pantin to Foug. We had plenty of all kinds, and we had a sort of honor agreement as to use of key to have access to our special store of the good stuff. These people seem to have ample supply of their ordinary red and white wines, but these special sorts have, as yet, not been restored sufficiently.

The people of this town are just going out of their ways to make us feel welcome. I hope that we shall be able to ride out this war right here. This is "some way" to defeat the Germans. Oh, well!

February 14, 1945 France (Foug)

Yes, 'tis Valentine's Day, and we're a bit ahead of you. So, there!

Our "Big Three" have issued their declaration, and it just seems to me that the German people should find some means to throw Hitler overboard. But, his controls are still too firm, and this declaration will be carried through to full fruition.

Col. Cole, Major Grove, Lt. Ken Lane (our adjutant), and our Chief Warrant Officer, Willard McMaster, occupy a large vacated home, across the street and about three houses down from the Baudins. Close by lives the man who was the "Chef de la Resistance" here in Foug. The Germans never learned his identity, and he instigated certain doings which kept the German irritated. These people avoided physical assault and contact, and never a killing—for the German were zealous to exact a penalty of ten for one. M. Baudin wanted me to meet this gentleman, and we stopped in. We were actually on our way to invite Col. Cole to go on the next Sunday's hunt for sanglier. Well, between the two stops, it took us from 8:00 to 11:30 to accomplish our mission. At the home of the "Chef" we had to have several toasts of wine, some little pastries, and two or three snorts of mirabelle. I have never quite experienced the extent of hospitality which these people are determined to show us. We did manage to find Col. Cole before he had retired, and he seemed quite pleased to be invited to go hunting.

This mirabelle is just "something else." I think that each man produces his own, and he would be highly insulted were a guest to refuse to imbibe. And, when they mix it with their "coffee," it is even worse. Ha! As we returned to the house, I warned Monsieur Baudin that Madame would probably meet us at the door with a rolling pin—un rouleau a patisserie. But, she had gone to bed, and we were saved from our punishment. He is more fun, and he just goes out of his way to make me feel completely welcomed and at home. What a place to be riding out this war!

My use of the French language is rapidly improving, and not difficult to understand if one will slow up a little. Of course, each person talks as always, and for me the words just run together and I tend to put the end of one word with the beginning of the next—result being that it does not translate.

Baudin has informed me that I am to have each Sunday meal at evening with them. They are, as yet, quite rationed, except for what they produce in their gardens or butcher locally. I protested, and told him and her that our system supplied us with our daily supplies for meals, etc. But, to no avail—I was to eat with them. So, I insisted that I furnish the aperitifs and liquors—and even champagne now and then, with some Benedictine for "good measure." We entered into a pact.

The Germans gleaned all greases from these folk. Bars of soap became virtually nonexistent for them. Via our military "ration," I receive a bar of soap each week, and this I just leave in the upstairs wash room. From what I understand, there were times during the war when they would have sacrificed much for a little soap. Their clothes became dull in appearance, because they could not adequately clean them. Slowly, but gradually, normal activities are returning.

About three days ago, while wandering around in nearby woods, I just happened to spot something that had a shine to it, and it proved to be a German helmet. I found a long stick, and from behind an adjacent tree I poked to overturn the helmet. I feared it might contain an explosive of some sort. But, it was not "loaded" and proved, when cleaned and polished, to be a rather handsome souvenir. When I showed it to the men in the office, they were quite determined to go out to do some searching. I did not know it, but learned that several relics of the German "occupation" had been found in the rooms of the vacated "usine"—some of which had been tucked away and hidden. As elsewhere in France, the German withdrawal was a rushed affair, and certain so-called treasures, hidden away, had to be abandoned.

Well, two or three days without rain, and maybe this Sunday will be a better day to hunt the sangliers. We shall see.

February 17, 1945 France (Foug)

Was out to dinner last evening. Captain Stroh is now rooming with the local doctor and wife, name of Ravault, and they like to play bridge. So, again, it was my good fortune to be a guest. I was OD the day before, and it was an uneventful job. Our business is picking up a bit, but we are under no pressure, whatever. I have thanked my "lucky stars" that we were relieved from that Paris ordeal.

These French folk must have been frustrated "to no end" while having to live beneath the heel of the German boot. The more of them I meet, the more certain I am that they are a "happy-go-lucky" sort and are fully accustomed to a free way of life.

Ravault had butchered a lamb, and we had some of the liver and then some of the "lamb"—with all the rest of the marvelous meal, to be topped with a burnt-sugar pudding, just one of the most delicious desserts I have ever eaten. Their home is nicely furnished, but everything is considerably worn and in need to be upholstered anew. Their house has central heating, the first I know of, here. For my room at the Baudin's, I have a little charcoal-burning stove in my room—similar to the ones in their other rooms, except the kitchen. As is the general custom, here, we had aperitifs before the meal, then to the table for about two hours, then time for a round or two of bridge, and then well after midnight before I was back to my bedroom. I tell you, this is some life most of us are leading in this town. Yessirree!

This poem was in a recent issue of "Stars and Stripes"—quite cute, I think.

LONG JOHN JENNY

>An Alsace maiden in a small café
>Keeps the boys happy in the cutest way,
>She entertains them with a strip routine

That's a bit naughty but not obscene.
The gal in question has a brand new pair
Of government issue woolen underwear.
So as not to risk pneumonia in the early dawn
She does all her stripping with her long johns on.
Her name is Jenny and she's quite a chick,
And to watch her stripping gives a solid kick.
The band starts swinging and she goes to town
While the boys shout, "Jenny, let your drop seat down."
Jenny is the only teaser of her kind
Who shows them nothing but her cute behind.
The lads sit drooling in their beer and schnapps,
And when Jenny lets her bottom out, they blow their tops.
First, she disposes of her lace silk bra
As the Yanks all holler, "Whoopee, Hurrah!"
The Tommies give out with a brisk "Hip! Hip!",
As Jenny saucily lays down her slip.
As she kicks a shoe to the balcony,
Completely exposing a shapely knee,
Off comes her stockings, one at a time.
She tosses her garters in a GI's wine.
Jenny stands lovely in her underwear,
A maiden undaunted and without a care.
She looks like a queen without her crown,
And the boys yell, "Jenny, let your drop seat down."
She wows them nightly in the cold café,
But she never goes below her wooly negligee.
Your ought to hear 'em whistle when she does a dump,
The fascinating lassie with the air cooled rump.
Long John Jenny is the toast of France,
Knocking them dead with her ventilated pants.
The customers flock from all over the map
Just to see Jenny let her drop seat flap.

Tomorrow we again hunt the sanglier. I hope it will be a nice day, and that we shall have some good shooting. Last Sunday, I didn't even see one. Better luck, tomorrow, eh? The sun will be out, probably.

Much on our radio about the American bombing of Japan. Seems to me that MacArthur will be recognized as the truly outstanding American general of this war. He is some sort of wizard—maybe.

February 19, 1945 France (Foug)

Had one of our drivers pick up for me a pair of overshoes at the PX in Nancy. Now, I wont have to go traipsing around in all this mud with my shoes being in need of scrubbing each time I come indoors. It is often a matter of just leaving the shoes inside a doorway—on a mat, or in a box, or on something provided.

These men do so much enjoy every minute of their hunting. They are now free to congregate for whatever purpose and wherever they wish—no more under the heel of a tyrannical conqueror. This sort of hunting is thoroughly organized and according to established custom. It is something they thoroughly enjoy. It is my understanding that the Germans often hunted the sanglier, but the French only on occasion—in limited numbers and then always in company of their German "superiors."

Our hunt, yesterday, was successful as far as having a good time and lots of walking and good exercise, and we did get back. The colonel and Charley were along, and we set out with Baudin about 9:00—and to reach the spot for rendezvous at 10:00. We deposited our musette bags with our lunches in a small cabin and then took up our assigned stations, etc. The beaters, or trackers, did roust out one beast, and the colonel could have had a shot at it, but he couldn't get the safety to release—the animal just trotted past him. But it was only partially grown, and I couldn't tell if our French friends were disgusted or amused. So, we moved to another area, and tried again; but, no prey found. We returned to the little cabin to eat our lunch.

For lunch, I had taken a jar of peanut butter, a fruit cake (American made), some cookies sent from the U.S., some cheddar cheese, and a bottle of wine (from our cache). Charley had two cans of sardines, a loaf of French bread, some wine, etc. Col. Cole had a similar supply. Baudin had two hard-boiled eggs for each of us, etc., and about six of those chaussons de pomme—the apple turnovers that look like slippers. Madame Baudin's brother, Louis Duboc, was with us, and he had his supply of good stuff to eat and drink. He may have bicycled in from a nearby town. There were the five of us in our little circle, but so much exchanging!

We had taken along a good supply of cigarettes, which we made available for all our French hosts—and did they take full advantage of this special treat. They have tobacco and paper, and they must roll their own. So, to have a supply of prepared cigarettes is a real treat. One would have thought we were turning over to them our most precious life possessions. Well, this noon-hour for repast continued until nearly three o'clock, and the camaraderie was genuine and at times quite hilarious. The wine disappeared, completely, and Charley and I laughed because we were not sure but that the sangliers, were we to see any, might be skipping about, dancing, or just running in circles. One of the men had brewed two large containers of "coffee" in the cabin, and he then filled our cups, to which were added generous amounts of mirabelle—all supplied by Monsieur Baudin and Louis Duboc. Teague and I managed to get ours "down," but Col. Cole found opportunity to pour his behind a tree. This strong "coffee" mixed with mirabelle is "something else," but these French just guzzle it down without so much as a need for additional breath. As yet, to me, the stuff is awful,, and with coffee it is worse. Ho! Ho!

These men make their own shells. They buy the casings, and then put in the powder and lead pellets. Baudin had furnished me with a sixteen-gauge gun, and I fired it one time. There was virtually no "kick," and my hunch is that one must be close to a sanglier to be able to kill it or to cripple it sufficiently to be taken.

The excitement for the afternoon came when a couple of the dogs flushed a large boar, and it turned and hooked with its tusks one of the dogs in the flank. The wounded dog had quite a rip in its side, and the dog's owner was more than just a little upset. He had raised the dog from a puppy, and had carefully trained it for hunting. We made a large wad from handkerchiefs, pinched the wound together, and then tied the wad against the wound by use of a jacket and sleeves. There was a window-shutter available at the cabin, and they used this as a sort of litter to carry the dog back to town. Our return to town resembled a sort of procession of honor. I was not certain as to how seriously injured the dog was, and it didn't move its head, even.

Maitre Baudin had invited the three of us to have evening dinner with them, and Madame had prepared a sumptuous meal—the usual pottage, something called "queche," roast chicken, green beans, etc., all preceded by a marvelous assortment of "hors d'oeuvres" and followed with cake and tarts. I had put two bottles of champagne in the refrigerator, and Charley brought a bottle of Madeira. We also brought in a bottle of Benedictine. That all of this had come from our special supply, all gathered for us by our German "friends," made it all the more tasteful and delicious. Yes, that this was captured "German stock" made it all the more desirable.

We were at the table from 8:00 to 11:00. After Charley and the colonel left, I insisted that I help with the dishes. Well, I was put in my place pronto, for this sort of doing was not to be permitted in France, for I was a guest. So, I just went to bed.

This morning, the man, whose dog had been wounded, showed up at our office about 8:45 to see if he could get a ride to take his dog to a veterinarian in Toul. This was quickly arranged, and the job was accomplished—with man and dog returned. This gentleman, according to Baudin, is one of the town's more influential citizens. So, I think we made an important friend. He had lost an arm, but was considered to be one of the better hunters (chasseurs).

Many wild rumors here and about. War news is good for our side. We can only guess as to how long it will take to corner Hitler. Then, we must deal with the Japanese in the Pacific. With our experience, we could be sent to the Pacific—once finished, here. Who knows?

Days continue to be a mixture of sunshine and clouds and drizzle. The Russians have not, as yet, entered Berlin. Over our radio, we hear some marvelous music which comes from a German station. It has been nearly three weeks since we have received letters from home—a real mess somewhere in the APO references. But, they will reach us—eventually, no doubt. All of us are just hungry for news from home. So it goes! For many of the men, Foug is a "far cry" from Paris, but most are content to ride out the war right here. The men are making friends of so many of the families—just as before in Trevieres and even in Pantin. But, Paris was GAY PAREE!

A dark, rainy, and dismal day. Am spending the morning in the office, and the men and I have been visiting about everything—and I do mean "everything"! (February 20, 1945)

Late yesterday afternoon, a little girl was killed when run over by an American vehicle. A convoy had stopped, and soldiers in a truck were handing candy and gum to some children. This particular truck had a loaded trailer. We just do not know what happened, but this six-year old tyke must have dropped some of her candy and was retrieving it just as the convoy began to move. The driver did not know that the little girl had stepped forward to get her candy, and the trailer ran over her—killing her on the spot. It was just the saddest of all possible things to happen, and no one was to blame. The people who saw it happen all said it was not the driver's fault. It was not a matter of reckless driving.

Monsieur Baudin took me to see where four sangliers are being kept cool and to be carved up to be shared with members of the hunting club. Another group of members had good luck, and these were two grown beasts and two small ones—the larger weighing well over 100 pounds and the small ones, just partially grown, about 15 to 20 pounds. They dip each pig in a vat of boiling water, and then remove all hair and scrape the skin until nearly white. Then, they disembowel their prey for butchering.

I must be OD this coming Sunday, and will not be able go hunting, but there will be other days.

When I told Baudin that duty would keep me at the depot, he was just very disappointed. He is determined that I shall "bag" a sanglier. When these men go hunting, they are just visiting and laughing all the time—while walking to the selected hunting sites. So many of them let me know how pleased they were to have me along. I have a hunch that they consider me to be a guest of the club. It is known as "La Société de la Chasse"—"Club of the Hunt." Monsieur Baudin was telling me some of the particulars about the Club, and I think that there are occasions when the members give some of the meat to the poor of the town.

News told of the death of one of Russia's more important generals, spelling something like Chernikorvsky. His career had been quite brilliant. It seems to me that the Russian "general staff" must be about as good as any other. The Germans are being sent in tailspins from both sides, and they will have to cry "Uncle" pretty soon, I hope.

Our company has had the most continuous and most gruelling responsbilities of any of the supply depots. Our men have worked with great diligence and should have received special recognition. We have had a definite drawback which has worked against us, and this centers upon a particular person. Were it not for him, we should probably have remained in Paris. But, I am grateful, for had we remained there, I should never have met this remarkable Baudin family and these other wonderful folk who live here. Blessings do come in disguise.

Moyer, our mail orderly, reports that no mail for today. Well, one of these days!

February 21, 1945 France (Foug)

The sun rose this morning without a cloud in the sky. So nice to be free of the drizzle. My French friends all say that this constant rain is unusual. Some of our men came across some sort of portable disinfector, and they turned it into a shower unit. At any rate, we officers now have good showers twice a week—this evening being one of them, and much superior to what we had in Paris at the depot. Hot water—even slightly warmed—was a rarity at our hotels. Our colder weather is nearly behind us, I think, and we shall all welcome the warmer climate. We are all hoping we can sweat out the end of the war right here.

The Yalta Conference has put finishing touches to this business of war, and the people of Germany can have few doubts as to their fate if they continue to support Hitler. But, to continue to resist may well have become a matter of pride.

Played several rounds of bridge last evening at Monsieur Chenot's. Charley was one of the foursome, and the other was Chenot's cousin, a Monsieur Gaigneur. We had some "battle royals," and we switched partners after each game. A few differences in rules and in counting, but the contest is much the same. We had fun, and more fun. Gaigneur had high total, and I was low. One aspect to our life here—evenings are usually "open," unless one is officer of the day or unless we are involved in some sort of emergency transaction which takes extra time.

I try to improve my French, and am reviewing about two lessons per evening in my grammar. These friends keep telling me that my use of their language is improving. So, maybe it is, actually. Charley jabbers along quite well. So far, we have played "auction"; but Chenot and Gaigneur want to learn "contract." When it comes to raising a bid, the points figure in rather than tricks to be taken. A three bid in a major suit counts 90 points, and a four bid in a minor suit counts only 80 points; so, it takes 5 diamonds or clubs to raise a 3 bid in hearts or spades. We have warned them that when it comes to "contract," the tricks to be taken, not the points, determine the bidding. Ha! It could bring an end to this Franco-American Alliance that we have created. Oh, well!

Well, about three weeks since we have received mail from home. It has to be accumulating somewhere—probably down in Dijon. But, eventually all these letters will arrive, as before. It is just difficult to write home when one has no recent news.

Last evening, Chenot served us a sort of beer, and it was awful. Since he had purchased it, I could refuse to drink it. When it comes to the mirabelle, awful stuff, too, one cannot refuse to sip it through to completion because they produce it themselves. It is a matter of honor, to them, I think. And, the mirabelle, when mixed with their very strong ersatz coffee, is even worse. Yes, we have to undergo some torture—just to be friendly. But one new tidbit was a small apple which had been seared in a hot oven, and then left to dry—the outer crust sealing in the juice and flavor of the fruit. Chenot served us quite a large bowl of these apples, and they are surprisingly good. One needs only to discard the core and seeds, but the French just munch it all—no waste whatever. So, Charley and I will have to make a small adjustment if we wish to acquire more of these French customs. But, we are making good progress.

This evening, we are to gather at the Baudins for bridge and for chess. Larry Ryley, one of our lieutenants, is a good chess player, and he will be a challenge for Baudin. Colonel Cole is invited for bridge So, we should have quite an evening.

Work at the depot is picking up, but we have nothing which comes close to the pressures we endured in Paris. Once we had put on skids the plan to unite two companies for that Pantin operation, the "higher ups" would not enlarge our company with a few men to make the operation a wee bit easier. We have learned that the outfit now operating the depot has the equivalent of an extra platoon—men and officers, and they do not begin to have the demands placed upon them that we had. Furthermore, more French—men and women—are employed, too. The women who worked in our records office removed and replaced the stock-record cards from and to the files, and two of them typed up replacement cards as we needed them. Pay for these people came via "reverse lend-lease"—I think. Ho! Ho!

Monsieur Baudin brought to Madame Beck a "ham" from one of the recently killed sangliers—to be for one of our meals. He had inscribed quite a card—my translation being: "The Association des Chasseurs de (Foug) have great pleasure in presenting this jambon de sanglier to the American Officers."

As for this hunting club, as I have sort of figured out, each time a member goes on a hunt he pays a fee into the kitty. So, I argued that we Americans, when we join in the hunt, should pay in to the fund. Of course, he just turned his back on me and would not listen. I look forward to my next hunt, and I shall attempt to argue with him, but will again have him turn away. Yessirree!

February 23, 1945 France (Foug)

My crew in the office just takes care of all the duties there, and it leaves me free to roam about. Much of our time is often spent in just visiting and enjoying each other's company. These men are just the best of the lot, and I cannot repeat this too often.

About eight from our company had attended the funeral of the little girl killed the other day. It was in the church which stands just off the main street—about three-fourths of the way up the hill. It was quite a turning out of the townsfolk to express sympathy, and I think they appreciated our presence.

At Baudin's the other evening, Col. Cole complained about not feeling well; so, I filled in at bridge after his departure. Ryley and Baudin had a real match at chess, but France eventually triumphed. I think they managed to stretch the one game throughout the entire evening. Madame Baudin had prepared a plum cake and a sponge cake for our dessert, and each was delicious. Of course, we had the usual mirabelle on hand, and then that awful blending of coffee and mirabelle!

Had opportunity to visit the Guebourgs—where Stroh and I managed to survive the mirabelle pudding. They are the friendliest of persons—Monsieur, Madame, and their son, Claude. My French wasn't flowing well, but they told me of their experiences with the German "guests." Being one of the town's butchers, Guébourg was of significance, and the Germans wished to supervise his trade. At first, a German commandant wanted to house ten soldiers in their home. But, it is not that spacious, etc. So, Madame, who is a somewhat buxom little woman, put her hand on her hips and told them she did not have the rooms. So, they compromised on five. The Germans kept close watch, were always very "correct," and were very attentive to make sure that no meat was secreted away to the F.F.I and the maquis—that most would be held in reserve for the German troops. This sort of supervision went on during the four years of the "occupation," and Guébourg's business become pretty lax and with virtually no profit. He has made sufficient recovery, except the railroad is not operating, as yet. So, "things" are slow, and profits are low. They do make me feel welcome.

Well, we were at the piano, much of the time. I returned to my room about 9:30. Claude attends a secondary school nearby, is sixteen years old, and very much wants to learn English. I promised to give him some help, and we shall try to have about two sessions each week. Madame Guébourg's name is Georgette, and his is René.

Well, today we received mail. Just great! According to my count, it has been 25 days since private letters have found our hiding place. Am going to read mine once I'm in my room—just don't want any interruptions.

There is, as yet, virtually no supply of gasoline for these people. So, for several of the hauling needs within the town our drivers and trucks are helping extensively. This creates a good bit of camaraderie and good will. We are under strict orders that no fuel is to be given to the people. So, we must do what we can and are, in the process, becoming more and more involved in certain local affairs. It is becoming a sort of back-scratching situation, with both sides seeming to be quite comfortable with the doings. My next two evenings are to be taken up with fun at Chenot's and at the Ravault's. So, it goes for me. Some war, methinks, for us here!

February 25, 1945 France (Foug)

Mail is pouring in—just 18 more letters, today. So, we are really back in business. Nice! I told Moyer, our mail orderly, that he had managed to escape the hangman's noose, for we were all just about ready to string him up to the nearest lamp post. Poor guy! We had been threatening him for several days with all sorts of consequences were he not to find us some letters. He was never without a fitting comeback, and always with overtone of sass. He is one good egg!

Such wonderful news from the Philippines! The recovery of all those Americans, among them being more than fifty nurses! And, of course, MacArthur continues to make the calls that are working. We certainly were happy to hear that Manila was again in "our hands." Admiral Nimitz is certainly directing the right plays for the navy. Whoopee!

Gave a pint of blood for our "bank," and I thought I would just have to scream. The captain, a medical corps doctor, just couldn't hit a vein, and he kept poking—first in one arm and then in the other. Finally came success. I had begun to think that this mirabelle had shrunk all my blood vessels. Oh, well! I hadn't given blood since in England. We had success, this time, once the captain changed the rubber tubing—after discovering the first tubing had a hole in it, etc. The poor fellow apologized "all over the place." I have two black and blue arms, just below the elbows on the inside. The gang in the office think I should put in for "the purple heart"! We have had several good laughs, all because of my "battle injuries."

The Baudins butchered a hog, recently. They had been fattening it for some time. This evening they insist I eat what is for them a speciality. They call it "boudin." They catch all the blood, once the poor pig has been strung up and its throat slit. They mix onions and garlic, and other seasoning, along with some sort of grease, into the blood, and all is then stuffed into the intestines. Along the way, clotting takes place. The stuffed intestines are then stretched out and tied into short sections, and it resembles a string of connected sausages, or little rings of salami. It smells something like a liverwurst. As yet, I am not very eager. I am to eat supper with them this evening, and this Baudin "boudin" is to be on the menu, I'm sure. They may roast this for a while in an oven. I shall know more about it. Oh, well!

Chenot wanted me to come up the street for an evening of bridge, but I had agreed to eat with the Baudins. I will be OD when the next hunt is scheduled. So, I shall again miss it. We had an adjustment in our roster, and this has caused me to miss two Sundays successively. This being OD just means that I can not sleep in my comfortable bed, and must make my rounds about twice during the night—just to make sure that the "guards" of the depot area and of the vault are not snoozing. We do have quite a supply of gold and silver for dental purposes, and then there are the whiskey and opiates which are to be issued for medicinal and other purposes—all to be secure, here, in a room "under lock and key."

Another beautiful day, today, and indications are that this weather may continue for a spell.

No change in my instructions as to putting so much into bonds from my savings account, and we could use a resupply of sardines, rye krisp, olives, Nestle's chocolate, etc. So, keep the stuff a-coming. The hunting season for sanglier will close, but I do not know just when. They probably breed in spring.

February 27, 1945 France (Foug)

The money-order arrived. Thank you for sending it. It was in my yesterday's stack of letters, and it was mailed more than a month ago. I was sure that it would eventually make its appearance. So, no worry and no problem to get it cashed. Bravo! These letters are rolling in by the bagful, now—just about every other day. We'll have a let up before long.

Stroh and I did have a marvelous time with the Ravaults last evening—wonderful dinner and then bridge after. They do enjoy to eat, so sing, to play cards, and to entertain. To be a guest in their home is just a delight, and so it is elsewhere. Dr. Ravault is working on his English with much vigor, and he keeps asking me about this word, and that word, and the meaning of this phrase and that phrase, etc. We finally completed a full game of bridge. The men who are making friends with the families keep saying the same—that they are just being treated as if they were favorite people. We were certainly fortunate to have reached this place. It is a far cry from Paris and its many "attractions," but these men are making some very good friends and seem to appreciate being here.

Have a bridge engagement for this evening—with Charley, Chenot, and Gaigneur. We do have so much fun.

Some rail connections into the town are now in use, and use of the RR has begun—but not much. There is a sort of little truck-like vehicle that is on the track, and the French use this to switch the cars. Well, it jumped the track this morning, and it took the entire day to get it back on track. Our men have nothing to do with operation of the RR, but about half the company and many of the townsfolk were watching. Had the feeling that this sort of thing had never happened before—here. After all had been accomplished, there were a few rails that needed to be reset. At least, it made for a different sort of day. The depot agent has set up an office in a small building about a block from the "station" in which we have our office.

You make reference to the "liquid fire" we must drink, now and then. This is, of course, the mirabelle. The ad from Gold's about the Tabu perfume gave me a chuckle. You should take your large bottles of this "forbidden fragrance" to the department—just to strut about with the stuff. The French word for taboo is "tabou." Get the idea??

You have never written to me that censoring had ever resulted in any cutting from my letters. I know that our letters, even when initialed by our company's censors, and I am the chief of the crew, are haphazardly rechecked when approved. Joyce wrote Pete that one of his letters had had part of a page removed. He could not recall what it was that had been deleted. Not often have I felt it necessary to return a letter to have it "corrected." Our men have been very careful as to what they say. And, as yet, we are to name no town in which we are "stationed," etc. Only when in Paris could we do it.

March 1, 1945 France (Foug)

The weather is nice, and the mail is coming in regularly—eighteen letters for me yesterday, and two today, the latest posted on the 19th. Most of them have been piled up some where for three or four weeks. What a system!

Dr. Ravault invited some of us to take a look at his dispensary, which is in one of the rooms in a former foundry—with part of the building having been damaged by some sort of explosion. I was somewhat surprised to find he had it so well furnished, and he has several electric appliances. In an adjoining room are several stalls for shower bathing, but he said the people rarely use them. He wants me to prepare a lecture on personal hygiene and the benefits to be gained from such. This will take some doing, and I will have to give the talk in French. He and Madame Ravault are almost rabidly working on their English, and he said they would help me to compose the talk. He seems to think that the people might listen to me. Well, we shall see!

Had not done anything with the popcorn you sent me, but did pop some last evening for the Baudins. They had neither seen nor eaten it before, and were simply amazed and fascinated. They couldn't believe that the kernels went into the kettle yellow, and then came out enlarged and white. Jean-Francois was frightened by the popping and cried as long as the "explosions" continued. They liked it, but wanted sugar sprinkled on it, rather than salt—and J-F ate quite a bit of it. So, maybe next time we wont have to put up with his screaming We shall be popping corn quite regularly, now, and please send me more. I may have enough to stretch through about four or five more poppings.

Pete came to my room the other evening, and we had quite a chewing session with respect to Col. Cole, our CO. Neither of us has much respect for him as a commanding officer, and we are considering making applications for transfer. Charley Teague is our only officer who gets along with him, and they are both "southerners." This is a good place to ride out the war, and Pete and I do not have our minds set in concrete. Ha!

Our "business" is picking up considerably, and it is good to have our time better occupied. Things have really been slow in our "records office."

Am supposed to hunt the sangliers with Baudin this Sunday. He is so certain that I shall have a lucky day. He furnishes me with shotgun and ammunition. I think one needs to be quite close to the beast in order to wound it sufficiently to stop it. We shall see!

March 5, 1945 France (Foug)

Bought a rather nice looking jacket for $14. Went into Nancy with our mail run, and went to the PX. This is patterned after a style which Eisenhower designed, also called "battle jacket."

Received a letter from Madame Rivet. I had written that I hoped to get some time off with chance to visit Paris. She ordered me to report immediately to their home and to stay with them. Monsieur Rivet often referred to the American "liberation"—and Charley and I would jokingly refer to ourselves as their "liberators." She addressed me as "Mon Cher Liberateur." I shall have to refer to myself as "Votre Bien Cher Liberateur," and I can hear them chuckling.

Have played more bridge with Chenot, Gaigneur, and Charley. We do have a good time—at least one evening each week.

Must make inquiry about this "post-hostility instruction" program. Our points are not very high, and most of us would not be on any list for early return to the U.S. once this war is over. But, as long as it usually takes to get any sort of inquiry acted upon, it could well be next summer. Gee, but I hope this European action will be finished by then. This being a "property officer" would be a very dull work—were we not having such a good time with our friends, here.

Went on the hunt, yesterday, and it was rainy, snowy, and cold, and no luck to find a wild boar in the morning. The noon repast was the good part of the ordeal. We found a somewhat sheltered nook beneath overhanging branches and had our usual exchange of food, wine, and mirabelle. Later, one of the men mortally wounded an animal of about 100 pounds. So, "la chasse" proved to be successful. Each man brings his own mirabelle, likes it, and may be insulted if you refuse to accept some from his bottle. I bring a little jigger of Madame Baudin's and attempt to keep it full. But, some of these more than friendly "chasseurs" expect me to put my small supply "down the hatch"—so they can refill my glass. Whew! What a life!

We have an assignment of German prisoners, and these remain with us. They are quite "German"—compared to those we had in Trevières. Stroh is to supervise them. They are housed in the "usine" and are under the "watch" of our armed guards—day and night. They are fed on our "C" rations, which are canned and are heated. Treatment of them is strictly according to the Geneva Convention. From reports, their treatment is far better than they administered to their POWs. We have received detailed instructions as to their treatment, confinement, work, etc. They receive nothing "fresh" in the line of food—except the bread.

Had dinner with the Baudins last evening, after we returned from the hunt. Madame is a real whiz when it comes to preparing meals, for her supply of good flour, sugar, shortening of any sort is so limited. Very few cows in this vicinity, for the Germans herded most of them away when they left. A butchered pig will provide some lard, of course, and this is then used sparingly. I always bring in a bottle of champagne, a bottle or two of wine, and maybe a bottle of Madiera. They no longer protest, but just smile. Yes, times do change, a bit. Ho! Ho!

Am OD through to tomorrow morning, and will have some time to write several letters. Will make my rounds two or three times, and may do some snoozing on the cot in the office. We have added about four men to the guard detail each day—now that the POWs are with us. It is my hunch that these men were well screened before being turned over to us for use.

This war against Germany has certainly been speeded up, and the Siegfried Line appears to be on its last legs. It seems to me that the Germans are so foolish to continue their struggle, for they will increasingly face into complete destruction of their cities, etc. But, they will put up a determined defense along the Rhine River, and the Allied armies will pay a heavy price to cross—the Americans, most of all. But, Hitler and his ilk remain in power, and they have no compunction, whatever, about the sacrifices of lives. It is woeful!

March 7, 1945 France (Foug)

Bridge last night at Monsieur Chenot's. He and his cousin, Gaigneur, do like to play, and Charley and I just fit in. We switch partners after each rubber. I told Chenot that I have two uncles—one named Griot and the other named Jouvenat. Without hesitation, he dubbed me to be named "Mickeynot" and refers to me as "Cher Cousin Mickeynot," He pronounces his name as if "shay-know"—and you know how to pronounce "gree-oh", and I have become "mickee-know". He addresses me as "Mon Cousin"—"My Cousin." We just grin from ear to ear!

Chenot and Gaigneur do love their mirabelle. Last evening he brought out the stuff in two bottles, one an old bottle for gin and the other one of Charley's Pepsi Cola bottles. He asked me which I preferred—gin or Pepsi Cola. I told him that I preferred neither, only mirabelle. I had wanted to stump him, but he went to his cupboard and brought a bottle labled "Mirabelle" and poured me considerably more than I wanted. Well, he is a mischievous rascal, and we laughed for five minutes.

This evening, Stroh and I shall play bridge with the Ravaults. Dinner will be at seven, and then will come the game—when we get around to it. I will not get away before midnight. Much of our conversation will be about the English language, and they both want exact translations. Stroh told me that he would be furnishing champagne and a liquor—from our special cache, of course.

The war news continues to be good—particularly promising here in Europe. The struggle for Iwo Jima is already so costly in lives. This will become increasingly awful as we are forced to close in on Japan. I do not know what can be done to bring about a cessation of the fighting until we have actually invaded and conquered the nation. It is quite beyond my capacity to imagine.

A few of our men have left the company, and a few promotions came as result—to fill the vacancies created. One of the men in my office was not one to receive advancement, and he has been a real sore thumb for me. He has sulked for a week, now, and just gripes about everything. Finally, I had all I could take, and we went into a little side office. I went over our T/O with him and noted that there was no chance for promotion for me, et cetera. He remained resentful, talked about how long the hours had been and remained to take care of the "records," and told me of friends of his who had come into the service after he had and now held ranks of sergeant and higher. I told him that Teague and I had been in the same OCS class and that he had received promotion to be captain, not I. He began to soften his hostility. We agreed that what each of us really wanted was the war to end and that we should be able to return to our homes. He is one of our corporals. We parted with a handshake and grins. Had he not swung around to a better frame of mind and behavior, I was prepared to tell him that he might suffer demotion. I was happy that it did not come to this.

Well, I later pondered the situation with our company and did some speculation as to how much better things would have been had we not been saddled with Cole as our CO. He has no comprehension with respect to the psychology which enshrouds the relationships between persons thrown together in the various relationships of the armed service. He is so rank-conscious and has such an out-of-balance opinion of himself. He is simply blind to the attributes which should make of one an excellent CO and leader. He enjoys his position of authority, and seems to relish it. He is the big toad in our very little puddle, and he does not let opportunity pass to let one of lesser status know where the latter's place is. Oh, if Grove could have replaced him! Grove, as our Major, does his duty and makes no issue of anything. I have never visited with him about this situation, and he has never offered to visit. The extent of his frustrations have to be almost beyond measure.

Well, the colonel and I have had our differences, and he knows that I speak my mind. He never stood behind us when we had difficulties with the central surgeon's office in Paris, and I told him of my disappointment. He will never acknowledge that he might have helped to make "things" better . Unfortunately for all of us in this outfit, it just happens to be as it is. Ouch!

We officers are no longer eating at Madame Beck's. She became increasingly difficult to cooperate and to get along with. I do not know the reason for the growing discontent. At any rate, we have returned to our company mess and are once again feasting from the expertises of our very good cooks. At first, Madame's French-style preparations of our furnished supplies was excellent.

(Years later, when I had opportunity to return to France and to visit the Baudins, I asked the Maitre if the French government ever paid the people who furnished us rooms, etc. He said, "Non, ne rien." She may have become much out of sorts if not receiving some sort of compensation for her work. But, we had been eating with her for just four weeks. On the other hand, I had been told that she had a quarrel with Col. Cole about the meals. Maybe she had developed a dislike of him to such extent that she no longer wanted to cook for us.)

March 10, 1945 France (Foug)

Our fortunate crossing of the Rhine on the 8th at Remagen has certainly thrown all strategy for a German defense line to the winds. And, with Von Runstedt out, Hitler must fall back upon his old-line generals. "Things" should now be speeded along considerably. We finally got a magnificent break of good luck. With clear weather, our planes will plaster the remaining German strongholds with much effect. The Americans may yet meet the Russians in Berlin.

Hitler's hide is now wearing thin!

Monsieur Baudin has explained the difference between the F.F.I. and the Maquis. The Maquis was composed of the younger men who fled into the woods and interior to escape the German labor draft, and of those men who managed to escape from the trains or from Germany. André Jacquet of Trevières was, I'm sure, active in the Maquis. The French Forces of the Interior was made up of the townsfolk who outwardly cooperated with the German captors, but who did all sorts of things to disrupt and delay and confuse. Often, coordinated actions between the two "groups" were carried on in order to thwart the German from achieving many of their goals. Members of both were meticulous in their avoidance of injury, or killing, of the Germans. The reprisal of "10 for 1" simply had to be avoided. Baudin wants to take me to two places where, respectively, 40 and 30 French men and older youth were executed and buried in mass graves.

Baudin is also much concerned about need for a rapid recovery of France's economic systems and channels. Socialism had become rather basic to the economy and politics of France, but he wants that there be no recurrence of a communistic upsurge. As mayor of the town, as notaire by profession, and as "President of the Hunting Club" he would prefer a more vigorous capitalistic upswing. I do not think he is an enthusiastic "Gaullist." He wants nothing to do with any sort of dictatorship. Capital and labor must become cooperative and resort to open and fair bargaining. If I understood him—even somewhat accurately, it is my impression the the F.F.I. was very active throughout this part of France.

Monique, daughter of the Baudins, has been quite ill with some sort of flu—at least, a severe nasopharyngeal inflammation. That she had a high fever was evident. So, I took over, insisted that she take two of my APC capsules and drink lots of water, go to bed, and prepare to sweat it out. Well, these people would rather do most anything than drink water. I had a clinical thermometer, and her temperature was nearly 103. She did as Dr. Quack prescribed, and broke out into a good sweat, after about three hours, and had a quick return to normal temperature. I told her to stay in bed and to rest for two days—then to get back into her usual activities. Seemed to me that it was about time to hang out my shingle. Madame Baudin thinks I should be a doctor.

Have written to the Nebraska State Journal to nominate the cottonwood to be selected as our "state tree." The French word for tree is "arbre"—a masculine noun. So, here is part of what I wrote about the cottonwood:

> …He's not a handsome tree, nor is he refined. He's plentiful to the extent that we curse his leaves in the fall of the year. His rugged bark is characteristic of his very nature, and he has continuously supplied us with shade in the summer and warmth in the winter. He's as dependable as the seasons and as willing to serve as the most gallant knight. Afterall, he's every where in our State, too.

My letter was a bit corny, I thought. My other suggestion was the box elder. I identified myself as a 1st Lt., MAC, APO 667, as being in France, and with home address—5324 Madison Ave., Lincoln. So, we shall see!

Went to see the Guebourgs yesterday evening, and we had a good time. They talk so fast, and it is often difficult for me to understand. Claude wants me to teach him English, and we'll attempt to have a session or two each week. I am also to assist the Ravaults. So, we shall see how all of this turns out. When I go to see these people, I take some of the candies you have sent, and they do enjoy this sweet stuff. Madame G. always has something tasty to put on the table for us to share.

Will be eating with the Baudins tomorrow evening. Some very good and old friends are coming from Paris, and they want me to have supper with them. I told Madame that they shouldn't feel they should invite me, and she just laughed at me. He added that I was "en famille"—and to be included. It will be another grand meal, with hours at the table. I shall put two bottles of champagne in their refrigerator, and will have another bottle or two of something. The three truck loads of stuff we brought from Pantin show few signs, as yet, of running out. Ha!

Bridge this evening. Last time, I was on the losing side in each of five rubbers. It would be nice to have better cards, for a change. Cannot go hunting tomorrow, for the colonel has called a meeting of the officers. I have a suspicion that he timed it purposefully. Maybe I shall be free next Sunday.

We are using three of the German POWs in our office, and they do all the cleaning. Two of them are experienced "bookkeepers" and seem much interested in our techniques and methods. Degner, if I have his name correct, is inclined to act as if he were somewhat superior. They are puzzled because our men and I are so friendly and chat informally all of the time. When I enter the office, the men never arise to their feet and stand at attention until I put them "at ease." But these German prisoners are immediately on their feet when I come in, stand at attention, and do not relax until I order them to get back to work. All these formalities will soon be shelved, but we are not about to engage in any sort of camaraderie. I told Thirlby to attempt to get Degner to relax and to accept the fact that Americans are different from Germans, etc. We shall see, eh?

Latest letter from home was dated the 26th of February. So, not bad!

March 15, 1945 France (Foug)

War news continues to be good for our side. All of us, here, just agree that we want this affair to finish so that we can head for home. The POWs who come in to work in our records office are quite concerned about what has happened to their towns and families. Is my understanding that their people know they are POWs and alive—maybe via the Red Cross, but their whereabouts remains secretive. Five are now assigned to clean our rooms in this "station house," and they remain available for other work throughout our installation. They continue to jump "to attention" when I first come in each day, but they are much more relaxed. Two or three are assisting with use of the stock-record cards—recording of items received and issued, etc. We are busy, but nothing as was the situation in the depot at Pantin.

I have submitted application to be considered for this post-hostility instruction work. Should there be decision to consider me seriously, I shall receive instructions to appear before a board or committee—probably in Paris. Well, we shall see. One thing is for certain—with our company under its present CO, it would be nice to get a change. But, I should not be happy to leave these French friends—for they are so very kind. We do have the best of times together.

You have asked about my getting a promotion. Out T/O, Table of Organization, is complete, and this leaves us just as we are. We are stymied. As often as I have openly disagreed with Col. Cole and in many instances to have proved him to be in error, he would be most reluctant to give me a captaincy—no doubt about this. I am persuaded that I shall "go down with the Titanic" still a lowly lieutenant, still with my silver bar. I am shedding no tears!!

We play bridge as often as possible at Monsieur Chenot's. My hopes are that I will be free to go hunting this coming Sunday. Another dinner with the Baudins, and I made certain that some champagne was in the refrigerator, and I always drag in a bottle or two of something they are, as yet, unable to purchase. No more protests. Ho! Ho!

Was OD yesterday. The colonel, I, and three of our men attended a memorial service in the local church. It was held for a man who was in the F.F.I. and was killed near Chartres when that city was being "liberated." I do not know the circumstances. Maitre Baudin asked that we have a representation at the service, and we were pleased to go. Many of our men are Catholic, and some of them attend Sunday morning worship in the church, and this has pleased the people. The interior of this church has some very nice and beautiful fixtures. The service followed the Catholic ritual. The priest is not an older man, and his homily was directed to the mourners who were seated directly before him. He spoke with good enunciation, and I could understand much of what he said. Yes, much blood had been "drained into the soil of France as result of the barbarism of Germans." He closed his remarks with this: "Many often must perish that others might live. A new France would rise, a France better than the one before!"

I need more tea, and two or three pounds of coffee would come in handy. Madame Baudin is fond of tea, and the coffee will find its place in her cupboard, too. Many thanks!

We have rigged up very good shower facilities, here, and we officers use it twice a week. While in Normandy, it was to sponge oneself out of his helmet filled with water. One thing about it, we are getting this place all into good working order, just as we did at Trevières and at Pantin. Our "superiors" seem to enjoy letting us get a place into fine working order, and then they send us elsewhere, with our successors "in" to enjoy the results of our labors. Oh, well!

Weather is warming, and we shall be shedding our woolen underclothes, soon. We've had no mail for five days. Beautiful day, but we do often have very dense fog in the mornings.

Our "carpenters" constructed a stock-records table for us, with several compartments on top, and it is a humdinger. One of our POWs designed it and made an impressive drawing of it. When Posypanko and Vanderwyst brought it in, we had a sort of celebration. I think our office POWs thought we were "nuts". Ha! They will just have to get used to us.

Must head over for our evening mess, and will probably shave before I go to bed. Our upstairs wash room at the Baudin's is much more available in the evening.

March 18, 1945 France (Foug)

We have had some nice days lately—with plenty of sunshine.

Work at the depot keeps picking up, and it is a matter of being at work in the office by shortly after seven, and then on the job until nearly six in the evening. But, this is nothing like the hectic situation in Paris. Charley and I gave Baudin a tour of the depot, and he was quite impressed with the adjustments we had made. If I understood correctly, this "usine" was a tile-making establishment. The machinery had been dismantled and stored in two or three of the rooms, and had largely rusted. No one knows what will be done with these buildings in future, but they do appear to be sturdy.

We have our occasional evening of bridge at Monsieur Chenot's. Charley and I must always munch on those dried apples, and we must appear to be enjoying them—and, likewise for the mirabelle and the strong ersatz coffee. Of course, scoring is always as done in France.

Am hoping to have a few days to sneak into Paris—to see the Rivets, Scheys, and Lurquins. Too, it will be nice to stroll about the city and to have time to look at the displays in the windows of the many shops and stores. I need to do some shopping—for a few gifts.

Have had my final day of hunting the sanglier. Stroh went with us. He is rather short and pudgy, and I think all the walking just about did him in. Baudin had a shot in the morning, but did no more than wound the animal, perhaps. We had the usual two and half hours for the lunch break. Madame Baudin had provided us with much good food, and we had several bottles of wine and mirabelle. The camaraderie of these lunch breaks is memorable—the sampling of the various "specialities" and the many, many "toasts" that eventually drain the bottles of wine and mirabelle.

After lunch, we walked to and took up our positions along some of the trails. The trackers rousted a full grown boar, and he came right to my corner. Well, the safety seemed to be stuck, and I was delayed too long to have a good shot—which I made anyhow. Those nearby knew that I had fumbled my chance. When we assembled to move on to another area, they were disappointed that I had not been successful. I did not want to tell them that I had goofed; so, I gave this explanation—which all knew was a "cock-and-bull story." I told them that during the lunch break, I had drunk too much wine and mirabelle; thus, when the sanglier appeared, I saw three, shot to kill the one nearest to me, but without luck, and all three just ran into the woods. Well, I had to use my best "French" to make my explanation, and once understanding what it was I was attempting to say, my comrades burst forth into laughter. (The story spread throughout the town after our return. For a week, as I would pass along the street, people would give me big grins and just wave me on. This was about as close as I ever came to being a celebrity.)

The hunting season closes the end of March. I have a hunch that Baudin pays a fee to have me along for a hunt; but, he says not—that I am always a guest of the club, "La Société de la Chasse."

For supper, Madame Baudin had prepared her usual repast. To begin came something I had never had before—a soft boiled egg served in a dish of sweetened gelatine. It was delicious, as was the rest of the meal—lamb, rabbit, vegetables, and three desserts. We had had quite a day, and Stroh admitted that he had never had an experience quite like it. These men just go out of their ways to make us feel welcome.

And, yesterday was St. Patrick's Day. Several of our men attended an early mass; but, I am not certain that the French make much of it.

March 23, 1945 France (Foug)

Just seems that each day is just about the same as the days before. News for our friend, Adolf, continues to give him little encouragement. Our POWs who work in our office seem to be keeping their ears open when any newscasts are on. Only Degner is able to catch the gist of the reports, and he relays to the others. The clear days are always good for air attacks on German cities, and often the reports do identify some of the cities targeted. Concerns of some of our POWs must be on sharpened edges. I keep telling myself that the Germans brought this on themselves. Oh, well!

The colonel and I went to (Nancy), and each of us, including our driver, did some purchasing. It was nice to take a little jaunt. Nice little stores, particularly with several having items of French embroidery available. Two or three luncheon sets caught my fancy, and they will make nice gifts for the future. Some scarfs caught my fancy, and also a guimpe—a fancy front for a blouse, but without the rest of the blouse. You probably know what it is, but you will know for sure when you see it. Ho! Ho! I was hoping to find some small handbags made of petit-point, but none were available—the sort of fabric just not yet back in production. I like to get things that are "Made in France."

About twice a week we have a movie for the company, and the most recent one was Laurel and Hardy in "Always in Trouble." When it comes to slap-stick, those fellows are not to be bested. Many of the "locals" come to see these movies, and they laughed right along with us at this pair. They do tickle our funny spots.

Was to the Guebourgs a couple evenings ago, and Madame initiated me into the art of making crepes—large, very thin pancakes that one smears with jam or jelly, then rolls them, and then eats them. They are good, and we had lots of fun. This was another evening of too much to eat, a good sampling of French wines, along with some liquors I had brought, and lots of pounding on the piano and some singing—much of it off key. Oh, well!

Received four letters from Lincolnites, yesterday, and they were postmarked December 4, February 20, and March 7 and 8. One has to wonder about the whereabouts of those two earlier letters.

While walking up the street to go to Chenot's to play bridge, I met the man whose dog had been gored by the boar. He greeted me as if I were a long-lost brother and told me the dog was fully recovered. He gave me such a vigorous hand shake that he almost disjointed my arm from the shoulder.

Broke a pair of my glasses while playing volley ball. Should never have left them on. Now I have the two pair of GI glasses, but they are steel rimmed and heavy. The optical unit which is attached to us will grind me out new lenses, but the shape will be altered—but without the heavy rims. So, just a few days without my rimless spectacles. No real inconvenience!

March 25, 1945 France (Foug)

Such marvelous weather for us, and this means that the air attacks against Germany are constant.

The Germans are definitely on their last legs. Our supply business remains constantly at good pace, but we have time to do lots of odd jobs. Use of our POWs is largely to clean up the entire "usine" and to make the surrounding grounds as neat as possible.

Across the railroad tracks and what seems to me to be to the east of town is an extensive hillside that is wooded. At various spots a number of the people have covered hot beds in which they start their garden plants, and these little beds have old storm windows to catch the sun and heat up the ground. Our men who regularly stand guard duty are required to have target practice now and then. The other day, they set up on a post an upward extended target and blazed away. This extended wooded hillside was in the background, and unknown to them was one of the hot beds—directly in the line of fire. It belonged to a Monsieur Queney, a very good friend of the Baudins, and this elderly gentleman had become an acquaintance of mine. He was quite angry, for he thought our men had purposefully used his hot bed for a target, and they had destroyed his panes of glass—which were irreplaceable. He came to Baudin to register his complaint against "les Americains"!

When told of the situation, I invited Monsieur Queney to go to the depot with me, and there I showed him where the men had engaged in their target practice—unfortunately his hot bed being at the very point on the hillside where the bullets struck. That there had been no malice eased his anger a bit. I knew we had several abandoned panes of glass somewhere in the storage rooms of the "usine," and there we found four double paned storm windows that were just what he needed. Some of our men carried the storm windows up to his hot bed, and he had become a very happy "little old Frenchman," who once again thought the American soldiers were just great people, etc.

No need to get upset because I am interested in this "post-hostility" instruction program. Except for two or three of our noncoms who were regular army, we do not have service points to get early release from the service. My hunch is that most of us in this depot company will not be eligible for release until late summer, and we might even be sent to set up a medical supply installation in the Pacific—maybe in China for completing the war against Japan. Who knows?? I certainly will not be among those who are eligible for early demobilization. Yes, the Rhine River is no longer a barrier, but much remains to be done. Patton is having a heyday.

Have been having some sort of stomach upset the past two or three days, and it must be a bug—for I haven't been eating anything strange or greasy. Had our company barber give me a good clipping, and maybe I'm just light headed. Have been taking my two showers each week, and I doubt if my cleanliness is the cause of my malaise. Oh, well! This, too, will pass.

More bridge a couple evenings ago at Chenot's. Tomorrow is my turn again to be OD, and this prevents me from opting to go hunt a sanglier, but I knew "duty" was going to interfere with pleasure.

This rift between F.D.R. and deGaulle is, in my opinion, not of Roosevelt's doing. "Le Grand Charles" should not ignore the fact that Roosevelt, Churchill, and Stalin have, as a cooperative threesome, been calling the plays quite successfully to bring ultimate finish to the Nazi power. An overrun France has been liberated in the process, and France will play a highly significant role in Europe's future. But, as of now, I think deGaulle has blundered and should cool his heels. Rumor is that Stalin is not an admirer of deGaulle. We do not need a thorn in the side of the Allied front. So, we shall have to keep an open ear to the news. The U.S. will have the war in the Pacific, yet, once this European chapter is written, and Russia's continued support is vital to our action versus the Japanese.

Have purchased another of these short "Ike" jackets—in "greens" and really dressy with pink trousers. It will soon be warmer, we will be going into summer garb, and the thing was on sale. I may not wear it much. Who knows? Our "blouses" are a bit heavy, and these jackets are both practical and sensible.

Palm Sunday, today. It had escaped my attention until some of the men returned from mass. Last year for Palm Sunday we were on the Queen Elizabeth, and many of us attended a service and had communion. Wouldn't it be wonderful if this war were long gone and behind us for Palm Sunday, 1946!

Am to go to the Guebourgs for supper tomorrow evening. My guess is that we shall finish the feast with another round of that mirabelle pudding. Whew! Do not know if I am to be the only guest. So many of our men have become good friends with various of these people, and often half are absent from the evening meals at our mess. It has been quite fascinating to hear of the very nice friendships that have developed. Monsieur Baudin has mentioned that our men have gained the high respect of the people of Foug.

It just seems to me that the people of France, in general, just let the vigor of their heritage slip into one of weakness, with inability to respond effectively to the challenge of nearby powers hostile to democratic processes. I just hope that we of the U.S. will take note of this and make certain that we do not under any circumstances permit the strengths of our heritage to be in any ways lessened. I fear that the percentage of voters who cast ballots in our elections, generally, may be indication of mounting problems in future. We ought to have a minimum of 80% of voters participate in each election—local, state, and national. Ha! I sense a long lecture coming up.

March 29, 1945 France (Foug)

Am finally feeling much better—back to normal, more or less. I am still of the opinion that it was a bug which caused my problem; but, no other victim could be found. Can always blame it on the mirabelle.

News from the German front is almost delightful—with some seven Allied armies running rampant over much of what is left of the Nazi realm. We hear much about Patton, but the news is virtually of "black out nature"—perhaps to keep Hitler's generals "in the dark." Who knows?

This getting up shortly after six o'clock each morning does not bother me, but I am so tired of having to put up with the over-bearing presence of and caustic slurs from our CO. He and others of his ilk had better stay in the army when this war is over, for they will find it difficult in public to meet people "on even ground." They get along because they have brass and silver on their shoulders . Our poor company has had our one big millstone hanging around its neck since its personnel were assigned.

You seem quite intrigued by my reference to mirabelle—this is a brandy which comes from a sort of plum juice, and about three thimblefuls of it will send one reeling. As yet, I don't care much for it, and I'm not fond of the champagne, for some of it tastes something like soda water. I'm certain that I am insulting the entire nation of France! Most of the "liqueurs" I like—Benedictine, Zinzano, etc.; and, their sweet wines are nice—ports, Madeira, etc. I much like their "vin rouge ordinaire"—the regular red table wine. It is a bit sour and just goes so well with most of the food—particularly red meat. The white "table wines" go well with all foul and with ham. I think this is somewhat as it is.

We have just heard that FDR has instructed all diplomats to remain at their posts 24 hours each day. Of course, we are all atwitter and guessing as to what is stirring.

This "Post-Hostility Program" is to offer classes of all sorts to our military personnel who await return to the U.S. Credits for the courses will be applicable toward gaining a high school diploma, or may be applicable for college credit. Having taught two years at Oshkosh and with my M.A., my application may find favor. I do not know. As for riding out this war, this is a good place to do it, for I can find no nicer people to be with than here in (Foug).

March 31, 1945 France (Foug)

Have been able to sneak in an extra hour of sleep each night, and it is improving my disposition. Also, I am making certain that I avoid certain foods. Our cooks do a fine job of it, but they do like to fry, and fry, and fry.

Rumors are a dime a dozen. We hear so often references to our Allied generals—Patton, Patch, Bradley, Hodges, Montgomery, et al. Seems to me that we may see end to this European struggle as early as June.

As our units advance into Germany, new field hospitals are set up and many accompanying advance stations. We must be issuing much of the materials, the materiel, needed, for we are very comfortably busy. Many of the truckers who come for these supplies are now driving considerable distances.

Madame Baudin and Jean-Francois have gone to visit her parents who live in a town not far from (Reims). She has gone for the Easter holiday. So, until her return, we will not have any of those marvelous feasts. Ha!

So many of the French are now returning from their long sojourns in German prisons and labor camps. Many of the accounts I have heard are somewhat pathetic, but the endings now have the awaited happiness. One of the men who works at the foundry, here, had a telephone call from his son who had been with the Maquis for at least two years. This son had been injured and suffered loss of a leg, and had been in a hospital in south-central France since last August or September. He was to arrive by train at (Nancy), and his father asked if one of our vehicles could take him to meet his son. This young man returned home, yesterday, and there was much rejoicing. Again, we had opportunity to strengthen much our relationship with the people of this town.

One of our men has just received a commission, as 2d lieutenant. He is a skilled engineer by profession, and should never have been assigned to a medical supply company. But, this is the army, I guess. He submitted his application seven months ago, and I helped him put his papers in order. He requested that I "administer the oath." This I did, told him he had paid me a great honor, and gave him a vigorous French hug.

This is the closing day for the hunting season, and Baudin wanted me to go. But, my schedule was just too full to break away. The weather is great, I shall be taking a shower this afternoon, and we shall have a contest at bridge this evening. And, tomorrow is Easter. Col. Cole, Charley, I, and two or three of the men may head to a nearby hospital which has for its chaplain an Episcopal minister. We shall take communion, of course. As for me, I am so very thankful for so much!

April 3, 1945 France (Foug)

Some of us did make it to a communion service Easter morning, the 1st, and it was held in a hotel dining room. With all the kneeling, the hard floor was just a bit rough on our knees. We were about fifteen minutes late to arrive, for the announcement we had received referred to a different hotel. The chaplain paused when we arrived, and then proceeded with the service. Others were late. His homily was appropriate, and he was an effective speaker.

Easter is a time for family gatherings here in France, I think. Madame Queney had Monsieur Baudin, Monique, and me at the table for Sunday evening, and we had a jolly, good time. I took some bottles of this and that, but they came up with good stuff stored away somewhere—even some champagne not of our supply. Then, yesterday noon, Stroh and I had a noon feast with the Ravaults, and it was to be a humdinger of a good time. Stroh had told me that he would furnish most of the bottled goods, and many of the bottles had the marking stamped on them, that they were reserved for the WEHRMACHT. Our French friends get a real charge from these labels—for the Germans had looted it all from the French, we Americans had rousted the Germans from the warehouse in Pantin with such speed that it was left for us, and now, from the Americans, the French were getting it returned to them. Well, we do have many a good laugh over review of these circumstances.

The biggest party of all was last evening at Chenot's. Several of his relatives are here, and Charley and I, along with Monsieur Baudin and Monique, joined in on all the fun, feasting, and frolicking. Chenot and Baudin enjoy cigars, and Charley and I always have an ample supply "in pockets" for an evening, or for whatever is to be on the docket. Nearly everyone smokes cigarettes,, and we come well stocked with packages galore—saved up from our rations. This turned into quite an evening—one that lasted until nearly four in the morning. I was often at the piano, and we made valiant attempts to sing whatever songs came to mind.

Chenot's cousins were right in the middle of it all, and his niece, Ann Marie Brun, is from Paris. Am not sure as to where all the food had been stored away, but we just kept stuffing it in. Charley and I had seen to it that no shortages of liqueurs and champagne were to arise. Larry Ryley was also with us, and he and Baudin repeatedly challenged each other at chess. And, occasionally, when the spirit so moved us, we attempted to dance. These people do get such a kick from their "celebrations," and they do make it so evident that they enjoy our presence. Chenot, now, always refers to me as "Mon cher cousin," and we must often drink toasts to someone or to something—every few minutes. Charley and I have learned to pace ourselves, and we ride out the storm pretty well. Before we went over to Chenot's, Monsieur Baudin told me of two French expressions which fit very well what we Americans refer to as a "hangover"—"mal aux cheveux" and "gueule de bois." The first translates into something like "aching hair" and the second into "mouth of wood." Am sort of under an impression that Ryley and Baudin may have imbibed "un peu trop." Oh, well!

Mail arrives somewhat out of order, but a letter slips in quite often within just a week after posting. As for my letters, it is not clear to me that "V-mail" is any better than airmail. Have you an opinion? Do not understand it, but we are, as yet, not to mention places that disclose unit locations. And, it has been raining, but spirits have not been dampened.

April 7, 1945 France (Foug)

My "Newsweek" magazine arrives nearly always just three weeks after issue. Sort of interesting to note.

My OD duty comes around regularly, and it usually means that I get little sleep. A couple nights ago was sort of an exception. Made my rounds about eleven, and then went to sleep and didn't awaken until about 6:45. Nothing was stirring to interrupt my snoozing.

Our POWs, those who clean up this old station and our office, keep their ears open for news about the war. They desire, I think, for the end to come soon, for it would mean for them a quicker return home. One of them asked us, using his best English, if we thought the end would come soon. We agreed that it would be several weeks, yet, for Hitler would never surrender until he had no more place to hide. These men regularly and efficiently do their work and cause us no concern; but, it seems to me, they have become quite downhearted—with so much of the reporting to deal with the bombings of cities. Only one or two understand much English, but they do catch the names of cities.

We have heard more and more of the abuses of prisoners held in Germany. My understanding is that prisoners under the custody of the German military were treated according to the Geneva Convention. The prisoners who were mistreated were those who had fallen into the hands of ardent Nazis. These Nazi fanatics may be no better than their counterparts in the Pacific, the Japanese to be referred to as "little Yellow Bellies."

Spring has really sprung, here, and some of the fruit trees are in full bloom—to appear to be gigantic snow balls. It would be nice to be around to share in the fresh fruit, but heaven forbid that we be here until then.

Monsieur Baudin, Monique, and I were at Chenot's for supper last night. Charley was there, of course, and several of Monsieur Chenot's relatives. It was a party par excellence, again, and we did not quit the fun until after one o'clock. Whew! They just seem to think that Charley and I are "members of the family."

Prospects have become quite certain that I shall be going to Paris to attend instruction for this "post-hostility" teaching. This has to do with "Information and Education," and it falls to me to go. It may be that we who attend these classes in Paris are to return to our units and lead the discussions which are to treat of the problems to arise from return to civilian life. My application to transfer may be of no avail. We shall see. But, I shall be in Paris again, and on some sort of "duty." I hope I can stay with the Rivets, but I know we shall have quarters and meals provided.

April 9, 1945 France (Foug)

Seems that my trip to Paris is assured, and it will be a great pleasure to see the Rivets, Billots, Scheys, Lurquins, and maybe some of the office workers at the depot. I just do not know what my schedule will be at the school.

Some bright and very nice days, here, and I have done some strolling about and have sort of thought through some matters—some of which you have asked about. Hit my office typewriter last evening and batted out quite a dissertation—much too long, but am sending it. Then, I revised it, and this is the shortened version. Have fun reading both. Ho! Ho!

◆ ◆ ◆

From the beginning, it has been my intent never to become embittered about anything that might happen. It has been a struggle, and the only way one can manage is to be ever mindful of his luck and good fortune. Members of this man's army become "bitter" for many reasons.

Promotion is a bug-bear and at the bottom of much bitterness. Every man, with any self-pride, wants to be promoted. Some will stoop to the bottom of the gutter, and we call it "ass-kissing," to get their promotions. Most, I believe, try their level best to do their jobs well—knowing that sooner or later their efforts will become recognized. However, one may find himself to be out on a limb.

We all know what a Table of Organization is. When it is filled, there is no chance for further promotion, unless a person of higher rank departs. Capable individuals will remain static in their grades for months, and it makes no difference as to the quality of their work. For many this may become source of discontent, etc. But, advancement in rank in the army often is not based on efficiency. Too often, favoritism and being a "yes man" enter the picture, and a unit's "politics" can be the determining factor. Have a hunch that these factors do not exist in the extreme in the field units—infantry, artillery, etc.; but they do seem to run rampant throughout the service units, and particularly those in the rear echelons. It is rather sickening, if the scuttlebutt has any truth behind it.

Many of our commanding officers are "rank conscious" and inclined to conceit. There is nothing quite to compare to stupidity which arises from conceit. Such as this becomes dulling, disgusting, and even nauseating. Some of these "uppers" seem to lose contact with the common soldier and with the officer of low rank. Situations can become sad, and it is here that we see how undemocratic our military system is. Such can give the enlisted man a wrong slant on that which he thinks he is fighting for, and many soldiers conclude that many officers are incompetent and often in positions of control. Low morale within a company will soon spell trouble.

Those of us who are in the rear echelons need to remind ourselves of what the fellows at the front have gone through, are going through, and will go through. We should not become embittered because of our present status, for we will most certainly return from this war with little blemish to mind or body. We need to be mindful of the thousands and thousands who will not return at all.

A cause for bitterness arises because of the "4-Fs." It is a sort of human frailty to be suspicious of people who are not present. Each of us has heard of this person and of that person who managed to keep out of the service because of this, that, or something else. We easily fall prey to hocus-pocus and deceit. The salaries that people are receiving back home sound very large when compared to the salary of the soldier, and it may seem that the fruits of war go to those not "in service." It is the soldier who wins a war. This entire matter can become very touchy, and much so if we believe this world or ours has become "money mad"!

This is more a war of production than most of us are prone to realize. A man can be as much a "warrior" on the assembly line as he is in a service unit over here. His work on the assembly line is almost as important as if he were over here using the weapon. The weapon must be perfect, good, and better than that of the enemy; if not, the man who is using it is fighting under a terrible handicap. And, we say this is "total war"—our way of life against that of the Nazi or the Jap. Our American system is being tried on an international battleground, and this war is far more than a test of gallantry to kill or to die trying. When the final whistle is blown, we Americans want to have proved that no other nation, no matter the extent of its head start, has been able to defeat us.

The thorn in the side is there, nevertheless, for those who see others in the luxurious positions back home, and the whirlpool of discontent swirls the more. When one is in the army, he loses most of his civilian rights. No matter what service one enters, he likes to think he is still somewhat of a civilian. But, he soon learns there are hundreds of "things" to remind him, daily, that he is not. Often, the lot which puts one man in the army and retains another in a position in industry may seem almost negligible; yet, the results are vastly different. A soldier's or an officer's rights in the army are quite outside those of the civilian. All of these regulations of the army are necessary to maintain discipline, assure action, and preserve unity. We all know it, we know it is a must, and we know that because of it our armies are winning this war. This seems to be well and good, and a bitterness is part of the picture.

We say this is "total war"—for the member of the armed forces and for the man who remains behind in industry. The man who remains behind squawks loud and long at the slightest implication that the government will regulate his activities "on his job," and he then demands that the government regulate prices and hours. But, how about salaries and wages? In many respects, should the government act decisively and vigorously, the howling and the protest mount. The soldier is in this war to win it, and there is virtually no chance that he will become enriched from any spoils, and he is even restricted from gathering for his own "collection" most of what he may find once an enemy has been driven from the battlefields and vicinities. At home, labor has retained the right to strike, and such action in any of our armed services would be called "mutiny"—and with a conviction possibly to bring a death sentence. Our factory worker may be late to work or decide to take "a day off"—but not sufficiently ill to stay home from the seashore or to have an afternoon for golf. Your soldier, were he to engage in such absenteeism, would be declared AWOL—with probable consequence of fine or restriction . The civilian is not frozen to his job as is the soldier. The risk to life and limb lies decisively with the soldier. There are many other comparisons and contrasts that could be noted. And, I have quite a bungled picture here of what turns round and round in a soldier's mind.

Well, I'm sure that our American public is fully conscious of the fact that there is a war on. I also believe that no person or groups of people should realize immense profits from this war. That this has become part of our picture is about the only "thing" that gives me any inclination to become more than just mildly unhappy. When I think of the conditions that many of these men have had to live under, to suffer because of, and then to die from, I become somewhat infuriated because of the underlying stupidity of it all. I also have a hunch that many of our people have not been fair with our men in the services, and that many of our people back home just do not know what "total war" is all about. Just ask those who have lost husband, son, brother, cousin, uncle,, or nephew. These can tell you what "total war" means.

Each service in our armed forces—Army, Navy, Marine Corps, Coast Guard, and Air Corps—has good reason to feel its branch to be superior. That is as it should be. We judge others on bases of our own individual skills and specialties. Some of our services will always lack the "glory" that may come from the battlefield. It is so often as in the case of the football team, for it is the ball-carrier who is usually hailed as the hero—not the tackle or the guard who opened the hole for him.

Yes, despite all the bungling and abuses of favoritism, we are close to victory. We are achieving a goal which not too long ago seemed beyond reach. We have been certain that right was on our side, and we have kept the course. And, I have had a good time in this bit of rambling. Even our weather agrees with my sunny disposition. But, we all want "to come home"!!

April 13, 1945 France (Foug)

Was over to Guebourg's last evening, for supper and just lots of fun. They are the darndest family one could know—not only to gather about the piano and sing, but to crawl through the broomstick, to crawl under the broomstick, to play every card trick known to man, and always to make their guests feel welcome. Claude wants me to show him through the depot. Was to my room shortly before midnight, and straight to bed.

Was up this morning at the usual time, and descended the stairs to go to the mess hall for breakfast. Baudin met me at the foot of the stairway and asked a question: "Qui est Truman?" My reply: "Il est Vice President des Etats Unis." He said: "Non. Il est President. Roosevelt est mort!" This is how I learned of the death of Franklin Roosevelt.

So, our flag is flying at half-mast. Charley had heard the news about midnight—over his radio.

We met at the breakfast table, and neither had much appetite. In some of our company sessions I had referred to reports about F.D.R.'s increasingly delicate health; but, we were stunned, nevertheless. He was never a favorite of our family, with so many of his domestic policies seeming to smack often of governmental over-reach into the traditional relationships of our citizenry—particular economic and social. Many may have condemned him for his domestic policies, but he became one of the greatest of our historic personages in the area of foreign policy and action. In this respect, he became magnificent. Harry Truman now has the extreme difficulty of stepping into the shoes of one of our strongest presidents, and I do not envy him—his task.

Six other of our vice presidents succeeded to the presidency in this way. The records of their presidencies have not been unkind. Theodore Roosevelt is the stand out. Franklin Roosevelt's influence may be greater, now that he is gone, and I think of the role which the U.S.A. must play in international affairs.

The beauty of our system of government is shown right here and now, and our effort in this war will suffer no interruption. We have just changed captains of our ship. Our "ship of state" will not alter its course, even though the heart of its crew is greatly saddened. Yes, one president has died, and his successor was "sworn in" within a few hours.

Roosevelt's influence internationally has been so extensive, and he seems to have symbolized many of the hopes and prayers of the downtrodden of this world. For so many, he personified the United States and seemed to become more than an individual. The coming conference at San Francisco will surely disclose the reach of his ideas. Stettinius is fully aware of these aspirations, and my guess is that Truman will not attempt to be a "foreground figure." Henry Wallace needed to be replaced, and I think there may well have been a "guiding wisdom" which turned the Democrats to this man from Missouri—yea, even a senator. The Republicans muffed their chance when they turned their backs on Willkie. I shall not be surprised should events prove the Democrats have focused their eyes upon a person of strength—perhaps yet to be revealed.

Am to head to the Ravault's—for good food, ping pong, more bridge, and another late hour.

April 14, 1945 France (Foug)

Am still pondering the impact of Roosevelt's death. Truman will make a solidly good president—of this I am confident. F.D.R.'s influence may be more far-reaching in death than had he continued to live. Our nation will not falter. Our constitutional succession discloses some of the beauty of our system, of our "way of life." Our role in foreign affairs will be vital, and we must not falter as we did after World War I.

I have become almost haunted by the awesome loss of life from this current war—all to have come from the predatory ambitions of Hitler, Mussolini, and their Japanese counterparts. A few days ago I copied this poem—from "Yank" or from "Stars and Stripes"—?? And I keep thinking of Merlin Stackhouse, Bob Duncan and Ralph Johnson, and of their mothers—Jennie, Stella and Lida K.

REMEMBER

We have a right to be heard,
For we are the grim price of freedom—
The best a country could give.
We were the young of America—
The hope of a strong, free future.
We need to be much more than a number,
A yellow telegram from the War Department.
But we don't want your tears or monuments,
Your thanks or pity.
We had a job to do, an expensive payment
To be made on the long-standing obligation
We owed to you, America.
A debt we paid with the most precious
Possession we had, Life.
Remember.

We were your youth,
The young in mind, body and spirit,
The youth of whom you despaired,
The wastrel, the decadent, the soft.
Have we not redeemed ourselves?
We hated war with a holy hate.
We loved, instead, rattling cars
Straight, hard roads to drive on
Sunday afternoons,
Football games and chrysanthemums,
High school proms and hired dress suits,
Beach parties and picnics in the fields,
Hunting trips with the frosty grass crumbling
Beneath the padded feet of a yipping dog,
The moonlight nights in a crazy roadster
With a girl with whom we made so many plans,

The quiet dignity of a job, and the opportunity
To make our way in the world,
The graciousness of a Sunday dinner
After church with the family's best silverware
Shining proudly on the white linen tablecloth,
The long talks with Dad on an Autumn evening.
All these, America, we sought of you.
You gave them gladly, for we were young,
So very young.
Remember.

We were the young, on whose shoulders fell
The terrible burden of a nation unprepared,
Unprepared for the grim reckoning of War—
Knowing and loving only peace,
But unable to have it without fighting.
We were the young men at the stations—
Thousands of us, planning on only a year,
A year of youth, to be given to the art of killing,
The first payment on a note falling due.
We were the young, raw men in a hundred camps
And naval stations throwing off civilian ways
For the military uniforms we were to wear.
We were the young, and we first felt war
In only its simulated role, that's true—
But, first knew the deadly figure of the doomed—
The world apart, from which there was no escaping
Except in death.
Remember.

We were the young who first embarked
And landed in the enemy-infested Solomons;
Who fell in Guadalcanal and Tulagi;
Who met the steaming, stinking, stalking

Jungles of Rendova, New Britain, and Bouganville;
Who fell in the murderous cross-fire at Tarawa;
Who did not even reach the land, but had
Our bodies washed ashore by the gentle waves.
We fought and fell at Eniwetok, Tinian,
Saipan, Palau; and always it was the same
Inexorable pattern of death for some
That many might live.
We paid the price in blessed life—
A dreadful price.
Remember.

We were the young men at Casablanca,
Tunisia, Sicily, Salerno, and Naples.
The only difference in the manifest was the time and
Place, and place meant nothing as long
As it was not home—America.
We stormed the beaches of France,
Stalked and were stalked in the hedgerows of Normandy,
Bled the caked roads red to St. Lo
And fought to the very gates of Germany.
There we shunted warm and living flesh and blood
Against the cold repelling steel of War.
Some shall break through, take the long road home.
We shall never, never move again,
For we are the dead; and though few hours ago
We lived, and loved and planned for life,
We are the dead.
Remember.

You say the use of past tense is harsh to hear,
Harsh with a finality that knows no recall.
We do not wish it so;
But, it must be, and does it not remind you of

>   The sonorous intoning of some dry professor—
>   "Quod Erat Demonstratum,"
>   That which has been demonstrated.
>   There is no more, the end has come for us, and
>   There is no hope or thought of returning.
>   We know we can't, and know not that we can be heard.
>   But, we have fought and given the last full measure
>   Of life. We loved it very much.
>   We loved you more, America.
>   For we were your young, America—
>   But we are your dead.
>   Remember.

It may have been submitted anonymously.

April 17, 1945 France (Foug)

You might send me a good shipment of popcorn, and this about all that I need. Everything else I can get at our PX.

Finally broke down and sent my little radio into a Signal Corps shop. It has not played, except to warm up and then click off, since we were in Normandy at Trevieres.

Had our barber give me a good clipping—quite short, again. The weather is warming up rapidly. So, I now should have a cooler head. Oh, well!

Listened to Truman's speech last evening and was not disappointed. He is not the speaker Roosevelt was, but he comes across as honest and sincere. He is going to be a stabilizing influence, and I think the "fates" have been kind to us.

A report is circulating that German resistance is expected to collapse in less than 72 hours. This is, as I look at the picture, just somebody's talking through his hat. My guess is that Roosevelt's death will spur Hitler and his Nazi gang to attempt to hold a line, in hope that Truman will be more willing to agree to some sort of compromise. They will find that our little friend from Missouri will press on for nothing else but total surrender—no strings attached.

April 22, 1945 France (Foug)

Was again at the Guebourg's evening before last, and what a time we had—playing the piano, singing, crawling under the broomstick, and acting silly. For a chubby little women, Madame G. has more energy that she can exhaust. Ha! She brought out canned cherries, plums, and gooseberries—always so many good things to eat. I keep giving her the dickens because she insists on using their stored-up good things to feed me, but she and Monsieur just laugh and shrug their shoulders.

Maitre Baudin has been down with this flu bug. So, I took over and prescribed the same as for Monique. He seems to be recovered and he is due to go to Paris. He has legal work to do and is not certain about his schedule and place to stay. I am to go and will stay at the Rivets. He will leave message via telephone with Madame Rivet as to his locale. I am eager for Baudin and Rivet to meet each other. They are not at all alike, however.

Had to chuckle at what Col. Cole said to me. He said he was sure the office could get along without me, that I should not worry, and that I should enjoy my return to Paris for this week of special classes. He knows as well as I that those men in our records office are a most capable and reliable group, just tops; but, he may have been telling me that I had become a sort of unneeded fixture. Oh, well! He is also going to Paris, and we will travel by our command car.

My little radio is working again, but it is now on batteries. It runs well at night, but gets good reception only with a long antenna or an aerial. It may be on its last legs, for its tubes are weak, and we have none to make replacements.

Yes, we seem to be doing a log of "swigging"; but, we, and I can speak for Charley and me, try to make it "sipping." These hosts of ours must think that they are negligent if they permit our glasses to become half empty. Then, I conclude that it is an insult to fail to drain your glass when the meal is over.

I am scribbling this at 1:40 a.m., this Sunday morning. Madame Baudin's father and brother had arrived, and they insisted that I join them for the evening repast, etc. Everything was as to be expected—such good food and such good "sipping"—mirabelle, marc, cognac, Benedictine, and champagne. As you may guess, much of the good nectar had come from our special "German supply." Monsieur

Baudin has two younger brothers, and a cousin, who became POWs and to be held in Germany. With no word from them for many months, and even years—in one brother's case, Baudin had feared they might be dead. We had some rather serious conversation, from time to time. One recurring theme was that the Americans had "saved" France. We did much toasting. I learned at the table that Baudins have a little cabin in the adjoining woods—not very far from town.

Have done my packing, must get some shut eye, and departure for Paris is this morning.

April 24, 1945 Paris

Here I am, going to school for a week at the Cité Universitaire. Rivets live just thirty minutes away if to walk, and about five minutes if to take the Metro. After this afternoon's session, am to meet Monsieur Baudin, Monsieur Lurquin and Monsieur Rivet—at the latter's office. Then, Baudin and Lurquin and I are to go to Lurquin's for dinner.

Paris is beautiful. The horse chestnut trees are fully leaved out. The city seems to have recovered nearly its normal life.

We arrived in Paris about 4:30 Sunday afternoon, and the Rivets were waiting for me. I'm tucked away in a nice small bedroom, and it is such a nice break to be away from the depot and in this lovely home.

April 26, 1945

Classes were finished yesterday at 12:30. So, I took the Metro to Pantin to see our old office gang. These women just about embraced me to death—French style! One of the ladies has gained her American citizenship, and will be going to New York as soon as passage, etc., can be arranged and her "papers" gathered and put into proper order. My guess is that it will take several months. Two daughters live in New York, and she has three other children who live in the Paris area.

Last evening, Baudin and I had dinner at the Lurquins, and we just kept visiting, etc., until after midnight. Well, the last Metro had passed, and I had to walk across town to the Rivet's, and it took me nearly two hours. Howzabout that!

Prices are just outrageous. I want to buy a chess set, but a good set of wood comes to no less than about $500. As yet, I find only plastic ones within my price range. Ha! But, Monsieur Lurquin is certain that we can fine a set for my choosing, at reasonable price, in some small shop on a side street. We shall see.

Some of us are having dinner together out in Pantin, and I will not be missing the Metro, this time. The "gals" at the office just insisted we must have a meal to celebrate our reunion. So, I shall see what it is to be all about. My hunch is that it is going to be a sort of "cover dish affair." Will just have to see.

April 29, 1945

Have had opportunity to visit a bit more with Lurquins and much with the Rivets. They have told me much about some of the problems the people had while living in the city under the German occupation. Paris, in contrast to so many of the cities in western Europe, experienced little damage. They think that the Germans expected to make Paris the administrative center of their new realm. The two or three aerial bombs which stuck the city on December 16 did not do extensive destruction. It is a beautiful city, and the scars of war, such as they were, have been almost completely removed. Monsieur Rivet, with a grin, keeps calling me, "Mon Cher Liberateur." But, what has not been pleasant to hear are the accounts related by the men who are returning from imprisonment in Germany. Those who survived the atrocities, experienced in Germany, have not been reluctant to give some gruesome details. Treatment of the French was, as I understand, somewhat in contrast to that meted out to the English and Americans. Monsieur Baudin is very anxious about his two brothers and his cousin.

Had brought a package of tea with me for Madame Rivet. She is very fond of tea, and was much pleased. Then I really got into trouble, for I bought a dozen pink carnations for her, and she just gave me a good scolding. I just laughed at her and told her that American officers were never to be assaulted, verbally or otherwise, by the French. She just shook her finger at me. We had quite a standoff. Ho! Ho!

These Education-Information classes we have been having are designed to instruct regarding the procedures whereby our men may take courses to complete studies to gain high school diplomas or to gain college credits. Also, there is the purpose to engage in discussions which will help prepare the men to set aside their "military thinking" and to become some what "demilitarized"—to turn their eyes and minds to civilian responsibilities.

Have purchased several sets of ear rings—boucles d'oreille. They are plastic, but the darned prices are so high. They will be strictly Parisienne for your American ears. I shall be sending them as soon as I return to (Foug), and some of them will be going to Boston.

The Scheys were out of the city, and their return was just in time for us to have a brief visit. Then, I have also had a good, but short, visit with Anne Marie Brun, Chenot's younger cousin. She lives in Pantin, and when she last visited Monsieur Chenot, Charley and I were able to "spirit away" about a couple pecks of potatoes for her to bring home. It was nice to see her. She hopes to return to (Foug) before our departure—which could be fairly soon, maybe.

The French municipalities are holding their first elections for about nine years, and women are voting for the first time—in the history of the nation. Do so hope that their governments which emerge will become far more effective and much less cumbersome than before the war.

Too, we keep hearing rumors about some sort of "redoubt" Hitler and the remaining Nazis are putting together—hoping to make a final assault to be too costly to attempt. We shall see, eh? And, I shall write when back to the depot.

May 1, 1945 France (Foug)

Am now back on the job. Arrived, here, yesterday about eight in the morning. By train from Paris to (Toul), and had to wait for two and half hours for transportation to come from the company to get me—less than ten miles. Everything was just humming along in fine shape, here, and I do not think they missed or needed me much. Ha!

To an extent, I was not ready to return. The Rivets were just simply grand hosts, and they spoiled me almost stinky—Monsieur, Madame, Nicole, and Jean-Pierre. Had kept secreted in my luggage another carton of cigarettes and a bottle each of Vielle Cure and Benedictine. These are just out of reach on the black market for all except the wealthiest. Monsieur Rivet was certain that I had purchased the stuff, and he insisted he pay me for them. As for the carnations, he and Madame took me to task for being "trop gentil!"—"too nice!"

In the compartment of the passenger car on the train, class "1" coach, were riding two French officers, probably on the younger side of middle aged. They had been imprisoned, recently liberated, and after many days for medical treatment released to return to their homes. They spoke no English, but I'm certain they had been prisoners since 1940. One of them appeared to have been worn to a frazzle and not well, actually. They said that as military prisoners they had received much better treatment than those persons who had attempted escape from the labor draft or who had fallen prey to German occupation and had engaged in activities of the Maquis and F.F.I.

Monsieur Baudin, on his return from Paris, had passed by Epernay to visit his parents, and on the previous train one of his brothers had just arrived—had been a prisoner of war since 1940. Of course, there had been much rejoicing. There remains one brother and a brother-in-law, I think, yet to return.

In Paris, the day before I left, Madame Rivet had received some particularly saddening news, moreso because of the circumstances. Prisoners, liberated by advancing American forces, marched when able to repatriation centers. To make certain that American pilots, flying overhead, would know they were released prisoners, they waved white handkerchiefs or towels. Well, German snipers were cowering in the woods along the way, and they would fire into the columns of the returning men. Madame Rivet's cousin was one of the several killed by these snipers, and this made it all the more difficult. But, as Monsieur Rivet summed it up: "C'est la guerre!"—"This is what war is all about!"

Had about fifty letters waiting for me, and what a time to get them read. Now, I am so far behind with my correspondence.

One of Baudin's favorite ditties is this little song—J' ai du bon tabac
        Dans ma tabatière,
        J' ai du bon tabac,
        Tu n' en auras pas.
        J' en ai du fin at du rape
        Le ne sera pas pour ton vilain nez!
        J' ai du bon tabac
        Dan ma tabatière,
        J' ai du bon tabac,
        Tu n' en auras pas.

What it adds up to is this, that the fellow has some very good tabacco in his tobacco can or box, and his friend will not get any of it. It has been very finely ground, but it is not to be for his friend's naughty nose. My guess is that we may be chanting about snuff, here. Oh, well!

Another rumor that the war has officially ended, but not yet. Will soon be heading for a good shower, and I need one, for had been just sponging off now and then. Ha! Also, the two quarts of popcorn had arrived, along with the Nestle's, etc. Thanks to you, we shall be having some extra treats, here and there.

May 3, 1945 France (Foug)

Monsieur Baudin's other brother has finally returned from Germany. He will be coming, Friday, with his wife and two sons. He had never seen the younger boy. Friday is also the Fete of Ste. Monique on the Catholic calendar. So, Friday we are going to have a double celebration, and Teague and Stroh have also been invited. Others will be on the guest list. Hunch is that this double celebration will surpass anything we have had. It is going to be joyous!

It has been unusually cold—with some intermittent snow, sleet, rain and drizzle, and sunshine. And, despite the somber weather, this happy little poem appeared recently:

> 'Twas in a restaurant they met,
> Romeo and Juliet.
> He had no money to pay the bill;
> So, Romeowed what Julie et.

I am sure you have been listening to the news. This surrender in northern Italy of more than a million Italian and German troops is the greatest such submission in the history of the world. And, Mussolini met his somewhat fitting end—to be strung up by his feet, as if no better than a butchered pig with its throat slit. We are a bit suspicious of the news as first released via the German sources; but, so many German generals are now throwing in their towels, and Hitler and Goebbels have supposedly committed suicide. I guess the "Chancellory" is no longer defended... Rumor is that the last of Germany's force have been used to slow the Russians.

Had about an extra forty-five minutes of snoozing this morning—didn't even go for breakfast. Col. Cole has not returned from Paris, and we are taking a few "things" a bit easier. Some of us are guessing that he is confabbing with some old cronies, maybe, in effort to get support for promotion to a full colonelcy. He doesn't deserve it. We should have been much better off without him. Oh, well! I slept late and didn't even hit our mess hall for breakfast. The Colonel nearly always counted noses to make certain we were all on deck and ready to go.

May 4, 1945 France (Foug)

News of the en mass surrender of Germans to the British at Hamburg was very encouraging.

The conference in San Francisco is of the utmost importance, and there will be much nudging and bargaining. This may well prove to be the "peace conference" which will set the balance of things for the future. Americans need to realize the great extent to which the people of Great Britain contributed to the defeat of Germany. To be sure, there were shortcomings, but we had our share. The British suffered much loss of cities and properties from bombardents—in contrast to our complete escape. The Russians, too, have grounds to expect much compensation—and security of their borders. Their creation of the Lublin government in Poland is a scheme to push far to the west their controls, etc. When compromise in future is to be the eventual outcome of the bargaining, then one must make the utmost claims if there is to be an acceptable drawing of lines for what is to be a somewhat just product of the give and take. Too often our so-called "great patriots" fail to see beyond the tips of their noses.

Our U.S.A. will need to be more than a little gracious, perhaps. For some sort of a workable international assembly and tribunal, we may need to grant the Soviet Union its three votes and the British Commonwealth of nations its six. Our single vote must shine all the brighter and ring forth the clearer, and our voice should be heard from the very pinnacle of this new structure. We, as a people, shirked our responsibilities after World War I, and there was no chance for any sort of enduring peace. Now, we must make our weight felt—and from our "united" and singular position. Franklin Roosevelt had, in so many respects, become the symbol, the hope, the inspiration of the peoples of the occupied nations. Churchill was marvelously defiant, but the outreach of his influence was not equal to that of Roosevelt. Stalin lacked even a semblance of that personal touch which could reach forth to warm the hearts of suppressed peoples, and his own regime permitted so little room for any expression of individualism—so central to our American heritage.

Yes, many of our political aspirants are so ready to cry "Wolf!" and to point their fingers at Great Britain or the Soviet Union. They are of the same ilk as those who manipulated the putting of Wendell Willkie on the shelf. I have a hunch that Harry Truman is going to emerge as one of the greater political surprises in our history, maybe to approach that of Abraham Lincoln. We, as a nation, must not falter in this opportunity to offer the world a chance for an enduring peace—which, at its best, is going to be relentlessly challenged by political leaders, here and there, who are motived by the material selfishnesses of their personal aspirations. These leaders surround themselves by others who seek their own larger slices of the pie. I guess I am still young enough to have hope—not shallow, but of depth.

Did I tell you I had nearly 50 letters waiting for me when I returned from my week in Paris? Now, I must again engage in the game of "Catch Up." And, this evening a big party is in the offing at the Baudins. Monsieur Baudin's other brother, also just returned after more than four years of being a POW in Germany, is coming from Epernay—with his wife and two sons, the younger whom he had not seen. Also, on the Catholic calendar, today is Ste. Monique's Day, and a day for a special fete for Monique. Oh, these French do enjoy having a big party.

May 6, 1945

Just had a hair cut, and I was looking a bit shaggy.

Must give you the info about our big party evening before last. Charley and Stroh were invited to join in the celebration. I had put three bottles of champagne in the refrigerator and had added a bottle of Porto and a bottle of Grand Marnier Orange Liqueur. Charley brought three or four bottles to add to the store. Of course, Maitre Baudin had tapped some of his hidden reserves. A few other guests were on hand. It all began about 8:00, with hors d'oeuvres served in the office and hallway of first floor—with many "toasts" and much lifting and sipping from glasses of champagne. Then, upstairs to the dining room.

The dining table had been extended and stretched nearly from wall to wall. It was an eight-course repast, at least, and continued through three desserts. Jean-Francois went to sleep in his high chair, and his mother put him to bed. The two boys held out until well after midnight and then went to sleep on a couch in the dining room—actually Monique's bed, for she had given her room to one Lt. Mickey when he arrived in (Foug).

Baudin"s brother was quite frail in appearance, very thin, and spoke slowly. He had lost about half his weight during his years as POW, and had regained several pounds. I was enthralled as he gave us certain details. He spoke clearly, and to the degree that I ceased to translate and was absorbed into the French language. When I realized that for more than an hour I had forgotten the English language, it sent a chill up and down my spine.

This man was not imprisoned at Dachau or Buchenwald. He spoke of the problems to arise because of lice and vermin. With no heat for the barracks, the prisoners bundled together in winter for warmth. They were fed regularly and were not physically abused. Each morning, guards entered the barracks, called all to attention—with arms extended. Should one not be able to stand, he was simply dragged out and thrown bodily onto a pile of deceased persons, etc.

The final morning, the day of the arrival of the Americans to free the camp, a guard gave the order to stand in line at attention, but he did not give the order to extend arms. This brother was too weak to rise from his bed, and his friends lifted him to his feet and held him. The guard was anxious and hurried, but he did warn them not to look out of the windows, or they would be shot. The guard left, slamming shut the door. Soon to follow was the sound of many motors and much activity and movement, with lots of shouting. Then silence!

He guessed that an hour passed, and then more motors and some shouting. The door to the barracks was virtually kicked open, and a "giant" stepped in, looked around, and departed. Within a few minutes, some American soldiers came in with litters, and checked the men and then carried those in the most feeble conditions to awaiting ambulances. This brother was taken to a nearby field hospital, given a shower and deloused, clothed in a sort of set of pajamas, fed a small bowl of thick porridge, and put into a bed—of sheets, no less, and with case for the pillow. Well, this man said he feared he was having a dream, and that he would awaken back in the barracks, etc. The following day, he and others were transported to other hospitals. I gathered that he was cared for about three weeks before returning to Epernay, just a few days before coming to (Foug).

This account was very similar to that which a Major MacKenzie told us at the "school" I had just attended in Paris. MacKenzie was a syndicated writer for U.S. newspapers, and he had been to Buchenwald. He first told us of diaries he had read, written by two electricians who had prepared the lighting for the executions of the generals who had plotted the assassination of Hitler last July. Hitler had ordered that the executions be filmed. It was done. It is my understanding that the film is now being viewed by certain selected persons. This has to be one of the most glaring evidences of the sickness of Hitler's mind and a glaring evidence against tyranny.

Major MacKenzie then turned to his visit to Buchenwald, and he must have been with the American troops who first reached the place. Just well into his narrative, he became noticeably ill—very pale and much distressed. He simply had to stop, turn his back to his audience, and cover his face with his hands—his shoulders trembling. He could not continue.

Well, back to our party. No thoughts of retiring, and we were still at the table come 6:30. I simply splashed water on my face, and headed for the depot. Col. Cole had returned, and we knew he would be watching to make certain no one was engaged in any sort of absenteeism, if only for a few minutes. Oh, well! With my crew with their work so completely "in hand," I have time to get all of this written for you to read.

Well, my thoughts did a lot of wandering about and into some remote corners. This war has surely shown man the limits to which he can carry forth with his "art of warfare"—and still manage, somehow, to survive. Our good Lord, who created us in his image, must certainly be discouraged., for in certain respects man has failed miserably. But, as we all know, there is such an abundance of goodness in this old world of ours. So, we just must keep on a-hoping! We may just need to heed more those admonitions—"Know thyself!" and "Unto thyself be true!"

Time passes rapidly. As our "Property Officer" and also in charge of "Information and Education" for the company, there is always something I must do. Then, my social calendar just keeps me going so often—to be with these wonderful friends. Last evening I was to the Ravaults for another wonderful feast and more bridge, ping pong, etc. Stroh talks no end about all this Dr. and Madame

Ravault do to make his stay with them a very happy one. We learned last evening of the return of Madame Ravault's brother-in-law. Along with about 600 other Frenchmen, who had been held prisoners near Leipzig, I guess, he was returned to Paris. These men were transported in 24 planes, C-47s. He would have soon died from starvation and illness—when liberated, and more than 300 had already perished in the "camp." He referred to the lack of toilet facilities, of the lice, rats, and other vermin, and lack of blankets, etc. Well, his wife did not recognize him until he stood before her and spoke. Baudin's brother had had more time to regain some of his former self, physically.

We've had popcorn for Baudin's brother and family. They have just been amazed at this "maïs"—mah-eese—which "explodes." The boys are all for it. This brother is more relaxed, now. I have visited with him, and he has seen some "things" very difficult for him to relate. In an almost pathetic way, he said he had often thought he would never be able to laugh again. He has been able to laugh again. Baudin told me that his brother had changed very much. We have engaged in numerous silly antics, and all of his is helping, to be sure, to break the grip of his long incarceration away from his family. Even until a few days before the American troops arrived, his captors had kept feeding to their prisoners misinformation about the events of the war, just to keep them thinking in terms of hopelessness. He has no sympathy for Germany and the vast destruction that has befallen her cities, etc. He kept using a word which I think means "to become numbed to" or, "because of"—from so much he had personally experienced and witnessed.

Well, the German positions in parts of Norway, Austria, Yuogoslavia, and Bohemia remain as holdouts versus the Russian assault, and Admiral Doenitz wants, apparently, to make no concessions to the Russians. Despite the "conflicts of interest" which lie between the Soviet Union and the western Allies, a "common ground" will be found upon which the victors of this awful conflagration can take a stand, together.

Well, to sum it up, I have been most fortunate throughout my military experience. These people, here in (Foug) do just top it off. What a way to wind it up as this war in Europe draws to its close. Amen!

May 8, 1945 Victory Day in Europe Foug, France

Yes. Today is V-E Day, and I am actually writing this the day after, but want to date it. So much was just almost "out of this world." Rarely in the history of the entire world has a nation stood so thoroughly defeated as Germany, today. This little town of Foug has just been celebrating. Talk about a Franco-American "Alliance"! Well, I can no more than just touch upon the celebrations, here. Of course, everything that had anything to do with "business as usual" was put on a shelf. Such an intermingling of people, French and Americans, and to such degree that one could hardly tell who was who. The men of the company virtually disappeared into the homes of the people, to celebrate, and one could not walk along the street except to greet and hug nearly every person met.

Monsieur Baudin and I had promised Monsieur Chenot and Jean Gaigneur that we would come to drink a "victory toast," so we did. Chenot's home is nearly to the height of the street, and we had many business places and some distance to return to the Baudin home. Once we had drunk our "victory toast," we began our descent of the street. Maitre Baudin is mayor of Foug, and we could not pass any place of business, etc., without being stopped "to toast victory." Often, we simply had no choice but to enter the home or the "store" to engage in the "toast," and more often than not it was to be a dash of mirabelle. Well before we were half way home, I was not sure if I were afloat or on land, on foot or flying, or whatever. So many of the men were members of the hunting club, and we had to stop to lift a glass to the victory. Madame was waiting for us—the noon lunch, and we were several doors from the gate. But, we finally made it, and then came more rejoicing. I had warned the Maitre that we would, no doubt, be met at the door by Madame Baudin, with rolling pin in hand, for we were an hour late.

The official signing of the papers took place in Reims, yesterday. Colonel Cole had directed that our company's store of champagne be released to the men—to the extent of one bottle for each two of them, and this is good indication of the quantity of the stuff we had brought with us from Pantin—our loot gathered by our German predecessors. We have about 160 men in the company. They also had access to the local resources, etc., along with whatever was to be brought out for the rejoicing. To my knowledge, we did not have an unpleasant incident to occur throughout the town.

Well, at the magic hour of 3 o'clock, we were to have a parade. To lead would be a combined band of the townsmen who played something and our men who played something. One just joined in and marched as much as he wished—even I for a full ascent and descent of the street. The French would strike up with their "Marseillaise"—for which the Americans had music, but lacked the beat and rhythm, to such extent that it was laughable; and then, the Americans would strike up with the "Star Spangled Banner"—for which the French lacked beat, rhythm, etc. It all just added to the hilarity of the celebration. The parade went up and down the street at least three times, with the national anthems repeated whenever the spirit so moved. Each time the flags passed, all on the sidelines saluted enthusiastically.

Church bells and sirens rang and sounded off and on, and occasionally firings of guns could be heard. At the foot of the street is a small square which enabled the paraders to turn about to ascend the hill. Watching from our depot area were our German POWs. Except for a few, our French friends just ignored them. It was so completely evident that Nazism had been uprooted, and without a shred of gloria left for its ignoble cause. Too, there were many of the folk who watched briefly, and then just retreated into their homes. This long war had simply drained them dry of emotion to celebrate. Many homes had those "empty chairs"—never to be filled.

For our celebration, on "a table" within the Baudin's abode, I had supplied three bottles of champagne, a bottle of cherry brandy, and a supply of rye krisp to be eaten with the cheeses. This brother of Monsieur Baudin was just about the happiest person to be seen. He is making a splendid recovery—spiritually, as well as physically. His wife often looks at him with amazement and near unbelief. They just treat me as if I were one of the family. But, they never use my given name, David—it is always "Lieut'nah Mickey." So,, it goes!

For the evening came the dances. Our large mess hall was the school auditorium, and it was cleared for one gathering. Its stage was reserved for the band. The other dance was in a second-floor large hall, off the main street well up the hill. As Mayor, Maitre Baudin made appearance at each dance, and he insisted that I accompany him. He issued for each group a sort of victory proclamation, etc. One thing I noticed, and this was for the first time that it struck me—that there was in the town a definite division of classes; professionals and proprietors did not associate socially with laborers, etc. Members of the hunting club were among the crowd to celebrate in the mess hall.

When we had our evening meal to celebrate the victory, Madam Baudin presented me with a bouquet of tulips and then bussed me, French style, first on one cheek, then on the other, and then back again. Then each of the others took turn, and I was well embraced—even Jean-Francois, held by his father, gave me three little smacks. The gist of the "toast" was that France owed her liberation and restored freedom to the United States. The bouquet for me was a symbol of their profound gratitude, etc. We could not linger too long at the evening dinner, for we had the darned dances to attend. Upon our return from the ball rooms, we just all continued to visit, laugh, drink another toast, now and then, and finally to retire about 1:30—"the morning after." And, I was expected to be at the depot by 7:30—as OD, "Officer of the Day." Oh, well! And, here I am at the typewriter.

May 12, 1945 Foug, France

(So little of any military significance happened with respect to our company and its activities. We kept up with "issues" to the units which depended upon us for their medical supplies. We expected that the depot would experience a decrease in its importance. Incoming supplies would keep up as earlier routine shipments had been made; but, we knew there would be a lessening of action. We wondered if we might be in line to be shifted to the Pacific—somewhere. It was all "let down" and denouement.)

(I had been keeping up an off-and-on-again correspondence with the Jaquet family of Trevières. André, the elder son, wrote me occasionally, and "normal life" had quite well returned to that area. He was amused, because of my reference to mirabelle, and he recalled that I would drink cider, but never brandy, while in the home of his parents. He wrote that his parents much hoped I would be able to visit them before returning to the United States.)

(These "liftings" from a few days of letters.}

We of the company are just thoroughly disgusted with our CO. The man just has no judgment when it comes to an understanding of keeping an outfit's spirit in high gear. Our men have given such a grand account of themselves. So, he issues an order that all men and officers must be on duty from 7:30 a.m. to 6:00 p.m., and all are to be in "Class A" attire for the evening meal. In addition, he expected that all would be present for the meals. Well, so many were often guests in the homes of the people for evening meals, and the Colonel but rarely. My opinion is that the man is simply jealous. I had opportunity to request that he reconsider his directive, and his curt remark was that he was the commanding officer and expected no departure from his rule. He is going to have a delegation from the men, and a host of our NCOs will be confronting him. I have a hunch that he will attempt some sort of face-saving compromise, and which will lead to an attempt to forget the whole "thing." We shall see. This poor man has been a sort of albatross around this company's neck since its beginning, and we are not able to rid ourselves of his presence. Humph!

I have been almost swept away by the occomplishments of the forces against Hitler and the Nazis in Europe and against the Japanese in the Pacific. Eisenhower is not a field commander, but he put together a combination of generals that were fantastically successful. He is a master coordinator, and he managed to keep the British and the Americans in a telling cooperation. The masterful coordination of relationships with the Russians is equally as remarkable. This has to be one of he most amazing accomplishments to bear the review of history. MacArthur has directed the campaigns in the Pacific with utmost skill and effectiveness. We Americans will have much to be proud of whenever we should seek to remember these two great generals. And now that this European scene has been so remarkably cleansed of the Fascist-Nazi contagion, the Japanese leaders should be contemplating that their turn is inevitable. Their toeholds in China, Malaya, and the Dutch East Indies will crumble, and then will come an invasion of their homeland. I dread to think of the cost in human lives. It could be of the worst nightmare.

These French people do enjoy waltzing, I think. The other evening at the victory dance in the school hall, their small orchestra often played waltzes. It was a good thing that I had learned to waltz when back in Wood Lake, for some of the dances were the sort where at a break in the music came a change of partners. This proved to be a challenge and some fun, for I hadn't engaged in the pirouetting and reversing since a "ball" at N.W.U. These people do not like a slow tempo, and they really swing in a hurry. I think Madame Baudin and her sister-in-law like to dance. Only three or four of us officers were invited to this dance. Many of the enlisted men were at the other.

It is my understanding that throughout France much praise and honor have been bestowed upon the men who were in the French army and upon those who were in the F.F.I. and Maquis. And, rightly so. We observed a rather interesting "switch-over" within the group of our German POWs. Degner, who works in our records office, refused to dress in the GI fatigues furnished them. Rather he wore his military uniform to keep his identity as a German soldier. Well, as of Victory Day, he discarded his overworn uniform, and donned American fatigue attire. Since the war was over and the German army no longer existed, he felt free to make the change. The men in the office just offered their congratulations, as did I, but without much ado.

Well, I keep thinking of that most fortunate crossing of the Rhine which our troops made at Remagen. The Rhine, thus, never became the formidable barrier to our eastern advance—as it most certainly would have been. Then it seemed to be so evident, that German leaders threw all possible reserves to slow the Russians, and the western Allies never experienced a "redoubt" so designed as to slow their progress.

Just announced is the "point system" to be used to determine order of release from our services—1 point per each month in the service; 1 point per each month overseas; 5 points per each decoration; 12 points per child. Thus, your sonny boy, having no children, finds himself involved with
      37 points for total service
      14 points for overseas service
      15 points for my 3 battle stars. Grand total reaches to 66 points, total.

So, if one needs 84 points to get out, I shall need a minimum of nine more months overseas. It will not work for officers as for the men, and speculation is that for officers a different sort of "system" will be at work, and may well be with certain additional delays. I do not know. My three "battle stars" are for Normandy, Northern France, and Germany. I am not necessarily pessimistic, but it will take several months for me to reach the qualification line. You can just be safe to bet that I shall not be home to light firecrackers this 4th of July. Ho! Ho!

All censoring restrictions are now lifted. You will know that I am in Foug, a town not far from Nancy, in Lorraine—northeastern France. We are just about six miles from Toul, a small city which may appear on a map. Meurthe et Moselle is the division of Lorraine in which Toul and Foug are located.

Some of us have been playing some tennis on a nearby court we have somewhat resurfaced. I took a swift walk to see the Guebourgs, and I will be having supper with them tomorrow evening. Monsieur Guebourg's brother has recently returned from a long sojourn in Germany, and they want me to meet him.

Too, Monsieur Baudin's other brother has now returned to his home in Chateau Thierry. He, as for the other brother, was reduced to a little over half his normal weight, was able only to walk with two canes, was ill with dysentery, and now sleeps about 18 hours per day. I do not know where he was finally imprisoned, but there were many Russian prisoners there. From what I understood from Monsieur Baudin, who hurriedly gave me some of the information, a few Poles and Jewish people were also in this camp, and most of them were at death's door. I believe this brother is now able to walk without the canes, and the dysentery has been cleared up. The "endings" for these two brothers have reached points of happiness; but, for so many others, this was not to be the case.

May 16, 1945 Foug, France

Three days since Mother's Day, and so many precious remembrances crossed my mind, and often I just kept fighting back against an angry mood—for I wanted to be home. Yessirree!

Enjoyed my shower yesterday, and it is always nice to feel refreshed. I had missed my turn three days earlier when we two handfuls of officers were scheduled. But, the sink in the upstairs washroom at the Baudin's is much better than the helmet which I had resource to when in Normandy. Ha!

Thoughts just keep swarming through my mind—about this war and about the utterness of Germany's defeat. She is a battered, beaten, and completely gutted nation—one which has reaped an awesome harvest from the seeds so maliciously sown. A philosophy such as that which inspired Nazism and Fascism, which inspired such suppression of freedom and desire and which led into a barbarism rarely perpetrated earlier in recorded history, simply had to be uprooted and cast aside to wither—and quickly.

If the Japanese fail to muster a courage to concede their defeat, they will arrive at the same direful consequence. Japan will become increasingly vulnerable, and particularly to aerial assault. As came for Germany, her cities will be destroyed, one after the other. There is a justice that waits to breathe forth its righteous fury. I wonder if there remains as a saving grace for those people a hidden wisdom that may spring forth from within their collective soul. Such was not to be for Germany.

It bothers me much to contemplate that a people too often seem to accept willingly, and perhaps enthusiastically, the ends which their power-hungry leaders spread before them. The Allied accomplishments on land, at sea, and in and from the air will become in future another "story to tell to the nations"! The cooperation, though strained from time to time, which the Russians, British, and Americans have so miraculous maintained to gain triumphant victory, must somehow continue if we are to have hope for enduring peace; and, the French will enter into this picture—along with a new Italy, etc.

We had an evening of fierce bridge playing the other evening at Monsieur Chenot's, and we often interrupted the contest to toast "Victory"—along with certain of our national leaders, and even ourselves. Ryley and Baudin carried on with their warfare, and they are now just a game apart. I can hold my own in bridge; but, as for chess, I am a "loser." Ho! Ho!

Received a nice letter from the Rivets, with all four signing. Madame informed me that they had adopted me. Am hoping that opportunity will permit some sort of a run into Paris, just to give them an "Adieu"—one that will come from the heart. We shall see!

Am not sure of the significance, but all of us had physical examinations. A team of military physicians put us through the paces. If we could breathe, blink our eyes, and wiggle our toes and fingers, we passed. It was a farce. Only explanation for it we could figure was that we may be in line for duty in the Pacific. Only time will tell.

I have no reason to be anxious about my future. Should I get into this "Information-Education Program," my sojourn in Europe could well be extended to a year. It would be a great relief to be freed from our CO's presence, but I do not expect to find another group of men who can, in general, come up to the level of our 3lst Medical Depot Company. Yes, we have a few "exceptions," but they hardly "count." From the beginning of this military experience, Dame Fortune has smiled for me. So be it!

May 20, 1945 Foug, France

Received your latest box day before yesterday. Am reserving the tea bags for future use, and gave the coffee to Madame Baudin. She was much pleased, and asked me to thank you. We sliced the Babe Ruth bars for a bridge game, etc. So, keep up the "good work." Ha! And, we pop corn at the Baudin's about twice a week. Charley keeps the popping busy at Chenot's, for Adelaide keeps him supplied.

We are having some very warm days, and it sort of adds to the dullness of our routines—quite a slowing of demand since no casualties coming in to the local hospitals, etc. It seems that we are settling down to "first aid" needs, here and there.

The people are much in earnest about their gardening, and they will continue this year to be quite dependent upon local production. This is similar to the situation at Trevières. I am of the persuasion that the French are great gardeners. As for other reasons for not much excitement, our dear Colonel just leaves so much to be desired. Oh, well! Sometimes, I wonder what I would do were he not around for me to gripe about and because of, etc.

Really, we are just in a sink of relative inaction. Am OD, today, but the Baudins want me to have noon meal with them—for something special she is concocting for us. So, Pete is going to cover for me while I am "off base." May continue this when I return.

Am back, and nearly 3:30. Monsieur Baudin had managed to buy a gallon or two of gasoline, and we went by auto to their little cabin in the woods, about a mile and a half out of town. We had walked to it a time or two. This time, Madame took the food along and did the cooking on the stove of the cabin. Monique and Jean-Francois just beamed to be at this cabin. Madame Baudin's mother is here, and this was the first time for her to be at the cabin since the beginning of the war.

Later, and back to my room after having been to the Guebourg's for supper. My social calendar keeps me running. Ho! Ho! You'll have to put up with my scribbling. Monsieur Guebourg's brother and family were here from a town in the Vosges Mountains—not very distant from here and not with high peaks, etc. We first went to a nearby café and had some Alsacian beer. It was awful! But, they liked it. Then to the house for another marvelous meal. At the piano, next, and with much chording, playing, singing, and laughing. Claude loves to sing, and he often picks the melody on the keys. I think he aspires to be an entertainer. I took my departure just after midnight and managed to get to my room before a rain hit the town

Monday, May 21—will add a note before putting this in the mail. Have been putting up with the old "Hanna curse"—a kink now and then in a back muscle. Well, it hit me again this morning, and I have not been able, by my usual stretching, twisting, and turning, to work it out. I'm going to give it another stretching or two; but, if I can get no relief, it may be a swift trip to our nearest army hospital. Whew! My "crew" are more amused than sympathetic.

May 24, 1945 Foug, France

Col. Cole and Charley took a sight-seeing tour drive into Germany, and they say that the destruction in so many cities is just beyond description. The people of Germany have found out what modern warfare is all about. How long will it take for them to recover?

Got my kink worked out. Went into Nancy to make inquiry about this new education-information program I may transfer to. But, I did not learn much. So, we shall make further pursuit, should my desire persist.

Well, Pete, Ken Lane and I are madder than a tribe of hatters. Captain Stroh has been put in charge of our "colony" of German POWs, and this special assignment removed him from the company. One of our other 1st lieutenants, who was not with us originally but transferred into the company and who is another "southern boy," has been promised the captaincy—if it is to be filled. As I wrote before, Cole is from the "South" and Charley is from the "South"! Lane and I received our promotions from "second lieutenant" at the same time and ahead of Pete, and Lane has been the company's adjutant, etc. He or I should receive this promotion if it is to be made

Yesterday evening, Monsieur and Madame Baudin and I went up to the cabin and hunted for escargots—large land snails that thrive in the shaded and moist undergrass of these dense woods. In about an hour's time we had picked up about 65 of the poor little creatures. When one is stretched out and moving, it appears to be about four inches long. These snails are considered to be a delicacy. They have invited Charley and me to come to the feast, tomorrow evening. Neither of us is at all excited about this eating of snails. All I know, as of yet, is that when we returned with the harvest, Madame Baudin soon dumped them into a large kettle of boiling water. Then, following a transfer of all into cold water, each snail was taken from its shell and was a little ball about the size of a nickel. The shells are rinsed clean. The snails may be further cooked in a sauce. Before the eating, each snail is put into a shell, with open side up and with all neatly and tightly arranged in large pans, and with the sauce poured upon each. From the oven and piping hot, they are ready to be eaten.

May 27, 1945 Foug, France

We've had more bridge at Chenot's—our usual foursome of Chenot, Gaigneur, Teague and Mickey.

And, came the feast of snails last evening at Baudin's. I fully expected to be on sick call this morning. The thought of eating the "things" was just fixation of mind. They have the "texture" of oysters. I may have downed six of them, and Charley at least four. Baudin kept after us to eat more of them, and then told us in his jolly way that the less we ate the more they would have for themselves. So, you see, we did have quite a time with our first eating of these escargots. I think I shall be a bit more courageous for the next round.

Maitre Baudin's brother from Chateau Thierry arrived yesterday. He has made a rather remarkable recovery from his experiences as a POW, but he just has a sort of "shrunken look." His mind has not been affected, and his sense of humor is definitely restored. He was among those who nearly starved to death during the final weeks of the war. If I understood him, he estimated there were in this camp about 20,000 Russians, 2,000 French, and no more than 200 Americans. The Americans received ample food and were favored with certain amenities, and the Russians very little. The French were sort of in between. The fence which separated the Americans from all others was closely meshed and watched, and the guards would permit no passing of food through or over the fence. He believed that between 200 and 500 Russians died each day during the final two weeks. He had little "good" to say when referring to his German captors.

Have decided to pursue transfer into this "education program." Must go to Nancy, tomorrow, to confer with a Major Lewis. Colonel Cole promised to approve my application, but he was somewhat reluctant. Perhaps, he was just indifferent. When he asked me to give reason for my request, I said he was somewhat at the center of the situation, gave him a salute, and departed. I'm sure their was no love lost on either side. So it is!

Weather is a mixture of sun and clouds—warm. And, the work for the depot is slow

May 31, 1945 Foug, France

And, yesterday was Memorial Day. It was for us, I think, just another day. The sacrifices of this war are yet to be rightfully measured, and we are just too close to it all to have cleared heads for thinking in terms of challenges, responses, and accomplishments. Those awesome losses of blood and life on the battlefields of Europe and Africa are behind us. We do not know to what extent our additional losses shall be in the final push against Japan.

One of my top NCOs put our situation in this way, that "our main reason now for being in the army is to get out of it." Several of our men will meet the "point requirement" to gain soon release from the service. So, within a couple months we shall see quite a change in our GI personnel. There is some speculation that our company will soon be returned to the U.S. for "orientation" and reassignment. Guess it will all depend upon the progress of he war versus Japan. As a company, we have been so fortunate, and not a "purple heart" to be found in our midst.

We'll be having another session at Chenot's this evening—a foursome of bridge, and Ryley and Monsieur Baudin will square off on the chess board. We will have more dried apples to crunch, and I think I am beginning to develop a taste for this darned mirabelle. Ha! But mixed with coffee, it is awful. But, we shall also have some good wine, and the crumpets that are nearly always delightful.

Have my regular duties as OD, about every 8th or 9th day, and the only exciting responsibility is to wander about the grounds twice during the night to make certain that our guards, particularly those about the vault, are not sleeping. We must keep under lock and key our supply of gold and silver for dentistry, and the narcotics and alcohol.

Many of our men have nearly become a part of this community. All are sprucing up a bit for our evening mess, but no one pays attention to that part of Cole's dictum which seemed to call for regular eating of the evening chow. Several of our men have an easy knack for picking up this French language. They understand and they speak. As for writing, it is a "no way" street. Ross Donaldson, one of my sergeants, is fluent in French, and he often is translating written notes which our men have received. It is fun, really.

June 4, 1945 Foug, France

Not much to do, here, before the anniversary of D-Day. Some water over the dam, since, eh?

We seem to be marking time, but no one seems to know what lies in store for us. About all we have to do is to lounge around to await instructions. The big job here is going to be to gather and to log all the surplus medical supplies and to box them for transfer. We have rumor that another company, or supply unit of some sort, is to replace us to close out the depot. We are simply involved with a sort of inventory. Is confusing, for nearby units are continuing to bring in their requisitions. My guess is that this is to continue to be a source of medical supplies for this area.

Weather is nice and warm. Seemed wise for me to get my personal belongings in order. So, I went through everything in my room and closet at the Baudin's and found beneath a pile of stuff two cans of sardines, a can of Vienna sausages, a box of rye krisps, and a box of Nestle's cocoa... So, I turned all over to Madame Baudin to add to the menu for our next trip to the hut in the woods.

Am hoping something will come in because of my application to get into this teaching program. But, these decisions are so much delayed, and we could be long gone before any word to arrive. My application will lie in a pile of communications to be read and taken for consideration; and, then, it will lie in another pile of outgoing "stuff" for several more days. There is no urgency to almost anything, here—now that the war is over in Europe.

Have been putting in a bit of time to write a summary of what I call "Just a Bit of Travel"—an account of our changes of locale, beginning with our departure from Ft. Lewis, Washington. I am nearly finished with it, and it is more than twenty pages—typed and single-spaced. Plan to mail it to you tomorrow. So, be prepared.

The other evening, a group of three officers and 12 enlisted men were in town, and they stayed with the company over night. Bob Sorenson, a graduate of the Engineering College at Uni of Nebraska, was one of their officers, and did we have a good visit. His younger brother was a good friend of Bob Duncan. Home address is 835 South 37th St, and he would appreciate a call to his mother. He has been in Germany to study the designs and constructions of bridges, and his unit is headed back to the U.S.—maybe to be assigned to the Pacific. So good to see another Nebraskan!

Would hold up on sending any packages to me, now. We just do not know how long we may be here. Our APO remains 513, as it has been for some time, as you know. Will be sending you a package of some of my stuff, and in it I am going to include a couple bottles of French liqueur. This is good "stuff," and I hope some postal examiner does not decide to confiscate it. Am willing to take the chance. Anyhow, I shall have a supply in my footlocker.

Had another round of snails with the Baudins, and I downed about ten of them. Maybe after a third round or four, I shall become an old hand at the business of eating these escargots. For these people, these snails are a real delicacy. Yessirree! This little cabin in the woods is just a charming place to be. They do so much enjoy being there.

June 8, 1945 Foug, France

We have not received personal mail for several days, and expectations are that we will soon have a different APO. This is the way it has been before. Our "higher authorities" know what the plan is for us, and the army postal service is notified pronto.

Had to study up on a military topic a few days ago, for the colonel asked me to lead a discussion on the matter. He doesn't hesitate to put an extra duty on my shoulders; but when it comes to possible promotion, I am definitely from the wrong side of the "Mason-Dixon Line." Ha!

It will be difficult to leave these grand people of Foug, for so many of them have been so generous and kind. We may have been left with the task to continue, here, and to close out the supplies, but this is not to be. I shouldn't be surprised were our CO to have requested a move. He may think that a change will enhance his opportunity to become a full colonel. His chief problem just lies in his incompetency. We may, again, be on the receiving end of a smelly stick—because of his efforts to do some manipulation. It has been very warm the past few days, and the "heat" is getting to me, and I am grouchy. Oh, well!

Received a letter from Madame Jacquet of Trevières, and what a time I had to read her writing. It would have been difficult had it been in English. The gist of her note was that they would be having a celebration for the anniversary of the landings in Normandy, and she wanted to thank, again, the Americans for their liberation. She is a sweet little soul. I must write in French to respond, and this will take me a while. Her elder son, André, and I have kept up an on-and-off correspondence. He tells me he is studying English, and wants me to write part of each letter in English.

Have been to see the Guebourgs. Bridge again at Monsieur Chenot's. And a third feast of snails with the Baudins—up in the little hut. As in the case of mirabelle, eventually I might learn to enjoy the snails. Howzabout that! Last evening was for dinner, ping pong, and bridge at the Ravault's. Stroh, of course, will not be departing with us. His supervision of the German POWs will end when they are to be processed for return to Germany.

It is a bit dull for us, to be sure. Not time, yet, for me to hear of any assignment to be in on this education business. So, I shall just wait it out. What a relief it would be to be free from this CO! But, I shall never find another group of men who, in general, can come up to par with ours of the "31st."

Monsieur Baudin had been wanting me to see two mass graves, each about 25 miles away, I think. Of course, the gasoline shortage has prevented our going there in his car. The Germans exacted a "ten for one" penalty against the French should one kill a German soldier or cause on purpose serious injury to a German soldier. In one of these graves are buried 40 men and older youth, and in the other there are 30. In this area, there was no further killing of Germans, nor any physical assault upon them. The citizenry resorted to other means to be "uncooperative."

June 11, 1945 Foug, France

Had another round of being Officer of the Day, and this will certainly be the last for here. We are to return to the United States. So, you can start to hold your breath. Tell Don I shall be needing a dental appointment. Now, isn't this just something! We know nothing as to schedule, etc.

Am sending another package, and will put my German helmet in it. Also, two more bottles—one of cointreau and one of Benedictine. There will be mostly "knick-knacks" and I hope all will arrive. One never knows what will walk away should someone open the box to inspect contents. Perhaps, we should use the word, "confiscation."

Have taken photos of all my friends, and will have them developed when I get to Lincoln. They are happy for us that we shall be returning home, but they insist that they will never have other American friends to be like us.

We've been playing some tennis, but it is just a bit too warm for me. When I last walked up the street to play bridge at Chenot's, two or three of my acquaintances along the way invited me in to have a sort of "au revoir" glass of wine. These folk have a genuine feeling of warm friendship for our company, and I became just a little "unhorsed" emotionally. My stomach was churning a bit, and all evening I had to put up with recurring nausea—but no crisis. It could have been that some of the wine didn't sit well.

Major Earl Grove has received transfer from the company, and I know how pleased he is. He would have been a peach of a C.O. So often Col. Cole would simply ignore his suggestion, or would just sort of "put him down." Grove just did his "thing"—constantly circulating and offering assistance and advice. He was well liked by the men, and they admired him.

We are so full of rumors and speculation. No one knows when we shall pull out from here, but our mail is certainly being delivered elsewhere—to await us.

Last evening when I returned to my room, Monsieur Baudin and Lt. Ryley were hard at it on the chess board. After Larry's departure, Baudins and I visited until nearly one in the morning. It is going to be difficult to tell them "au revoir." Our friendship has become so very "dear." Monsieur Baudin most of the time resorts to humor and to josh and to resort to a prank. This time he was somewhat to the contrary and quite sober. As we sipped away, we—Madame and Monique, too—were now and then somewhat tearful. There will be several other rather tearful partings throughout the town.

When we depart, we will take only our personal belongings, of course. For the company, only the official records pertinent to personnel records, recorded minutes of meetings, etc. Some file cases will be the extent of it—those which contain the official documents.

June 14, 1945 Foug, France

We are practically on our way to go to a camp to prepare for our return to the U.S.A. This will be my final letter from here. In some respects this is almost too good to be true! I shall phone as soon as I can, once we land.

Had another "run in" with the colonel. My "gang" and I had everything in order and ready for departure, but the officer with the advance cadre of our replacement company asked for some sort of document or summary of volume of goods, etc., and we had all such packed away. Thirlby and two or three of the others of our "records-keeping" gave him the info, generally. It had something to do with "accountability," and this officer in charge made a sort of protest to the colonel. So, wanting to get at me for something, Col. Cole called me in and proceeded to reprimand. He even reviewed a few of his personal grievances. When he had finished, I gave him a smile, saluted, said nothing, and about faced and departed. I hope my silence conveyed my thorough disgust and that I deemed his accost to be such that merited no reply. For some reason, this did not make me angry; rather, it amused me. As for important records, the stock-cards were up to date, and this info was all the newcomers needed for their "accountability."

(The following afternoon we were to board a train, in Foug, for Reims, near which had been established "Camp Philadelphia," where we were to be prepared for return to America. The cars had already been pulled in, and we were to be "all aboard" and ready for departrure at about 2:00 p.m. It seemed as if the entire village had turned out to wish us well and to say final "good-bys"! There was much hugging, embracing, and some shedding of tears. It was what I expected to be my final "au revoirs" to my many friends. But, no engine had arrived to take us away. It was a warm day, and we were sweating and not a very happy bunch. Come time for evening meal, and some sort of rations had been issued for the trip. Baudins asked me to come for a quick supper, which I did. Others, also, made hurried get-a-ways. Then, back to the train. It was the next morning before the engine arrived, for there had been a mixup with respect to the day of departure. The night was one during which everyone had to depart and return because of often needed toilet calls. Some of the people had returned to wave us a fond farewell. Thus was our departure from Foug! We would arrive at Reims in the early evening, and then to "Philadelphia" via trucks. We bedded down for a good night's sleep, actually.)

Camp Philadelphia

June 17, 1945 Camp Philadelphia, near Reims, France

We must just sweat out our homeward movement—know nothing about time, from what port, etc.

Will go into Reims, tomorrow—via regular military bus service, to check with a personnel officer to see is he has any suggestions to make concerning my request for reassignment into this Information-Education Program.

Again, it was difficult to say goodby to Baudins, and we all had tears in our eyes, My stay with them was such a very happy chapter in my life here in France. They said they would not have asked another American to stay in their home, for our "au revoirs" had just been too difficult. My stay with them was such a marvelous dividend. And, then the other folk, too. Whew!

June 20

Once back in the States, we shall receive leaves for 30 days. So, we shall have plenty of time for much to happen. Of course, should this reassignment come through, then my return will be much delayed. But, here, we are much relaxed, enjoy frequent games of cards, and have time to take in a movie if we want. A possible ride into Paris, tomorrow—may get to do some further checking on my reassignment, and will try to see the Rivets.

June 24

Didn't get into Paris until yesterday—departure from here was via command car at 4:30 in the morning, and return was by 3:30 in the afternoon. We had breakfast at a military mess hall near Place d'Etoile. I then made inquiry in a nearby headquarters about my transfer, and no one knew anything about anything. Had just enough time to dash via the Metro to see the Rivets, and arrived while they were having a sort of noon reception to announce a betrothal—that of a cousin's daughter, I think. At any rate, I shared in some marvelous pastries and a glass or three of champagne. With not much time to loiter, it was back to the command car and the others for our return. What a day!

June 28

Much has happened, in a way. An administrative officer, here, made some inquiries about my possible appointment into this education program. The teaching jobs have been assigned, but there remain some administrative "desk" positions. I told him I was not interested, etc. So, that is that, and I shall be definitely on the way home. Then, Col. Cole came by to chat—gist of his purpose was to tell me that he wanted me to stay with the company, and he expressed regret that we had had our misunderstandings and difficulties. He was sincere, I think. We shook hands. But, I want no more of him, really!

Was able to catch another ride into Paris, and I was with the Rivets over night. What a break for me! Nicole has begun her studies to lead to a career in medicine, and I think she wants to become a physician. She and Jean-Pierre much want to visit in the United States, and I told them that their welcome would be a warm one. Jean-Pierre is just eleven years old. We had a grand visit, and not to bed until after midnight. Oh, what wonderful hospitality! They kept telling me that my "French" had so greatly improved. Monsieur Rivet does well with his English, and Nicole will attempt a phrase now and then.

We are in tents, here, and the nights have been almost below a bit chilly. We are on cots, and my feet are cold unless I wear heavy socks. I'm tempted to put my sleeping bag on the ground, as I did in England.

June 29

When we arrived here, we had such a backlog of letters waiting for us, and they continue to come. It has been great to hear from you. With much time to write, my correspondence has been nearly "caught up," but this writing to friends in France takes me a while. Foug is just too far for a possible quick run, and we have been keeping the mail busy with our correspondence. So many wonderful people in that town.

It is rainy and chilly, and we want sunshine. We engage in rather lengthy "bull sessions," and often our subject turns to our CO, whom we hope we shall lose once we reassemble after our 30-day leaves. Sometimes, I just feel sorry for him.

As someone to rant and rave about, he has become a worn-out "subject." Oh, well!

July 2

Once in the U.S., I shall be sent directly to Ft. Leavenworth, Kansas, my place of original classification. From there I shall receive papers for my 30-day leave. And, as you now know, we shall all be heading to Boston.

Charley has a can of chicken, and two or three of us are going to help him eat it this evening. Each of us brought along several bottles of this and that with us and will enjoy the camaraderie. We nearly "cleaned out" our store of bottles brought to Foug from Pantin, and what remained we distributed to our friends, there.

We will be making another visit to Reims, and we have some very good military facilities there—good for meals and showers and for relaxing. Bus service back and forth is hourly. We do not have difficulty to find the hours moving along at good pace. As for mail, Bin, your letter of June 25th arrived today. Not bad, eh?

July 4

A letter postmarked June 27 arrived, and we should have no complaints. This morning I just became ambitious and washed all my dirty clothes. One of us does something, and then the rest of us just follow suit. Ha! Some have attempted a little sun-bathing, but I'm not interested in chancing a burn.

A little jaunt into Reims, yesterday, and spent the time to see the city's marvelous old cathedral. It is just magnificent, and we spent nearly two hours just in, and out, and all around. I just cannot imagine how the people "back then" were able to build it. It received some bullet wounds during the war, but they are attempting to obliterate these. There were so many American military personnel running around that it seemed as if we had occupied the city.

We have been instructed to keep close to our company area. This may mean something.

July 5

We are still marking time. And, this morning I received "word" that "University Center # 2" was going to request me for a position. Any assignment would come from the chief surgeon's office in Paris. The written and official notice must come through immediately, or we may be on our way home. This assignment could keep me in France for several months. If you have heard nothing from me, you will know I am on the way home.

30-Day Leave

(Our departure for Le Havre was within a few days and by train, as I recall. Arrival was timed for immediate boarding of the carrier ship, "General McRae." Not a large vessel, it was well filled with returning troops. We encountered some rough seas en route across the Atlantic, and again so many were seasick. As before, when aboard the "Queen Elizabeth," I experienced no nausea. As landlubber from north-central Nebraska and native of the Sandhills, my only explanation could be that I was already used to the "waves."

(From New York City by train to Ft. Leavenworth, Kansas, to receive my papers for a 30-day leave, and then by bus to Lincoln. The joy of return and reunion with family was simply wonderful. "Gas stamps" had been saved for our drive to Boston, for I was to be married August 11. My mother, my sister and brother-in-law, and I would take the highways to Hyde Park, Massachusetts, in the family Chevrolet. Wedding would be followed by short honeymoon on Cape Cod. These were also the days when the uranium and plutonium bombs, "Little Boy" and "Fat Man", were dropped on Hiroshima and Nagasaki and of Japan's acceptance of "unconditional surrender." The five of us would be returning to Lincoln, and our departure was the day the government lifted gas rationing and the need for the "stamps." The war was over.

(When my leave expired, I returned to Ft. Leavenworth . Our 31st Medical Depot Company was to reassemble at Ft. Benning, Georgia. Mim returned to Boston by train.)

Ft. Leavenworth, Kansas

August 30, 1945 Ft. Leavenworth, Kansas

No chance to get a change in my "orders," and so must proceed to Ft. Benning. So, no reason for Mim to delay her return to Boston.

Ran into Luke Barringer, and did we have a grand chat. They are releasing men from the service by the droves, hourly. We have a rumor that the point-score for release is to be lowered. I doubt if it will affect my status to any essential degree. But, what a perfectly wonderful "leave" of 33 days I did have!

Do not know what can possibly lie ahead for us as a company. Times are going to be dull, indeed. Well, it won't be for long, certainly. I just hope that when my time for release comes, I can go directly to Boston. The army "game" may rule that my release must be from Ft. Leavenworth. If so, I shall just have to take an extra ride by train or plane. A small cluster of us are to gather here for our return to the company.

Ft. Benning, Georgia

September 1, 1945 Ft. Benning, Georgia

Pete is our only officer not yet arrived. Rudy Kelemen, Captain, was also married—as were about fifteen of the men. Adelaide and Joyce are coming to Columbus, and Charley has been in town to find rooms. Mim and I decided that she should not come down. It is almost impossible, from what we are told, to find suitable rooms or apartments—the nice ones are taken, of course.

September 3

Charley and I attended a communion service yesterday, in a Baptist church in town. It was nice! We then went for a chicken dinner, and returned to camp.

Several of us are going to submit letters to request early release. The colonel may attempt to stall us, for he seems to be his usual self. He'd better stay in the service, for he'll never find a job outside to pay him the salary he receives. Ho! Ho!

September 4

Charley and I had a round of golf and will be playing again. We must rent the clubs . New golf balls are scarcer than hen's teeth, and we were permitted to use some real "oldies" that the locals had thrown into a basket. We also have a very fine swimming pool. Traipsing around this golf course, with the temperature as high as it is, has sort of tuckered me out. Ha!

I remain in charge of "plans and training," and the colonel directed me to draw up a program. Frankly, as one of our sergeants once said, we are in this army for just one reason, to get out. Well, what sort of "training" do we need for this? Just returned from their furloughs of thirty days, our men do not need instruction for return to civilian life, or for anything else.

September 8

So good to visit over the telephone day before yesterday. We get in a golf game each day, and by chance just happened on the scene when the manager opened a case of new balls. Each who needed them could buy two. It has been just loads of fun to be on a golf course, again. We do need lots of practice. Ha! But, what a way to be earning my salary! No luck, as yet, for Adelaide and Joyce to find suitable places in town to reside. Fortunately, a sort of visitors' barracks is available on camp, nearby.

For church, Sunday, I shall go in town to the Episcopal church. Then, I shall join Petersons and Teagues for dinner. They are just great, and so much fun to be with. They want to meet Mim, but I think we made the best decision for her to stay at home.

September 11

Nothing to write about, and our brief telephone calls just keep us posted.

September 25

No reason to write, for we have our short telephone chats every third day. These discharges and releases are moving so slowly. Has to be another example of bungling on the parts of some of our "higher ups." We did see Abbott and Costello in "In Hollywood." These two are always good for a barrel of laughs.

One of our sergeants suggested that we schedule a hike of nine or ten miles—just to roam about to see some of the nearby countryside. So, two of us borrowed a jeep and driver from a nearby motor pool, took a wee tour, and mapped our route. This sergeant and I felt somewhat foolish. But, we did it, and the company, as left, did it, and, with lunch-break of issued "rations," we spent about four hours along some wooded roadways within the vicinity of Ft. Benning. We were never beyond the limits of the "reserve."

As for other "training," we do regularly review the news, have gathered some information relative to job opportunities, and spend time going through the literature relative to educational opportunities. The so-called "G.I. Bill of Rights" is of great significance. Several of our men have written letters to colleges and universities. But, cause for discouragement is the fact that many men of other units have been here for more than eight weeks—awaiting "papers." We have been here just a month. Some have surmised that these delays keep the number of troops still on deck in higher numbers so that more of these higher paid administrative officers can continue to drag down their fat salaries. Several of our men have scattered about and are helping new friends with their work in other outfits. So it is going! Well, John Q. Public is having to foot the bill, eh?

October 3

Am enjoying the letters from France. Will return them to you, and will give you translations when next in Lincoln. Yes, I may enroll at the University of Nebraska. Did see the movie, "Winged Victory," and what a "whitewash"—in my estimation it just stunk.

(This was my final letter from a military base. My instructions were to go to Ft. Bragg, N.C., to receive my release from the service. My "farewells" with the men of my "records crew" became somewhat emotional. Except for one, all were still around. Our accord had been both gentle and warm. From there, it was directly to Boston. Mim needed time to terminate her secretarial job, and we then returned to Lincoln, by plane. It was well into December, and my alma mater, Nebraska Wesleyan University, had a job for me—to direct the recruitment of new students. This I agreed to do until the following September. The war for me had come to its end. Yessirree!)

Love u loads,
Dave

Just a Bit of Travel

as of June 5, 1945, Foug, France

The consternation over the whereto of our destination was of no little measure as we awaited notification for movement from Ft. Lewis, Washington. Rumors had been running rather wickedly that the South Pacific was to be the lucky region to receive the more than capable 31st. All through February and the early part of March we had been feverishly meeting the tests for overseas movement—with emphases on malaria control, gas warfare, exercises in embarkation and debarkation, etc. All our personal and organizational equipment had to be in # 1 condition, and each man was given a thorough physical examination.

Once our unit received word that it was soon to be headed overseas, furloughs for the EM were much increased. Despite our stepped-up program, movement orders came with many of the men home on their "last furlough" before movement; they had to be called back, even though many of them had just reached home. The company reassembled for final checking and packing.

We left Ft. Lewis at 2:00 p.m. the 22nd of March, 1944, along with our sister company, the 30th Medical Depot Company. No one knew where we were going, but it was almost a certainty that it would be the east coast. It took us until early the following Monday morning (the 27th) to arrive at our destination, Camp Kilmer, New Jersey.

There, for nearly three feverish days, we went through all sorts of final check-ups; for the first time all outgoing mail had to be censored, and it was my job, as unit censor, to see that the men were fully informed as to the existing regulations and limitations. While at our POE station, many hoped to receive passes into NYC. However, none were forthcoming, for we were to proceed almost immediately to our transoceanic means of transportation. We left Kilmer about 7:00 the evening of March 30th, proceeded by train—crowded two to a seat with all our personal equipment—to a pier on the NJ side of the River, took a ferry boat over to the NY side, picked up our barrack-bags or duffle-bags, and marched off.

Before leaving Kilmer, we had a potent rumor that we were to sail on the "Queen Elizabeth"—the report coming from the detail that had gone down to load our footlockers, TAT Equipment, etc. Col. Cole, in his usual authoritative manner, pooh-poohed the idea, for he knew confidentially that we were going "in convoy." No one was sure about anything. After leaving the ferry on the NY side, we marched quite a bit and were directed into a large enclosure on one of the piers. The Red Cross served us with coffee and doughnuts, and we awaited boarding orders

We officers were conducted onto the ship via a different gangplank from that of EM. We were given mess and billet cards which told us on which deck and in which compartment we were to bunk and at which hours we were to eat. It WAS the "Queen Elizabeth"! She was immense! The men were billeted down in the very lowest hold of the ship—about three levels below the water line.

As I remember, Teague, Ryley, Pete, Lane, and I were all in the same stateroom—nine of us, altogether, counting four other lieutenants. Captains were in better staterooms, and the majors and colonels in better ones, yet. Ha! After we got settled, there was little to do except explore the ship. But, we had loaded in about midnight and were advised to stay in our bunks. The ship was completely blacked out. As instructed to do, Col. Cole set up a roster for us company officers who were to stand two-hour fire watches down in the hold where are men were. This was a ship regulation and was not an odious task. Breakfast was, for us, at 8 o'clock.

As mentioned, this ship was just immense. One could easily become "lost"—at first. We did become acquainted with its many halls, decks, corners, etc. It is a magnificent ship. Publicity had stated that the "Elizabeth" had hauled, at one time, more than 15,000 troops—not to count the ship's crew. We did not have quite so many for this voyage. A few companies experienced what was called "double-shift occupation" of certain billets—twelve hours in and twelve hours out, and the ship was crowded. We pulled out of New York harbor at 1:00 p.m., March 31st. Staten Island, Statue of Liberty, etc., just slipped past. Everyone, who could, was out on the decks. We had "lumps" in our throats as the skyline disappeared from view.

We ate twice a day—in many shifts, but our times were 8:00 a.m. and 6:00 p.m. We officers ate from nice, white table cloths, and our waiters were all in tuxedos. It was pretty fancy and very much "English." Our food was good, and we had fresh buns with each meal. Most of us were certainly quite surprised to be faring so well. We ate from china. Of course, the EM didn't fare so well—had to line up to be served into their mess kits, etc. This was not, altogether, conducive to democratic ideals, I fear. Ha!

We had understood that our passage over was a part of British "reverse lend-lease"—our meals, also. But, due to another of Col. Cole's whims, we later had to pay for our meals through deductions from our pay vouchers. We were virtually alone among the many outfits whose officers paid for their mess while crossing the Atlantic. The meals were well worth the price. What irked us was that our colonel was so stupid… We could do nothing about it, and this was to prove to be just the beginning of many such idiocies.

Pete became desperately seasick. It was more mental than otherwise, and he played the game to its fullest. Except for his first, he escaped from standing fire watch for the men below, and he managed to have his sleep uninterrupted. The rest of us who stood watch were thoroughly disgusted with him. I have wondered what might have been his "condition" had we been on a small ship and into rough waters. He ate very little during the voyage. He was my "relief" for the watch below. Col. Cole refused to change the roster. So, each of my sojourns below was for four hours. The camaraderie with the men was a marvelous dividend.

Our trip across was nearly uneventful. We had our daily "alerts," the crew had their target practices, we met the "Queen Mary" on a return voyage to the U.S., we encountered a westbound convoy, and we were "saluted" by their planes. Our fourth night out, the ship's sonar detected submarines. It was known that Hitler had placed the two "Queens" on a priority list, along with the "Aquitania." These three vessels never sailed in convoy, but used their speed as chief defense against subs. The ship made a sharp turn to the right, and then did some zigging and zagging along lines a bit to the southeast. Not until the morning of our sixth day did we sight the coast of Ireland, and through our binoculars the Emerald Island looked pretty good. About six that evening we pulled into the Firth of Clyde and dropped anchor.

We, for the first time, were permitted to open our portholes. Ships were everywhere—naval and otherwise, British and American, etc. Each of us was "all eyes." The coastline of Scotland was beautiful, and on both sides of us! Our voyage had been a good one, and we had experienced none of the discomforts we had read about. Most of us had taken salt-water showers, and we always had hot water for washing and shaving. We officers tipped our waiters, for they deserved ample rewards for their excellent services in our behalf. As for Pete, he recovered pronto when we sighted land. Oh, well!

Our final night aboard ship was one to remember. Each of us had received a full day's "K rations"—a Thursday. Next day was "Good Friday." Most of the EM were hungry, and they had their rations for the next day, to be eaten while en route by train to southern England. Our Catholic men opened their rations to eat the "meat" portions, and this started further development. To me, it became an exercise in hilarity.

Our cooks had become friendly with the ship's cooks, and a surplus of potatoes had, for whatever cause, come about. From this connection, no less that two bushels of these spuds ended up with our men, who proceeded to peel and devour their delicacies—and with salt brought down from the kitchen. The peelings accumulated on the floor, and it became as slippery as an ice rink—all of this to welcome me when I descended for my watch. What followed I have related—it becoming one of the funniest incidents to occur. It became a Maundy Thursday eating never to be forgotten.

We ate breakfast aboard ship and awaited our time for the ferry boats to take us ashore. We left ship about 5:00 p.m., and landed at the little town of Gourick. Many things attracted our attention, but most of all was the rollicking welcome we received from Scottish bagpipers who paraded "up and down" for us. They were in their kilts, and they really played for all they were worth.

A train was waiting for us. After women of the Red Cross served us coffee and doughnuts, we boarded the train and took our places in the funny little compartments. Ours would be an all night's journey to southern England. We speculated as to what our missions would be. We expected we would be assigned to some sort of supply depot or center. We felt primed to get to work.

As we journeyed up the Clyde valley to Glasgow, the beauty of the landscape much impressed us. It was so green, neat, clean, pastoral, and peaceful—in appearance. The hedgerows, garden plots, huts and homes, and meadows seemed to explain why it was that this country was so envied for its natural beauty. Soon after the train left Glasgow, darkness set in, and we settled down to spend the night. We munched on our "K" rations, felt the chill of the breeze, closed the windows, and attempted to sleep. Snoozing was no more than fitful.

Down the east coast of Scotland and England, we went through Edinburgh and London, and arrived at Andover, in Hampshire (Hants), the afternoon of the 8th. The RTO had procured trucks to haul us to "Chilbolton Camp A"—a distance of about 12 miles. Of course, we drove on the left side of the road. Our camp was a desolate appearing spot. No depot was in sight, and we were somewhat disheartened. To meet us was a QM officer from a nearby military hospital, and he had on hand two days' rations for us. Certain other items were awaiting us. Our stomachs had a sort of pitted feeling.

Our "camp" was located in a grove of pine, cedar, and ash trees—all somewhat in the middle of a large mud hole. The buildings consisted of Nissan-like huts, and they were filthy dirty. It was about three o'clock, and we had time to do a bit of cleaning. The water flowed, and we wondered what we were going to make of it. We had no mission. We were not known by any supply installation. It was, at first, virtually impossible to draw our TO equipment. We soon discerned that the "red tape" was almost more than stupefying. We were not happy. All was SNAFU! Our visiting officer had indicated that we should engage in a "training program," and we had, of course, become quite sickened of such while back in the States. Col. Cole had taken leave from us in London.

"Camp A" was located just more than a mile northwest of the village of Crawley, the center of much of Thackeray's writing. Crawley is about six miles southwest of Winchester. We were about 12 miles from Andover, with Stockbridge being but three miles away on the way to Andover. All of these are approximately twenty miles to the north of Southampton. We were in southern England!

The rainy season was on, and the dirty little huts, the muddy area, and the dismal coldness made the atmosphere quite uninviting. Our first task was to clean our surroundings—to scrub all walls and floors up and down, and to sweep the area of all the leaves. For heat in each hut was a charcoal-burning stove, a somewhat quaint contraption which proved to be quite efficient. We had an ample supply of the charcoal, and there was a trick to get it to burn and to glowingly give off sustaining warmth. The huts were a bit breezy, but the weather warmed. Quite a large pile of bricks was nearby, and the men soon had a walk laid throughout the area. The place soon appeared to be quite presentable. Many of us caught a fever to purchase a bicycle. Mine cost equivalent of $40, and it was new. It was enjoyable to tour along the many roads and to see the countryside.

Spring must have come a bit late, for the leaves did not burst forth until after May first. Temperature remained chilly. The landscape was so green, the little pastures and farms were so clean and well kept right into the corners, and it seemed a little difficult to realize we were living in the midst of a people at war. For entertainment, we saw movies at neighboring units, or into town; and, we set up our own screen. Local "rules" required that passes into town be given to groups of men, and that each group we accompanied by an officer. We played baseball, softball, and volleyball. We had stakes and horseshoes. Time passed.

Most discouraging was the "red tape" encountered to draw supplies. We had been told in the U.S. that the "drawing of equipment overseas" was simple and without the delays so often encountered. Well, in England it was worse. We seemed always to face into scarcity, and almost by accident were we to receive a requisitioned item the first time 'round. For us, it was both ridiculous and disgusting. We were under instructions to complete our authorized equipment, and until we were placed on a "high priority status" it was a slow process. We were puzzled. But, once we gained "status," change set in, and we gained attention—and even the rest of our vehicles. May 2nd the company received its "alert."

However, on April 30, our "base platoon" had been directed to go to G-55, a nearby general depot at Lockerly. Major Grove put me in charge, and our mission was undisclosed. It was nearly dark when we arrived, and no one knew where we were to bunk. About 11:30, we were "grounded out" in tents. It was beastly cold, and none of us was happy. A Major Hebert told us we were to load "skids"—whatever they were!

Next morning, we were located in the "2nd troop area" of the depot. The mess and sleeping facilities, latrine and washing accommodations, etc., were far below what we had left at peaceful Chilbolton. Our place in the chow line had been fixed at six o'clock, morning and evening. We would sleep and eat about three miles from the warehouses. Transportation was by one truck, and it took three trips to get our sixty men back and forth. Our job was to fit boxes of medical supplies on to "skids," to wrap each load in heavy canvas, and to strap each together with steel bands in such manner that it could be loaded onto ships, and then removed, by use of cranes. We had an initial deadline to meet, and the number of skids to be prepared was almost beyond hope. No doubt about it! Somebody had been caught napping, and we were to meet the crisis.

I've never seen a group of men waylay a task to the degree that our men did this one. Our sergeants organized their crews, and I encouraged them. By end of the second day, it was evident that the deadline was not altogether beyond reach. The pace was to be almost "killing," for it became a 7:00 a.m. to 11:30 p.m. ordeal. The men walked around like zombies much of the time. Only illness granted any "time off." The men saw this to be their first mission, and they were not to be daunted. They licked the challenge right to the last box and were within two hours of the deadline. From then on, it was to be always ahead of the game.

It seemed to me that during the first ten days of this ordeal the men just sort of shrunk. I lost fifteen pounds and did practically no physical labor. By end of the second day, we had taken over the project in its entirety—except, perhaps, the "responsibility." In the end, it proved to be a most valuable experience, for it geared these men to be able to handle any challenge that might face them when they were to receive, store, and dispense medical supplies—even "units" for advance station hospitals, etc.

We had been at this game for more than a week, when we had visitors from our home base—Major Grove, Captain Stroh, and Lieutenant Ryley. They came to inform me that I was to spend some time back at "Camp A." A higher headquarters had discovered our presence and decided we should undertake a vigorous training program, one that would prepare us to storm beaches and establish emergency medical supply stations. I was now to become a liaison person, between our two locales, and to direct our new "program." I also learned that our two advance sections had pulled out for Dursley, near Bristol. Their mission was a mystery, and we would not see them again until our second day on French soil.

The job at G-55 continued, but without the pressure. The "skids" were loaded and assembled for future movements. Our men eventually returned to Camp A for housing and food, and the skidding crews were hauled back and forth daily.

The last of the skids were loaded on July 6. From the end of May, I was spending most of my time at Chilbolton. We played softball, baseball, volleyball and cards; pitched horseshoes; and enjoyed our days of leisure—really, to be among the most peacefully care-free of my more than three and a half years in the service.

Toward the end of May, "D-Day" fever was running rampant. Nearby airfields were increasingly active, and we could feel the quickened beat of an "invasion pulse." We were directed "to train" by sleeping in our pup tents. This process "to toughen up" proved to be more than ordinary, for the local population of rats wished to join us. What irked us were the frequent inspections we had from various clusters of "upper brass" who seemed to be almost "mad driven" to give evidence of doing the duties for which they received pay. But, whatever, an approaching "invasion" was central to all thought and concern.

Just after midnight, June 6, the drone of airplanes began, and noticeably increased and without any let up. We had returned to sleep in our huts by this time, and we were soon gathered out of doors to watch the formations fly overhead. We seemed to be in the very center of the path. A battalion of MPs had bivouacked adjacent to us, and those men were also out to watch the show. We were certain the invasion was underway. But, our radio was silent, as far as any news of invasion was concerned. Not until about 9 o'clock that morning did we hear, officially, an announcement that the invasion was underway. Earlier, a German station had announced that the invasion had begun.

The number of planes was simply astounding. Of course, we had no way to know if the landings had been successful or repelled. Somehow, we just knew it had to succeed! For us, the aerial show was simply magnificent. By mid morning, we had reports of casualties being flown in—to a nearby "general hospital." We knew loss of life would be heavy, and it was sickening. Several of our men were often on their knees, with prayers in their hearts. Yes, it was exciting, and we knew one of the greatest events in all of history was occurring. Most of us openly wondered when we should be called upon to cross the "ditch."

Three or four of our men had relatives in England, and each if them received time off for a short visit. We continued to play our games and to observe the planes. The first of the so-called buzz-bombs landed the day that Major Grove and I had our visit to London. No more than two of the bombs landed within hearing distance of our Camp A. We knew we were destined to head across to

France, but we wondered if our turn would come after the WACs had made it safe for us. Mail ceased to arrive from home, and we knew our letters were being directed elsewhere. Morale sags when mail from home has become directed elsewhere. We simply had to lay back to await orders.

On a Friday evening, about 9 o'clock, July 6, a Rail Transportation Officer (RTO) informed us via telephone that we were to be loaded and ready to go by 6:30 "in the morning"! Ho! Ho! So, we worked all night long, and it was a mighty scramble. It rained liked fury, and it was a night to be remembered. Those "higher ups" should have had their ears burned off, for we cussed them from head to toe, and back again—over and over again. We went by train to Southampton. We then spent three days in the large staging area—sleeping, eating, going to movies, and just relaxing,—it being three days of much needed rest. We were well taken care of, and our motor personnel were somewhat amazed from the careful inspections made of our vehicles.

The 11th, we shouldered our duffles, etc., marched through Southampton to the docks, and boarded the "Princess Charlotte," a former Belgian cross-channel excursion ship. We officers were directed to little state rooms, and we were to eat in a reserved "hall"—our menu to consist of warmed "C rations." The EM fared the same, down in their hold. The ship moved out and anchored near the Isle of Wight. A convoy was forming. Barrage balloons were all over the place. It was interesting!

We crossed the channel on the 12th, and we saw ships, more ships, and even more ships—of all sorts. Of course, barrage balloons were everywhere. As we approached the coast of France, it seemed that half the merchant marine of the world had been sunk—as of there. These old vessels, we were told, had been scuttled to make breakwaters for the Omaha and Utah Beaches. Later, in the afternoon, we transferred to an LCT, were taken to a little pier that jutted into the shallow water, and went ashore without getting our feet wet. Utah Beach was not an impressive place—just sand. Some German cement fortifications were here and there. It was hot and dusty, and our packs and duffles were heavy.

As instructed, we stacked our packs, etc, on the beach and marched about four miles to an "in-transit area." We had "K" rations to eat, a light rain was falling, and some of us attemped to visit a bit with the French people who were watching us and lived in the nearby homes. Not too far away, an ammunition dump was in process of blowing up—not result of enemy action, but due to "a careless match." I guess ours was to be a typical "first night" on the continent, but certainly far better than that of the assault troops. We had no latrine facilities, except the nearby woods, and these woods had been long overused and required very careful stepping. All rules for "army sanitation" had long been abandoned. Thus, it was!

We were up bright and early the morning of the 13th, were loaded onto trucks, and were taken for a short ride to a medical supply installation—one operated by our advance sections. We had a "royal reunion" with our men, and so good to see Charley and Pete. According to them, we were to have followed much sooner than we did. Saint Marie du Mont was the little village near which we landed, and our advance sections had set up their supply point but a short distance beyond. They had landed about 1:00 a.m. the morning of "D-2"—just after midnight. They had some wild tales to tell. They had dug many holes to crawl into, and no one had been wounded. So, no "purple hearts," thankfully. They had accumulated quite a cache of German military souvenirs.

Transportation delivered our duffles and other baggage, and we bedded down for the night, making certain we had some holes to dive into should need arise. What impressed me most was the manner in which these men had fixed up their quarters. One can hardly imagine the very excellent things done with scrap lumber, scrap canvas, etc.—the very stuff we had used to use for skids and to enclose them. By pairs, they were several feet below the surface of the ground, had waterproof canvas tops above, used boxes and crates for shelving, and claimed to have some of the comforts of home. Nicest of all, they had been receiving and storing our mail. All of us late arrivals just spent hours to catch up on our "reading from home"! The "home literature" was nearly overwhelming.

Our advance sections had been attached to First Army. Were we to become again a united company? No one seemed to know. We wondered if Col. Cole, back in London, knew. The next day was Bastille Day, July 14. Very early, drivers with trucks arrived. They had our duffles, etc., and they knew our destination. We journeyed through Carentan, to Isigny, and finally to Trevières. We unloaded onto a little green meadow which spread beneath an apple orchard. An advance section of our sister company, the 30th, was there, and these good friends had received and stacked supplies that had been delivered for us. It was good to see them. All they could tell us, for sure, was that about nine o'clock each evening some "Jerry planes" would fly over to entertain us. They then departed. We had time to pitch two pyramidal tents—cover for us officers; and the EM pitched their puptents here and there. We did some shifting the next morning, and Lane, Ryley, and I were together. We wasted no time to dig two, deep slit trenches.

We were yet on "C" and "K" rations. After supper, we settled down for the night. An anti-aircraft battery was in place just across a hedgerow. When "Mr. Jerry" came over, the fireworks began, and we could not tell if the bullets clipping the leaves of our tree tops came from the plane or from the aircraft battery. We hovered in our trenches, just as trained veterans would have done. Next morning, we dug down another foot. As for our EM, they dug in, fixed their abodes to patterns after those of their compatriots of the advance sections.

A command car rolled in, and a letter of instruction informed Major Grove that we were to be the receiving point for medical supplies to be unloaded at Omaha Beach. We knew all would be on our "skids" and that at least two advance field hospitals were to be "assembled." In the meantime, nearly each of us was out to find anything that would improve our facility. And, each of us was surely pondering our impressions after having been for seventy-two hours on French soil.

We knew our enemy was not too many miles away. The sandy and dusty conditions of the beach and of the road that ran parallel to the beach did not add to the beauty of the countryside. Nearly all houses we had seen were well battered and seemed symbolic of so much that we would see in future. German "pill boxes" were everywhere. Burned and destroyed vehicles, abandoned cannon, and the many shell holes were grim reminders of the struggle that had crossed this narrow strip. Many signs had been posted to warn us that land beyond a certain point had not been cleared of land mines, etc. One dared not stray from a beaten path.

Hedgerows were everywhere, and they enclosed the little fields. No one needed to stretch his imagination to realize the excellent defense measures these very hedges had afforded the Germans—and would continue elsewhere. We who had bicycles did some riding, and all wandered here and there, and into Trevières. The people, everywhere, met us with great warmth and friendly smiles. They seemed to have hearts of gold, but they were desperately poor.

We were never to be an outfit geared for battle. Our rides through St. Marie du Mont and St. Mere Église, on to Carentan, and via Isigny to Trevières had revealed to us the scars of battle which now surrounded these stricken people.

The village of Trevières was more than half reduced to near rubble. But, these people had not lost their "esprit de vivre" and to offered us a warmest of welcomes.

The field in which we were to establish our depot was called "L'Étard." It was green as could be, had about ten large apple trees well loaded with ripening fruit, and was completely surrounded by hedges. Throughout these hedges, one could find evidences of the Germans having been there—the scattered .30 caliber rifle shells. As for "souvenirs," the grounds had been well searched over before our arrival. Our officers' tents, our Motor Pool, the mess and kitchen tents, and the administrative tents were along the west and south side of the place. The EM were generally "dug in" along the northern and eastern sides. Without any buildings, we combined squad tents and ward tents to house most of out items for issue. To safeguard drugs, opiates, and dental gold and silver, we had a tent within a tent—with padlocked flaps, and always "under guard." Four ward tents were joined to provide for a sort of "loose issue" facility. We painted red crosses on several of the "roofs." A nearby engineering company laid down a crushed rock roadway throughout the depot area. Within a week's time this orchard had been transformed into a fully functioning medical supply depot. And, we were very busy. Eventually we had expanded to occupy two adjacent smaller fields. No doubt about it, ours had become a major supply installation.

Our beach receiving points were also at Longueville and Mosles, and we became known under many names—Millwheel, Miser, M-3, Medical Intransit Storage Area, Beach Receiving Point, etc. We finally settled in as "M-403"—but not long before our departure.

The signal corps finally installed a telephone switchboard, and we could make contact with higher headquarters. But, little could be done directly, for we had to go through one station in order to reach another—to use "Adeline" to get to "Sugar Maple, or "Tiger Bear" to reach "Oboe"; it was a three-ring circus—with names of girls, birds, animals, grains, etc., to identify the various outfits. Our code books were constantly changing, and couriers kept us up to date. If our German foes were to listen in, they were to be kept confused. Yessirree!

On our second day at Trevières I became acquainted with the Jacquet family. The younger son, Jean, proved to be a most unusual person. He was our initial contact, and about six of us who dealt with "records" were often in the home. We shared tears when they learned of the death of their daughter, from the bombings of Caen. We rejoiced when their son, André, returned. We hugged before our departure.

This small town was less than 20 miles from St. Lo, and we were in direct line taken by the planes which focused upon the city. The two days of bombardment which preceded the break through was, for us, a repetition of "D-Day." Of course, we were yet in the earlier stages of getting our supply depot into full operation. We were not to be for long near to a "front line." But, our volume of business grew rapidly, for our medical aid stations and advance hospitals had many wounded. New depot sites were located at LeMans and Chartres. Out heaviest day came when we loaded more than 200 trucks and trailers with 970 "long tons" of medical supplies and materiel.

Our "supply of labor" became greatly eased when we received our POWs on August 18. Most of these men were daily carted back and forth from a nearby stockade. Most were not the arrogant Germans we had expected. They constructed a small stockade for local use and worked throughout the depot, except in the "property office" where we kept all records, stock cards, files, etc. They worked at night when needed, and made no attempt to wander away. They spoke many of the Slavic, Ukrainian and Byelorussian dialects, and our Sergeant Myron Posypanko could communicate with them. They said they were better fed and more comfortably "housed" than they had been as soldiers in the German army. Of course, they professed their hopes that the war would not long endure and that they could safely return to their families and homes.

Toward the end of August, rumors circulated that we were to be transferred to Paris, as soon as the city was "secure." We were to establish a central medical supply depot. We also learned that the outfit we virtually replaced at G-55 in England would replace us, and we were confident that they would inherit an installation "in good order." Major Grove and ten of our headquarters men pulled out for Paris on September 6. The rest of us were to follow a week later. Our advance sections had long since rejoined us.

After the "breakthrough" at St. Lo, our EM quit their pup tents and occupied squad tents over in an adjacent orchard-field. We had procured some generators for power and enjoyed the better lighting. We had some excellent scroungers who had managed to acquire a couple movie projectors, and we had regular showings each evening. Our French friends nearly always crowded in to watch. Many of the ladies of the town did much of the laundry for the men, and they seemed pleased to receive the garments along with the soap. Our shower unit worked well, and the water was circulated through some sort of portable "disinfector." Our successors were to inherit many of the "comforts" of the best of army camps. Oh, well!

The operation in Paris was to be as different from Trevières as night can be from day. In Pantin we had two large warehouses, each of five stories—with adjoining rail facilities and a usable canal. At first, all seemed just a bit unreal—a sort of "pinch-me-to see-if-I'm awake" affair. The apple orchards in Normandy are quite scenic. The trees are systematically planted, are well pruned, and produce only for cider. The people drink cider at each meal, as we drink water. This cider is mild, not sweet, and not considered to be intoxicating. The apples are not eaten, and they remain green. Most of these orchards are owned by larger land owners, and the "little people," or peasantry, must purchase cider from the owners or buy apples to produce their own. Each family seemed to have plenty of it, and they passed it around freely to us Americans. The cider barrels were huge.

When our planes began the bombardment of the German positions at St. Lo, we received warning to be alert to possible "gas attack"—as possible effort to counter the Allied offensive along the front. We knew what our masks were for, and each was supposed always to be within reach. Our "superiors" decided to have a trial run, to see how long it would take for a "gas alert" to move from the front to Cherbourg. Units had been forewarned by telephone, but our "connections" were too recent to get our number on the list. About 12:30 a.m. came the sound of klaxons and cries of GAS—from the front. Our guards received the signals and passed them along. We had heavy rains, and certain local farmers had done some mowing of hay. To sniff the air was to smell odor resembling one or two of our worst gases.

Some of our men had found their pup tents to be a little humid, and had brought their bedrolls into the larger tents used for offices and storage—for dryer quarters. What many had forgotten to do was to bring their gas masks with them. When "alarm" sounded, there was mad dashing to retrieve masks, and with much of the ground underfoot more than just a little muddy, some of the men slipped, fell, became covered from head to foot with mud, etc., and etc. Panic for some took over. Others, who had their masks with them, sniffed to detect presence of fumes, were sensitive to the whiffs of recently cut hay, may have caught fumes from cans emptied to provide fuel for our cooking stoves, and prepared to await an "all clear." Three or four in the pyramidal used for our "records" climbed onto the tables and put their noses as high into the air as possible—hoping that the higher the nose, the weaker the gas.

Ryley, Lane, and I were awakened, and Lane and I simply reached down, picked up and put on our masks. But, Ryley couldn't find his, and he went into panic. He searched high and low, upturned his bed, emptied his footlocker, and rushed from the tent—having remembered his mask was in the seat of a command car. Outside, he encountered Major Grove, who was our "gas officer" and who was not wearing his mask—having detected there was no poisonous gas present. It took a bit of doing for Grove and the men with him to calm Ryley. He had been thoroughly frightened, and it had not been something amusing to watch. Of course, during later reviews of the incident, all things became more humorous with each retelling.

One of the men, who lacked his mask, went into shock—insisted that he could not breathe, suffered from severe pains in his chest, and choked violently. Our Mess Sergeant was sleeping soundly in his nicely arranged dugout. While putting on his mask, he knocked over a can of talcum powder on a shelf near his head. To sniff for clear air, he detected a sweet telltale smell of "gas" and may have been the last of our gang to remove his mask. This, too, became a "laughing matter."

Because of the Red Cross insignia on many of our tents and with a large banner flying at the entrance to our area, we had almost each day people come in who wished to see "le medecin." Of course, we had no doctor or physician. As you may have read, we did do some bits of surgery, but our skills in "first aid" were to prove to be our forte. I do not remember that we turned any one away. We became artists at removing slivers and splinters and at painting sores with Merthiolate. These were a poor people, but they were proud. We could never accept any of their money; so, they would bring eggs and fresh vegetables—on occasion, even, a kettle of stew. It seemed to me that our friendly relationship with these folk was not ordinary. But proof of the pudding was that wherever the men of our company landed, they quite universally hit it off in high gear with the people. I remain certain that we, as a company, were composed of an unusual group of men—and so many of them not long from high school.

En route to Paris we saw many abandoned German trucks and vehicles, but only few towns much damaged by bombings and/or artillery. There was little to compare to Caen and St. Lo—for instance. The German retreat across France had been swift. It was our understanding that Patton had to halt his drive only because fuel and other supplies could not keep up. The Germans, according to report had left Paris virtually unscathed and virtually without snipers. So, we headed to the big city without apprehension, but with expectations.

The Hotel Ambassador was first abode for us officers, and I had a large room all to myself—full bed, private bath, linens, and hardly believable. We would enjoy our comfort, but without hot water. Our men were nicely ensconced in a "chateau" and a large school complex in Pantin. Our late afternoon arrival on the l3th left us with sufficient time to marvel at out good fortune before heading to an officers' mess.

Our two large warehouses were "supervised" by a "Chambre de Commerce" and were adjacent to the Oeurcq Canal in Le Port de Pantin—to the northeast of the city, even with subway connections. The French had used them for storage of grain and flour, and we found some still there—even after four years of German occupation. We had four cranes and a freight elevator which would often stick if provoked because of the slightest imbalance of cargo. No doubt about it, these facilities loomed to be almost equal to some sort of "heaven"!

To our amazement, we discovered that our German predecessors had used these storage facilities for their "PX" and liquors—gathered by whatever means and under whatever pretexts and for what they expected to be permanent enjoyment. The quantities of boxes and crates, by far most not yet opened, could be counted into the thousands. Not only were there the best of French wines, cognacs, liquors, and champagnes, but stacks of canned Polish hams, Dutch and French cheeses, Belgian sweet breads and cakes, perfumes and eau de colognes, fine-toothed combs, playing cards, letter openers with fancy handles, hair oils, pencils, and pens and inks. Nearly all boxes and thousands and thousands of bottles had been stamped or bore labels—as reserved for the WEHRMACHT.

We had no way to know how much had been carried out and away by "French employees" and others. Our guards were instructed to prevent further looting. Our men had not hesitated to lay in supplies to be packaged and sent home. For purposes of "French relief," trucks by the dozens arrived, from the U.S. "post exchange", to haul into the city the bulk of the unbroken and "original" crates and boxes. The quantities of "spoils" which remained were just mind-boggling and not to be believed unless seen. A thought crossed my mind that the Germans had to pull out from Paris in such a rush that they had no time to take any of this loot. Of interest to note, was the increased number of packages sent home by our men and officers. The bottles of "Tosca" perfume were beyond possible exhaustion. We had fallen heir to a legacy—a most amazing "thing,"

Our earlier operations at M-407 were simply to clean up the two warehouses, the grounds, and the office facilities. The "Chambre de Commerce" removed the piles of grain and the sacks of flour; we irked the French because we pushed them to work more diligently than seemed to be their custom; my hunch was that the people knew but one pace, that of doing as little as possible—just as they had done for the Germans. The pace was to be slow. We may have engaged more than a hundred persons to engage in the "clearing out." It sort of added up into confusion, and was almost more amusing than irksome. It was my understanding that signed vouchers enabled these employees to receive pay from French sources, to be chalked up to "reverse lend-lease." Many of these people remained with us throughout our stay, and I do not recall that any of them complained because of non payment of wages.

With the German departure from nearly all of northern France, our supply systems underwent reorganizations as needed. Most medical supplies were directed into Paris (Pantin)—for storage and redistribution. As situated adjacent to the canal, and with shortage of parking areas, our two warehouses were not conducive to "rapid business." Ours was to become a "big-time operation," and we had to streamline nearly all procedures. Of major importance was to systematize the lining up and parking of vehicles. Adding to the complications and confusions was the presence in Paris of the Office of Chief Surgeon, ETO, whose officials often had special "projects" and pet interests to be attended to—often without delay.

Almost to the man in our company, we were willing to put in the long hours needed to make the installation work well. We quickly needed more manpower—American, not French. The 15th Medical Depot Company had arrived from England in mid October, and these men were, at first, meeting our needs. Not in my "Property Office," but elsewhere in the depot, frictions developed. From what I could detect, two factors had taken shape: first of all, the men of the new company were under the illusion that they were to take over the depot; and second, Col. Cole placed their officers and NCOs in nearly all of the "key positions." He was forced "to retreat," and our crisis eased when the Surgeon's Office assigned the 15th to proceed to Liege.,

Some half dozen ladies worked for and with us in the Property Office. Their duties were clerical, and they performed well. They were diligent. They never seemed, quite, to understand the care-free and generous nature of the American soldier. Each repeatedly attempted to express her "relief" because of the exodus of the Germans and of the arrival of the Americans. One of these women spoke some English, and understood it more easily. When we departed the following January, honest tears were shed. Ross Donaldson, one of my sergeants, and I could converse with them in French, and this did make it much easier.

Our hopes to have time to get out and to see the sights of Paris were hardly to be realized. Depot hours were regularly from 7:30 a.m. to 6:30 p.m. But, these hours were for little more than "posting at the gate," and the night crews became skilled at the game of "catch up." When the pressures slackened, the men could sign out to go into the city. Often, a "work day" ended only when one hit bed or cot for sleep. When the German counter-offensive began on December 16, "Battle of the Bulge," requests for medical supplies and all "things" needed to care for the wounded and dying just simply required for nearly three weeks an around-the-clock response. We met that challenge. We were also aware that the burden placed upon us was of vastly lesser significance—somehow, than for those on the front lines.

We had heard rumors, as early as Thanksgiving, that we might not be long in Paris. As the Ardennes campaign spread, we heard more rumors about an impending move for us. Official word told us, January 10 (1945), that we were to release the operation to the 11th Medical Depot Company on the 18th. The "word" also informed us that we were to be transferred to the control of SOLOC, Southern Line of Communications, southern France. Were we to go to Merseilles? We could be sent to Dijon. The latter proved to be the case.

In one respect, our morale took a beating. We felt that our highly successful work at the Pantin depot was being ignored, that we merited "recognition"—not reassignment. At best, it was no less than "a kick in the pants." (I did not know at the time of Col. Cole's probable central role in the affair.) With such pressures being laid upon the depot, due to the "Battle of the Bulge," it seemed an action of near insanity to turn over the depot to an untried outfit. Nevertheless, our "base platoon" and headquarters pulled out for Dijon—early morning of the 18th. My sentiments were mixed, for it was good to be rid of the depot and not so good to be quitting Paris.

A bit more about my living "quarters" in this big city. The "Ambassador" was on Blvd. Haussman, not far from Place de L'Opéra, and it was an elegant contrast to our pyramidals at Treviéres. An officers mess was nearby on a "Rez-Chaussée"—where the French waitresses were cute and the food was good. We knew that this hotel was not long to be for company grade officers. When British officers requested the hotel, we Americans of captaincies and below were sent to the "Louvois"—Rue de Richelieu, reserved for company grade officers, with captains to have their room singly, and lieutenants to be two in a room. Pete and I were together, and Charley was by himself. We were just a block from Place de L'Opéra. Two or three entrances to the Metro were handy—with one to give direct passage to Pantin, a ride of ten minutes. Only on a rare day would the hotel have any heat, or warm water. We were comfortable, and would stay here until the day after Christmas.

Charley, Pete, and I often did snacking in our rooms—nearly always together and to share our "goodies" from home and the stuff we brought from the "German deposit" left at the depot. We munched, and sipped, and read to each other much of the news we received from home. On occasion, we were joined by others of our crew. Charley and Pete soon were placed on alternate schedules for night duty at the depot. So, our camaraderie became a bit altered. The arrivals of our Christmas packages made each evening a marvelous time for special snacking. We were within easy walking distance of the Opéra and two or three other "show places" to be attended.

We always ate breakfast and meals at noon at the depot's mess—French women to prepare the food, etc. Occasionally, for evening, when work permitted, we might hit an officers' mess at Circie Militaire, Place de St. Augustine. The French cooks were able to do much with the various "rations" furnished them by the U.S. government. Were we to opt to eat at a French café, we could use some of our French currency, with which we were paid our "wages." Oh. Well!

My associations with the Rivets, Scheys, and Billots—along with evenings as the Opéra and Follies—were experiences never to be forgotten. For genuine hospitality, the Rivets were just unusual. The beauties of Paris—and I refer here to buildings, places, landmarks. parks, monuments, etc.—have been of endless attractions. It will be my hope that opportunity will arise in future for me to return to this marvelous city. Our responsibilities at the depot were often to be nearly overwhelming, and we had so little leisure to poke around, here and there. I was physically tired when time came for our departure.

My last two residences in Paris were quite different from the rooms in the "Ambassador" and the "Louvois." The first of these, cold as it was and Paris without any coal for heating, was in a little fifth class hotel, the "Aviateur," 17 Rue Louis Blanc, in the Aubervilliers section of the city—about half way to our depot from the Opéra. Pete and I were there, each in a little two-by-four room, with temperature seemingly as cold as a north wind in January. Except to sleep, we spent no time in our rooms. But, a greener field soon beckoned us.

Pete gained access to a spacious apartment not far from the Hotel de Ville, and we had it all to ourselves. I think Monsieur Rivet put him on its trail. The large bedroom had a fireplace, as did the living room. We hauled in quite a load of scrap wood from the depot, and it was a joy to spend an evening before the fire in our "sitting room." For some reason, the sardines, rye krisps, wines from our cache, etc., just tasted much better in these surroundings. We were in this place for two weeks before our exit from the city. One evening, I invited my gang from the Records Office to arrive at 7:30 to be my guests for supper and the evening, and they did much enjoy the sharing of foods and wines which came from our "German donation." They were just dumfounded at the comforts of our apartment. I arranged for a truck from the depot to pick them up at 12:30. Pete also hosted an evening for about ten men from his warehouse gang.

It was soon to be off for Dijon, and we expected to take over a depot. What we found was a small operation which by no means could utilize the services of our entire company. Tired when we arrived on the 19th, we were afforded two weeks of relaxation and rest. Col. Cole, from Paris, had managed this assignment for us. He must have known little about the situation and its lack of need for additional personnel—let alone a full blown company. The action in Dijon simply served to give emphasis to the unusual "load" we had been carrying in Pantin.

We had heavy snow while at Dijon, and people told us that it was most unusual—the heaviest "in years"! Close to the coal fields of the Vosges Mountains, fuel was on hand for the local military installations and many of the public offices. We officers were billeted in a small hotel, had hot water for bathing each evening, and enjoyed our excellent cuisine. We remained quite mystified because of our presence. We also wondered about the future of our "advance platoon" which had remained at Pantin.

Apparently, our superiors in the Chief Surgeon's Office in Paris had to decide our destiny. We were directed to go to a town of Foug—located not far from the city of Nancy, in northeastern France. So, we who were in Dijon pulled out at a good hour, the morning of February 2, in trucks and other vehicles. We found Foug to be a relatively small town, the farthest cry from "Gai Paree." But, we were also to find a town full of some of the most marvelous people. Dame Fortune was smiling on us, indeed!

Foug was about five miles from the larger town of Toul. Our men were quartered in a large school house, and two adjacent empty homes. To begin, we officers were placed in private homes, some of us to remain with these families for our sojourn there. We all, officers and EM, just seemed to be absorbed into the community, and we soon became "the talk of the town." Whatever may have been argued to account for our dismissal from Paris, we felt richly rewarded by the friendliness of these people; and, our men responded with a propriety which "toed the line," almost without exception, during the five months of our stay.

For our depot, we acquired an old "carlage", which in its better days had been a tile factory. It was almost grotesque—single storied, of umpteen chambers, and with certain pieces of defunct and long abandoned machinery in one room after another, here and there. The Germans had used some of the rooms for storage of grain and hay—much of which remained and of no use because of dampness and mold. Some ovens for baking bread were in one of the rooms. It would require two weeks of ardent labor for our effort to become a smooth one, but was never to become overwhelmingly busy as had been the Paris enterprise.

Our stock records and unit files would show that we served eventually over thirty hospitals, the units within four field armies, and many service establishments. Build up of business increased rapidly; but, once the crossing of the Rhine River at Remagen, March 8, had its full impact, our volume of requisitions decreased somewhat. VE-Day found us comfortably in full operation.

Yes! Nazism had been crushed, and we felt satisfied that our operations at Trevières, Pantin, and Foug had contributed substantially to the accomplishments of our American mission. Our concern, in its collective sense, focused upon redeployment and the possibility of service in the Pacific. We wanted to return to our U.S.A., but we knew that so many others had more than earned their priorities and merited the earlier "homecomings."

We are proud of our record!

978-0-595-41199-3
0-595-41199-1

Printed in the United States
63069LVS00002B/358-384